Egypt

Fodor's 92
Egypt

Kay Showker

FODOR'S TRAVEL PUBLICATIONS, INC.
New York & London

Copyright © 1992 by Fodor's Travel Publications, Inc.

Fodor's is a trademark of Fodor's Travel Publications, Inc.

ISBN 0–679–02037–3

Fodor's Egypt

Editor: Andrew Beresky
Maps: Pictograph
Drawings: Edgar Blakeney
Cover Photograph: Owen Franken/Stock Boston

Cover Design: Vignelli Associates

Special Sales

Fodor's Travel Publications are available at special quantity discounts for bulk purchases
(100 copies or more) for sales promotions or premiums. Special editions, including
personalized covers, excerpts of existing guides, and corporate imprints, can be created in
large quantities for special needs. For more information, write to Special Marketing,
Fodor's Travel Publications, 201 East 50th Street, New York, NY 10022; or call 800/800–
3246. Inquiries from the United Kingdom should be sent to Fodor's Travel Publications,
20 Vauxhall Bridge Rd., London, England SW1V 2SA.

CONTENTS

Author's Foreword vii
Editor's Foreword ix
Map of Egypt, x–xi

FACTS AT YOUR FINGERTIPS

Planning Your Trip: When to Come, 1; Holidays, 1; How to Get There, 3; Airfares, 3; Packaged Tours and Costs, 5; British Operators, 9; Passports and Visas, 9; Health Regulations and Inoculations, 10; What to Take, 11; Sources of Information, 12; Suggested Reading List, 12

Arriving in Egypt: Arriving at the Airport, 15; Transportation from Cairo Airport, 15; Landing at the Port, 16; Customs, 16; Registering upon Arrival, 17; Currency Regulations and Exchange Rates, 17; Tipping, 19; Women Traveling Alone, 20

Staying in Egypt: Tourist Facilities, 20; Time, 21; Electric Current, 21; Languages, 21; Conversion Chart, 22; Business Hours, 22; Post, Cables, Telephone, Telex, 22; Photography and Equipment, 24; Health Precautions, 25

Getting Around in Egypt: How to Get Around, 25; Trains, 27; Lower Egypt, 27; Upper Egypt, 29; To Sudan, 29; Distance Between Cairo and Other Cities, 30; Air Travel, 30; Intra Egypt Flights, 31; Nile Steamers, 31; Visiting Upper Egypt, 35; Driving in Egypt, 36

Leaving Egypt: Exporting Gifts, 39; Customs Going Home, 39

THE EGYPTIAN SCENE

By Way of Background 43

Egypt's Marvelous History—A 63-Century Epic 50

Egyptian Food and Drink—Coffee, *Fool,* and *Zibib* 68

THE FACE OF EGYPT

Cairo—City of a Thousand Years 75
  Map of Cairo, 78–79
  Pharaonic Cairo, 81
  Coptic Cairo, 93
  Islamic Cairo, 98
  Modern Cairo and Other Sites of Interest, 107
  Suggested Itinerary for Cairo, 111
  Excursions from Cairo, 112
  Practical Information for Cairo, 116

Upper Egypt—Luxor, Karnak, and the High Dam 162
  Luxor, 163
  Map of Luxor–Karnak and the Valley of Kings, 164
  Plan of the Temple of Luxor, 166
  Plan of the Temple of Karnak, 167
  Aswan, 177
  Map of Aswan Area, 179

Abu Simbel, 182
Practical Information for Upper Egypt, 185

Alexandria—Ancient Queen of the Mediterranean   189
   Map of Alexandria, 190–191
   Practical Information for Alexandria, 199

The Suez Canal, the Red Sea, and Sinai—Passage to the Orient   202
   Sinai, the Land of Turquoise, 206
   Practical Information for the Suez Canal and Sinai Areas, 209

APPENDIX

English–Arabic Tourist Vocabulary   217
Pharaonic Gods and Symbols   223

Index   224

AUTHOR'S FOREWORD

In preparing a guide on a country 7,000 years old, the biggest problem that faces a writer is deciding what to leave out. Egypt's antiquities alone fill volumes. After examining the current literature, I found that much of it tends to be of two types: history books, scholarly treatises, and art books—all serious in tone and profuse in detail—or nostalgic ramblings by former European residents, which are entertaining and charming but somewhat irrelevant.

The scholarly books can be invaluable when one is standing in front of a strange drawing on the wall of an ancient tomb or temple, but they are not much help for planning a trip from a distance of 6,000 miles. The sentimental type of book offers its readers the vicarious enjoyment that helps get today's travelers out of their armchairs and into plane seats, but they are neither practical nor timely.

This book is meant to bridge the gap. I have tried to give readers enough historical background to understand the broad changes that took place in the long span of Egypt's history without becoming lost in its maze. For those interested in more detail, I have, where appropriate, mentioned books that will provide this type of information.

At the same time, Egypt is a bustling modern country where a visitor can have fun, eat well, enjoy sports, shop and spend time among warm and generous people who will become lifelong friends. I have devoted a great part of this book to making this facet of the country more approachable and accessible to the newcomer.

Yet, more than anything else, this book attempts to be concise and practical—to help you plan your trip before you go and to help you enjoy your visit after you arrive.

Reading about Egypt's history in advance will greatly augment the pleasure and meaning of your visit, and I urge you to do so. The *Suggested Reading List* later in the book is intended as an aid in selecting books. I have relied heavily on these sources myself.

Egypt is the result of my personal experience and impressions as a traveler. The choice of information and opinions are mine without any obligations whatsoever. I welcome suggestions from readers for information to be included in any future edition, and I will be grateful to learn about any experience encountered by a reader that did not match my description.

Consistency in the transliteration of Arabic names and in the spelling of ancient Egyptian ones is an insurmountable problem. A few examples will illustrate the difficulty: The name of the Prophet is written as Muhammad, Mohammed, Muhamed, Mohamed, and Mehmet. Among the pharaohs one encounters most often there is Ramesis or Ramses or Ramesses; Thutmosis or Tuthmose; Hatshepchut or Hatchapsut.

I have tried to be practical by using the spellings most commonly employed. Names of places, shops, etc., are rendered as they appear locally so that a newcomer will recognize them, but even this has its inconsistencies. It is not unusual, for example, to find the Egyptians writing Menia, Minia, or Minya for the same town in Upper Egypt.

No guidebook can be written without the help of many people, and this one is no exception. I have been dealing with the Egyptian Government Tourist Office, both in the United States and in Egypt, for more than 20 years and no matter how small or how big the request, I have found their directors and staff always willing and eager to help.

Special thanks are due to Joanne Zembal, an American freelance writer and photographer living in Egypt, and to Fawzeya el Sawy, whose invaluable research helped to update this edition.

K.S.

EDITOR'S FOREWORD

The lure of ancient Egypt is so great that travelers are seldom aware of the country's other attractions. But it is no exaggeration to say that if there were no Pyramids or Abu Simbel, no Valley of the Kings or Karnak Temple, Egypt would still be one of the most interesting countries in the world to visit. Cairo has more magnificent Islamic treasures than any city in the world. They alone are well worth a visit.

While every care has been taken to assure the accuracy of the information in this guide, the passage of time will always bring change and, consequently, the publisher cannot accept responsibility for errors that may occur.

All prices and opening times quoted here are based on information available to us at press time. Hours and admission fees may change, however, and the prudent traveler will avoid inconvenience by calling ahead.

Fodor's wants to hear about your travel experiences, both pleasant and unpleasant. When a hotel or restaurant fails to live up to its billing, let us know and we will investigate the complaint and revise our entries where the facts warrant it.

Send your letters to the editors of Fodor's Travel Publications, 201 E. 50th Street, New York, NY 10022.

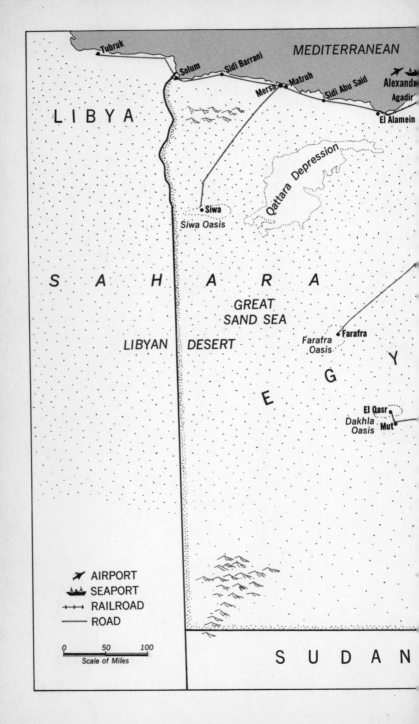

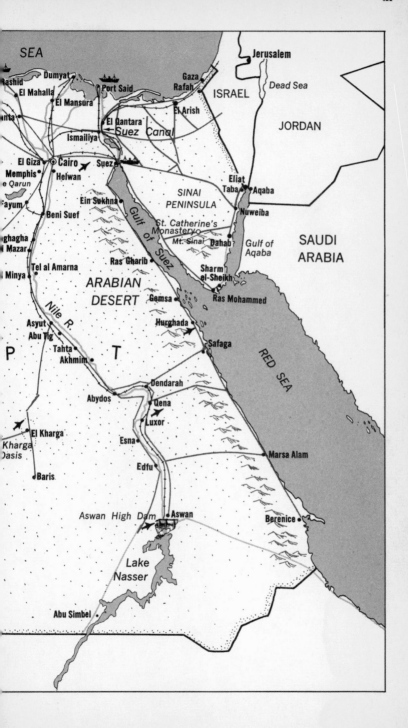

FACTS AT YOUR FINGERTIPS

Planning Your Trip

WHEN TO COME. Egypt is a year-round travel destination, but October through May is the ideal time to visit. Winter is considered the high season—especially at Luxor and Aswan in Upper Egypt, which has been a popular winter resort for Europeans since Edwardian aristocrats made it fashionable.

The year-round climate in Cairo is very dry. During winter the days are sunny, but from mid-December to mid-February they are often cool enough for wool suits and sweaters; the nights are cold enough for a coat. April tends to be a month of unpredictable weather and can still be cool and windy. You may encounter the *Khamseen* (sirocco) during the spring, when high Sahara winds blanket the atmosphere with a haze.

From June through September, Cairo is hot and Upper Egypt is very hot. However, leading hotels in Cairo, Luxor, and Aswan are air-conditioned, and if you do your sightseeing in the early morning or late afternoon, it is not unbearable. On the other hand, those who suffer from exposure to intense, direct sun and heat should not attempt a trip to Abu Simbel during the summer months.

EGYPTIAN MONTHS OF THE YEAR
COMPARED TO THE GREGORIAN CALENDAR

Gregorian (A)	Solar (A)	Coptic (B)	Hijra (C)
January	Khanun II	Tuba	Gumada II
February	Shabat	Amchir	Ragab
March	Azar	Baramhat	Shaban
April	Nizan	Barmuda	Ramadan
May	Ayar	Bashans	Shawal
June	Haziran	Bauna	Thul-Kida
July	Thamuz	Abib	Thul-Higga
August	Aab	Misra	Moharram
		Nasi (D)	
September	Aylul	Tut	Safar
October	Techrin I	Babeh	Rabi I
November	Techrin II	Hatur	Rabi II
December	Khanun I	Kiyahk	Gumada I

(A) Solar and Gregorian months are same.
(B) Coptic month is 30 days.
(C) Hijra-month is 29 or 30 days; the year is 354 days.
(D) Nasi lasts 5 or 6 days.

HOLIDAYS. *National:* April 25, Liberation of Sinai Day; May 1, Labor Day; July 23, Revolution Anniversary; Oct. 6, Armed Forces Day. Festivals: Sham en Nessim (Celebration of Spring), first Monday following Eastern Orthodox Easter.

1

AVERAGE TEMPERATURES IN MAJOR TOURIST CENTERS

| | Winter | | | Spring | | | Summer | | | Fall | | |
---	Dec.	Jan.	Feb.	Mar.	Apr.	May	June	July	Aug.	Sept.	Oct.	Nov.
ALEXANDRIA: (high)	F.69	66	67	70	75	80	83	86	87	86	83	77
(low)	F.54	51	51	54	58	63	69	73	74	72	68	62
CAIRO:	F.69	66	69	75	83	90	95	96	95	89	85	78
	F.49	45	47	51	56	62	68	71	71	68	63	57
LUXOR:	F.78	74	79	86	95	103	106	107	106	103	98	87
	F.45	42	44	50	59	69	70	72	73	71	65	54
ASWAN:	F.78	75	79	88	97	103	108	107	106	103	99	88
	F.52	49	51	57	65	73	77	78	80	74	71	61

Religious: Muslim religious holidays are calculated by the lunar calendar and occur 11–12 days earlier each year. Ramadan is the Muslim month of fasting from sunrise to sunset. During these hours not even water may be taken. In 1992, Ramadan begins on about March 5.

Ramadan ends with the Id al Fitr, or Small Bairam. The Id al Adha, or Big Bairam, comes 70 days later at the end of the period of the pilgrimage to Mecca and commemorates Abraham's sacrificing his son to God.

Islamic New Year's Day is the first day of the Hijra year, and it marks the flight of the prophet Muhammad and his followers from Mecca to Medina in an effort to save his prophetic mission. The Moulid El Nabi celebrates the birth of the prophet.

On major holidays Egyptians tend to take three- to five-day vacations. Government offices are open only from 10 AM to 2 PM during Ramadan, and most offices and many businesses close for several days during the Bairam feasts. Businessmen in particular should try to avoid visiting Egypt during Ramadan and the Bairam feasts as they will accomplish little.

HOW TO GET THERE. Cairo is today as it has been throughout its history—a crossroad. The air routes between Europe, Asia and Africa crisscross at the Egyptian capital, making it readily accessible by the major international airlines from almost any country of the world. Following the reopening of the Suez Canal in June 1975, Egypt quickly regained its preeminence on the sea routes and now several cruise lines offer a voyage through the canal as part of a Mediterranean or Red Sea cruise or on around-the-world itineraries.

By air: *Egyptair,* the national carrier, flies between New York and Cairo three times weekly. On Tuesday, the flight from New York is nonstop; on Friday and Sunday, it flies via Paris. *TWA* also has direct flights from New York to Cairo, but their schedules change too often to be included here. Another dozen or more international airlines fly daily from major U.S. gateways with interim stops and connecting flights to Cairo via almost any European capital.

Egyptair and the leading carriers of Europe offer regular flights from major European capitals to Cairo. The airlines of the Middle East also have daily connections between Cairo and the capitals of the region.

Although Cairo is easily accessible from the United States and almost any European or Middle Eastern capital, travelers should be aware that the demand for airline seats is sometimes greater than the supply. Book early, reconfirm, and get to the airport early—especially when you are traveling to Egypt from any other capital in the Middle East.

Regularly scheduled air service between Cairo and Tel Aviv is available from *El Al Airlines* and *Air Sinai.* The flight takes 1¼ hours.

Generally, it is advisable to purchase return tickets prior to coming to Egypt as the government now adds a 10% tax on all international tickets purchased in Egypt, even if the payment is made by credit card.

AIRFARES

Among the more confusing aspects of travel these days is the matter of airfares. The following fares were valid at the time of writing but are subject to change. All prices are New York–Cairo round-trip:

Individual Fares

First Class: $4,934—available year-round.
Business Class: $2,998—available year-round.
Economy Class: $2,702—unrestricted year-round; $2,166 with certain restrictions.
6–60 days PEX: $926 plus $100 surcharge Dec. 8–Jan. 13, basic; $1,231 shoulder season; $1,323 peak, with restrictions.
14–90 day Excursion: $1,500 basic fare; $1,664 peak.
  Youth (12–26 years): $696 year-round.
  Student (ages 18–31): $875. Must be able to prove that you are a bona-fide student.
Egyptair has a standby fare for $600 adult, $450 children 2–12, Oct. 1–Dec. 19 and Jan. 6–May 14; $700 adult, $500 children, May 15–June 20 and July 11–Sept. 30. Passengers must stand by for available seats on the outbound flight from New York but get a confirmed seat for the return flight.

Group and Discount Fares

Some group fares can be advantageous for as few as 5 or 10 persons traveling together. At the same time, discount fares in the aftermath of the 1978 deregulation are a fact of life, and travelers should try to take advantage of them when applicable. The lowest fares are usually available from consolidators, some of whom work through travel agents and others who deal directly with the public, advertising their fares in city newspapers on a regular basis. Ask your travel agent to check; these fares change too rapidly to be included here.

By sea: At present there are no all-passenger ships in regular service from the United States to the Mediterranean. However, cruise lines that offer Mediterranean cruises have combined air-sea programs that include a stopover in Alexandria or Port Said with an excursion to Cairo. Local travel agents arrange to meet passengers at the port and provide them with a sightseeing program to Cairo while their ship waits. The tours to Cairo, usually by motor coach, offer a very quick look at the Pyramids and bazaars. These tours tend to be very hurried and overpriced. Many such combined air-sea programs can be purchased in the United States.

Among the cruise lines that call at Egyptian ports are *Cunard, Epirotiki, Paquet, Royal Viking Line,* and *Sun Line Cruises.* Your travel agent can give you more details.

Adriatic Lines, 5 World Trade Center, New York, has year-round ferry service connecting Venice and Alexandria. From Oct. to May, the Maritime Co. of Lesvos operates between Pireaus, Ancona, and Alexandria.

The *Egyptian Navigation Company,* 1 El Hurreya Avenue, Alexandria, tel. 800–050; 20 Talaat Harb, Cairo, tel. 392–8287, has regular ferry service from Suez to Jidda, Saudi Arabia. It also operates a daily ferry departing at 11 AM from Nuweibeh in Sinai to Aqaba, Jordan. Additionally, *Misr Edco Shipping Co.* (Mena Tours) has a reliable ferry service linking Suez, Aqaba, and Jidda.

North African Shipping Company, 171 Mohamed Farid St., tel. 391–4682, operates the new, sleek, M/S *Princesa Marissa* from late Mar. through Nov. between Port Said; Limassol, Cyprus; and Haifa, Israel.

By land: Transportation between Egypt and Israel is available by motorcoach, taxi, and private vehicles. Buses go between Cairo and El Arish (Rafah), where passengers cross the border and continue into Israel via Israeli bus. Or, if you are starting out in Israel, transportation is available from Tel Aviv and Jerusalem to Cairo via El Arish. There is also frequent bus service between Eliat, Israel, through the Taba border to resorts of Nuweibah, Dahab, and Sharm el Sheikh on the Gulf of Aqaba.

Travel time from Cairo to Rafah is about six hours. There, clearance through customs for the onward trip to Tel Aviv can add several hours to the trip.

Passengers who plan to make a round-trip from Egypt must have a multientry visa for returning to Egypt. While it is preferable to have your visa for reentry in advance to save time, Egyptian visas are issued at the border. You should take food and water, as there are few facilities en route in Sinai. (If you are a member of a tour group, food and formalities are provided by the operator.) This trip is long and tiring. Do not undertake it unless you are prepared to withstand delays and inconveniences.

Several companies offer seat-in-bus service from Cairo. Individual travelers must book in advance.

Travco Egypt, 3 Ishaak Yacoub, Zamalek, tel. 340–0235, telex 92926, has Sun.–Fri. motorcoach departures from the Cairo Sheraton at 5 AM to Tel Aviv and Jerusalem. The price is L.E. 61 one-way and L.E. 115 round-trip.

East Delta Lines (tel. 839–589) has bus departures from Abassiya Station in Cairo to Tel Aviv and Jerusalem. Inquire locally for departure times and fares.

American Express, 15 Kasr el Nil St., tel. 750–444, also operates daily, except Saturday, deluxe buses to Tel Aviv for $25 one-way and to Jerusalem for $25 one-way. Payment can be made in local currency if you show official exchange receipts. The buses depart from the front entrance of the Egyptian Antiquities Museum at 6:30 AM.

Another possibility, but only for students and others prepared for long inconvenience, is to share a taxi—from Ramses Square in Cairo to Rafah, cross the border, and pick up another taxi to Tel Aviv or Jerusalem. The total cost is about $20, and the trip takes up to 12 hours depending on border delays. As with bus travel, you should take food and bottled water.

In 1989 Egypt and Libya normalized relations and opened their borders. It is now possible to drive across North Africa from Casablanca to Cairo, a distance of about 3,000 miles. Nationals of most countries need visas for the border crossings. Also, there is direct, luxury bus service from Cairo to Tripoli, via Benghazi, in Libya.

PACKAGED TOURS AND COSTS. Many American tour operators offer packaged tours to Egypt that include transportation, hotels, sightseeing, and most meals. Such inclusive packages are the most economical and convenient way to visit Egypt and are strongly recommended, particularly for first-time visitors.

A large number of packages combine Egypt with several other Mediterranean or Middle Eastern destinations. For a first-time traveler to this part
of the world, multistop packages are enticing but are not recommended.
On such a tour, you will see the Pyramids and the Sphinx and visit the
Egyptian Museum and the old bazaars of Cairo—*but you will not see
Egypt*. There is too much to enjoy in Egypt to combine it with a hurried
trip through four or five countries in two or three weeks. Of necessity,
the emphasis of any Middle East tour is on history, monuments and antiquities, and even the most avid history buff or amateur archaeologist may
tire of too many museums and temples in a day. Moreover, if you combine
too many countries on one tour the impressions run together. Egypt alone
is more than worth a visit.

The following examples of tours are meant as an indication, not a complete list, of what is currently on the market. Every effort has been made
to provide the most current prices, but *all prices* are subject to change.
The information should give readers a reasonable idea of the types of tours
available and the approximate costs of a trip to Egypt. You should consult
a travel agent for the most up-to-date information, as new programs are
being added all the time. In most cases, a high-season supplement will increase the airfare in June, July, and August.

The tour operators are listed here in alphabetical order. No other
criteria have been used, nor have we attempted to evaluate their products.
All prices are land arrangements only, per person for two sharing a double
room; airfare is additional, unless otherwise stated. The airline named is
the principal one for the program; it or your travel agent should have the
program's brochure.

Abercrombie & Kent International, 1520 Kensington Rd., Oak Brook,
IL 60521; 708–954–2944; 800–323–7308. Four different tours of Egypt,
ranging from 11 to 17 days, feature a Nile cruise (5 to 11 days). All programs include the operator's own *Sun Boat or Sunboat II* and are escorted
by Egyptologists. Extensions are available to Israel, the Red Sea, Alexandria, the Western Desert, and other parts of Africa. Prices start at $1,995;
year-round departures. Tours include most meals, sightseeing, deluxe accommodations, and internal Egypt flights.

American Express Vacations, 300 Pinnacle Way, Norcross, GA 30071;
800–241–1700. A variety of programs featuring Egypt alone or in combination with Israel or Greek Islands cruise. *The Nile in Style,* 10 days, includes a cruise on the new *Diamond Boat* between Luxor and Aswan.
Ancient Wonders and Nile Cruise uses Sheraton Boats and includes a visit
to Abu Simbel. New this year are two-night city packages for Cairo,
Luxor, or Aswan. Another version offers three nights in Cairo with two
full days of sightseeing and an optional extension to Luxor.

Esplanade Tours (rep. Swan Hellenic Ltd.), 581 Boylston St., Boston,
MA 02116; 617–266–7465; 800–426–5492. Cruises are 12 days
Aswan/Luxor or Luxor/Aswan, from $3,635; and 20 days Cairo/Aswan
or Aswan/Cairo, from $4,785. Prices include outside, twin cabin on the
Nile Monarch, round-trip airfare from New York, overnight stay in Lon-
don before and after Egypt, airport transfers, sightseeing, meals, tax, and
gratuites. Land tours, offered twice yearly, are the 15-day Art Treasures
Tour/Northern Sinai and the Siwa Oasis, from $3,505; and the 19-day
Art Treasures Tour/Egypt-Western Desert and Sinai, from $4,355. Rates
are per person sharing a twin room and include round-trip airfare from

London. Swan Hellenic was scheduled to launch its new *Nile Monarch* in autumn 1991. The boat is expected to be one of the most luxurious boats cruising the Nile. The company also operates special "Ornithological Cruises" in conjunction with the Royal Society for the Protection of Birds, which provides tour leaders.

Maupintour, Inc. 1515 St. Andrews Dr., Box 807, Lawrence, Kansas 66044; 913–843–1211; 800–255–4266. One of the longest established, most reliable operators offering Egypt tours has five year-round escorted programs, lasting 14 to 17 days. "Egypt Exclusively" takes 13 days to tour Cairo, Fayoum, and Upper Egypt, including Abu Simbel. "Egypt/Nile Cruise" lasts 16 days and includes a four-day Nile cruise.The "Presidential Nile Cruise" offers a 10-day cruise plus a visit to Simbel. The 17-day "Sultan and Pharaohs," introduced in 1990, combines Egypt and Turkey. Prices start at $2,179 and include hotel, sightseeing, most meals, transfers, and domestic transportation.

Naggar Tours of Egypt, 605 Market St., Suite 1310, San Francisco, CA 94105; 800–443–NILE; 415–979–0161. *Egypt as Never Before* is a quick reference guide to Naggar's 22 itineraries with daily and/or weekly departures. Tours range from three days in Cairo to a 14-day program that includes Cairo, Luxor, Aswan, Abu Simbel, or a seven-day Nile cruise. A second brochure features Naggar's ships, which sail on four-, six-, and seven-night cruises that can be combined with tours.

Olson-Travelworld, 5855 Green Valley Circle, Culver City, CA 90230; 800–421–2255, 213–670–7100. One deluxe, escorted tour of 14 days features Egypt exclusively and is priced from $2,790 from New York including air transportation. Prices cover sightseeing, transfers, and all meals, à la carte. The six-night tour visits Cairo, Luxor; Sheraton Nile cruise includes Abydos, Dendera, and Aswan, plus Abu Simbel.

Overseas Adventure Travel, 349 Broadway, Cambridge, MA 02139; 800–221–0814; 617–876–0533. Adventure program in Egypt: "The Eternal Nile," 16 days, includes Cairo, Abu Simbel, and Aswan. From Aswan you'll take a three-day Nile trip on a felucca to Luxor, visiting Kom Ombo and Edfu. The tour continues to Hurghada for two days of Red Sea snorkeling. Prices start at $1,630; groups are limited to 15 persons.

Park East Tours, 1841 Broadway, NYC 10023; 800–223–6078; 212–765–4870. The "Nile Odyssey" is an 11-day deluxe program of Egypt exclusively, with year-round departures from New York. It includes several days of sightseeing in Cairo, a four-night cruise on an Oberoi or Presidential ship sailing between Luxor and Aswan, a sound-and-light show at Karnak, and a special excursion to Abu Simbel. Prices start from $2,795, with air transportation from New York and land arrangements. Extensions to Kenya, Tanzania, and Morocco are also available.

Persepolis Tours, 501 Fifth Ave., NYC 10017; 800–666–1119; 212–972–1333. Two all-Egypt programs have year-round weekly departures. The 13-day *Egypt Complete* tour combines Cairo with a six-night Nile cruise plus an excursion to Fayoum. The 10-day *Egypt* offers Cairo and four nights on a Nile cruise in Upper Egypt; the others combine Egypt and a Kenya safari, or Morocco. New this year is a five-night optional extension to Greece. The programs are hosted and use deluxe hotels and cruise ships.

Sunny Land Tours, 166 Main St., Hackensack, NJ 07601; 201–487–2150; 800–783–7839. Five itineraries cover Egypt exclusively and feature

Cairo and Upper Egypt Nile cruises between Aswan and Luxor; others combine Egypt with Jordan and Israel, with a Kenya safari, and other Middle East destinations. Tours are locally hosted, provide extensive touring, most meals, and most of them include three- or four-day Nile cruises.

Travel Plans International, 1200 Harger Rd., Box 3875, Oak Brook, IL 60521; 800–323–7600; 708–573–1400. An established firm in arranging tours of Egypt, TPI, now offers a 12-day Nile cruise between Cairo and Aswan on the *Nile Sovereign,* a new 56-passenger ship, as part of a 17-day Egyptian excursion. Luxury service with white-gloved waiters and Egyptologists used exclusively by the company are part of the trip. Price: from $3,200 in summer; $3,815 in winter.

Travcoa World Tours, Box 2630, Newport Beach, CA 92658; 800–992–2003, 800–992–2004 (CA); 714–476–2800. Two deluxe, escorted programs with year-round departures have luxury accommodations, three meals, and lectures by prominent Egyptologists. The 11-day tour includes Cairo and a four-night Upper Egypt Nile cruise. The 16-day tour extends the stay in Luxor for visits to Abydos and Dendera, and it includes an excursion to St. Catherine's Monastery in Sinai.

TWA Getaway, 28 South Sixth St., Philadelphia, PA 19106; 800–GET–AWAY. Seven escorted tours, ranging from 10 to 15 days, combine Egypt with other countries of the Middle East and depart frequently year-round; three have a Nile cruise. Prices have several levels of hotel accommodations and sightseeing, meals, and internal transportation.

Special-Interest Tours. Egypt's appeal goes far beyond antiquities, and a growing number of innovative tour operators are making it possible for visitors to discover this with new programs designed for scuba diving, mountain trekking, felucca sailing, and visiting the oasis of the Western Desert.

Dive Programs. Experts consider the Red Sea one of the prime locations in the world for viewing spectacular underwater life. Four specialists— *South Sinai Travel, Travco Travel, D.I.V.E.,* and *Spring Tours*—offer programs to resorts in Hurghada and Sinai; *Misr Travel* includes diving in packages for their resort in Hurghada. The Egyptian Tourist Office in New York has a brochure, *Dive Red Sea,* that provides useful information as well as the addresses of the dive specialists mentioned above. Most major hotels in Hurghada and Sharm el Sheikh operate their own dive centers where it is possible to become certified in a week. Ayman Taher, Egypt's best-known underwater photographer, conducts dive trips from his boat, *Espedal,* which departs from Sharm el Sheikh.

Trekking. Adventure tours for trekking and camping in Sinai or sailing the Nile by felucca are now available. *Trafalgar* and *International Travel Planners,* 506 Fifth St. (Box AC), Greenport, NY 11944 (tel. 516–477–2046), offer a five-day felucca sail trekking from Aswan to Luxor, and stopping at the temple sites of Kom Ombo, Edfu, and Esna, where the boats pass through locks. Trekking and Sinai camping safaris combine Cairo with four days in Sinai and two days in Upper Egypt. Similar programs are available through *Mountain Travel* of Albany, CA and *Overseas Adventure Travel* of Cambridge, MA. The four dive specialists mentioned previously also offer camping safaris in Sinai.

BRITISH OPERATORS. British tour operators offer similar programs; however, some of the best have the added feature of an Egyptologist or well-known archaeologist to accompany the tour. Among the most outstanding and best known is *Swan Hellenic Cruises Ltd.,* 77 New Oxford St., London WC1A 1PP (tel. 071–831–1515/1234). Their programs are two-week Nile cruises starting from either Aswan or Cairo with stops at more archaeological sites than are generally offered on programs by U.S. operators. Swan's tours are usually booked for a year in advance, but you should make inquires, as late requests can often be accommodated. (For more information on Swan programs, *see Esplanade Tours* above.)

Bales Tours Ltd., Bales House, Barrington Rd., Dorking, Surrey (tel. 0306–885991), has a similar 21-day version, priced from £1,425. The operator also offers a 15-day program that flies to Luxor, where it picks up the Nile cruise to Aswan. It costs £1,245. Bales offers a 15-day economy package with weekly departures from London, traveling to Upper Egypt by air. It costs £948 and drops to £699 in summer. There is also a one-week program covering Cairo and Luxor, with an optional excursion to Aswan.

Among the other operators with programs to Egypt are *Speedbird Holidays,* Alta House, 152 King St., London W6 0QU (tel. 081–741–8041); *Fairways & Swinford Travel,* Sea Containers House, 20 Upper Ground, London SE1 9PF (tel. 071–261–1744); *Thomas Cook,* 45 Berkeley St., London W1A 1EB (tel. 071–437–9080); *Thomson Holidays,* Greater London House, Hampstead Rd., London NW1 7SD (tel. 071–387–8484); *Kuoni Travel Ltd.,* Kuoni House, Dorking, Surrey RH5 4AZ (tel. 0306–885044); *Tradewinds Faraway Holidays,* Station House, 81–83 Fulham High St., London SW6 3JP (tel. 071–731–8000); and *Orientours,* Kent House, 87 Regent St., London W1R 8LS (tel. 071–434–1551).

PASSPORTS AND VISAS. All visitors to Egypt must hold a valid passport or document in lieu of passport. Egyptian consulates abroad are authorized to issue entry visas for tourists valid for 30 days and renewable for six months.

Egyptian consulates in the *United States* are located at 2310 Decatur Pl. NW, Washington, DC 20008; 1110 Second Ave., New York, NY 10022; 505 North Lake Shore Dr., #6503, Chicago, IL 60611; 2000 West Loop S, #170, Houston, TX 77027; and 3001 Pacific Avenue, San Francisco, CA 94115; in *Canada* at 3754 Côte de Neiges, Montreal, and 454 Laurier Ave. NE, Ottawa; and in the *United Kingdom* at 19 Kensington Place Gardens Mews, London W8 4QL (tel. 071–229–8818).

When applying for a tourist visa you will need: a passport, one photo with application, $12 for U.S. citizens; $38 (or about £22) for British citizens; fees vary for others; in cash or certified check, if applying in person; money order or certified check if applying by mail, a self-addressed envelope with required registered mail postage.

Please note that although tourist visas are valid for one month, the visa application form at the Egyptian Consulate may ask you to state specifically the length of your visit. Your visa will be issued for the exact time you state, e.g., one week, two weeks, etc. To give yourself flexibility, state "one month" even if you plan to stay a shorter time.

A six months' extension of a tourist visa can be obtained by applying to the Passport Department, Mogammaa Building, First Floor, Midan Tahrir (Liberation Square), Cairo.

Visitors may also obtain a visa on arrival at the port in Alexandria, the airport in Cairo, and at borders. The visa is valid for one month. At present, to extend your visa for one month or more, you must show evidence of having exchanged a minimum of $180 into Egyptian currency for each month of your stay.

A group (collective) visa can be issued on personal passports or collectively to a group of tourists organized by a travel agency, steamship, or airline. Such visas are used only when members of a group remain together as a group and do not separate.

Transit: If you are in transit by ship or plane and will not be remaining in Egypt, you do not need a visa. You will be given a landing permit valid for the time your ship or plane is calling at an Egyptian port or airport.

Transit passengers with three or more hours' delay may want to try *Egyptair's* minitours of Cairo run by Karnak Tours. These can be purchased at a desk inside Terminal One. Prices include car, driver, guides, entrance fees, visa formalities, and are for one person. Prices for 2–14 people are half the following rates.

Tour A: Pyramids and Sphinx—three hours. Price: U.S. $33; $20 per person for a group of 3 to 7 persons.

Tour B: Pyramids, Sphinx, and Egyptian Museum—four hours. Price: U.S. $37; $25 per person for a group of 3 to 7 persons.

Tour C: Tour A and B plus Citadel and City tour—five hours. Price: U.S. $50.

Student visas: Granted at the beginning of the academic year in October and valid for one year. Inquire at the Egyptian Embassy, 2310 Decatur Place, NW Washington DC 20008, for details.

Business visas and work permits: Foreigners coming to Egypt to take up employment or residence require special permission. Inquire for details from the Egyptian Commercial Office, 2715 Connecticut Avenue, NW, Washington, DC, Egyptian Economic Mission, 529 Fifth Avenue, New York, NY 10017, or the Egyptian consular offices mentioned above, under *Passports and Visas.*

HEALTH REGULATIONS AND INOCULATIONS. A valid vaccination certificate against cholera is required of all travelers (except children under one year of age) coming from or in transit through an infected area. A cholera vaccination certificate is valid for six months beginning six days from the date of inoculation.

Those coming from a yellow fever area must have had a yellow fever shot at least 10 days prior to their arrival in Egypt.

Inoculation against typhoid and malaria is recommended.

If you are coming from or transiting an area internationally considered to be an infected one, you should inquire about current regulations from the nearest Egyptian Consulate in order to avoid delay upon arrival.

Egypt is a member of the World Health Organization and adheres strictly to immunization requirements. Anyone who arrives in Egypt without proper records or inoculations will be quarantined.

WHAT TO TAKE. Pack with a plan so that you will not be burdened with useless items. Limit weight and luggage to what you can carry—and leave enough room for the gifts and souvenirs you are sure to buy in Egypt.

Although Egypt is thought of as having a hot climate, you will be surprised to discover how much the temperature varies within a given day or from one month to the next. Your wardrobe should therefore be planned according to the time of the year and the extent of your itinerary.

In early summer and fall, cotton and cotton-blend dresses and slacks for women and slacks and suits for men are comfortable, provided they are made with the type of fabric that breathes. In the dead of summer, only pure cotton dresses, blouses, and skirts and shirts and trousers are recommended, especially for those who suffer from the heat.

In December through March, women will need sweaters, wool or knitted suits and dresses with long sleeves or jackets. Even April can be cool, especially in the evening, so be sure to include a versatile dress with jacket or knits with long sleeves. Include a coat, a warm housecoat, nightgown and slippers, and a stole or a warm wrap for evenings year-round. It is amazing how, in the middle of summer when the sun goes down after a scorching day, there is sometimes a chill in the air. You will feel it all the more because the day was so hot. Moreover, houses, old hotels, and guest houses are not centrally heated, and it is frequently cooler inside than outdoors. Hats are seldom worn except as protection against the sun.

Egyptians are accustomed to foreigners and to the bizarre ways in which some tourists dress. Nonetheless, Egypt is still a conservative country as far as women are concerned. Slacks are readily accepted; shorts and bareback sundresses are not, except at the beach. Unless you are eager to attract attention to yourself, modesty in dress and decorum in manner are wise.

For men, most first-class hotels and restaurants prefer tie and jacket during meals, although there is much less emphasis on formality of dress than was the case in the past.

Hotel laundry service is fast and reasonable, so you do not need to burden yourself with a great deal of clothing. Also, don't forget that Egyptian cotton is among the finest in the world. You can buy shirts already made or have them tailored at reasonable cost.

As a reminder—the average rainfall in Cairo is 3.1 days in December and drops to zero on many days from July to October. In other words, it's dry.

Include in your suitcase: binoculars, a small flashlight (especially for visiting tombs and temples), a washcloth, disposable premoistened facecloths, insect repellent, collapsible hanger, face soap (kept in plastic bag), packaged soap powders, and a collapsible drinking cup. Always have an ample supply of facial tissues on hand—you will be amazed at their many uses. Only the better hotels supply facial tissues in your room.

Sunglasses are a *must,* and a shade hat for sightseeing rounds in the open and for the beach is useful. A raincoat and boots may be necessary in Alexandria during January and February. From April through October, bring a bathing suit for sunbathing or a swim in Alexandria and Cairo, year-round for a swim in Luxor and Aswan—and don't forget to pack the suntan lotion, or sunscreen lotion for sensitive skin. A small canteen for water will be useful for sightseeing rounds in out-of-the-way places.

SOURCES OF INFORMATION. *Government Tourist Offices:* United States: Egyptian Government Tourist Office, 630 Fifth Ave., New York, NY 10111; 212–246–6960. Egyptian Government Tourist Office, 323 Geary St., Suite 608; San Francisco, CA 94115; 415–781–7676.

Canada: Egyptian Tourist Authority, Place Bonaventure, 40 Frontenac, Box 304, Montreal, Canada H5A 1B4.

United Kingdom: Egyptian State Tourist Office, 168 Piccadilly, London W1. Tel. 071–493–5282.

The Egyptian Government Tourist Office functions solely as an information center for tourists. For inquiries pertaining to subjects other than tourism, contact:

In U.S.A.: Press & Information Bureau, Egyptian Embassy, 2310 Decatur Place, NW, Washington, DC 20008.

Egyptian Education and Cultural Program, 2200 Kalorama Road, NW, Washington, DC 20008.

Egyptian Commercial Office, 2715 Connecticut Avenue, NW, Washington, DC 20008.

Egyptian Economic Mission, 529 Fifth Avenue, New York, NY 10017.

In Canada: Egyptian Consulate, 3754 Côte des Neiges, Montreal, P.Q. H3H.

In the United Kingdom: Egyptian Consulate, 19 Kensington Place Gardens Mews, London W8 4QL.

SUGGESTED READING LIST. Background: Naguib Mahfouz, Egypt's Nobel Prize for Literature winner in 1988, has written a number of books depicting Egyptian culture. One of the most famous, *Midaq Alley,* has been translated into English and published by the American University in Cairo Press. His books—many in English—are available in major bookstores.

Al Sadat, Anwar. *In Search of Identity.* Harper and Row, New York, 1978. An autobiography of Egypt's second president.

Aldridge, James. *Cairo.* Little, Brown & Company, Boston, 1969. Of all the books on Egypt, none is better written, more informative, and more useful for a visitor to read before a visit. Using the vehicle of the tale of a city that is over 1,000 years old, the author tells the history of Egypt. Through his extensive research, he was able to include many details often overlooked by writers on Egypt and he writes with an understanding seldom found.

Billard, J. B. *Ancient Egypt.* National Geographic Society, 1978. Chapters are written by scholars and recognized specialists, and profusely illustrated with photographs from the Society's superb collection.

Carter, Howard. *The Tomb of Tutankhamen.* E. P. Dutton, New York, 1972. The story of the discovery by the man who made it. Beautiful color plates as well as black-and-white photographs.

Casson, Lionel. *Ancient Egypt.* Time-Life Books, New York, 1965. Excellent summary of ancient Egypt's history, culture, and religion. Strongly recommended as an introduction or as a refresher.

Ceram, C. W. *Gods, Graves and Scholars: The Story of Archaeology.* Knopf, New York, 1952. This book was written for the layman and is one of the most popular books ever written on archaeology. Informative and easy to read. Available in paperback. It is especially good for the chapter on Howard Carter's discovery of the tomb of Tutankhamun.

Creswell, K. A. C. *A Short Account of Early Muslim Architecture*. Pelican, London, 1958; Verry, 1972. The leading authority on Islamic art and architecture. The book is available in paperback.

David, A. Rosalie. *The Making of the Past: The Egyptian Kingdoms*. E. P. Dutton, 1975. Excellent detailed descriptions, drawings, and diagrams of the major antiquities; to be studied in advance of your visit and upon return.

Fagan, Brian M. *The Rape of the Nile: Tomb Robbers, Tourists and Archaeologists in Egypt*. Charles Scribner's Sons, New York, 1975. This book will give you an appreciation of the history of the antiquities of Egypt, which is more tragic and more glorious than any fiction. Better read before you go, but this is good reading upon return. Richly illustrated, succinctly written, it offers another dimension to the understanding of Egypt.

Jobbins, Jenny, *The Red Sea Coasts of Egypt*, American University in Cairo Press, 1989. Gives history along with new recreational and diving facilities.

Moorehead, Alan. *The White Nile*. Penguin, London, 1963; *The Blue Nile*. London, Four Square, 1964. Available in paperback, and in a handsome hardcover edition with good illustrations. Originally based on articles that appeared in the *New Yorker* magazine in 1961–62.

Megalli, Mary D. *On the Road in Egypt: A Motorist's Guide*. American University in Cairo Press, 1989. Well-referenced set of maps covering major roads and desert tracks. Also includes Arabic-English vocabulary of motoring terms.

Sitwell, Sacheverell. *Arabesque and Honeycomb*. Robert Hale, London, 1957. If you read Sitwell before going to Egypt, you might never go, but if you overlook the classic colonial bias, you will find interesting vignettes on Cairo, especially on the mosques.

History and culture: Breasted, James. *History of Egypt from the Earliest Times to the Persian Conquest*. Charles Scribner's Sons, New York. This is the classic work in English on Ancient Egypt by one of the best-known and most respected Egyptologists. Although the work of latter scholars has clarified or changed some of Breasted's theories and assumptions, this book is the place for any serious student to begin.

Cromer, E. B. *Modern Egypt*. Macmillan, New York, 1908. Two volumes. For anyone planning to spend some time in Egypt, this book is very important. Cromer was the British high commissioner in Egypt for over two decades and for all practical purposes ran the country single-handed.

Guillaume, A. *Islam*. Penguin, 1954. The traveler who reads about Islam, in addition to Egypt, will enjoy his visit to Egypt much more.

Baines, John, and Malek, Jaromir. *Atlas of Ancient Egypt*. Phaidon Press Ltd., 1980. Attractive coffee-table book with good maps of Egypt's past.

Hardy, Edward. *Christian Egypt: Church and People*. Oxford U.P., New York, 1952. One of the few books in English on the subject.

Russell, Dorothea. *Medieval Cairo and the Monasteries of Wadi Natrun*. Weidenfeld and Nicolson, London, 1962.

Wynn, Wilton. *Nasser: A Search for Dignity*. Arlington, New York, 1959. As a young American teacher in Egypt, the author taught many of the leaders who staged the revolution of 1952. For many years he served as the Associated Press correspondent in Egypt and senior correspondent for *Time* magazine. Few Americans writing on the modern Middle East are as well acquainted with their subject.

Aids to sightseeing: Budge, E. A. Wallis. *The Book of the Dead*. Arkana, London and Boston. A translation of hymns and religious texts that the ancient Egyptians inscribed upon tomb walls, coffins, papyrus, amulets, etc., to ensure the well-being of the deceased in the afterworld.

Cairo: A Practical Guide. American University Press, Cairo, 1988. Sixth edition revised by Cassandra Vivian. Referred to several times in this book. It is the only one of its kind and is indispensable for someone planning to live in Cairo, especially for the shopping guide, list of doctors, and other such material not readily available elsewhere.

Guide-Poche Univers. *Egypt*. Editions Marcus, Paris, 1976. Originally written in French, the book is especially useful for its detailed maps and drawings of ancient sites and explanations of ancient religion and mythology. It is not, however, accurate in some of its material on Islam.

Devonshire, Mrs. R. L. *Rambles in Cairo*. Les Editions Universitaires d'Egypte, 1947. For detailed descriptions of mosques and Islamic monuments, the book is useful for background details and includes map.

Dodge, Bayard. *The Azhar*. Middle East Institute, 1961. The author traces the history of the ancient mosque and university.

Fakhry, Ahmed. *The Pyramids*. University of Chicago Press, 1975, paperback. A highly readable account of the building of the Pyramids by a scholar who spent his life studying them.

Kamil, Jill. *Upper Egypt, Historical Outline and Descriptive Guide to the Ancient Sites*. Longman, London/New York, 1983. A useful paperback guide for those touring on their own and others who want more information than tour guides usually give. The author also has written separate guides for Luxor and Sakkara that are equally useful. They are available in Cairo and Luxor bookstores.

Parker, Richard B., and Robin Sabin. *A Practical Guide to Islamic Monuments in Cairo*. American University, Cairo, 1974. By far the best easy-to-read (and carry) guidebook on Islamic Cairo and a must for anyone interested in this aspect of the city. With its maps and detailed information, it makes sightseeing on your own very possible. It also gives readers enough historic background and definition of terms to help them enjoy it. Mr. Parker, a foreign-service officer who served a tour of duty in Cairo, was disappointed by the lack of an adequate guidebook to the great Islamic antiquities of Cairo and so wrote one. We can all be grateful. It is available in Cairo bookstores.

Arriving in Egypt

ARRIVING AT THE AIRPORT. Cairo International Airport, built over three decades ago, has been expanded several times to keep up with the increased flow of passengers. Now it consists of two terminals: the older Terminal One, which is used for all Egyptair flights (both domestic and international) plus several Middle East carriers; and the glossy new Terminal Two for all other international airlines. The new terminal is a blessing; travelers familiar with the hectic atmosphere of the old terminal will be amazed and delighted by the difference. The new building has all modern amenities along with an efficient staff that works hard to ensure smooth procedures. Most of the officials at the airport speak English and you should be able to communicate with them without difficulty. If you keep smiling, you will find most Egyptian officials pleasant and helpful.

Before you leave the plane, your stewardess should hand out Egyptian entry forms to be filled in and presented to airport officials on arrival. These forms are supposed to include a currency declaration form, known as Form D. In practice, however, neither this form nor any other form that requests a declaration of the amount of currency you are bringing into the country is given out. But that does not relieve you of the requirement to prove preentry possession, in case you are questioned by officials upon departure. To avoid problems — including having your money confiscated—do not bring in large amounts of cash. Rather, carry traveler's checks or letters of credit, and *always* keep all receipts of currency transactions made during your stay in Egypt. (See *Currency Regulations and Exchange Rates* for more information.)

To reexchange your unused Egyptian pounds you will need to show buying invoices and your hotel bills, which indicate that you have spent a minimum of $30 per day. Otherwise you will not be able to make this exchange, and there's no use in arguing with any of the officials about it. That's the system and they follow it to the letter. If you want to reexchange your leftover Egyptian currency, there is a bank near the airline check-in counters and before entering the security departure point.

To repeat, be sure to keep all buying invoices in order to reexchange unused Egyptian pounds at the time of your departure.

From the immigration entrance area, visitors proceed into the large main hall of the terminal to claim luggage. Customs inspection is usually perfunctory. Unless there is a large number of passengers in your group or other planeloads ahead of you, entry formalities and customs normally do not take a long time. Egypt has adopted the European system of a green zone exit marked "Nothing to Declare." It is generally used by tourists.

In the luggage claim area there are porters to help with your bags.

There are a few duty-free shops for basic items and a small gift shop and snack bar in the departure lounges. Major airlines, tourist agencies, and the government tourist bureau have offices in Terminals One and Two.

At no time is it more practical to be in a tour group or to use the meeting and transfer services of a local travel agency in Egypt than on arrival and departure and transfers from the airport or port into town to handle formalities. It can save you a great deal of wear and tear.

TRANSPORTATION FROM CAIRO AIRPORT. A taxi stand is located immediately in front of the airport building. Getting a taxi is often chaotic, as there appears to be no system for deciding who takes which taxi, but be patient; eventually it gets sorted out.

Even if you are not traveling in a group you should ask your travel agent to arrange for your transfer from the airport to the hotel. You'll avoid the hassle of having to get a taxi when you're tired after a long transatlantic flight.

Limo Bank Nasser has Mercedes cars on radio call. Its airport offices are located at the main exit door of Terminals One and Two; a dispatcher is on duty outside the main doors of both terminals, where cars are stationed. Prices are fixed and posted at L.E. 25 to the area of the Nile Hilton, L.E. 28 to Cairo Sheraton and Gezira Sheraton, and L.E. 35 to the Mena House, and other hotels in the vicinity of the Pyramids. All Heliopolis destinations are L.E. 20. For the central office, tel. 915–348 or 915–349.

You should make a point of collecting small change in Egyptian currency and having it handy at all times. Egypt is a poor, overpopulated country where there are always lots of people around doing things for you—whether you want them to or not. You will need to hand out tips, or *baksheesh,* as it is known in Arabic, all the time. Never give a lot. Instead, give a little, but give it often.

Taxis in the cities are metered. The rate is 25 pts. for the first kilometer (1 kilometer = .62 miles) and 10 pts. for each additional kilometer. The drive from the airport to downtown Cairo is about 12 miles and the taxi fare should cost about L.E. 3 on the meter, but, depending on your destination, expect to pay L.E. 15, which is a reasonable amount considering the distance. Most important, settle the price *before* you get into the taxi and you can avoid an argument later.

If you arrive by day, the drive through the suburbs of Heliopolis, Abbassiya, and along the Corniche Road by the Nile is a pleasant introduction to the city. When traffic is light, the ride takes about 30 minutes, but in heavy traffic, allow an hour or more.

LANDING AT THE PORT. In Alexandria, entrance formalities will be completed on board ship prior to embarkation. Passengers walk directly from the ship into the port building, past the offices of the steamship companies, travel agencies, and government tourist office. The entrance corridor also has a post office, telephone service, and bank. A few feet away is the customs room where luggage is inspected.

After formalities are completed, visitors who are making the excursion to Cairo proceed to the main entrance of the port building to board chartered buses. Passengers on their own proceed by taxi to downtown Alexandria or the railway station. Taxi fare should be about L.E. 5. From a downtown hotel, a taxi to the railway station costs about L.E. 5; from downtown or rail station to Montazeh Sheraton, L.E. 10. A tour of Alexandria may be arranged with a travel agent at the port before proceeding to Cairo.

Several express trains run daily between Alexandria and Cairo. The three-hour trip through the Delta region is very pleasant and will give you a delightful preview of the Egyptian countryside. At the railway station in Cairo, visitors are usually met by a hotel or travel agency representative. If not, you may entrust your luggage to a station porter wearing a number. He will help you get a taxi. Just outside the Cairo station, you will see the first of many colossal statues of Ramses II, the builder of Abu Simbel and many other great monuments in Egypt.

The trip from the station to a downtown hotel takes about 15 minutes and costs about L.E. 5.

CUSTOMS. *Personal effects,* including furs and jewelry, are exempt from import duties provided they are for personal use and will be taken with the visitor upon departure from Egypt. These include new and used clothing and other articles reasonably required by a tourist, such as cameras and film, radio, typewriter, 200 cigarettes or 50 cigars, one liter of alcoholic beverage, and reasonable quantities of foodstuffs, perfume, and medicine intended for personal use. Portable televisions are subject to duty. You may be asked to list cameras on the customs declaration form, especially if you are carrying more than one. Valuable personal jewelry, although exempt from duty, must be declared on Form D on arrival.

Commercial articles: Duty must be deposited on articles of commercial value and will be refunded upon departure.

Firearms: Importing firearms into Egypt is prohibited. Customs authorities may grant tourists temporary licenses for firearms and hunting equipment provided an application has been submitted to the Minister of Interior, Cairo. The application must include the tourist's full name, nationality, passport number, period of stay in Egypt, and a full description of the weapons for which licensing is required. Two photos and an official receipt specifying that covering fees have been paid should be attached to the application. Under no circumstances may you dispose of firearms thus licensed during your stay.

If the necessary documents are not obtained, the firearms will be taken by customs officials on your arrival and returned to you when you leave Egypt. On arrival at Cairo airport anyone in possession of a gun must declare the serial number and kind of gun in his possession at the customs office to facilitate departure formalities.

Animals: Animals need a veterinary certificate stating that the pet is in good health, as well as a current rabies inoculation certificate. A small government tax is levied on all dogs brought into or bought in Egypt. On payment of the tax, a small identification tag is issued that should be attached to the dog's collar where it can be spotted easily.

REGISTERING UPON ARRIVAL. Foreigners must register with the proper authorities within seven days of their arrival in Egypt, the day of entry being excluded from this period. Those staying in a hotel are saved the bother as the hotel does it for them. You will be asked to surrender your passport for 24 hours in order to complete these formalities. If you are staying only a very brief time in the hotel, be sure to alert the desk clerk so that your passport will be returned in time for your departure.

If you are staying with a friend in a private home, registering with the authorities will be your responsibility or that of your host. It can be done at the *Passport Office,* Al Mogammaa Building, El Tahrir Square, Cairo, or 136 El Saraya Street, Alexandria. Those who register late are fined L.E. 25.

CURRENCY REGULATIONS AND EXCHANGE RATES. The unit of currency is the Egyptian pound (L.E.). It is divided into 100 piasters. Each piaster is subdivided into 10 milliemes. Pounds can be written in the following way: L.E. 1 or L.E. 1.000 or 100 pt. (i.e., 100 piasters). The following banknotes and coins are in circulation:

Banknotes: 1, 5, 10, 20, 50, 100 pounds. (L.E.); 25, 50 piasters.

Coins: 5-1, 10-1, and 20-10 piaster silver coins with the Salah-ed-Din Eagle or the Sphinx on one side and the value and the date of issue on the other.

Some old coins of several different shapes and sizes are still in circulation and are becoming collector's items. Memorial silver pieces for 25 and 50 piasters that have been issued on special occasions are also in circulation.

Exchange rates and facilities: Visitors to Egypt are obliged to convert currency at authorized exchanges only, found in all major hotels and banks. At Cairo airport and five-star hotels, exchange facilities are available 24 hours daily; at ports, the bank opens upon arrival of ships.

In an effort to wipe out the black market, the government devalued the Egyptian pound by 37% in May 1987. It was the first stage of a long-range program to create an open market for currency exchange. The government set a new rate and, subsequently, released the Egyptian pound to float freely against international currencies in the open market. At press time, the open market rate was L.E. 1=U.S. $.31, or U.S. $1=L.E. 3.20. Conventional wisdom ways the rate will probably reach L.E. 4 to the U.S. $1 by late 1991. Meanwhile, you should be aware that some U.S. banks and well-known exchange agencies are lagging shamefully behind the market. While the open market rate, published daily in the financial pages of major U.S. newspapers, was L.E. 3 or more, these institutions were still paying only L.E. 2.20—pocketing a neat 30% profit.

In the process of revamping the exchange system, some regulations that had been troublesome in the past were dropped. For example, visitors are no longer required to exchange a set amount of money into Egyptian pounds upon arrival. However, the rules have not been relaxed totally. Foreigners must still pay hotel bills with Egyptian pounds that have been officially exchanged and be able to show evidence of such transactions.

CURRENCY CONVERSION TABLE*

Egyptian Pounds/Piasters	U.S. Dollars/Cents
L.E. .25	$ .08
.50	.16
.75	.23
1.00	.31
2.00	.62
3.00	93
4.00	1.24
5.00	1.55
10.00	3.10
15.00	4.65
20.00	6.20

*Rates are approximate and subject to change.

Currency regulations: Tourists are allowed to bring in up to L.E. 20 in Egyptian currency. There is no limit to the amount of foreign currency in the form of banknotes, letters of credit, and traveler's checks that tourists may bring into Egypt. Upon departure, you may reconvert your unused Egyptian pounds *provided* you can show the buying invoices for them and your hotel bill to prove you spent $30 or £25 for every day of your stay in Egypt. There is no point in arguing with the bank teller or customs official; if you do not have the proper documentation, they will stick to the letter of the law and will not budge.

To repeat, keep track of all bank receipts. You will need to submit them to customs authorities upon departure in order to reconvert any unused Egyptian currency. The bank windows at the airport for reexchanging money are located in the main hall *before* entering the departure lounge.

Note: Over the years nothing has given visitors more trouble than the currency exchange laws. The recent reforms are certainly a step in the right direction, but visitors should recognize that they are *still responsible for obeying the laws and their failure to do so could lead to trouble, including having their money confiscated by authorities*. The problem is that Egyptian authorities themselves are lax in helping visitors comply with the regulations, but they can be unbending in applying the law.

To be specific, the Egyptian Consulate in the United States issues the following instructions: "You may enter Egypt with any amount of foreign currency, but if you wish to leave Egypt with the same amount or part of the foreign currency you originally carried upon entering, you must fill a Customs Currency Declaration Form upon arrival stating the amounts of foreign currency in your possession. This form should be stamped by Customs and you must keep a copy in your possession that you will be required to show upon departure. Failure to show this Customs Currency Declaration Form may result in the confiscation of all foreign currency in your possession and would be of great inconvenience to you. You may get the Currency Declaration Form from the airline carrier or the Egyptian Customs Authority at the airport or any other port of entry in Egypt."

The instructions seem clear, but the reality is that you cannot get Customs Currency Declaration Forms from the airline carrier as they do not have them. This was particularly true of Egyptair, which, in our most recent experience, did not even have supplies of the standard entry form. Foreign passengers had to obtain those upon arrival at Immigration. As for obtaining the Customs Currency Declaration Form from the Egyptian Customs Authority at the airport, that becomes even more of a myth. Not only did they not have it when we asked for it, but they said we did not need it and told us to "just keep all of our receipts to show customs." However, past experience has shown that this last course of action is insufficient to satisfy Customs officials.

To help keep your currency problems to a minimum, follow these steps: **Do not** carry large amounts of cash into or out of Egypt; instead, carry traveler's checks or letters of credit; **Always,** when buying Egyptian pounds, get a receipt; **keep ALL receipts**—currency exchanges, hotel bills, store purchases—until you depart the country; and **exchange only** small amounts of dollars or sterling for Egyptian currency as you need them so that you will not be left with unwanted Egyptian pounds at the end of your trip.

Credit cards and personal checks: Egyptian merchants are accustomed to credit cards, but their use is still limited to deluxe and first-class hotels and restaurants and to stores that deal with tourists. It is difficult to cash personal checks drawn on foreign banks. Do not plan to use them. Instead, bring enough traveler's checks or a letter of credit.

TIPPING. In most restaurants and hotels, droves of men hover about you to give you service. If you have been served well, a little baksheesh is appreciated. Fifty piasters will go a long way, and you will be handing out plenty before the trip ends. Carry a change purse for coins, and always ask for change in small denominations when paying a bill. Many people tip as they go, assuming this alleviates the necessity for tipping at the end of their visit. On the contrary, your departure, especially from a hotel, is the moment when tips are expected. You will swear you never saw most of the people before—and you probably haven't. For the occasion, be ready with a handful of piasters, distribute them with largesse, and hope the right ones are in the crowd. As a rule of thumb, remember that your *total* tip should not exceed 10% of your bill *before* the tax is added. Hotel bills have a 12% service charge, a 5% government tax, and a 2% city tax added to the total amount of your bill.

WOMEN TRAVELING ALONE. Unless you are a seasoned traveler, your first trip to Egypt will be more fun and less costly if you join a group—especially for the trip to Luxor, Aswan, and other sites in Upper Egypt. It is easy for an individual to join such groups, as leading travel agencies in Cairo and Alexandria have groups leaving daily for major sites of interest.

On the other hand, if you do not like to travel with anyone else, you need not hesitate. There are so many tourists roaming all over the country that Egyptians, even in the most remote places, are usually accustomed to foreign women on their own.

It is only fair to add, however, that if you do travel alone, your behavior must be circumspect and your dress modest. For example, bare-back dresses and shorts should be kept for the beach, and very short skirts and low-cut dresses and blouses must be avoided on city streets. Egypt is a Muslim country, and while it is not as conservative as others, discretion is necessary. It is especially important for women entering a mosque to be respectably dressed. Egyptian men have a habit of staring, which can be unsettling to a foreigner. Unfortunately, too, the new religious fervor stirring in other parts of the Middle East has spilled over into Egypt. For the first time in my 30 years' association with Egypt, I have seen a change in attitude toward unaccompanied women, that prompts me to caution them against going alone into areas of towns where they would clearly be the only foreigners, unless accompanied by an Egyptian friend or guide.

Egypt has one of the lowest crime rates in the world. There is some petty theft around hotels and sightseeing locales, but it is trivial compared with the crime in large American cities. Crimes of violence, outside of family feuds and vendettas, are almost unknown.

Staying in Egypt

TOURIST FACILITIES. *Tourist police,* stationed at major points of entry and sightseeing, wear either a white or black uniform, depending on the time of the year, and a blue badge that says Tourist Police—in Arabic!

Tourist Police:

Head Office, 5 Adly Street	Tel: 390–6028
Airport, Cairo International Airport	291–4255
Khan el Khalil, Khan el Khalil	904827
Main Railway Station, Ramses Square	847–611
Pyramids Zone, Pyramids Road (near Mena House)	850259

Tourist guides are available for hire by the day through hotels, travel agencies, and the tourist information offices for about L.E. 60 and up per day. Guides are licensed by the Ministry of Tourism and are required to pass examinations on the history and antiquities of Egypt. This, of course, does not mean that you will not be approached by those who are not so licensed and qualified. If you think you are being hustled, enlist the aid of your hotel concierge or the nearest policeman to deal with the situation.

Egypt is one of the oldest tourist countries in the world—and so are some of the guides, known here as dragomen. Except for the older men, the dragomen no longer wear the once characteristic turban and sweeping robes. Most dragomen, especially at sites of antiquity, are colorful, if not always accurate, and are inclined to embellish the facts to make a good story. They are being replaced by younger, better educated guides who have been trained for the job.

For those who visit Egypt on their own and not as part of a tour group, the *Government Tourist Office* can be helpful. These are the major locations of the Tourist Information Offices:

Cairo: Head Office: 5 Adly Street	Tel: 391–3454
Cairo: Pyramids Office: Pyramids Road	850259
Cairo: International Airport Office, Terminal One:	667475
Cairo: International Airport Office, Terminal Two:	291–4255
Alexandria: Saad Zaghloul Square	807611
Alexandria: Port	492–5986
Port Said: Palestine Street	238068
Luxor: The Tourist Bazaar	382215
Aswan: The Tourist Bazaar	323297
Suez: By the waterfront	223589
Hurghada	40513
New Valley	901206

The Association of Tourists' Friends, 33 Kasr el Nil St., Cairo; tel. 742036, is a private organization of volunteers formed to help visitors who are interested in meeting Egyptians.

TIME. Greenwich mean time plus two hours, or seven hours earlier than Eastern Standard Time; six hours during summer daylight savings time. Time changes take place on October 1 (one hour ahead) and March 1 (one hour back).

ELECTRIC CURRENT. 220 AC, 50 cycles. Wall plugs are the round two-prong European type. Adapter plugs for American products should be brought with you. American appliances need transformers. Save yourself trouble by carrying electrical devices with built-in 110/220v. converters and a set of adapter plugs.

LANGUAGES. Arabic is the national language of Egypt. In large towns and major tourist centers you will find English-, French-, German-, and Italian-speaking personnel among the staff in hotels and stores. Educated Egyptians almost always speak fluent English and French.

CONVERSION CHART

Metric Unit	U.S. Equivalent
Length	
meter (m)	39.37 inches
kilometer (km)	.62 mile
millimeter (mm)	.04 inch
Area	
hectare (ha)	2.47 acres
Capacity	
liter (L)	1.057 quarts
Weight	
gram (g)	.035 ounce
kilogram (kg)	2.2 pounds
metric ton (MT)	1.1 ton
Power	
kilowatt (kw)	1.34 horsepower

$$\text{(Fahrenheit) } °F = (°C \times 9/5) + 32$$
$$\text{(Celsius) } °C = (°F - 32) \times 5/9$$

BUSINESS HOURS. *Banks:* Daily—8:30 AM to 1:30 PM, closed Friday and Saturday. All major hotels have banks and exchange facilities that are usually open 24 hours daily. There is also a bank at the Egyptian Antiquities Museum, located in the east wing.

Stores: 9 AM to 1 PM and 4:30 to 7:30 or 8 PM summer; 10 AM to 5 or 6 PM winter; most shops in the Khan el Khalili bazaar stay open until about 8 PM. Most close on Sunday. Check with your hotel for store hours. The hours change from one season to another, and past efforts to standardize them have been unsuccessful.

Commercial offices: Summer—8 AM to 2 PM Winter—9 AM to 1 PM and 4:30 or 5 to 7 PM. Majority close Thursday afternoon and Friday; some close Saturday afternoon and Sunday.

Government offices: Daily: 8 AM to 2 PM; closed Friday and national holidays.

Note: For those who are coming to Egypt on business, it is very important to know the work days of the offices with which you will be doing business. Most embassies and some businesses close Friday and Saturday; others close Saturday and Sunday.

POST, CABLES, TELEPHONE, TELEX. **Post:** Delivery of airmail letters from New York to Cairo can take up to two weeks. Surface mail from the United States takes three months or longer. The Central Post Office, Attaba Square, is open 8 AM to 7 PM daily, 8 AM to noon on Fridays. All other post offices are open from 8 AM to 3 PM daily except Fridays. Front desk clerks in hotels have stamps and will mail ordinary letters and postcards for hotel guests. Postage on letters and postcards to the United States cost the same—70 piasters.

Letters to tourists with no fixed address in Egypt may be sent in care of "Poste Restante," but the addressee must personally pick up mail from the Central Post Office at Attaba Square. (We have never tried it.) As an alternative, visitors may receive mail at American Express, Sharia Kasr el Nil, Cairo. The Client's Desk, where mail is kept, is closed on Friday.

Packages require export licenses, which may be obtained from the Post Office on Ramses Street, near the train station. Shops catering to tourists will send packages for a fee that includes the license and packaging.

Parcels sent by surface mail from the United States take three to six months to reach the addresses in Egypt, or several weeks by air, and are subject to very heavy customs duty.

Telegraph: Cables and telegrams (in English) can be sent from hotels or at Telephone Offices. Telegrams must be written in block letters, and the sender's first and last name must be included.

Full rate to New York is approximately 70 pts. per word, with the address and signature counting as words. Full rate to London is about 67 pts. per word. Night letters cannot be sent. Telegraph service within Egypt is also available.

Sending cables to Cairo from the United States has been unreliable lately; they may not get delivered. Generally, telex or telefax is reliable, but if messages are important, it is better to phone. In addition to private courier services, reliable overnight delivery of letters and small packages is guaranteed worldwide through a service of Egypt's National Postal Organization. The major Express Mail Center is off Attaba Square, with customs on the spot. This service is consistently reliable.

Telephone: Major cities have dial systems. In small towns telephone service is available through local operators. Public phone booths are located at railroad stations, main squares, airport and tobacco stands or kiosks throughout both cities, and at several large hotels, such as the Heliopolis Sheraton. A local call in Cairo costs at least 25 pts., and you will need coins for the machine. For Cairo Information, dial 140. Shops will usually allow you to use the phone for a quick call.

Direct-dial long-distance service is available to the United States and most of the world. The cost to the United States is L.E. 21.80 station-to-station for three minutes, L.E. 32 person-to-person; night rates, 8 PM–8 AM, are slightly lower. Collect calls cannot be made from Egypt. However, Americans with an international AT&T credit card may use it by dialing 146 for an English-speaking operator. Ask the hotel switchboard operator for help if you need specific information. It is possible to place a call outside a hotel on your own if you have patience. The National Telecommunications Center on Adly St. has an English-speaking staff and is open 24 hours daily. The greatest improvement has been the availability of direct dial to the United States from most areas of the city and from certain private and business phones enabling calls to go through immediately.

The telephone country code for Egypt is 20; for Cairo, 2. When dialing Cairo from the United States, the numbers 202 should precede the local Cairo telephone number. Some other city codes are Abu Simbel and Aswan, 97; Alexandria and Mersa Matruh, 3; El-Arish and Ismailia, 64; Hurghada and Suez, 62; Luxor, 95; Port Said, 66; Sharm el Sheikh and St. Catherine, 10. A complete list is available from the Tourist Office.

Telex and Fax: Facilities are available at major hotels for guests and many private offices. Business Service Centers at major hotels offer telex service to outside customers at a 25% service charge over the cost of the telex. Meridian rates (based on Egyptian Telecommunication tariff) to the

United States are L.E. 7 per minute. Europe is the same. Telex and fax machines have become a normal part of operations for many businesses.

PHOTOGRAPHY AND EQUIPMENT. Egypt is a paradise for photographers, but remember that the sun is deceivingly bright, especially at sites of antiquity. You are not allowed to take pictures inside the tombs in the Valley of the Kings or inside most of those in the Valley of the Queens and Nobles. Attempts to do so could result in the confiscation of your camera and film.

Recently, the Egyptian Consulate in the United States issued these regulations: "You may enter Egypt with your video camera and other photography paraphernalia provided you register the equipment at the Customs Authority upon arrival. Failure to register your photography equipment may result in imposing the Egyptian Customs duties." But, as with so many of Egypt's regulations, the reality can be quite different. Discussions with some photographers about their experiences has led us to conclude that visitors with video equipment or amateurs who carry unusual amounts of cameras and lenses that give the impression they are professionals might be hassled. Fancy equipment, it seems, is one more opportunity for unsavory officials and gatekeepers at antiquity sites to extract baksheesh.

You are not allowed to take pictures of military zones, bridges, public works installation, or at certain strategic places, such as the Aswan Dam. Your guide will show you where you can take photographs at the Dam site. You are also not allowed to photograph police and military personnel.

To photograph in the Egyptian Antiquities and Coptic museums, you will need special permission, which is usually extended to professional photographers only. Inquiries should be made through the press office at the Ministry of Culture and Information as soon as you arrive in Cairo. (For more details on photographing antiquities, see the chapter on Upper Egypt.)

In the past, film was very expensive in Egypt, but at present, due to favorable exchange rates for the U.S. dollar and the British pound, film is reasonably priced. For example, black-and-white film is L.E. 10; Ektachrome, L.E. 20; Agfachrome, L.E. 11; Instamatic, L.E. 5. Also, you do not need to worry about the quality of the film, provided you buy it from a reputable, air-conditioned outlet. Two of Cairo's best are Kodak, 20 Adly St., and Actina, 4 Talaat Hart St. (Both are closed Sundays.) Actina also does camera repair. One of the best repair shops in the city is Khatchig, 27 Abd el-Khalek Sarwat St., Shop No. 4, Central Cairo, tel. 392–8747. Open Tues.–Sat. 10 AM–3 PM and 4–7 PM.

Slides of important sites are on sale at leading hotels and gift shops and at sites of antiquities and museums. The quality of the colors varies considerably from one vendor to another.

Keep your camera, lens, film, and other photographic equipment in plastic bags. At sites of antiquities particularly, there is a very fine sand dust in the air that can seep into your camera case.

Serious amateur photographers should carry a light meter, because unless you are familiar with desert conditions, you will probably overexpose the film. If you are ever in doubt, use one stop under a normal setting. There is an enormous amount of reflected light, especially during midday. On black-and-white film, you will be happy with the results of a yellow filter. Film with a high ASA reading is terrific for inside temples but too fast for normal outside shots in the bright sun at antiquity sites. As for color, wonderful results can be had with low ASA film such as Kodacolor 25 or 64 because lighting conditions are ideal. If you can overlook the fact that your photographs will have shadows, the best times of day for picture taking are early morning and late afternoon, when colors are deeper and sharper, and the color of the antique stone is mellow.

Black-and-white film, color prints, and Ektachrome slides can be developed in one or two days in Cairo. Kodak on Adly St. can process color prints in an hour. Kodachrome 25 and 64 slides cannot be processed here. Unless you have some special need to have your used film developed quickly, you should plan to develop film on your return home.

The Nile Hilton photo shop is open from 9 to 9 Monday through Saturday; Sunday to 7. The shop develops film, and if you need passport-size photos, these can be made in a hurry for a reasonable price. There are also good photo shops in major hotels and many in the downtown shopping area around Talaat Harb and Sharif streets.

HEALTH PRECAUTIONS. *Food:* In leading hotels and restaurants, food is usually clean and well prepared; nonetheless, reasonable caution should be exercised. Eat only food that has been cooked and fruits and vegetables that can be peeled, unless you are well traveled and know what your system can adjust to quickly.

Do not be alarmed if, after a day or two, you get the local version of *turista,* which in Egypt is commonly known as gyppie tummy. A doctor or pharmacist in Cairo or Alexandria will most likely prescribe Sulphur Guanidine, but our experience has been that nothing is better than Lomotil, obtainable from the same sources. The most important thing to remember is to take the medicine the moment you feel something coming on. Do not try to be a hero or think that ignoring it will make it go away. Call for a doctor if you find that you're running a fever. If you take medicine immediately, the upset should not be serious. As a further precaution, always cover yourself when you go to sleep. There is a marked difference between inside and outdoors in the daytime, and temperatures drop considerably at night. Sometimes a chill can bring on or aggravate a stomach upset. Also, drink plenty of liquids to avoid dehydration when you have an upset stomach. Try to avoid iced water.

Water: Drinking water in Cairo and Alexandria is safe in leading hotels. If you have a sensitive stomach, it is a good idea to drink only bottled water, which is available in hotels and restaurants throughout Egypt.

Getting Around in Egypt

HOW TO GET AROUND. For supercharged Americans or Europeans, Egypt is often an exercise in patience. Public transportation in particular can be a trying experience. There was a time when the use of public buses could be recommended for experienced travelers, provided they did not use them during rush hours. These days you would have to be a little masochistic to get on a city bus. They are packed solid. In Cairo, new minibuses with guaranteed seating have begun to appear, especially between

Tahrir Square and Zamalek, Giza and Heliopolis. They travel specific routes and cost about 50 pts. More will probably be added as they prove their popularity.

As a consequence visitors must rely on taxis, and although they are not expensive, there are not enough of them in Cairo to meet the demand. During rush hours it is almost impossible to find one. If you become stranded, the wisest course is to walk to the nearest hotel. Taxis are more likely to show up there to drop off passengers. Also, do not hesitate to hail one that already has a passenger. Most Egyptians are very willing to share. *Limo,* a radio-taxi service, offers 24-hour, citywide cabs at fixed rates. Tel. 915–348 or 915–3490. You can also hire a Limo or other car with driver by the day.

A taxi ride in Egypt could be one of the most eventful experiences of your life. Egypt is a flat country and most of the roads are as straight as an arrow, so it takes a bit of doing to make a simple car ride memorable. Yet the traffic jams that sometimes develop are unbelievable, and they materialize out of nowhere. With a healthy sense of humor and a great deal of patience, you will be able to come through the ordeal intact. Otherwise, you could easily be reduced to tears. Whatever happens, logic is your least useful tool. Somehow, and only Allah knows how, after a short time and a great deal of horn blowing and gesticulating, the traffic begins to flow again.

Taxis: In Cairo taxis are painted dark blue and white, and in Alexandria, black and orange or yellow. The fare is registered on a meter on the driver's right side. The flag fall charge is 25 pts. for the first kilometer and 10 pts. for each additional kilometer.

Taxi drivers might speak a smattering of English, but do not count on their understanding anything but Arabic. They seldom know the names of any but the major streets. Since street names seem to change with the political winds—you might find them a better barometer than the newspapers—it is possible to sympathize with taxi drivers for not being able to keep up with the trend.

If you do not know the direction to your destination, ask your hotel concierge or doorman to write the address in Arabic on a piece of paper and to instruct the taxi driver. If you want to direct him yourself, you should learn these words: *doughri* or *ala toul* (straight ahead), *yameen* (right), *shamal* (left), *'andak* (stop).

The average taxi ride in downtown costs about L.E. 5 or more when taken from a luxury hotel. There is no extra charge for night service, but taxi drivers might want to charge more. Also, because the official taxi fares are too cheap, cab drivers have taken to the age-old trick of saying the meter does not work. In this case, try to determine the price in advance or be prepared to be generous. Even when a meter works, drivers expect to be paid triple the meter reading—and still the price would be a bargain.

As an aid to tourists, when visitors take a taxi from a hotel or major tourist attraction a tourist policeman records the date, time, destination, and taxi number. If you have any problems with a taxi driver, he can be traced. Another benefit is that through the records of the tourist police, it is sometimes possible to recover an item left in a taxi.

Metro: The first stage of Cairo's new gleaming subway has been completed. (*See* the Transportation section of the Cairo chapter for a description of its routes.)

Car rentals: Renting a car with driver in Egypt is one of the true bargains left. *Hertz* rates start at about L.E. 67 per day for a four-seater Fiat with 100 km per day free. For another L.E. 24, you can have an English-speaking driver for 10 hours daily. From experience, we can recommend the company and its drivers, and in Cairo traffic, the drivers are worth every piaster. Be generous with your tip at the conclusion; drivers make so little one wonders how they manage to live. Hertz has an office at the airport and at the Ramses Hilton and Nile Wena hotels. Its headquarters is 195 July 26 St., Agouza. Tel. 347–4172. Reservations can be made through the company's offices in the United States. *Avis, Budget,* and other chains are also represented.

In Alexandria, *Avis* (Cecil Hotel, Saad Zaghloul Square; tel. 807–055) rents Peugot 505 at L.E. 58 per day with 100 km free; a driver can also be provided.

Horse carriages: These are tourist attractions rather than a means of transportation. Nowadays they are seen in Alexandria, Luxor, and small villages, but very seldom in Cairo. The fare should be agreed upon before engaging the carriage and generally should not be more than L.E. 10 for a short ride.

TRAINS. A network of trains connects Cairo with the major towns of the Delta and with the important sites of antiquity in Upper Egypt. There are three classes on Egyptian trains. The third class should not be used by visitors. By Western standards, first-class travel by train is comfortable and cheap and the air-conditioning systems—winter or summer—are good. Second class is adequate for short trips to Alexandria. Reservations must be made in advance at the Cairo Railway station at Midan Ramses, Alexandria Railway station in the central part of town, or through a travel agency. Demand is greater than supply. You must book several days in advance.

On your first trip to Egypt, first-class travel by express trains is recommended, especially for the trip between Cairo and Alexandria; it is a pleasant introduction to the Egyptian countryside and way of life. First-class Cairo-Alexandria passengers may reserve in advance seats in air-conditioned cars. The train ride between Cairo and Alexandria is very comfortable and enjoyable. Coffee and other beverages, sandwiches, and cakes are served at a small cost. Trains are very punctual.

LOWER EGYPT

First- and second-class trains are air-conditioned. Train schedules are usually consistent and reliable, but travelers should reconfirm departure times given here before finalizing an itinerary.

Fares: 1st class, L.E. 10.60; 1st-class Express, L.E. 13
2nd class, L.E. 6.50; 2nd-class Express, L.E. 8

Alexandria Depart	Cairo Arrive	Cairo Depart	Alexandria Arrive
7:30 AM	10:20 AM	6:20 AM	8:55 AM
*8:00 AM	10:00 AM	*8:00 AM	10:00 AM
9:20 AM	12:10 PM	8:55 AM	11:25 AM
10:30 AM	1:20 PM	9:30 AM	12:10 PM
11:50 AM	2:20 PM	11:20 AM	2:00 PM
2:00 PM	4:00 PM	12:15 PM	2:45 PM
3:30 PM	6:15 PM	1:05 PM	3:55 PM
5:10 PM	8:00 PM	*2:00 PM	4:00 PM
7:00 PM	9:00 PM	3:35 PM	9:00 PM
7:25 PM	9:25 PM	5:50 PM	8:30 PM
		*7:00 PM	9:00 PM
		8:10 PM	10:50 PM

Note *Fast trains to Alexandria are now known as *Turbini* and take only two hours. The cost for first-class travel is L.E. 13 one-way; Ramses Station, tel. 753–555. The trains officially called Express have become slow and are usually dirty. Normal trains take approximately three hours.

UPPER EGYPT

Wagon-Lits manages new, well-maintained trains with two-berth sleeping compartments from Cairo to Luxor and Aswan. The price for these overnight air-conditioned express trains includes dinner and breakfast. Beverages, including bottled water, are extra. As the price to either Luxor or Aswan is the same, L.E. 170.20, you may wish to start an Upper Egypt trip in Aswan. Reservations for trains operated by Wagon-Lits can be made at their office: 48 Giza St., Orman Building: tel 348–7354; telex 20973.

Tickets can be purchased only *one week* in advance from Ramses Station. However, advance reservations can be made at CIWLET, 48 Giza St., Cairo. Tel. 348–7354. Also, travel agents can secure tickets.

Express Train for Upper Egypt: *Fare:* L.E. 265.65—single compartment; L.E. 170.20—per person, double compartment

Cairo	Luxor	Aswan
Depart: 7:00 PM	Arrive: 5:30 AM	Arrive: 9:30 AM
7:20 PM	6:00 AM	10:00 AM

Aswan	Luxor	Cairo
Depart: 3:45 PM	Arrive: 7:30 PM	Arrive: 6:30 AM
6:30 PM	10:40 PM	9:30 AM

Other Trains to Upper Egypt:
There are also two regular, air-conditioned trains to Upper Egypt; these are much slower than the express ones but far cheaper. Generally, the only tourists using them are students and cross-Africa travelers. Sleepers on these trains are reserved for Egyptians and are next to impossible for foreigners to obtain.

Fares: To Luxor	1st class	L.E. 26.80
	2nd class	L.E. 15.60
To Aswan	1st class	L.E. 33.20
	2nd class	L.E. 18.60

Upper Egypt Train Schedule:

Cairo	*Luxor*	*Aswan*
Depart: 7:30 AM	Arrive: 6:00 PM	Arrive: 11:20 PM
noon	1:00 AM	

Aswan	*Luxor*	*Cairo*
Depart: 5:00 AM	Arrive: 10:00 AM	Arrive: 8:55 AM
	5:20 AM	4:20 PM

TO SUDAN

The Nile Valley Navigation Corp. (offices at Ramses Station) operates two new boats from Aswan to Wadi Halfa, with onward train connection to Khartoum, twice a week. A first-class ticket in a two-berth cabin is L.E. 85; second-class, is L.E. 48. Land-Rover transport is approximately L.E. 135. Individual tickets can be purchased at Ramses Station, but vehicle bookings can be made only in Aswan. The Cairo office is open daily except Fri. 9 AM to 2 PM

DISTANCE BETWEEN CAIRO AND OTHER CITIES

From Cairo to:	Kms.	(Miles) by road	Kms. by rail
El Alamein	304	(182)	326
Alexandria (Via the Delta Highway)	225	(135)	208
Alexandria (Via the desert road)	221	(132)	
Assiut	380	(228)	375
Aswan	890	(534)	879
Baliana (Abydos)	556	(304)	518
Delta Barrages	25	(15)	
Damietta	191	(114)	205
Edfu	785	(470)	776
Ein Sukhna	189	(113)	
Esna	732	(429)	724
Fayyum	103	(62)	130
Helwan	32	(19)	
Ismailia (Via Bilbeis)	140	(84)	159
Kharga Oasis	600	(359)	737
Kom Ombo	835	(560)	834
Luxor	676	(406)	671
Maadi	14	(8)	
Mallawi (Tell-al-Amarna)	288	(173)	
Mersa Matruh	490	(294)	510
Minia	243	(146)	247
Port Said	220	(132)	237
Rosetta	263	(157)	269
Sallum	714	(428)	759

AIR TRAVEL. *Egyptair* operates between the major cities, with regular daily flights from Cairo to Luxor/Aswan, Abu Simbel, Alexandria and Hurghada and twice weekly to Kharga in the New Valley. Air travel is recommended for anyone whose time is limited. Fares are reasonable. The carrier can also arrange combined air-and-hotel tickets to Luxor, Aswan, and a day tour to Abu Simbel. In fact, the tour to Abu Simbel by air offered by all travel agencies in Egypt, the United States, Europe, etc., is the same one and is a monopoly of the airlines.

Egyptair Offices: Cairo: 6 Adly St., 9 Talaat Harb St., Opera Square, Nile Hilton, Cairo Sheraton, 22 Ibrahim el Lakani, Heliopolis.

Alexandria: El Ramal Square.

Port Said: Sharia al Gumhruia.

Air Sinai provides regular service to Sharm el Sheikh, St. Catherine's Monastery, El Arish in the Sinai Peninsula, Hurghada on the Red Sea, and Tel Aviv. Its main office is located in the new wing of the Nile Hilton Hotel. Tel. 760948. In the Unites States, Canada, and the United Kingdom, information is available from *Egyptair*.

ZAS, Airline of Egypt, Novotel Airport, tel. 290–8707 or 290–7840, was started as an Egyptian cargo carrier with international headquarters at Amsterdam's Schipol Airport. Recently it began offering domestic and international passenger service. Through Z tours (at Novotel), individual passengers may buy seats on daily flights (which are primarily charters) to Luxor, Aswan, Hurghada, Sharm el Sheikh, and Alexandria. User reports have been positive on ZAS's reliability in maintaining its schedules and honoring confirmed bookings.

Airport Information Office: tel. 665–599.

The airlines have requested a 15% fare increase; at press time, these had not yet been approved.

INTRA-EGYPT FLIGHTS

One-way airfares (subject to change)	U.S. Dollars	
	First Class	Economy
Cairo to:		
Abu Simbel	171	137
Alexandria	49	40
Aswan	122	96
Hurghada	95	75
Luxor	88	69
New Valley	95	75
Luxor to:		
Abu Simbel	88	69
Aswan	39	30
Hurghada	39	30
New Valley	74	59
Aswan to:		
Abu Simbel	55	42
New Valley	39	30

(Schedules are subject to frequent changes, which is why we no longer attempt to list them here. Check with Egyptair/New York and be sure to check locally and *always reconfirm all your reservations upon your arrival in Egypt.* Since the difference between first- and tourist-class fares is often small, you may wish to consider purchasing a first-class ticket. The first-class section is less likely to be overbooked, and confirmed reservations are more likely to be honored.)

The number of flights in and out of Cairo is not adequate for the demand. This is as true on international flights as it is on domestic ones.

Flights to and from Upper Egypt are constantly overbooked, but they do work on a first-come, first-served basis, so it pays to get to the airport early.

You should be at the airport a minimum of one or two hours before flight time. The trip from town to the airport in Cairo is 30 minutes to an hour, depending on the time of day and traffic.

NILE STEAMERS. A voyage up the Nile by steamer is one of the most delightful trips in Egypt, and even with 200 boats—a more than tenfold increase in the past decade—supply can barely keep up with demand. Most of the new vessels are in the four- and five-star categories and offer three- to five-night cruises between Luxor and Aswan. Some add Abydos and Denderah, which have the most interesting and important temples in Upper Egypt and feature longer cruises of six or seven nights as well as optional tours by land. The pressure of so many ships has also led more cruise companies to add longer 10- and 11-night excursions that travel to Middle Egypt or sail between Cairo and Luxor/Aswan. Among the newest, most luxurious ships are the *Nephtis,* which is part of the fleet of Hilton International; the *Nile Monarch,* which belongs to Swan Hellenic Tours, represented in the United States by Esplanade Tours of Boston; and the *Kasr el Nil* and *Radamis,* which are operated by Movenpick Hotels.

Prices of Nile cruises are now divided into three seasons:

High Season (October through April): Five-star ships range from $130 to $200 per person per night; four-star ships range from $75 to $140 per person per night.

Shoulder Season (May and September): Reduction of 15% off the high season rates.

Low Season (June through August): Reduction of 50% off the high season rates.

Generally, prices include all meals, service, taxes, and sightseeing in the company of a trained guide or Egyptologist. Quality varies even more than the price. Unless you have the opportunity to inspect the ship yourself, you would be well advised to deal only with companies that have established reputations in the hotel and cruises business. Companies whose five-star ships consistently get good reviews are Hilton International, Mena House Oberoi, Presidential, Sheraton, and Sonesta. These are the main ships used by major U.S. tour companies as well.

If you arrive in Egypt without cruise reservations and decide to take one, it is wise to make inquiries and reservations through the owning or managing company's offices in Cairo where cabin space is controlled. If you wait until you arrive in Luxor or Aswan to find space, you must walk from ship to ship, inquiring from the boat manager if space is available, and be willing to take pot luck. However, the latter method does have merit if you have ample time. First, it enables you to see the ship and its cabins before booking it, and perhaps, take a quick reading of its cleanliness (an important indication of how the ship is run, considering the large number of ships with little or no track record now available). And, if you are good at bargaining, you can probably negotiate a better price for an empty cabin on the day of sailing than if you were to book it in advance in Cairo. This is, after all, a matter of supply and demand, which tends to fluctuate wildly.

A cruise on the Nile differs from ocean cruising in several ways. Nile steamers, compared with oceangoing cruises ships, are small and cozy like a yacht and have an informal, comfortable atmosphere. Some ships accommodate as few as 20 passengers, while the largest take up to 152 people.

Staterooms, slightly smaller than those of standard cruise ships, are comparable in size to cabins on ships that sail the Greek islands. They are well-appointed and comfortable. Most are fitted with twin lower beds; some have wall pull-down bunks for a third person, dressing table or nightstand, closet, and private bath with shower. Ships with suites often have full bath with tub. Four- and five-star ships are fully air-conditioned.

Small ship size limits the recreational and entertainment facilities, but these are not important considerations on a Nile cruise, where the attractions are the antiquities and the scenic countryside. On the other hand, ships holding 80 or more passengers have lounges for reading and relaxing, bar, sundeck, swimming pool, pleasant dining room with full table service, and evening entertainment. Laundry services and hair salon are also available.

Nile cruises begin in one of three places—Cairo, Luxor, or Aswan. More and more companies are offering long cruises throughout the year because they are becoming increasingly popular and because the new ships are air-conditioned.

Passengers who begin their cruise in Upper Egypt usually travel to Luxor or Aswan by plane or train. In Luxor, a town next to the ancient site of Thebes, the ships dock on the east bank of the river near the PLM Azur and Winter Palace hotels, within walking distance of Luxor Temple and the Luxor Museum and a short carriage ride from Karnak Temple, the most colossal ancient monument in the world.

Sightseeing includes a full day on the West Bank of the Nile, in the Valley of the Kings, where the tombs of Tutankhamen and other pharaohs were found; the Valley of the Queens; the Tombs of the Nobles, which contain some of the most important art of ancient Egypt; and other great temples and monuments.

From Luxor, many cruises sail downstream (north) to visit the Temples of Abydos and Denderah; others take in only the sites between Luxor and Aswan. Abydos is one of the oldest sites of worship in the world and, because of its art, is considered the most important temple in Egypt. Tours beyond Abydos are available on longer cruises that stop at Tel al Amarna, the capital of Pharoah Akhenaton and his beautiful wife, Nefertiti; at Minya, the largest town of central Egypt; and at Beni Hassan, site of 12th-century tombs—unusual tomb drawings show ancient Egyptians practicing judo and playing ball games that appear to be similar to those we play today.

From Luxor, ships also sail upstream (south) to Aswan and stop for sightseeing at Esna, Edfu, and Kom Ombo—all sites of temples dating from the Ptolemaic and Greek periods. If the cruise begins at Aswan, the same itinerary is followed in reverse order, sailing downstream to Luxor.

Aswan was the capital of Nubia and an important trading place in ancient times. Today, it is primarily a winter resort and the administrative center for the High Dam and the surrounding region. Aswan is dotted with antiquities, most importantly the Temple of Philae, which is located on an island in the middle of the river.

Egypt without the Nile River seems inconceivable. Your first view of the river snaking its way through the desert will be a dramatic illustration of its importance throughout Egypt's history. Beyond the ribbon of green—the land irrigated by the Nile—the desert begins and stretches endlessly into the horizon on both sides.

The Nile flows so gently that ships glide almost imperceptibly. The banks of the river are never more than a short distance away, and passengers can enjoy a close view of rural life in Upper Egypt. Life on the land bridges centuries. Cruise passengers see scenes along the riverbanks and in the green fields that replicate ancient drawings on the walls of the temples and tombs. The sense of endless time and tranquillity is almost overwhelming, particularly in contrast to the roar and clamor of Cairo.

The following is a partial listing of companies and their operating Nile steamers:

Abercrombie & Kent, 1420 Kensington Rd., Oak Brook, IL 60521. Tel. 800–323–7308. Operates *Sun Boat,* 24 cabins; *Sunboat II,* 32 cabins.

Cairo Hotel & Nile Cruise Co., 23 Ismail Mohamed St., Zamalek. Tel. 341–1190. Operates *King Tut,* 45 cabins.

Egyptian Company for Floating Hotels, 17 Ahmed Heshmat St., Zamalek. Tel. 340–3748. Operates *Nile Beauty,* 56 cabins.

Helio Tours, 147 El Hegaz St., Heliopolis, Cairo. Tel. 245–4246. Operates *Helio,* 50 cabins.

Hilton International, Cornish St., Cairo Tel. 740880. Operates *Isis,* 48 cabins; *Nephtis,* 62 cabins; and *Osiris,* 48 cabins. Tel. 212–688–2240.

International Nile Cruise Co., 87 Ramses St., Cairo Tel. 744708. Operates *Golden Boat,* 50 cabins; *Diamond,* 50 cabins; and *Fleur,* 50 cabins.

Jolley's Travel, 23 Kasr El Nil, Cairo. Tel. 393–9390. Operates *Alexander the Great,* 58 cabins. Tel. 800–368–6500.

Eastmar Co., 13 Kasr El Nil St., Cairo. Tel. 753–216.

Nile Star, 40 cabins.

Mena House Oberoi, tel. 385–5544. Operates *Sheherayar,* 74 cabins; *Shehrazad,* 74 cabins.

Middle East Floating Hotels Co., 4 Karim El Dawla St., Tel. 758988. Operates *Arabia,* 28 cabins.

Movenpick Hotels, Luxor Movenpick Hotel Jolie Ville, Crocodile Island, Luxor, tel. 095–384–855. Cairo Reservations: 247–0077. Operates *Kasr el Nil,* 51 cabins; *Radamis,* 74 cabins.

Naggar Travel and Nile Cruises, 32 Sabry Abu Allam St. Tel. 742855. Operates *Ramsis of Egypt,* 40 cabins; *Queen Nabila,* 62 cabins; *King Ramsis of the Nile,* 83 cabins; and *Nabila II,* 82 cabins. Tel. 201–585–2180.

Presidential Nile Cruise Co., 13 Maraashly St., Zamalek. Tel. 340–0517. Operates *Nile President,* 68 cabins; *Nile Princess,* 31 cabins; *Nile Symphony,* 75 cabins and two suites; *Nile Admiral,* 78 cabins; *Nile Emperor,* 75 cabins; *Nile Legend,* 75 cabins; *Nile Ritz,* 78 cabins; and the newest of the fleet, *Nile Plaza,* 78 cabins.

Pullman International Hotels, Nile Pullman Cruises, 9 Menes St., El Korba, Heliopolis. Tel. 290–8802. Operates *Nile Pullman L'Egyptien,* 37 cabins; and *Nile Pullman Fleurette,* 51 cabins.

Pyramid Tours, 56 Gamet Dowal Arabi, Mohandessen, Cairo. Tel. 360–0146. *El Karnak,* 22 cabins; *Pyramids,* 22 cabins; *Queen Cleopatra,* 18 cabins; *Queen Nefertiti,* 22 cabins; *Ramses,* 18 cabins; and *Tutankhamen,* 18 cabins; *Luxor; Hatshepsut; Akhenaton.*

Sheraton Hotels, 48-b, Guiza St., Orman Bldg., Cairo. Tel. 348–8215. Operates *Ani,* 76 cabins; *Aton,* 76 cabins; *Hotep,* 76 cabins; and *Tut,* 76 cabins. Tel. 800–843–6453; 800–343–7170.

Sonesta Hotels, Sonesta Hotel Cairo, 4 El Tayaran St., Nasr City. Tel. 262–8111. Operates *Nile Goddess,* 68 cabins.

Sphinx Tours, 2 Behler Passage, Cairo. Tel. 392–0704. Operates *Nile Queen,* 50 cabins; *Nile Sphinx,* 50 cabins; *Rev Vacance,* 20 cabins; and *Le Scribe.* Tel. 212–832–3120.

Spring Tours, 3, Said el Bakri St., Zamalek. Tel. 341–5972. Operates the *Nile Spring* and *Spring I,* 43 cabins each..

Swan/Hellenic (Div. of P & O), Esplanade Tours, 581 Boylston St., Boston, MA 02116. Tel. 617–266–7465. Operates *Nile Monarch,* 48 cabins; and *Nile Princess.*

Time Machine Co., 9 Ahmed Labib el Kerdani St., Heliopolis, Cairo. Tel. 661561. Operates *The Time Machine,* 20 cabins.

Trans Egypt Travel, 37 Kasr El Nil, Zamalek. Tel. 744313. Operates *Triton,* 47 cabins.

For those who are truly ready for an adventure, *South Sinai Travel* and other tour companies in Cairo offer a cruise between Aswan and Luxor by felucca. Or, once in Aswan, you can arrange a trip with a felucca captain yourself. The cost, not including food, is about L.E. 100.

VISITING UPPER EGYPT. For the full excursion to Upper Egypt, a prearranged trip may be bought in Cairo. The package includes round-trip train, plane and/or steamer fare, food, hotel accommodations, and guides. If you are a seasoned traveler, you may prefer to go on your own and pay each item separately as your needs require. The latter plan is more costly but enables you to travel at your own pace. We cannot stress strongly enough, however, that for most people on a first trip to Egypt, a prearranged tour organized through a *reliable travel agent* is practical and more satisfactory.

Some Egyptian travel agents offer tours to Upper Egypt with all travel by motorcoach. They are sold locally and in Europe and provide for travel of about 200 miles per day from Cairo to Minya, Assuit, Luxor and Aswan, with stops along the way at sites of antiquity. The 40-passenger luxury coaches are air-conditioned and comfortable.

In planning your itinerary you should investigate the new alternatives that offer the possibility of more extensive and less costly modes of travel if you tend to travel on your own.

For the onward journey from Egypt to Sudan, boat passage to Sudan via Lake Nasser must be booked in Cairo and paid for in Egyptian pounds exchanged at the official rate. It is also possible to drive from Cairo to Aswan by car, ship the car to Wadi Halfa, and then either drive or send the car by train to Khartoum. All visas and permits must be obtained before you leave Cairo.

Intracity bus service. Travel between Cairo and Alexandria and other major cities by deluxe, air-conditioned motorcoach is comfortable and cheap. Tickets may be purchased at a kiosk opposite the Ramses Hilton Hotel, north of Midan el Tahrir, from which buses leave. A one-way ticket from Cairo to Alexandria in one of these air-conditioned buses is L.E. 10. The return ticket must be purchased in Alexandria.

Misr Travel and other well-established travel agencies have air-conditioned luxury motorcoaches that are available for local as well as long-distance travel, including excursions to Upper Egypt, and can be chartered for groups.

Daily service from Cairo to St. Catherine's and Sharm el Sheikh is available from *East Delta Line.* Buses leave for St. Catherine's at 7 and 10:30 AM and return from there at 6 AM and 1 PM. Buses for Sharm el Sheikh depart at 7 and 10 AM, 1 and 4 PM and midnight. Buses for Nuweiba and Taba leave at 7 AM. All buses leave from Sinai Terminal in the Cairo suburb of Abbassia. Buses for Hurghada leave from the Ahmed Helmy Station behind Ramses Station; for towns along the Suez Canal, they leave from Orabi Station, also near Ramses Station. *Note:* Luxury buses have music videos that often blare at ultrahigh volume.

For motorcoach service to Upper Egypt, *see* the section on Upper Egypt.

Intracity taxi service. Peugeot taxis, leaving from in front of the Ramses Railroad Station and Tahrir Square, are an economical way to travel around Egypt. The taxis are station wagons and usually hold up to seven passengers, plus the driver. One-way to Alexandria per person is L.E. 5; to Ismailia, L.E. 3; to Suez, L.E. 3; to Port Said, L.E. 5; to El Arish, L.E. 10. Since the prices are so cheap, foreign travelers often buy two seats to gain the added comfort.

DRIVING IN EGYPT. The *Automobile Club of Egypt,* 10 Sharia Kasr el Nil, can be helpful in supplying information on driving to the different regions of the country. Incidentally, the club has one of the best restaurants in town. It is for members only, but if you write ahead to the secretary, you will be welcomed as a visitor. Tel. 743355.

The *Touring Club of Egypt* is affiliated with the Automobile Club.

A tourist entering Egypt with a car registered in a foreign country is exempt from local customs duties for a period of 90 days under the following regulations:

   1) the owner must hold a triptych or *carnet de passage en douane* from a recognized automobile club (i.e., AAA); otherwise he or she must pay a deposit that will be refunded upon departure;

   2) the owner must have an international driving license valid for the 90-day period;

   3) the car must have an international motor vehicle license; and

   4) customs officials must verify that the owner has no fixed residence in Egypt.

At the customs house the car owner is given a label for a 90-day tax exemption to post on the car's front window. If the stamp is not displayed, you may be stopped by the police. If the car remains in Egypt after 90 days, the owner must pay L.E. 20 until the date of expiration. After that, payment of 1/10th of the value of the car is requested. The owner is also subject to road tax.

Importing other vehicles: Under a triptych, motor bicycles, scooters, motorcycles, small aircraft, minibuses with up to nine seats, boats, luggage, and caravan trailers, commercial passenger buses, and taxis may be imported temporarily.

Vehicles to be used for demonstration or exhibition purposes may be imported for 90 days against a deposit on the customs duty and taxes.

Nonmotorized bicycles may be temporarily imported duty-free as personal effects without customs documents.

Length of stay: Vehicles temporarily imported by tourists may remain in Egypt for up to three months. During the 90-day period there is no limit on the number of times you may enter Egypt, provided your visa and carnet are valid.

Tourists who want to keep a vehicle in Egypt for a longer period may apply to the Automobile Club of Egypt, which will forward the request for extension to the proper authorities, provided the visa is extended. Extensions are granted for another three months maximum. You should contact the Automobile Club at least one month before the document is due to expire.

If you are planning an extended stay in Egypt, a car will add tremendously to the pleasure of your visit.

Private cars for use during a long-term stay may also be imported into Egypt, but steep customs duties must be paid. If you intend to sell the car in Egypt, check first with the American Embassy on importation regulations. They change rather frequently.

Insurance: By law all car owners must carry third-party personal liability insurance obtained in Egypt. Good insurance coverage is advisable and is available at reasonable prices. Rates vary according to the engine size, horsepower, and value of the car.

License: An Egyptian driver's license is necessary and is issued upon presentation of four photos, certificate of medical examination, U.S. or British driver's license, and payment of a small fee.

Those who do not have a valid international driver's license will be required to take a driving test. A driver's license must be obtained before the license plate can be issued. Bring a valid U.S. or international driver's license to save yourself a great deal of time and endless trouble.

Rule of the road: Traffic moves to the right. Do not plan to drive at night except in major cities.

Garage and repairs: New cars will minimize the problem of repair and spare parts. Small cars are more practical to operate.

Spare parts are not readily available because of import restrictions, and they tend to be very expensive when they are. Those planning a long stay or a great deal of driving should bring spare parts for their cars, especially those most subject to wear, such as gaskets, fan belts, spark plugs (ignition points), fuel lines, pumps and filters, and headlights and taillights. Egypt has a local tire industry and Fiat assembly plant.

General Motors, Mercedes, Fiat, Peugeot, Volkswagen, etc., maintain agencies with their own repair shops. Most garages have good mechanics, and body work and paint jobs are inexpensive by U.S. standards.

Gasoline and service stations: In Cairo and Alexandria, petrol and service stations are plentiful, but outside of main towns they are scarce. Before starting on a long trip, be sure to get all the pertinent information you might need about road conditions and location of petrol stations from the Automobile Club or Tourist Administration.

Gasoline is called benzene and is sold by the liter. It costs about 55 pts. for regular and 60 pts. for high octane. Car engines and mechanisms function well but should be cleaned frequently because of the ever-present sand dust in the air and impurities in the gasoline.

Security regulations: Travel in the area near the Libyan border is restricted by the government for military reasons. Permits for travel in other security areas can be obtained from the Travel Permits Department of the Ministry of Interior, corner of Sharia Sheikh Rihan and Sharia Nubar (two blocks east of the American University).

Travel to Israel from Egypt by land is possible by private car as well as by motorcoach. Allow two to three hours for customs formalities at the border.

Inquire about regulations from the Automobile Club before starting out on a trip, and always carry your passport with you.

A chart of distances from Cairo to major towns throughout Egypt appears earlier in this section. A brief description of major roads follows.

Tourist Roads of Lower Egypt: Alexandria–Cairo (220 km–136 mi), paved desert road. Note that 109 km (68 mi) along the paved desert road, another road leads to Wadi Natrun, the famous valley where several ancient Coptic monasteries are located. Just before reaching Cairo, the road passes the Pyramids of Giza.

Alexandria–Cairo (221 km–138 mi), a direct road that links Cairo to Alexandria, passes through the Delta region by way of its main towns and through nearly all the *Muhafezat* (governorates) of Lower Egypt.

Cairo–Ismailia (120 km–72 mi), the best four-lane divided highway in Egypt, leaves from Cairo alongside the airport. Another road, known as the Agricultural Road between Ismailia and Cairo, parallels the desert road to the north and passes through El Qassasin, El Tell El Kebir, and Bilbeis.

Port Said–Ismailia–Suez (170 km–106 mi); a two-lane road that runs parallel to the Suez Canal.

Suez–Cairo (134 km–84 mi), a desert road linking the Red Sea to the Nile, follows the historic pilgrimage and trade route.

Cairo–Fayum (70 km–44 mi) is a good two-lane highway and an interesting and pleasant drive through the countryside.

Coastal road Alexandria–Sallum (508 km–317 mi) is an asphalt road along a fertile region near the Mediterranean coast that passes through El Alamein and Mersa Matruh.

Mersa Matruh–Siwa Oasis (302 km–188 mi); the route was used by Alexander the Great to visit the Amun Temple at the Siwa Oasis. A new paved road was completed in 1984. You must have permission from the governorate of Mersa Matruh to proceed beyond the town of Mersa Matruh. This is usually given automatically, particularly since Egypt and Libya normalized relations.

Tourist Roads of Upper Egypt: Cairo–Aswan (approximately 900 km–560 mi) is paved throughout and forms part of the international route from

Cairo to Cape Town. It passes a large number of antiquity sites. The drive from Abydos to Luxor takes under three hours and from Luxor to Aswan about four hours; from Aswan to Abu Simbel, 3½ hours.

Assiut–New Valley: the road from Assiut to El Kharga Oasis (137 miles) and from El Kharga to El Dakhla Oasis (118 miles) is paved.

The oases are scattered with historical monuments of the 18th Egyptian Dynasty and with Roman and Coptic monuments.

The Red Sea resort of Hurghada may be reached from Cairo via Suez, straight south through Ein Sukhna to Hurghada; from Qena to Safaga to Hurghada; from Edfu to Mersa Alam and Hurghada. In Sinai, there are roads to St. Catherine's Monastery and from there, a new road connects St. Catherine with the coastal resorts of Nuweiba, Dahab, Sharm el Sheikh, and Taba. New roads from Suez to Sharm el Sheikh cut driving time from Cairo to five hours.

Leaving Egypt

EXPORTING GIFTS. On departure, visitors may take out gifts and souvenirs made in Egypt provided the goods were bought with the currency properly exchanged on Form D. Gifts and souvenirs up to L.E. 35 may also be sent from Egypt through a local travel agent and through reliable shops that sell handicrafts, provided they are not for commercial use.

Antiques cannot be exported. The government has become very strict about their sale or purchase.

CUSTOMS GOING HOME. If you propose to take on your holiday any *foreign-made* articles, such as cameras, binoculars, expensive time-pieces, and the like, register them at the airport or local customhouses in major cities before departure. The registration is valid once and for all. Otherwise, on returning home, you may be charged duty.

United States. Americans who are out of the United States at least 48 hours and have claimed no exemption during the previous 30 days are entitled to bring in duty-free up to $800 worth of articles for bona fide gifts or for their own personal use. The value of each item is determined by the price actually paid (so save your receipts). Every member of a family is entitled to this same exemption, regardless of age, and the allowance can be pooled. Handicrafts from the developing world, which includes Egypt, are exempt from customs duty.

Do not bring home foreign meats, fruits, plants, soil, or other agricultural items when you return to the United States. To do so will delay you at the port of entry. It is illegal to bring in foreign agricultural items without permission because they can spread destructive plant or animal pests and diseases. For more information, write to: Quarantines, U.S. Department of Agriculture, Federal Building, Hyattsville, MD 20782.

Not more than 100 cigars may be imported duty-free per person, nor more than a quart of wine or liquor (none at all if your passport indicates you are from a "dry" state, or if you are under 21 years of age).

Antiques are defined, for customs purposes, as articles manufactured over 100 years ago and are admitted duty-free. If there's any question of age, you may be asked to supply proof.

Small gifts may be mailed to friends, but not more than one package to any single address and none to your own home. Notation on the package should be "Gift, value less than $100." Tobacco, liquor, and perfume cannot be mailed.

To facilitate the actual customs examination, it's convenient to pack all your purchases in one suitcase.

Purchases intended for your duty-free quota must accompany your personal baggage.

Canada. Residents of Canada may claim an exemption of $150 a year plus an allowance of 40 ounces of liquor, 50 cigars, 200 cigarettes, and two lb. of tobacco. Personal gifts should be mailed as "Unsolicited Gift—Value under $15." For details, ask for the Canada Customs Brochure "I Declare."

Great Britain. Returning to Britain, you may bring home: (1) 200 cigarettes, 100 cigarillos, 50 cigars, or 250 grams of tobacco; (2) two liters of table wine and, in addition, (a) one liter of alcohol over 22% by volume (38.8 proof, most spirits), (b) two liters of alcohol under 22% by volume, or (c) two more liters of table wine; (3) 50 grams of perfume and ¼ liter of toilet water; and (4) other goods up to a value of £32.

THE EGYPTIAN
SCENE

Re, the Sun-God

BY WAY OF BACKGROUND

Egypt is *Masr* in Arabic. It occupies the northeastern corner of Africa and is connected to Asia by the Sinai Peninsula.

Egypt is bordered by Libya on the west, Sudan on the south, Saudi Arabia on the southeast, Israel on the east, and the Mediterranean Sea on the north. Specifically its coordinates are 24° and 36° east Greenwich; 22° and 31° north.

Egypt's territory covers 386,000 square miles, but less than 4% is inhabited, cultivated land; the rest is desert. The Nile, like an elongated oasis, cuts Egypt from south to north for a distance of almost 900 miles from Wadi Halfa on the Sudan border to Cairo. There the river divides into two main branches, each 150 miles long. The Rosetta branch on the west and the Damietta on the east form the great Delta, the graphic name given it by the Greeks because it has the shape of a triangle.

Cairo stands at the apex of the Delta—a significant position for the capital throughout its long history. The area north of Cairo to the Mediterranean is known as Lower Egypt. The Nile Valley stretching south from Cairo to Sudan is referred to as Upper Egypt. In antiquity the area south of the first cataract near Aswan to the northern territory of the Sudan was known as Nubia.

Physical Features

Egypt is divided into three major regions:

I. The Nile Valley

In Upper Egypt south of Aswan, the Nile Valley is desert. Limestone cliffs on both sides of the valley reach 3,000 feet above sea level in the east and 2,400 feet in the west. The area is an extension of the Sahara and is the most arid and least fertile part of the country. From Aswan north to Cairo the Nile runs through a valley that varies in width from one to six miles and reaches its widest span of nine miles at Kom Ombo. On both sides of the valley, rock hills rise to 900 feet above sea level.

In Lower Egypt beginning 19 miles north of Cairo, the Nile forks into two branches between which lies the Delta, said to be the most fertile land in the world. East of the Delta, the Suez Canal zone extends north from the Gulf of Suez at the head of the Red Sea to Port Said on the Mediterranean Sea. The Suez Canal links the Red Sea at Suez with the Mediterranean at Port Said. Ismailia, also in the Canal zone, is connected by a canal to Cairo.

The heavy fighting in the 1967 war all but destroyed these three towns. At the start of the war the people living here fled to Cairo and Alexandria—almost doubling those cities' population overnight. Following the reopening of the Suez Canal in June 1975, the former inhabitants returned to their towns as reconstruction and new housing were completed. Because of the country's enormous population growth during the past decade, the canal cities are more populated now than they were before the war.

II. The Eastern Desert (Arabian Desert)

From the Nile Valley stretching to Sinai and the Red Sea are desert and limestone mountains. The southern portion of the Eastern Desert along the west coast of the Red Sea is a sterile area characterized by a range of barren mountains 6,000 feet high. It is rich in minerals and stone. The north portion, Sinai, is the gateway to Egypt from the east. It is triangular in shape and stretches for 240 miles from north to south and 120 miles from east to west. The northern and southern parts have water from rainfall, but in the central part water is scarce.

III. The Western Desert (Libyan Desert)

The area extending west of the Nile Valley to the Libyan border and from the Mediterranean coast in the north to the Sudan in the south represents two-thirds of the total area of Egypt.

This landmass is divided into frontier districts centered about its fertile oases. In the northern portion lies the Northern Plateau, the region of the Great Depressions—Siwa Oasis, Qattara Depression, Wadi el Natroun, and the Baharia Oasis. In the south are Farafra, Dakhla, and Kharga Oases. Fayum, one of the largest oases, is linked to the Nile by a 90-mile irrigation arm and is considered part of the Nile Valley.

The Western Desert is scheduled to have some of the most far-reaching and imaginative development of any area of the world. Already the area is being widely prospected for oil, and plans call for massive reclamation of the land from the desert by tapping underground water reserves. To date, $60 million have gone into research and much more will need to be spent before the effort can be meaningful. A study of the Western Desert by an American team in 1977 showed an underground lake containing an estimated 2.5 billion square-feet of water and extending 500 miles. It, of course, needs to be developed so that new lands can be brought under cultivation, but the discovery brightens Egypt's future.

The physical isolation of Egypt, hemmed in as it is by desert and sea, has had a profound influence on the course of its history. By being set apart from the other civilizations of the ancient world that rose in the Mesopotamian Valley and advanced to the Eastern Mediterranean, Egypt developed a distinctive culture, which persists to this day. Today, for example, despite modern influences and rapid communications, Egyptian art is distinctive and springs from its native traditions in a way that is unlike any other Middle Eastern culture.

Population

Approximately 56 million people make up Egypt's population, of which 95% live along the fertile banks of the Nile. The density, which averages almost 5,000 people per square mile in the cultivated areas, is one of the highest in the world and dramatically illustrates the meaning of the Nile to Egypt. Egypt also has one of the world's highest birth rates, adding one million babies every eight months.

Today the population in Cairo is estimated to be 14 million; Alexandria's is about four million. These numbers were greatly swollen by the people who fled from the Suez area during the 1967 war. Other large cities are Minya, Assiut, Sohag, Nag Hammadi, Qena, and Aswan in Upper Egypt; Tanta, Zagazig, Damanhour, and Mansourah in the Delta.

The people are grouped into four main categories:

The *fellahin,* who are peasant-farmers living in the villages along the Nile and in the Delta. They are the bulk and national strength of the country. A shift of population from the countryside to the cities in the past three decades has created an estimated proportion of 65% rural and 35% urban.

The Copts, who might be considered the most direct descendants of the ancient Egyptians. They are both urban and rural.

The Bedouins, who are nomadic Arabs and probably account for less than 2% of the population.

The European, Turkish, and Levantine minorities who are no longer as important in the life of Egypt as they were in the hundred years before the 1952 revolution, when they dominated the commerce and politics of the country.

Religion

Islam is the major religion in Egypt. Approximately 85% of the population are Sunni (orthodox) Muslims.

Christians make up an estimated 14%. Most belong to the Coptic Church, the Monophysitic branch of Christianity, which split from the general church at the Council of Chalcedon in AD 451. Others belong to various sects of European and Eastern churches. The number of Jews is very small.

Language

Arabic is the official language of the country. Most educated Egyptians speak at least one or two other languages, usually English and French.

Government

Egypt is a republic with a unicameral legislature, the National Assembly, elected by universal suffrage every six years. The 360-member National Assembly selects a president whose nomination is submitted to public referendum. The president appoints the Council of Ministers.

Administration

Egypt is divided into 25 governorates, five of which are towns—Cairo, Alexandria, Port Said, Suez, and Ismailia. The eight of the Delta are Behira, Damietta, Kafr el Sheikh, Garbia, Dakhlia, Sharkia, Tahrir, and Qalyubia. Another eight are in Upper Egypt—Fayoum, Beni Suef, Giza, Minya, Assiut, Sohag, Qena, and Aswan; and four are the frontier areas of the Red Sea, New Valley, Matruh, and Sinai.

The governorate is ordinarily made up of a city and its suburbs or part of a territory composed of a chief town and main district. Each governorate (*muhafezate*) has a governor (*muhafez*) and a governor's council.

Economy

Since ancient times Egypt's economy has been based on the Nile. Controlling its flow and benefiting from its annual flood was the major preoccupation of the people. The task was accomplished by diverting the waters and the fertile soil carried by the river into basins from which the farmlands were irrigated.

As the engineers became more sophisticated, they learned to store the Nile's waters in great reservoirs in Sudan and at Aswan in Upper Egypt, and they built a series of dams and barrages along the river to divert water throughout the year into the network of irrigation canals. In order to bring more and more land under cultivation, the level of the dams was raised. This system served about 80% of the cultivated area and made it possible to grow two or three crops a year. Finally, with the building of the new High Dam at Aswan, the Nile's waters were brought under year-round control.

Egypt's main crop is long-staple cotton, among the world's finest. The bulk is raised in Lower Egypt, and from the time it was introduced into Egypt by Muhammad Ali early in the 19th century, it has traditionally accounted for 80% of all exports. Following efforts at diversification and industrialization, this one-crop dependency however, has begun to change. Until recently Egypt grew enough wheat to meet its domestic requirements, as well as a wide variety of fruits and vegetables. Unlike most of the Middle East, where rice is a basic staple, Egypt's is *fool,* the fava bean.

Egypt's industry is centered primarily in Alexandria, Cairo, several Delta cities, and Assiut. Before the revolution of 1952, it was devoted mostly to textiles, and there was a small consumer goods and food processing industry.

Efforts at expansion and diversification were started during the 1960s, and Egypt now produces the bulk of its domestic requirements for consumer goods and has built the foundations for its industrial development.

Prior to the 1967 war, transit fees from the Suez Canal accounted for approximately one-half of Egypt's foreign exchange. After its closure in

1967 and the loss of revenues, coupled with years of war or threat of war, Egypt's economy was badly drained.

Following the October war of 1973 and the reopening of the Suez Canal in 1975, Egypt's economy temporarily gained a new lease on life. But the country's economic problems are so massive and the obstacles to reform so fundamental that anything short of total renovation is likely to have little or no effect. The year 1985–86 was a particularly hard period, with the sharp decline in the price of oil and lost revenues from remittances of Egyptian workers who had been employed in the Saudi Arabia and the Gulf States. Tourism is the shining star, with more than 2.5 million visitors, but it, too, has great peaks and valleys and is always hostage to the political events of the region. After its near devastation in 1986, Egypt's tourism bounced back and by 1988 was having such a boom that it was difficult to find a hotel room in Upper Egypt. By then, too, Suez Canal revenues had reached approximately $1.8 billion.

But once again, in 1991 as a result of the war in the Gulf, Egypt saw its tourism ground to a near halt. But within a month of the war's end, the country was hopeful and ready for the boom to resume.

Taboos and Customs

Although there is a Western facade among modern, young and educated Egyptians, Egypt is the East. You will find all the modern conveniences to make your visit comfortable, but do not expect Egypt to be like home. Its way of life is different from ours. This difference is its fascination and the reason so many journey 5,000 miles to see it.

If you are disturbed by poverty, remember that Egyptians are bitterly aware of their low standard of living, and against some of the worst odds in the world, they are working hard to improve it.

From the time Cambyses stormed into Egypt in 525 BC until the revolution of 1952, someone other than the Egyptians ran Egypt. Throughout history it has been a prize of conquest and, depending on how well it was organized and ruled, Egypt had the potential of making its rulers incredibly wealthy.

But that has passed. Egypt is now run by Egyptians. They are intensely proud of their country and want to move on as rapidly as possible to develop it into a modern nation, although their efforts are often frustrated by a stupefying bureaucracy and a legacy of traditions that sometimes run counter to modern society. During your visit you will frequently be reminded of the difficulties in transforming a nation whose patterns are 7,000 years old.

Most Egyptians are Muslims, and in this they take a pride second only to their pride in being Egyptians. This does not mean, however, that they stop whatever they are doing five times a day, face Mecca, and begin their prayers. On the contrary, most Egyptians you are likely to meet are urbanized and have altered their religious habits to cope with 20th-century city life. Yet many in the city and most in the villages observe Muslim traditions of prayer when they can and abstain from alcoholic beverages. Even the most sophisticated and urban Muslims seldom eat pork, although pork is available in Cairo.

Islam is one of the most pervasive religions in the world, and its hold on Egypt is unquestionable. As the seat of Islam's oldest and most important institution of learning, Al Azhar, Egypt has been a focal point for Islam for centuries. This, as much as any other factor, has given Egypt her bond with the other Arab countries and her leadership in the Muslim world. When one considers that there are over 700 million Muslims spread out across the world, the scope of leadership is significant and perhaps explains why Egypt often has been able to exert more influence than her size might appear to warrant.

Unless they have studied Islam, most Westerns have many false notions about the religion. Orthodox Muslims do pray five times a day, and the ritual of prayer prescribed by the Koran can be observed in the mosques at prayer time or even on a sidewalk or side street or in the fields. Muslims are not self-conscious about saying their prayers in front of others.

Women's Role

Modest dress, not veiling, is prescribed for women in the Koran, the holy book of the Muslims. A veiled Egyptian woman is an unusual sight in Cairo now, but even when the custom was prevalent, the style in Egypt was a fishnet affair and was never the heavy, hoodlike covering of North Africa or Arabia. Occasionally you might see a woman from the village in a semiveiled costume, but the veiled women you see nowadays in Cairo and Alexandria are likely to be those who visit Egypt frequently from the Arabian Peninsula and from other North African countries where veiling is still practiced.

Visitors should be aware that a conservative revival is enjoying a certain amount of popularity currently and is manifested by a surprisingly large number of young women on Cairo streets wearing long dresses and covering their heads (but not their faces). It is hard to assess its true depth at the present time.

While the Koran allows men to have four wives, it also requires them to treat them equally. These days, most men find that very difficult to do. Economics, if nothing else, is putting an end to polygamy.

The struggle for women's rights began in the 1930s during the British occupation, when women were active in the nationalist movement. It continued its militancy up to and through the early part of the 1952 revolution and then subsided. Most of these early fighters are now quite elderly, and the new generation of women have not taken up the challenge in quite the same way. Instead, the younger generation of liberated women seem to be pressing ahead with education, entering the job market at every level, and becoming economic assets to their families.

Women have been active in most professions for several decades, and they have held high government positions—including cabinet posts and seats in the National Assembly, where at present there are nine. The head of the nation's television is a woman—certainly one of the country's most influential positions. Although the changes in this century have been profound, one would have to say that during the past two decades the changes in the role of women have been radical. To find, as one does now, young girls from the villages working as waitresses in the hotels in Aswan, or as barmaids in Cairo—with family concurrence—would have been unthinkable a few years ago.

An Egyptian Welcome

In spite of the history of on-again, off-again relations between the United States and Egypt, you will find that Egyptians really like Americans and they are eager to tell you so. The visit by the American president to Egypt in 1974 was the first step in reconciling the relationship, which had been broken since 1967. The visit in 1975 of the Egyptian president to the United States began a new chapter in the relations between the two countries and was further strengthened by his repeat visits. The courage of President Sadat's visit to Jerusalem in 1978 and his subsequent efforts for peace won him admiration around the world, as the outpouring of emotion showed upon his tragic death in October of 1981. Sadat frequently has been at the head of the list of world leaders most admired by Americans.

Relations between Egypt and Western Europe, strained since the 1956 invasion and 1967 war, have improved even more dramatically. British visitors will often find, as they do in India, that the past is remembered more often for its beneficial aspects, and anticolonial bitterness has faded as Egyptian independence has flowered.

Egyptians are good-natured, friendly, and accommodating to visitors, but they are more reserved when dealing with foreigners than are Americans. Educated and urban Egyptians are worldly and sophisticated, but the majority of Egyptians living along the banks of the Nile have never ventured beyond their village and their way of life, except for radio and television, has changed little for thousands of years.

Egyptians are "body" people. They slap, hug, kiss, push, shove, and touch each other a great deal. They love their children and are openly warm, affectionate, and indulgent with them. At the same time, they demand respect, loyalty, and obedience from them. Important decisions such as marriage, divorce, careers, and travel are still family matters, and the opinion of the family is often the most important deciding factor.

Throughout the Mediterranean world, and more especially in Egypt, there is a total unconcern for time, which is frustrating and irritating for Westerners. Yet it is precisely the Egyptians' relaxed manner that accounts for a great deal of their charm. They are extremely patient. They cannot be hurried—don't bother to try. Instead, anticipate your needs much further in advance than you might at home and don't be timid about repeating them frequently.

Bukra means "tomorrow." It is an expression used constantly in Egypt. It is the tomorrow of the future. It has no time limit. *Bukra fil mishmish*—tomorrow when the apricots bloom—is a special Egyptian tomorrow stretching to infinity.

So relax! You will enjoy your visit far more if you adjust to, rather than fight, the system.

Anubis, God of Funerary Rites

EGYPT'S MARVELOUS
HISTORY

A 63-Century Epic

Four thousand years before the birth of Christ, a civilization emerged on the green ribbon that cuts across the Sahara wasteland; and in the 30 centuries of its preeminence it reached a stage of development and sophistication that none of its contemporaries surpassed and few to this day have equaled. For example:

—With our vast engineering technology, the building of the Pyramids remains a mystery.

—With all the miracles of modern science, we do not know the ancient Egyptians' secret of mummification.

—Papyrus, the first paper (and origin of the word from Greek), enabled the Egyptians to keep prodigious records—unlike their contemporaries, who used clumsy clay tablets.

Record keeping played a major role in the Egyptians' ability to organize society and maximize the benefits of the Nile's waters, which in turn led to their great prosperity. But what really set the Egyptians apart from all the rest was their ability to sustain their civilization almost without interruption for 30 centuries—a feat no others have achieved. The reason is found in Egypt's unusual relationship with the Nile River.

The river valley, protected by the desert on both sides, acted as a barrier that discouraged invasion and enabled the people to live in relative security. At the same time, to control the river's annual flood, the villages along the Nile had to cooperate in order to survive. Cooperation, in turn, meant organization. And it was this organization, more than any other factor, that enabled Egypt to endure.

By the time Herodotus, the great historian of the Greeks, visited Egypt in 450 BC, it was already an ancient land, since its first fixed date can be placed around the beginning of the fourth millennium BC Logic tells us that this civilization would have had to have been even older, since its system of writing did not spring into being full-blown.

Who, then, were the Egyptians and where did they come from?

The origins of the Egyptians remain a puzzle to historians to this day. From archaeological discoveries we know that in prehistoric times the area of the Nile Valley was green, forested, peopled, and rich in animal life. But over the millennia, the nature of the land was altered so drastically that these earliest inhabitants left or perhaps were forced to leave. The area had become denuded, arid, and barren. Scholars say there is no evidence of a connection between prehistoric man in Egypt and the ancient Egyptians with whom the country's recorded history begins.

Authorities do not agree on the origins of these latter-day Egyptians either. Early theories held that they were African. While historians generally agree that there were some African migrations into the Nile Valley, the current belief is that the Egyptians were tribes from the Libyan Desert on the one hand and from the Arabian Desert on the other. From their language, scholars have concluded that the immigrants were predominantly Semitic in origin and that they probably settled in the Nile Valley prior to 10,000 BC

Too many centuries of Nile silt have piled up in the Delta to enable Egyptologists to uncover the remains of the Red Kingdom—so named because of the red color of the Nile mud. At least we know that by 4000 BC there was a flourishing, sophisticated civilization.

It had already devised a calendar of 360 days that was divided into 12 portions of 30 days each. The difference was made up by having five sacred feast days at the end of each year. This civilization had developed a writing system, a measuring system, and it recorded this information on paper made from the papyrus leaf by a method that we have only recently learned to imitate.

Simultaneously, another kingdom had developed along the Upper Nile as far as the first cataract near Aswan. It was known as the White Kingdom, presumably for the same graphic reason—the land's color was white. Its leader wore a white crown; its emblem was a white flower.

Upper and Lower Egypt United

At some time around 3100 BC (some authorities say as early as 3400 BC; others as late as 3000 BC), a leader whom history has called Menes from Thinis (near Abydos) united the White and Red kingdoms. As Egyptologists interpret it, he united the crowns of Upper and Lower Egypt—a prerequisite for governing this land of potential wealth that was recognized by every ruler from Menes down to the Romans. The reason for this need was, of course, control of the Nile.

None of the tombs of the rulers prior to Menes has ever been discovered, but archaeologists have been able to piece together from funeral mounds

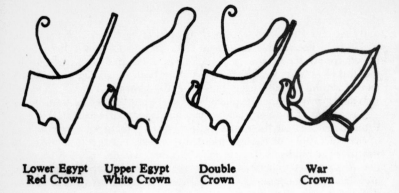

Lower Egypt   **Upper Egypt**   **Double**   **War**
Red Crown   **White Crown**   **Crown**   **Crown**

of lesser citizens a considerable amount of information on these early Egyptians. .

From Menes, however, the historical evidence is abundant, and for this reason we start the story of ancient Egypt with his reign, the first of 30 dynasties that ruled Egypt from 3100 BC to the coming of the Romans in 30 BC.

Menes moved to Memphis, where he established the first capital of the united land. The site is located only 20 miles from Cairo.

In the furniture, utensils, and jewelry of daily life there is compelling evidence that by Menes's time, the Egyptian civilization had already achieved an exquisite mastery of its crafts, as can be seen in the Egyptian Antiquities Museum in Cairo. The refinement and strength of the statues, the fineness of their utensils, the grace and precision of alabaster carved to represent natural objects, the magnificent design and craft of furniture inlaid with ivory and ebony, and the skill in the working of gold jewelry and precious stones are only a few of the examples of this mastery.

Furthermore, an inventory of the land was made at regular intervals. There ability to produce and maintain such an elaborate bookkeeping system is further evidence of the level of sophistication the Egyptians had reached by this period. We also know that a state religion began to develop, vaguely centered in the person of the king as the unifier of the land.

The union forged by Menes was not a peaceful one in the beginning, as might be supposed. For decades the two sections fought—the south having to subdue the rebellious north. The final reconciliation of the warring states was attributed to the most important god of ancient Egypt, Osiris, god of the netherworld, whose role was to judge those passing through the netherworld to eternity.

The Gods of Egypt

To understand the civilization of ancient Egypt, it is necessary to look at two aspects of its life that were so intertwined they can never be separated. One is the Nile, as has been described; the other is religion.

No force had greater influence on the life of ancient man than did religion. It permeated his life. Religion explained the world about him, his fears and hopes. Its outward manifestation was the motif from which art, architecture, literature, and science evolved.

The religion of ancient Egypt, of which one needs some knowledge in order to enjoy the monuments, temples, tomb drawings and the exhibits in the museums, is rooted in prehistory, long before the pharaohs. The Egyptians, like most primitive societies, revered nature and both feared and admired its traits—the strength of the lion, its tenderness toward its young. Throughout Egypt's ancient history, animals were associated with the gods in one form or another. They dwelt in the temples and were mummified in the same manner as human beings, although it was not until much later in history that they were worshiped.

In his surroundings—the trees, birds, and beasts—the Egyptian saw his gods. They were creatures like himself, but they possessed strange powers that he did not have, such as the flight of a bird, and spirits over which he had no control. Some of these spirits were friends who would help and protect him; others wanted to harm him. Misfortune, he believed, came from one of the evil spirits around him.

Beyond these local spirits, the Egyptian needed to explain the sky, the earth, and the other grand elements of his world. In a land where the sun is powerful and plentiful, it is no surprise that it was given special status. The Egyptians, we presume, perceived that life was dependent on the sun. Over the centuries, worship of the sun was almost universal, although it took different forms in different places, and two or more forms were sometimes blended into one.

The chief center of sun worship was On, a city in the Delta, which the Greeks called Heliopolis. Here the sun god was known as Re (Ra). The theory held that Re had two barques in which he sailed across the heavens, one for the morning and the other for the afternoon. When he entered the netherworld in his barque to return to the east, he brought light and joy with him. The symbol of his presence in the temple at Heliopolis was an obelisk. At Edfu, another center for the worship of the sun, he appeared as a hawk and was named Horus.

The explanation for heaven and earth also varied—some saw a huge cow with her head in the west, the earth stretched between her feet; her belly studded with stars representing the arch of heaven. In another place they saw a female figure bending over the earth, with her feet in the east and her outstretched arms in the west. Both of these representations can be seen frequently in drawings and temple carvings throughout Upper Egypt.

Eventually local ideas were mixed with myths from other places. Hence, the sun was born every morning as a calf or as a child, depending upon whether one believed the heaven was a cow or a woman. The flight of a bird and the movement of the sun became one, and the sun with outspread wings was one of the most common symbols of ancient Egypt. In a later form it became a protective goddess, as can be seen in many of the exhibits in the Tutankhamen collection.

As society became more sophisticated and the Egyptian less awed by the mysteries of nature, his gods underwent a transformation. Gradually the three aspects—nature, animal, and man—were fused. By the time of Menes (I Dynasty), the gods had come to be conceived in human form.

One of the earliest deities to undergo this fusion was Hathor, the goddess of love and childbirth. She was given a human body and head but retained an element of her animal manifestation—a pair of cow's horns.

Thoth, god of wisdom and truth, also acquired a human body but kept the head of the ibis. Anubis, who assisted Osiris as judge of the dead and guardian of the tombs, also took on a human body but kept the head of a jackal.

To explain creation, the Egyptians evolved a theory that reasoned: If the sky was a sea upon which the sun and the heavenly lights sailed westward every day, then there had to be a waterway by which they could return. They concluded that there was another Nile beneath the earth. Through its long dark passage the celestial barque sailed at night and reappeared in the east each morning. This other Nile was connected with the earthly Nile at the first cataract—the place where the people who first believed this myth thought the earth ended.

According to James Breasted in his *History of Egypt* (New York, 1909), this concept of the encircling sea was inherited by the Greeks, who called the sea Okeanos, or Ocean. "In the beginning only this ocean existed, said a flower, out of which issued the sun-god. From himself he begat four children, Shu and Tefnut, Keb and Nut. All these, with their father, lay upon the ocean of chaos, when Shu and Tefnut, who represent the atmosphere, thrust themselves between Keb and Nut. They planted their feet upon Keb and raised Nut on high, so that Keb became the earth and Nut the heavens.

"Keb and Nut were the father and mother of the four divinities, Osiris and Isis, Set and Nephthys; together they formed with their primeval father the sun-god, a circle of nine deities, the "ennead' of which each temple later possessed a local form.

"This correlation of the primitive divinities as father, mother, and son strongly influenced the theology of later times until each temple possessed an artificially created triad, of purely secondary origin, upon which an 'ennead' was then built up."

Besides these gods of the earth, the sun, and the heavens, there were also those who lived in the netherworld. As we said earlier, this world was conceived of as a long gloomy passage along which a subterranean river—the other Nile—carried the sun from west to east. Here dwelt the dead, whose king was Osiris. According to the legend, Osiris had succeeded the sun-god as king on earth, aided by his faithful sister-wife, Isis.

Isis and Osiris

Osiris had been a good and beloved ruler, but he was craftily misled and slain by his brother Set, who was jealous of him. Set cut the body of his brother into a million pieces and scattered them about the land. Where each piece fell, the land was fertile and a green blade grew. In her consternation Iris roamed the earth in search of the pieces of Osiris's body. When, after great tribulation, Isis had regained the body of Osiris, she prepared it for burial with the help of an old god of the netherworld, Anubis, the jackal-god, who thereafter became the god of embalmment. The charms Isis spoke over the body of Osiris were so powerful that he was resurrected; and although it was impossible for the departed god to resume his earthly life, he lived on as lord of the netherworld.

Isis later gave birth to a son, Horus, whom she secretly reared among the marshes of the Delta to become his father's avenger. When he grew to manhood, the youth pursued Set and in the terrible battle that raged from one end of the earth to the other, both were mutilated. Finally, Set was defeated and Horus was able to assume the earthly throne of his father.

Set went to the tribunal of the gods, where he challenged the birth of Horus and his claim to the throne. But, defended by Thoth, the god of wisdom and truth, Horus was vindicated. Some versions say that it was Osiris himself who was vindicated.

Thereafter, every pharaoh ruled on earth as Horus. When he died, he became Osiris and ruled the underworld. His son, the new pharaoh, ruled on earth as Horus.

The ancient Egyptians believed that upon death all persons had to pass through the netherworld for the last judgment by Osiris and 42 assistant judges, one for each of the nomes (provinces) of Egypt.

Death, the Egyptians believed, was a continuation of life, which is why they spent so much time and effort in preparation for it. Upon death, 70 days were needed to prepare the body for embalming, and during that time the body and the Ka (one's spirit and alter ego) wandered through the underworld searching for Osiris, who is represented in tomb drawings with either a white face (death) or a green face (vegetation or rebirth).

The dead person and his Ka had to pass through the judgment hall where he told each of the judges what he had done in life and answered for his sins. The sins were no different from ours today—murder, stealing, lying, deceit, adultery, blasphemy, etc. To test the truth of his plea and to pass judgment on his eternal life, his heart was weighed on a scale of justice with a feather (the symbol of truth) as balance. If the heart (thought to be the seat of intelligence) was as light as a feather, the judgment would be favorable. The standard was high. Those who failed the ordeal were condemned to hunger and thirst in the darkness of the tomb. In this judgment, the Egyptians introduced for the first time in history the idea of future accountability, where man's eternal life depended on the ethical quality of his earthly one.

Although it started in the Delta, Abydos in Upper Egypt became the main center of the Osiris myth and an important place of pilgrimage. An annual series of dramatic presentations in which the main incidents of Osiris's life, death, and final triumph were enacted drew audiences from all over the land. In some parts of the drama, the ordinary people were allowed to participate with the priests—and the spectacle was undoubtedly magnificent, not unlike the later passion plays of Christianity.

The Osiris cult covers only a few of the gods and their overlapping personalities that populated the region of ancient Egypt. But it gives some idea of the complexity of the role of religion in daily life. It further helps to explain why the Egyptians saw death as a continuation of life and spent so much of their earthly life preparing for the eternal one.

The cult of Osiris is the most basic and consistent theme of Egyptian history from ancient times down through the centuries, including the Christian period to the coming of Islam. The myth of Osiris was easy for people to understand; they could identify with it. Hence, it was easy for a cult to develop around it. Isis became the ideal wife and mother, and Horus, who originally belonged to the sun myth and had nothing to do with Osiris, became the embodiment of the good son and the ultimate triumph of a just cause.

Under the Greeks and later under the Romans, many of the Egyptian gods were merged with those of the Greeks and Romans. Osiris became a form of Zeus; Venus had many of the attributes of Isis and so on. It takes very little imagination to trace Greek and Roman myths from the Osiris legend and to see how many of the stories of Hebraic and Christian literature were derived from it.

The concepts of the trinity, the last judgment, redemption, resurrection, and many more were later to become cornerstones of the Christian faith and were adopted into Islam in modified forms.

The Three Kingdoms

The dynasty of Menes and the one that followed covered about 400 years, during which Egypt emerged from prehistoric obscurity. From that point its history, beginning with the III Dynasty, is divided into three main periods, each separated by intermediate periods during which the country's fortunes were temporarily at a low ebb. Each of the three kingdoms was characterized by great accomplishments:

The Old Kingdom (2700–2200 BC) was the period during which the Pyramids were built.

The Middle Kingdom (2200–1800 BC) saw Egypt's political and economic strength expand and its art reach a peak.

During the New Kingdom (1600–1100 BC) the nation reached its zenith as a political power and acquired history's first empire. After this period, Egypt's days as a great nation were over, although the pharaohs continued to occupy the throne for another eight centuries.

Egypt's political and social structure was formed early and changed little over the centuries. Power was in the hands of a pharaoh cast in the double role of king and god at the pinnacle of the society. And, like the Pyramids the pharaohs built, an elite group of officers and priests to whom the pharaohs delegated authority was situated at the top just below the ruler, while the entire structure was supported by a broad base of highly organized workers and peasants.

For four centuries the dynasty begun by Menes continued to consolidate his gains and develop a prosperity that laid the foundation for the first great epoch of Egyptian history. During the next 500 years, from the III to the VI Dynasty, building, government, and administration reached levels that were never surpassed in later periods.

For us today, this period can be seen in the masterpieces of the Step Pyramid at Sakkara, the first large structure in stone; the three Pyramids of Giza; and the collection of superb sculpture and artifacts that fills a quarter of the Antiquities Museum in Cairo and a part of collections in museums around the world.

The mere organization of labor involved in quarrying, transporting, and assembling this vast amount of material would tax the richest nations even today. The maintenance of a city of 100,000 laborers, who were nonproducing and a constant burden on the state, tells us something of the wealth and power of the early pharaohs.

During this period the first known seagoing vessels were built, making possible the expansion of trade north to Phoenicia and south beyond

Nubia to Somali. The power of the landed nobility developed into what was history's first feudal system.

By the VI Dynasty Egypt had begun to face several internal difficulties. Spiritually, the omnipotence of the pharaoh was diminished somewhat by the priests; economically, the strain of building and maintaining the Pyramids had severely weakened the country. Finally, after the 90-year reign of Pepi II, the country began to come apart. The organization so necessary for controlling the Nile and maximizing its benefits broke down.

After a brief 30 years (VII and VIII Dynasties), which historians describe as one of internal confusion, the seat of power shifted from Memphis to Heracleopolis, about 55 miles south of Memphis in the area of Fayum. Eighteen kings (IX and X Dynasties) were at the helm.

Meanwhile, a powerful family of princes in Thebes, near present-day Luxor, gained strength and ultimately triumphed over the north. They established the XI Dynasty from 2160 BC, and the center of power moved to the south. The period from the demise of Memphis to the triumph of Thebes covered about 300 years.

This period, designated by the XI and XII Dynasties (2160–1788 BC), is known as the Middle Kingdom, the classical period of Egyptian history during which Egypt was once again united.

The XII Dynasty was founded in about 2000 BC by another Theban family under Amenemhet II, who consolidated the power of the state by dealing with the powerful landed nobles one by one. His successors moved the capital back to the north and established their rule at Lisht, about 20 miles south of Memphis. They continued to reorganize the domestic affairs of the country, curbing the power of feudal lords and replacing them with governors and advisors from Thebes whom they could trust. It took five kings more than 150 years to supplant their power.

The kings of the XII Dynasty also expanded the Nile's irrigation system, especially at Fayum. In the artistic field, art, jewelry, and literature reached a peak never again equaled for their refinement. The rulers of the XII Dynasty also continued to expand the country's control beyond its borders, and under Amenemhet's grandson, Sesostris III, the Egyptians invaded Syria for the first time. The pharaoh personally led his army, and he became a legend as he extended Egypt's control over 1,000 miles of the Nile. (This period paralleled the biblical era of Abraham's arrival in the land of Canaan.)

Under Amenemhet III, the nation reached one of its greatest periods of power, productivity, and artistic achievement. The Theban rulers also elevated to national prominence an obscure Theban god, Amon, who was to become one of the great forces in ancient history. The image of Amon accompanied the Egyptian army through the ancient world. A thousand years later Alexander the Great would seek his aid in ruling Egypt. The most massive temple of all time—the Temple of Karnak—was erected in his honor. Here the most spectacular feast of the year was held at the time of the flood to honor him.

Once again a great era was followed by an unstable one under the XIII Dynasty in the 18th century BC This is known to historians as the Second Intermediate Period. The country again separated into its two natural geographical parts, Upper and Lower Egypt. The two sections fought from time to time; each was beset by internal squabbling, and one weak leader followed another.

Egypt Divided

The country disintegrated into petty kingdoms, of which Thebes was the largest in the south, where a regime maintained itself for about two centuries, holding a short strip of territory of about 125 miles in the area of Thebes.

Without central power to administer its irrigation system, the nation's resources became dissipated and authority weakened. Hence Egypt was easy prey to foreign invaders when, about 1730 BC, the Hyksos, an Asian tribe, swept over the northern portion of the land, leaving vast destruction in their wake.

Historians are not entirely sure about the origins of the Hyksos, known as the Shepherd Kings, but they generally agree that they were mostly Semites, probably from Palestine, who came across the desert, settled near the eastern border of Egypt, and from there eventually controlled most of the Delta. Apparently they had little difficulty overcoming local opposition, since the Egyptians were not as advanced in warfare as their invaders.

The Hyksos rapidly became Egyptianized, and although their rule lasted only about a century, they had a profound impact on Egypt—mainly because they brought with them new tools of war and taught the Egyptians warfare on a large scale. Of the new weapons introduced by the Hyksos, the most important was the horse-drawn chariot. When the Egyptians finally expelled the Hyksos, they did so by learning to use their enemy's weapons.

In spite of their military advantage, the Hyksos were unable to extend their rule beyond a point midway between Memphis and Thebes, and their inability to dislodge the Theban regime proved their undoing.

The family that founded the XVIII Dynasty (mid-16th century BC) was one of history's most remarkable. Under Ahmose I, the Egyptians' powerful army stormed the Hyksos capital in the eastern Delta and drove the foreigners out of Egypt in about 1580 BC It was not, however, until a half century later that the Hyksos were finally defeated, when Thutmose III won the battle of Kadesh in Syria.

Under the XVIII Dynasty, the first of the New Kingdom, Egypt was once again united and its rulers laid the foundation for the greatest period in the country's history. Under these pharaohs Egypt became an empire—the world's first—extending its rule in the south beyond the fourth cataract of the Nile in Sudan and the Euphrates River in the northeast.

In rebuilding the country, Ahmose I faced a task that differed substantially from the reorganization by the pharaohs of the XII Dynasty at the start of the Middle Kingdom. The latter had only to manipulate to their own ends established political power without destroying its base. Ahmose began by building a completely new fabric of government, shaped somewhat by events that had culminated in the expulsion of the Hyksos. He was now head of a strong, well-organized army, which in turn determined the character of the government—Egypt became a military state.

In spite of their traditionally unwarlike nature, the Egyptians became soldiers as a result of the long war with the Hyksos. The army, after years in Asia, had learned not only the art of war but also the enormous wealth and power to be gained by conquest. The entire country was aroused by the ambitions of empire building.

Ahmose I restored the boundaries that Egypt had held in the Old Kingdom. He destroyed the power of local nobles and confiscated their lands for the crown. In effect, all Egypt became the pharaoh's personal estate, and thus he created a new order that his successors further consolidated.

Hatshepsut and Egypt's Glory

Amenhotep I, the son of Ahmose I, moved the nation's boundary farther south and started the country on a period of prosperity that lasted for 150 years. Thutmose I, the third pharaoh of the XVIII Dynasty, pushed the frontiers still farther south beyond the fourth cataract and northeast to Palestine and Syria. After his reign, Egypt's military expansion was suspended for two decades by Thutmose's daughter, Hatshepsut, one of the most remarkable women in history.

Hatshepsut was married to Thutmose II, her half brother—not an unusual practice in ancient times. When Thutmose II died after a short rule, she took over the government as regent during the minority of Thutmose III, a child her husband had fathered by a lesser wife of the harem. He had become pharaoh by a bizarre incident in which the priests had singled him out during a feast.

Nominally, Thutmose III was pharaoh and at first Hatshepsut ruled in his name, but she soon abandoned the pretense and established herself as pharaoh. Historical evidence is too inconclusive to state for certain what took place, but Hatshepsut and Thutmose III were on and off the throne for over a decade.

The nomination of Hatshepsut to the succession and her descent from an old and illustrious Theban family apparently made her position strong with the nobles of her party. Although unable to eliminate Thutmose III entirely, Hatshepsut ultimately seized power and ruled as supreme co-regent. Thutmose III was relegated to the background while the queen played the leading state role. Both she and Thutmose III numbered the years of their joint reign from the first accession of Thutmose III.

Clearly, Hatshepsut could not have wielded so much power without powerful supporters. Chief among them was Senmut, the architect of the Queen's Temples at Deir el Bahri and the Temple of Amon in Karnak. It is said that he held 80 titles.

Hatshepsut was the first queen to assume the godship with the kingship and to wear the Double Crown, indicating sovereignty over the two lands of Upper and Lower Egypt. In addition, statues show her in the masculine attire of the kingship. One of the surest proofs of her amazing ability was her success in dominating Thutmose III so long. For 20 years the man who was to become one of Egypt's greatest pharaohs lived in her shadow.

Finally, when Thutmose III was able to gather the backing he needed to unseat her, he did so with a vengeance. After her death he had her name removed wherever it was written, especially at Deir el Bahri, Hatshepsut's famous mortuary temple at the west bank at Luxor—among the highlights of a visit today.

Thutmose III has been called the Napoleon of antiquity—a brilliant military strategist, leader of men, superhero of the then civilized world. His reign, known as the Imperial Age, marks the crest of Egyptian history. He built the first real empire and became the first universal personality in history.

At the time of his death the Egyptian empire stretched from Syria to Sudan. His reign marks an epoch not only in Egypt but in the entire East, for never before in history had one person controlled the resources of so great a nation. Thebes grew into a great metropolis from which, amid great wealth and splendor, the pharaohs of the XVIII and XIX Dynasties ruled their vast domain for 230 years.

Thutmose III administered the empire so well that the machinery he set in motion ran successfully for a full century after him. Egypt was at peace and trade flourished. Except for putting down a rebellion in Nubia, his successor had no need of military ventures. Instead, Amenhotep III went on a building spree that included the creation of colossal statues and temples throughout the land.

By 1375 BC, at the end of his reign and during that of his son, Amenhotep IV, a combination of adverse influences both within and without led ultimately to the empire's destruction. From information contained in a collection of clay tablets discovered in the ruins of Tell al Amarna, events that would later weaken the empire were taking place at the extreme edge of Egypt's territory. In particular, the Hittites from Asia Minor were advancing into Syria, and at the same time Egypt had loosened its hold on Palestine. Unaware or unconcerned about the situation, Amenhotep IV became absorbed in social and religious reform that caused internal convulsions such as the country had never before endured.

The World's First Universal God

Amenhotep IV may have been a religious fanatic; certainly he was an ascetic. He was physically weak, with a long, thin face and a misshapen body. He immersed himself in philosophy and theology and gradually developed ideas that made him the most interesting of all the pharaohs and the first prophet in history. In his immediate circle were his mother, Queen Ti; his wife, Nefertiti (known to us because of her famous sculpted head, which now rests in the Berlin Museum), and a favorite priest, Eye, the husband of his childhood nurse.

Whether his original intention was toward a social revolution or a religious one is not clear, but with single-minded determination he collided with the bureaucracy and the clergy, institutions that had become deeply entrenched and powerful since the time of Thutmose III. But to understand Amenhotep IV's role, one must place it in context.

Egypt's imperial position had had a profound influence on all the country's life and ideas. Even before the conquests in Asia the priests were beginning to interpret the gods in a more philosophical way. James Breasted, in his *History of Egypt*, notes that it was no accident that the concept of a universal god arose in Egypt during the time her pharaohs ruled an entire empire. A priest of this age had in the person of the pharaoh a tangible form of a world concept—a prerequisite to the notion of a world god.

None of the old divinities of Egypt had been proclaimed the god of the empire, although the sun-god Re of Heliopolis was highly esteemed. Already under Amenhotep III an old name for the material sun, Aton, had come into use and occasionally the sun-god was designated as "the god."

In a move to reassert a pharaoh's authority, Amenhotep IV openly challenged the priesthood, the most powerful and conservative group in the empire, with his new ideas. Under the name Aton, Amenhotep IV introduced the worship of one supreme and universal god, and he did not even try to camouflage the new deity with the old sun-god Re. He attributed the new faith to Re as its source, but claimed to have been himself the channel of its revelation. The new religion was not merely sun worship. Amenhotep IV had identified the source of life as the heat that he found to be present in all life. He concluded that Aton was everywhere through his rays. He used as Aton's symbol a disk whose ray resembled many outstretched arms ending in cupped hands.

In a further affront to the priests of Amon, the pharaoh built a temple to Aton between the temples of Karnak and Luxor in the garden of Amon, which had been created by Amenhotep III. (Amenhotep IV is supposed to have built eight temples in Thebes. One was uncovered only recently in the vicinity of Karnak Temple at Luxor.)

Other gods were still tolerated, but it was inevitable that the priests of Amon would be jealous of the new strange god, especially since the wealth formerly lavished on Amon's sanctuary was now being spent on the usurper. To make matters worse for the priests of Amon, Amenhotep IV had the support of the Memphis and Heliopolis priests who for so long had had to take a back seat to Thebes.

It was not long before Amenhotep IV found Thebes intolerable and decided to make a complete break. In one move he swept aside centuries of polytheism. The priests were dispossessed and official temple worship of various gods ceased. In particular, he replaced the traditional worship of Amon with that of Aton, the source of all life. With the frenzy of a fanatic he had the names and images of Amon removed from all temples and tombs, including that of his father.

Then, as the coup de grace, he changed his name from Amenhotep, which meant "Amon is content," to Akhenaton (Ikhnaton), meaning "serviceable to the Aton." (This is the name by which he is known in history.) He moved the capital to the site of Tell al Amarna, about 200 miles south of Cairo near the present town of Minya, and called it Akhetaton.

A new spirit prevailed in Egypt, Ikhnaton perceived his god as the creator of nature through which his beneficence for all creatures was revealed. According to Breasted, he called Aton "father and mother of all that he had made," and he saw in some degree the goodness of that All-Father as did he who bade us consider the lilies. He pointed to the all-embracing bounty of the common father of humanity. It is this aspect of Ikhnaton's mind that is especially remarkable; he is the first prophet of history.

"While to the traditional pharoah the state god was only the triumphant conqueror, who crushed all peoples and drove them tribute-laden before the Pharaoh's chariot, Ikhnaton saw in him the beneficent father of all men. It is the first time in history that a discerning eye has caught this great universal truth."

While Ikhnaton recognized the power and the beneficence of God, he did not have a very spiritual conception of the deity; nor did he attribute to him ethical qualities beyond those that Amon had possessed. Nevertheless, he placed a constant emphasis upon "truth." His search for truth and the naturalness of his daily life had a great impact on the art of the time. It was more perceptive than any art had been before and reflected a simple and beautiful realism. It opened a new chapter in art history and was to have a profound influence on future artists of Egypt. (Evidence of these changes are apparent when one compares the tomb and temple carvings during the period of Ikhnaton with earlier ones.)

It is not entirely clear what happened after Ikhnaton's rule, but he was first succeeded by his son-in-law, Smenkhkara, who died soon after and was followed by his half brother, Tutankhaton, a mere child of nine. For the first three years of his reign, Tutankhaton remained at Tell al Amarna, but finally he succumbed to the power of the Theban priests and returned to the old capital. He changed his name to Tutankhamen and revived the old religion. We know very little about him except that he died young, probably as early as 18. His tomb was the only one of the pharaohs' tombs from the Middle Kingdom or earlier periods to be found intact.

The army had enabled Ikhnaton to break with tradition, and now it was the army that returned Egypt to tradition. Harmhab, one of the able commanders under the fallen dynasty, survived the crisis and finally seized the throne. Under his vigorous rule the disorganized nation was gradually restored to order.

The army made peace with the civil service and the clergy and all three institutions shared power. In the new age that followed, the throne paid careful attention to the rights and prerogatives of all three. Harmhab was followed by the pharaohs of the XIX (1350–1205 BC) and XX Dynasties (1200–1090 BC), 11 of whom bore the famous name of Ramses.

The period spanned by these two dynasties was Egypt's most productive age, and because so many of its colossal monuments have survived until now, it is often taken to be her greatest period. Actually, it was the beginning of the end of Egypt's greatness as a major power.

Harmhab's immediate successors began the recovery of the lost empire in Asia, but the Hittites were too firmly established for them to regain Syria. Neither Seti II nor Ramses II was able to push the northern frontiers much beyond Palestine.

In some part Egypt's decline was brought about by forces over which the pharaohs had no control. Great movements of people were taking place throughout the east. But at the beginning of the 13th century BC when Ramses followed his brilliant father, Seti, no evidence of decline was discernible.

Climax of the Age of Pharaohs

Ramses, who has been called the king of kings, ruled Egypt for 67 years and from the evidence he was one of the most spectacular men in history.

He entered into diplomatic negotiations with the Hittites, with whom he signed what is probably the earliest recorded treaty in history. He campaigned in Syria and Palestine and raided the south. Accounts of his valor and courage survive on the walls of almost every major temple of his time.

He covered Egypt from one end to the other with monuments and temples. Among them are the Great Hypostyle Hall at Karnak; the Ramesseum, the funerary temple dedicated to himself and the god Amon at Thebes; the great temple at Abydos, dedicated to the god Osiris; several structures at Memphis and the most famous of all—the temple of Abu Simbel with its four colossal statues of Ramses.

The age of Ramses, with its imposing statues, grand temples, and great feats, marks the climax of the age of the pharaohs. From this period until the conquest by Alexander the Great, the history of ancient Egypt becomes one of steady decline. Although the country would enjoy occasional periods of prosperity and unity, never again would it be a world power.

After 1100 BC, internal dissension again split the country into its traditional northern and southern halves. At first merchant princes from Tanis ruled Lower Egypt, and the high priests of Amon who succeeded the last Ramses held Upper Egypt.

Around 950 BC, Sheshank, a Libyan who belonged to a family of high priests from Heracleopolis, seized control of both Upper and Lower Egypt. Under him the XXII Dynasty tried to restore Egypt's prestige and the country prospered. He raided Palestine and in about 930 BC plundered the Temple of Solomon in Jerusalem.

But rivalry between the powerful priests at Thebes undermined the dynasty and by 730 BC Egypt was once again ripe for foreign invasion, which came from the south this time. The Nubians remained in power for 70 years but were driven back to their homes by the Assyrians, who invaded from the east in 663 BC

Within the year, the Assyrians were tricked into leaving Egypt by a prince of Sais, Psamtik I, to whom they gave authority. He established the XXVI Dynasty, sometimes called the Renaissance period, and for 54 years the country enjoyed peace and prosperity once again. His successors were also able leaders and Egypt continued to prosper until 525 BC, when the country was invaded by the Persians. In 332 BC, as part of his campaign to destroy the Persian Empire, Alexander the Great conquered Egypt.

With this, the last of the pharaohs—the XXX Dynasty—was swept away.

Greeks and Romans

Ptolemy, the general whom Alexander left to govern Egypt, established a new dynasty that ruled Egypt for over two centuries. Cleopatra, the seventh Ptolemaic queen to have this name and the most famous queen of ancient times, was the last of the line. Alexandria became the capital and most important center of Hellenism. Its university and library were the most celebrated of their time, and among the great scholars who went there to study and work were Euclid, Eratosthenes, and Herophilus.

The Greek period closed with the arrival of the Romans in 30 BC. They turned Egypt into the personal domain of the emperor and the wheat basket of his empire. Within a short time of the Roman takeover, however, Christianity began to spread in Egypt. Alexandria was to become a great center of the new faith, second only to Rome and Constantinople. Particularly important in Egypt was the development of monasticism, the first in Christianity.

Arrival of Islam

In 641, only a few years after the birth of Islam, Egypt was conquered by the Arabs. The majority of Egyptians quickly adopted their faith, and Arabic replaced Greek and Coptic as the language of the country. With the center of the faith in Arabia and the capital of the empire first in Damascus and later in Baghdad, Egypt did not play as significant a role in the early days of Islam as it did in its later history.

In 969, the Fatimids, who were Shiite Muslims from North Africa, invaded Egypt and established their capital at Cairo. Under their reign Al

Azhar was begun, later to become the first university and the most important center of Muslim learning in the world.

During the time of the Crusades, a new dynasty, the Ayyubid, was established by Salah ed-Din, known to the West as Saladin. Under his rule Egypt became once again an important power in the East and extended its rule to Palestine and Syria.

With the last of the Ayyubids in 1245, and through the conniving and manipulations of a most unusual slave who became queen, a new group known as Mameluks came to power and, in one form or another, ran Egypt for the next seven centuries. The Mameluks were mercenaries and former slaves of Turkish and Eastern European origin who became influential soldiers and advisers. The ruthless Bahri Mameluks and later the even worse Circassian Mameluks ruled Egypt until it was conquered by the Ottoman Turks, most tyrannical of all, early in the 16th century.

Mameluk rule was characterized by incessant warfare and political chaos resulting from continuing palace intrigues. Seldom did a ruler last more than six years before he was eliminated by a rival. Despite this, the Mameluks lived lavishly and were patrons of the arts. Islamic art and architecture in Egypt reached their zenith under their rule, and many of Cairo's greatest mosques and mausoleums date from this period.

Egypt, long the benefactor of east-west trade, suffered the same fate as other countries of the area when the discovery of America and the circumnavigation of the globe revolutionized world trading patterns.

In the later days of Turkish rule Egypt again fell to the power of influential mercenaries, yet another group of Mameluks. Egypt remained nominally part of the Turkish Empire until World War I.

French and English Invasions

In 1798, as part of his effort to outflank the British and establish a trade route to the east, Napoleon occupied Egypt. His mission was a disaster for the French, but it opened a new chapter in Egypt's history and marked the start of modern history in the Middle East.

Napoleon's expedition included an army of scholars as well as soldiers. Their studies were the start of research into the mysteries of ancient Egypt that later developed into the science of Egyptology. On the other hand, the opening of Egypt to the West also meant exposure to Western ideas, which set in motion a chain of events that is felt to this day.

After the French withdrawal, Muhammad Ali, a soldier of Albanian origin at the head of the Turkish Army, was appointed by the Ottomans to rule Egypt. One of his first moves was to eliminate the power of the Mameluks once and for all—by having them massacred. Afterward he set about to modernize Egypt. He introduced cotton from India, redistributed land, and improved and expanded irrigation. He and his successors gradually obtained autonomy from the Ottomans.

Although history has tended to glamorize this chapter of Egyptian history, the fact is that Muhammad Ali dealt with the Egyptians as ruthlessly as he had with the Mameluks and in effect made Egypt into his personal estate. The nation became almost entirely dependent on its cotton crop. The combination of the concentration of power in the hands of Muhammad Ali's successors and the one-crop economy were to plague Egypt with many problems and much distress for the next 150 years.

In 1866 Isma'il, the grandson of Muhammad Ali, was granted the title of khedive (viceroy) by the Turks, and during his reign the Suez Canal was completed. But by 1875, through his own extravagance and the charlatanry of the British, French, and powerful European banking interests, Isma'il had become so heavily in debt that he was forced to sell his Canal shares to Britain. And in 1880 his successor, Tewfiq, had to submit to joint British-French control over Egypt's finances. (A full account of this period is available in James Aldridge's *Cairo*, and it helps one understand the background of events that followed over the next half century and finally erupted into the revolution of 1952.)

European manipulation of the khedive, Egypt's economy, and the general mismanagement of the country caused unrest throughout the land. What started as an army protest headed by Ahmad 'Arabi, a lieutenant, developed into a revolt, and, unfortunately for the Egyptians, it provided a pretext for British intervention in 1882. For the next four decades, Britain ruled Egypt through her high commissioners, the most famous—and most infamous—of whom was Lord Cromer, who ruled the country almost single-handedly for 20 years.

During World War I, Britain declared Egypt a protectorate and brought Turkey's rule to an abrupt end. At the close of the war Egyptian nationalists led by Said Zaghlul agitated for independence, with an appeal by Zaghlul to the League of Nations convened in Paris. A treaty providing for a constitutional monarchy under Fuad I (the father of Farouk) was concluded in 1922; but despite promises of independence, the British protectorate remained until 1936, when another treaty promised eventual withdrawal of British troops.

During World War II Britain undertook the defense of Egypt and defeated the Germans in a decisive battle at Alamein in 1942. After the war, friction between Egypt and Britain remained. The nationalist movement continued to grow and the Muslim Brotherhood became very strong. The aim of both was full independence and final withdrawal of the British. Outwardly, disputes centered around the Suez Canal and Sudan, which had been under a joint Anglo-Egyptian condominium since 1899. Also, Egypt bitterly opposed the United Nations' partition of Palestine in 1948.

Independence in 1952

Finally, as a result of long frustration in their attempts to gain full independence and disillusionment with the corrupt Farouk government, a group of young army officers staged a bloodless coup in 1952. The following year Egypt was declared a republic, the dynasty of Muhammad Ali came to an end, and for the first time in 2,000 years Egypt was again in the hands of Egyptians. Muhammad Naguib, a respected elder statesman, was made head of the new government, but the following year Gamal Abdel Nasser emerged as the power behind the coup and remained head of state until his sudden death in 1970.

At the beginning of Nasser's regime, relations between Egypt and the United States were very good. The United States supported Egypt's effort to enforce Britain's commitment to withdraw its troops and to turn over the administration of the Suez Canal to Egypt. However, as the conflict between Egypt and Israel heated up and the issue of U.S. participation in building the Aswan Dam erupted, American-Egyptian relations deteriorated.

When Egypt nationalized the Suez Canal Company and demanded the removal of British troops, the result in 1956 was a joint British, French, and Israeli attack on Egypt, which was halted amid U.S. and Soviet threats and counterthreats that were complicated by the Hungarian uprising at the same time.

For the next decade, the United States's position steadily declined as Russian influence grew. The Russians helped the Egyptians build the Aswan Dam, and supplied and trained the army, while becoming very active in the educational and cultural fields.

In 1958, and again in 1963 and 1971, attempts were made to form an Arab Union, first with Syria, then with Iraq and later with Libya.

From the time of the Six-Day War in June 1967 to a renewal of the fighting in October 1973, diplomatic relations between Egypt and the United States broke off. But with the United States's role in mediating the Sinai agreement and the reopening of the Suez Canal, relations greatly improved and were dramatized by Nixon's visit to Egypt in 1974 and the visit to America of Egyptian President Anwar Sadat the following year and a second visit in April of 1977. Indeed, the normally good relations that have characterized the historic intercourse between the two countries have returned.

British visitors will find a warmer welcome than before, thanks to the desire of most Egyptians to forget the unpleasantness in the past and to the respect and admiration for Britain that is still strong in cultural and business circles.

Recent Events

After the October War of 1973, events in the Middle East have taken many unpredictable turns and always Egypt has been at the center of them. The war itself was a turning point for the Egyptians. It helped them regain the confidence that was so badly shattered by their humiliating defeat in the Six-Day War of 1967. In practical terms, Egypt regained the Suez Canal and the desperately needed revenue from its traffic and began rebuilding the cities in the Canal Zone, enabling those who fled the war zone to return.

In 1974 President Sadat surprised the West by tossing out the Soviets, and in 1977 he dumbfounded the world by making his precedent-breaking visit to Israel. This was followed by the famous 1978 Camp David talks, and President Carter's visit to Egypt in 1979 was the gesture needed to bring the peace treaty with Israel into reality.

Efforts at achieving such a treaty had been the cornerstone of Egypt's policy since Sadat came into power in 1970. While Egypt's relationship with the rest of the Arab world was greatly strained by the signing of the agreement, Sadat's peace initiatives had the overwhelming approval of the Egyptian people, and following his tragic death in 1981, his successor, Hosni Mubarak, has continued the pursuit of peace, although with little success. Today Egypt is in a precarious position, caught between two worlds. On the one hand, Egypt is an integral part of the Arab World, struggling with modernization, moderation, and a Western outlook; on the other, she must deal with the fundamentalists who appear to be gaining strength as the country's economy continues to lose ground under the combined weight of shrinking resources and a population explosion that is out of control.

From the outset of the Gulf crisis President Mubarak took a strong leadership position against the Iraqi invasion of Kuwait, and for the most part he had the country behind him. Even his detractors lowered their voices after the war, once the extent of the catastrophe wrought by the Iraqis became known. At press time it was too early to know the long-term impact of the Gulf war on Egypt; but it is already obvious that the country has paid a heavy price in three ways:

Approximately 1.5 million Egyptians working in Kuwait and Iraq were uprooted, losing their livelihood and having to return to Egypt to face a level of unemployment that has already reached crisis proportions. The remittances these workers sent to their families in Egypt had long been an essential, stabilizing element in the country's economy.

Tourism, which is Egypt's largest foreign-exchange earner, had been set to break all records in 1990. But after Iraq's invasion of Kuwait there was a steady erosion, and as soon as the war began, tourism came to a standstill. Losses were calculated in the millions.

Revenues from the Suez Canal fell sharply, not only because of the drop-off in traffic through the Canal due to the embargo on Iraq but because insurance premiums became so exorbitant that all traffic was adversely affected.

Egypt's losses from the war have been estimated at about $20 billion. This is on top of a national debt that reached more than $48 billion in 1991. Some relief has come from the United States in its forgiveness of $7 billion of Egypt's debt, and other Western governments were expected to wipe out more than $40 billion, provided the Egyptian government committed itself to the economic reforms laid out by the International Monetary Fund (IMF).

Certainly, the foreign government debt-relief measures could go a long way toward alleviating Egypt's financial woes, but the IMF's reforms will not come without a political price domestically. Even after the debt relief has been given, Egypt will still be left with a debt of about $8.64 billion owed to commercial banks and other private institutions. In addition, this debt relief will hardly be enough to offset the other deep dislocations Egypt has suffered. Needless to say, true peace throughout the region would also help.

Isis, Goddess of Heaven and Earth

EGYPTIAN FOOD AND DRINK

Coffee, *Fool, and Zibib*

Egyptians usually eat a light breakfast and have their main meal at about 2 or 3 PM. Many take afternoon tea at about 5 or 6 PM, and have a light supper. When Egyptians go out for dinner or invite guests to their home, the invitation is usually for about 9, but dinner will probably not be served until 10 or 11 PM. Those who have the good fortune to be invited to an Egyptian home for a meal have a treat in store.

Restaurants serve lunch between 1 and 3 to 4 PM and dinner from 8 PM to midnight.

In most hotels, unless you specifically order an American breakfast, you get a Continental repast of juice, rolls, butter, jam, and strong French coffee or tea. Sliced bread for toast is available, but it is not as soft as American bread. Native Egyptian bread is a flat, round loaf called *aiysh*.

If you cannot start the day without a cup of American coffee, or if you can't handle strong French-style morning coffee, pack a jar of instant coffee in your suitcase. Also, Nescafé or powdered coffee is available in most restaurants and hotels, but neither decaffeinated coffee nor artificial sweetener is usually available. If you rely on these items for health reasons, you should bring your own supplies.

Drinking coffee is a tradition throughout the Middle East. You will always be offered a cup of Egyptian or Arabic coffee when you visit a friend or a business associate or stop at a shop in the bazaar.

Arabic coffee is thick and is ordered according to the amount of sugar: sweet *(ziyada)*, medium *(mazboota)*, or bitter *(saada)*. In Egypt the local

68

coffee house has traditionally been a meeting place for men who at the end of the day join their friends to smoke a *nargili* (hubble-bubble or water pipe), listen to Arabic music, discuss politics, and recite poetry.

Egypt has a variety of native dishes, and most good restaurants serve both Western and Oriental selections. Menus are available in English, French, and Arabic; the maître d' speaks English.

Appetizers

Batarikh: Egyptian caviar, pressed, dried, and preserved in salt and oil, is served in small, thin slices to be eaten with bread or crackers.

Baba-ghanouj: baked eggplant mashed and mixed with sesame paste, flavored with lemon, garlic, and olive oil. The same dish is found in several Middle Eastern countries, but in Egypt its preparation and flavor vary slightly from that found in Lebanon or Syria. It is served as a dip with toasted bread chips, as an hors d'oeuvre, or as a first-course vegetable dish.

Leban zabadi: Egyptian yogurt—thicker, creamier, and better than any yogurt you can get in the States. (Eating leban zabadi regularly helps to diminish intestinal upsets.)

Mish: dried cheese with spices added is made into a paste and served as an hors d'oeuvre.

Taameyya (or *falafel*): patties of mashed *fool* (fava bean) with finely chopped parsley, highly seasoned and deep-fried in oil—excellent with cocktails. This is an Egyptian specialty, and it is prepared better in Egypt than in any other Middle Eastern country, although many others claim it as their own.

Taheena: The oil paste from the sesame seed is often used as an ingredient in Arabic food. In Egypt, taheena alone is combined with lemon, garlic, and spices and served with toasted bread chips as a dip for hors d'oeuvres.

Turshi (often called *bickley*): mixed vegetables pickled in a spicy sauce. Especially good with cocktails.

Waraq anab: rolled grape leaves stuffed with rice and meat or lentils. Known to Americans by its Greek name, *dolma*.

Main Courses

Fool mudhammas: This is Egypt's national dish. Fool is cooked with spices, and sometimes tomatoes, into a thick sauce (something like chili con carne without meat). It is often topped with a fried egg for breakfast and served without the egg for other meals. Very few restaurants frequented by tourists serve fool mudhammas. The Cairo Marriott and the Nile Hilton coffee shops have it, and Tabie, a restaurant in downtown Cairo, is famous for it.

Kebab: Egyptian shish kebab is made of chunks of lamb or minced lamb *(kufta)* with spices added. In Egypt the flavor of kebab is different from that in any other Middle Eastern country. Lean pieces of lamb are cut into small cubes, then seasoned in a marinade of thin shavings of onion, parsley, marjoram, some lemon juice, salt, and pepper. The marinaded pieces of lamb are then placed on a skewer and grilled over hot charcoal. When the meat is minced or ground and formed into finger patties around a skewer for broiling, it is called kufta.

Moulukhiya: a steamed green vegetable (something like spinach), which may be eaten separately or used as a sauce on other dishes. The plant closely resembles mint and is scientifically known as Corete or *Carchorus alitorius.* The leaves are chopped and added to chicken or rabbit broth. Moulukhiya can be served as a soup or with crushed pieces of bread and some rice; the latter is known as *fattett moulukhiya.* The dish is available in several versions in other Arab countries, but to any Middle Easterner, moulukhiya is Egyptian.

Pigeons are broiled on an open spit, which gives the meat a smoky flavor. Several outdoor garden restaurants in Cairo specialize in the preparation of these birds. *Casino des Pigeons* by the Nile is the most popular.

Roz bel khalta: fried rice mixed with currants, nuts, meat, and liver.

Grilled shrimp: huge, succulent, and delicious shrimp from the Mediterranean and the Red Sea—more like small lobster tails. This is probably the best dish for American tastes to be found in Egypt—a real treat. Small shrimp are available, too.

Other Eastern dishes: Many of the better known Lebanese dishes are available in Egypt and are often served in Egyptian homes. Curry, presumably brought from India by the British, is available in several Cairo restaurants as mild or as hot as you like.

Fruits, Desserts, and Cheese

There is a year-round variety of fruit—citrus, melons (especially Ismailia melon), pomegranates, apricots, and figs. All are excellent. Eat whatever fruit is in season—peel it for caution. If you are lucky enough to be in Egypt when mangoes are in season, you will have an unexpected treat.

Egyptian sherbet, *dondurma,* is a white milk ice that is very sweet. *Umm ali,* a bread pudding topped with pine nuts and milk, served hot, is also an Egyptian specialty. *Aish el saraya* has a custard on the bottom, cake on top; *ata'if* is a special dessert for the month of Ramadan; and *kanafa,* a sweet resembling shredded wheat stuffed with chopped nuts, is flavored with syrup and rose water. All are very sweet, popular desserts of Syrian origin. *Muhalabiya* is a particularly good dessert made from cream of rice and decorated with pistachios.

The local cheese, *gibna beida,* is similar to what is called Greek or *feta* cheese in the United States.

Beverages

Several good, inexpensive table wines are made from Alexandrian grapes. Omar Khayyam (dry red), Rubis d'Egypte (rosé), and Gianaclis Village (dry white) are the best; they all run about L.E. 5 a bottle in retail shops. The markup in hotels and restaurants may be 200% or more. Quality is variable, and there are other inferior labels.

As a matter of interest, it is not known whether grapes were indigenous to the Nile Valley or were imported to Egypt in ancient times. Both tree- and vine-growing grapes were known, but from ancient drawings, the latter appears to have been more widespread. As far back as the Third Dynasty (about 2730 BC) Egyptians were planting grape trees in their gardens. One of the most interesting tombs in the Valley of the Nobles at Luxor is that of Sennefer. Its ceiling is designed to represent a grape arbor.

Local brandy comes in a variety of prices and grades, but the best, suitable for punches and mixed drinks, costs L.E. 9 for a large bottle. There is also a rum, Zattos, for L.E. 4.50.

Zibib is the Egyptian version of Lebanese *arak,* Turkish *raki,* Greek *ouzo,* or French *pernod* and makes an excellent before-dinner drink, either on the rocks or diluted with water, which turns it a milky color. The anisette-flavored aperitif comes in two sizes: L.E. 11 for a large bottle; L.E. 2.90 for a small one.

All the above wines and liquors can be purchased at the Egyptian Vineyards and Distilleries, 41 Talaat Harb Street, and in many grocery stores. At the rest house and gasoline station halfway between Alexandria and Cairo on the desert road, the Gianaclis Vineyards maintain a shop for their wines and spirits, as well as their olive and date by-products. The wines, especially, are cheaper than in Cairo.

Imported liquors, including whiskey, are difficult to find and cost about L.E. 80–L.E. 90 per bottle on the black market. In hotels and nightclubs, they are marked up 200% or more. Visitors should plan to bring the allowed three litres of duty-free spirits upon entering. Foreigners can purchase them in the duty-free shops at Cairo International Airport upon arrival. Dollars must be used. Drinks in bars range from L.E. 7 and up.

The local beer is good and costs about L.E. 4 for a large bottle in a restaurant. Stella is a light lager in green or brown bottles. Stella Export is sweeter, more expensive (L.E. 6 in bars), and comes in smaller brown bottles. You will almost always be served a large bottle. The small ones seem to be in short supply. Bock beer is available briefly in the spring season and is called *marzen.* Aswali is a dark beer made in Aswan. Major hotels and European-style restaurants have a limited selection of imported beers, which cost L.E. 7 and up.

Soft drinks, soda, tonic mineral water, and a variety of exotic fruit juices are available year-round and seasonally. Coca-Cola, 7-Up, Pepsi, and Schweppes sodas are made locally and cost about 30 pts. per bottle.

One of the most popular Egyptian refreshments is *Karkade,* a pretty raspberry-colored drink made from the flowers of sorrel, a plant grown in Aswan. Guests are often served this drink in government or business offices and in Egyptian homes. Local tradition says it is good for calming the nerves. It is served cold during the summer or hot, like tea, during the winter.

THE FACE OF EGYPT

Osiris, God of the Dead

CAIRO

City of a Thousand Years

The graceful minarets of stately mosques vie with slim modern buildings along the skyline. Shady parks overlooking the river and flowering gardens along wide boulevards refresh the eyes against the desert edges of this magnificent city astride the Nile.

Cairo, Egypt's capital and the largest city in Africa, sways with the movement of 14 million people—the ever-present multitudes. Located at the apex of the Delta, this great metropolis is the meeting place of Africa and Arabia, Europe and Asia.

Throughout most of its history, Cairo has been the bank and warehouse of east-west trade. Because of its location, it was the most convenient junction for the transshipment of goods, which arrived by ship from the East via the Red Sea and from there were carried overland the short distance to Cairo. Here they were stored, bought or sold, then floated down the Nile to the Mediterranean and on to Europe.

Few capitals in the world have quite the same all-encompassing position as Cairo does today. It is Egypt's economic, political, administrative, cultural, educational, entertainment, military, transportation, and historical center—all in one. Almost nothing happens in Egypt that does not happen in Cairo. This is at once its blessing and its curse.

Cairo's four universities attract men and women from all over the Middle East, Asia, and Africa, as they did in ancient times. Al Azhar, considered the oldest continual university in history, is the most important center of religious learning in the Muslim world. Cairo has fabulous museums,

75

churches, and mosques. Its bazaars are the best in the eastern Mediterranean, set in narrow winding alleys in an atmosphere permeated with spices and incense.

Actually, there have been many Cairos in the history of this great city. The first is so ancient historians do not know when it was begun or by whom. Known as On in antiquity, it was called Heliopolis, the city of the sun, by the Greeks. On was the center of worship of Re, the sun god, and reached its peak in about 2500 BC. For hundreds of years it had the ancient world's most advanced university. After the rise of Thebes, On lost its preeminence but remained an important center of the empire. Today an obelisk in Heliopolis, a modern suburb of Cairo, marks the site of ancient On. Ironically, Heliopolis is called Masr Gadid (New Cairo) in Arabic. Another city is believed to have grown around the royal farm and dwelling place of the workers building the Pyramids in the period between 2700 and 2500 BC. Today this settlement is somewhere under the homes and apartments of Cairo suburbs, which stretch unbroken from the Nile to the shadow of the great Pyramids of Giza.

After the Persians under Cambyses razed Heliopolis to the ground in 525 BC, the long history of the city was broken for a thousand years— significant for Egypt as much as for the city. The Greeks, who followed the Persians, shifted the capital to Alexandria and with one stroke lifted Egypt out of Africa and placed it on the Mediterranean. With it, the era of the pharaohs ended and a European era began. Athens was a village, but Alexandria was the capital of the empire.

All the more reason that a thousand years later, when the Arabs streaked across the desert to pitch their tents at Fustat, the forerunner of today's Cairo, the shift was more than geographic. It signaled the end of Greek culture and the Christian era and the beginning of a new Egypt— Arab and Islamic.

The oldest part of the city is still known by the Egyptians as Old Cairo. Here the Persians built a fort on the strategic point of the Nile and the Romans fortified the site known as Babylon. Near the Roman fortress where the Arab army camped, a mosque was built and around it the city grew. During the next three centuries the city shifted its center slightly— to Askar and to Katai. Then in 969, the Fatimids from North Africa conquered Egypt and established their capital in the area they called al Qahira, the victorious. Finally, during the 12th century under Saladin, all four locales were made into one.

While the name did not change, Cairo changed many times during the next five centuries under the Mameluks and expanded north along the Nile. Finally, in the period after the French invasion and the arrival of the Europeans, the city crossed the river to its west bank. But even after a thousand years the city's greatest expansion of all times has been in this century and more particularly since World War II.

Today Cairo stretches so far in each direction that the only place from which one can see its great expanse is the Tower of Cairo on the island of Gezira, in the middle of the Nile. In the panorama the history of Egypt and the tale of Cairo unfolds: From the south, the Nile comes up from Africa to just north of the city, where it divides to form the great Delta, and from there it continues to the Mediterranean. Behind the soaring minarets of the Muhammad Ali Mosque and the Mukattam Hills in the east, there is the desert stretching to Arabia. To the west, beyond the Pyramids, another desert stretches across the Sahara wasteland. The green, fertile land created by the Nile is sharply edged on both banks of the river.

From this dramatic scene a visitor can also spot the center of the modern city, Midan al Tahrir (Liberation Square), which is the best place in which to orient oneself to the city. From the square the roads on the north and northeast lead to Cairo's main business district, the fashionable shopping streets of Kasr el Nil and Talaat Harb, and the cinema district. Beyond is Bulac, Opera Square, the Ezbekiya Gardens, the heart of Cairo at the time of the Napoleonic invasion, and the Mouski.

Directly south of Midan al Tahrir lies Garden City, the former palatial residence of colonial Egypt, and farther south are Old Cairo and the island of Roda. The Corniche drive by the Nile leads south to Maadi, a suburb of beautiful villas and gardens.

East of Midan al Tahrir is the Bab el Luk district and beyond that the Citadel commands the city from the foot of the Mukattam Hills. This area is the most historic part of the city. Visitors will find many of the great mosques, old houses, and museums.

West of Midan al Tahrir is Gezira, a small island in the middle of the Nile, with the residential area of Zamalek. Beyond Gezira on the west side of the Nile are the residential areas of Dokki and Giza, Cairo University, and the road's to the Pyramids. This area, although a separate municipality under the governorate of Giza, is for all practical purposes a part of Cairo.

For a traveler in search of history or pleasure, a shophound or a sportsman, few cities in the world compare with Cairo.

Planning Your Sightseeing

What to see in Cairo depends largely on the length of your visit and your interests. There is something for everyone, but clearly there is a great deal more of certain things, such as antiquities, than in almost any other place in the world.

Itineraries can be based on visiting the sites in the order of their historic, artistic, or archaeological importance or by exploring one district of Cairo at a time. The first approach is probably more useful if your time is limited because you can quickly make a list of priorities and design a sightseeing day around it. On the other hand, exploring one district of Cairo at a time is more fun, especially for those who plan an extended visit. In the long run, it might even be more productive because Cairo is a very large, sprawling city. It has the same congestion problems that afflict all big cities and it is possible to waste a great deal of time in traffic.

If you are not already traveling in a group, we would strongly recommend that you join an organized city tour on your first visit to Cairo. It is the least costly way to tour and it will enable you to cover most of the essentials in a short time. Unless you have a special interest in one aspect of Egypt, a generalized tour will be more satisfying than concentrating on only one aspect for the entire day. If, after one or two city tours, you want to strike out on your own, you will have a better idea of what to see and how to see it.

Hiring a car or taxi with or without a guide and planning your own itinerary enables you to see and remain at the places that interest you most, but it can be expensive. If you do decide to go off on your own, be sure

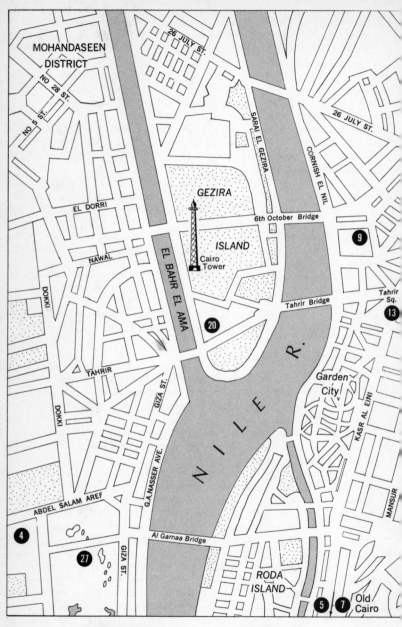

Points of Interest

1) Abdin Palace
2) Ezbakiya Garden
3) Blue Mosque
4) Cairo University
5) Church of Abu Serga
6) Citadel
7) Coptic Museum
8) Egyptian Library
9) Egyptian Museum
10) El-Azhar Mosque
11) Islamic Museum
12) Khan el-Khalili (Bazaar)
13) Metro's main stations

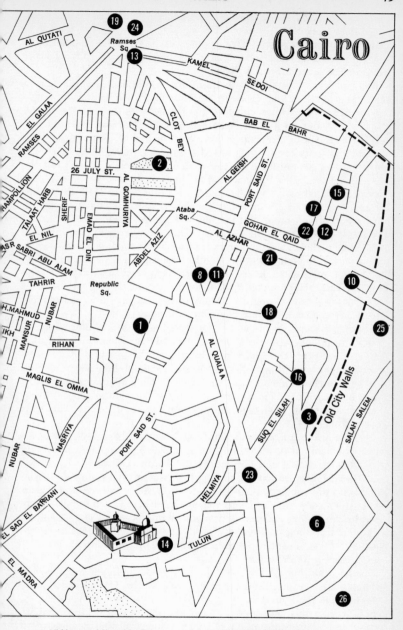

Cairo

14) Mosque of Ahmed Ibn Tulun
15) Mosque of el Akmar
16) Mosque of el Mardani
17) Mosque of Qalawun
18) Mosque of Sultan el-Muayyad
19) Railroad Station
20) Opera House and Cultural Center

21) School-Mosque of El-Ghuri
22) School-Mosque of Sultan Barquq
23) School-Mosque of Sultan Hasan
24) Statue of Ramses II
25) Tombs of the Caliphs
26) Tombs of the Mamelukes
27) Zoo

to set the fee *in advance* for a hired car, guide, donkey, camel, carriage, horse, or whatever.

If at any time you should have trouble with a taxi driver, peddler, vendor, guide, or dragoman, you should report it immediately to the Tourist Office or the nearest Tourist Police.

A list of local travel agents in Cairo and Alexandria is available in a local publication entitled *Cairo By Night and Day,* available from hotels and airlines. We have not included the list here, as the number of new agencies increases daily. Some, but not all, operate their own tours of Cairo and Upper Egypt or can arrange them on short notice. The large companies, such as American Express and Misr Travel, have regularly scheduled tours that you can purchase and join with other travelers. As an example, Misr Travel's half-day Pyramid and Sphinx tour is U.S. $45. An all-day Memphis and Sakkara, Pyramids and Sphinx tour is U.S. $110 with lunch. Either a city tour or a tour of Old Cairo is U.S. $35 for one person; $80 for a group of up to four persons; and $15 per person for a large group. The evening program for the sound-and-light show at the Pyramids is U.S. $17. Prices include guide and entrance fees. Tours for Cairo and its environs depart from both downtown and Heliopolis. Itineraries change daily, but the Pyramids and Sakkara are almost always available. Contact Misr Travel, 7 Talaat Harb St., tel. 750010, for a schedule. Be very careful about the agency with which you deal. Many of the new ones are inadequately staffed, incompetent, and are charging ridiculous prices.

At ports, airports, hotels, and major tourist areas, tourist officers selected from the police corps are on hand to assist tourists on arrival and during their visit in Egypt. They might not always have the answers to your questions, but they are willing to help. Most speak enough English to help you or to help you find someone who can help you. They wear a regular policeman's uniform (black for winter; white for summer) and can be distinguished by a small light blue bar worn on the chest pocket that reads Tourist Police.

There is also a guides' association (although we have yet to discover precisely where it is or who administers it), which gives practical training to candidates chosen and licensed by the Tourist Office, 5 Adly Street, tel. 391–3454. On a recent trip to Egypt, we were with a young guide who had taken a tourism degree at a local university. She was sweet and charming, but her knowledge of Cairo was not extensive. If you are genuinely interested in history and antiquities, you should be very exact about this with your travel agent. There are good, knowledgeable guides in Egypt, but the best ones must be booked in advance. A list of guides/phone numbers appears in the *Practical Guide to Cairo.*

On the other hand, even with the best guide in Egypt to show you around, there is no substitute for reading in advance. There is much more to Cairo than the Pyramids. We urge you to investigate it on your own, hopefully with this guidebook in hand and the specialized aids that we recommend where appropriate. If you rely solely on tourist guides, you will have nothing but the most superficial look at this city.

If you cannot see Egypt's antiquities in the company of a full-fledged Egyptologist, archaeologist, historian, architect, or Islamic expert, then your next choice is a dragoman. These are the traditional, handsomely robed and turbaned men who have been guiding tourists around antiquity sites and through the bazaars for at least a century—and they are now a dying institution.

The word *dragoman* is a corruption of the Arabic word *terjiman,* meaning "interpreter." In olden days that is what they were, but at the turn of the century, with the arrival of the rich Europeans and Americans who came to winter in Egypt, the dragoman expanded his services until he became all things to all people. He filled the role of guide, mentor, father confessor, bodyguard and, with luck, lasting friend. Most of the old gentlemen have never been to school, but they often know more about the sites of antiquity than some of the new guides who have not had proper training, and they are certainly more entertaining. Their information is often inaccurate in detail, but never mind; the good ones tell their stories with great drama and with such excitement that they pique your interest and make a good show of it. Most of the time you are glad to have them with you to call off the hounds of peddlers and children after *baksheesh* (tips).

Most dragomen are reliable, but, as with everything else in Egypt, you should agree on the price beforehand—and don't pay until you are finished. The usual fee is about L.E. 30 for half a day and L.E. 60 for an entire day, although the price seems to be going up rather rapidly these days, and many will insist on more. You can be sure that if you go shopping with him he will take you to his favorite shop (one that his cousin owns) and he will get a 25% kickback, or more.

For easy reference, the following section on the capital city has been divided into *Pharaonic, Coptic, Islamic,* and *modern* Cairo. Visitors are unlikely to visit the sites in this order, but it helps to read about them and to refer to them with some historical perspective.

The opening and closing times of museums are notoriously inconsistent. We have often gone to a museum after closing hours to discover that it is still open, or before closing hours and found it closed. The one that seems strictest about its hours is the Egyptian Antiquities Museum.

The itineraries at the end of this section are designed to enable visitors to see the most in the shortest time. If you are planning an extended stay, you might want to consult a travel agent or the Tourist Office in Cairo for more information.

NOTE: In 1990 entrance fees to all antiquity sites, museums, and other such attractions were raised considerably, and some places that did not have entrance fees in the past now have them. We have made every effort to give readers the most current information, but do not be surprised to find higher prices.

PHARAONIC CAIRO

Summary of Pharaonic Cairo: Within easy reach of the city are the Pyramids, the Sphinx, and Memphis and Sakkara. These should be preceded by a visit to the Egyptian Antiquities Museum.

The Pyramids

Located nine miles west of Cairo. Entrance: L.E. 14; Great Pyramid, L.E. 14; Solar Boat Museum, L.E. 27. Hours: 9 AM to 2 PM.

On arrival in Cairo by plane or train, the excitement of your visit will be heightened as soon as you have the first glimpse of the gigantic peaks of the three Pyramids of Giza rising in the distance on the western horizon. At a closer range, your first look at them—the last of the Seven Wonders of the Ancient World—will be surprising and perhaps even disappointing.

The Pyramids are the ultimate travel cliche and, what's more, they look exactly like their picture. But don't worry, the disappointment is fleeting. Within a short time, your mind will start to grasp the size of the Pyramids, the precision of their structure, and the effort it took to build them, and you will begin to marvel at them. Then, suddenly, the impact of their majesty and symmetry will overwhelm you and leave you speechless.

Famous writers down through the ages have written about this experience. One of our favorites is Julian Huxley in *From an Antique Land* (New York: Harper & Row, 1966):

"Familiarity . . . had led me . . . to discount [the Pyramids]. They had become international commonplaces, degraded to the level of the tourist souvenir. They had passed through so many million minds as one of the 'Wonders of the World' that their sharp edge of real wonder had been blunted. . . . I was sure I was not going to be impressed by them.

"But in actuality, they make an overpowering impression. It is not one of beauty, but on the other hand not one of mere bigness, though size enters into it, and there is an element of aesthetic satisfaction in the elemental simplicity of their triangular silhouette. But this combines with an element of vicarious pride in the magnitude of the human achievement involved . . . to produce an effect different from that of any other work of man."

Jomrad, one of the scholars on Napoleon's expedition, described his experience thus:

"Seen from a distance they produce the same kind of effect as do high mountain peaks. . . . The nearer one approaches, the more this effect decreases. But when at last you are within a short distance of these regular masses, a wholly different impression is produced; you are struck by surprise, and as soon as you have reached the top of the slope, your ideas change in a flash. Finally, when you have reached the foot of the Great Pyramid, you are seized with a vivid and powerful emotion, tempered by a sort of stupefaction, almost overwhelming in its effects."

The Pyramids stand on a hill overlooking the Nile Valley and are a testimony to the ancients' belief in the immortality of the soul. It took 20 years to build one.

Although there are some 80 pyramids in Egypt, the three at Giza are the most important and the most famous. The first in size and chronological order is Cheops (Khufu), erected in about 2690 BC. Its original height was 481 feet and its base covered 13 acres. Cheophren (Kheophren), Cheops's son, built the second pyramid in about 2650 BC, slightly smaller in size. The third pyramid, smallest of the three, was erected in about 2600 BC and named after Menkaru (Mycerinus).

The *Great Pyramid* is estimated to contain 2.5 million tons of stone; each stone weighs an average of 2.5 tons. According to Napoleon, its cubic content is enough to build a wall 10 feet high and a foot thick entirely around France. The area of its base is said to be large enough to hold St. Paul's, Westminster Abbey, St. Peter's, and the cathedrals of Florence and Milan all at once. To put it in American terms, this means that the base of Cheops's pyramid covers the same area as the four city blocks taken up by Lincoln Center in New York.

The Great Pyramid is still the largest and most massive stone structure in the world. The stones, put together without mortar, are fitted so perfectly that not even a razor blade can be passed between them.

The interior of Cheops's pyramid has several long empty corridors without decoration. The most important is the Grand Gallery, 153 feet long and 28 feet high, leading to a simple funeral chamber. Two openings pierce the entire structure and allow air to enter. Above the King's Chamber, five other compartments formed by huge granite blocks were designed to relieve the chamber of the structure's tremendous weight. The climb up into the chambers of the pyramid is not for the faint-hearted, the claustrophobic, or the out-of-shape. One can walk erect for quite a way into the pyramid to inspect the walls and passageways and then turn back.

Details on the history and building of the Pyramids are covered in many scholarly tomes, and the speculations over how and why they were built have been the basis of many popular books. Among those included in the "Suggested Reading List," one of the best and easiest to read is *The Pyramids*, by Ahmed Fakhry, a leading Egyptian scholar who spent his life studying them.

East of the Pyramids lie the tombs of the princesses; on the west, those of nobles and courtiers. Such tombs are known as *mastabas*, because their shape resembles a bench (mastaba) still found against the doors of village houses. Some scholars think it was, in fact, from these simple structures that the design of the Pyramids grew. At the foot of the Great Pyramid, a former royal rest house in pharaonic style is now a museum. It has a pleasant outdoor garden and commands a magnificent view of the Nile Valley and Cairo.

Solar Boat Museum. Entrance fee: L.E. 27. Hours 9 AM–2 PM; tel. 857–928. New discoveries are constantly being made in the area of the Pyramids, but none have been more exciting than the two well-preserved wooden funeral boats that were uncovered in 1954 south of the Great Pyramid. They are the only vestiges from Cheops's reign, other than the Pyramid itself, that have been discovered and they are considered among the most sensational archaeological finds of recent years.

The first boat, which has been reassembled and reconstructed in many parts, stands in a museum next to Cheops's pyramid. It actually carried the body of the pharaoh from Memphis to Giza. The museum is worth a visit to gain an appreciation of both the boats and the entire undertaking. The museum building has caused deterioration of the wood, ropes, canvas sails and reed mats, and authorities finally decided to open the museum to raise money to correct the building's structural problems.

Equally exciting have been the recent discoveries of tombs and treasures from the Old Kingdom in the area of the Pyramids and at Sakkara. Fifteen tombs were opened to the public in 1990; perhaps as many as 500 tombs lie in the necropolis. West of the Great Pyramid is the tomb of Ka-M-Ankh, a high-ranking priest. Carved from solid limestone almost 5,000 years ago, the walls are covered with brightly colored scenes of daily life; the sarcophagus is in the center. In another location, the archaeologists found a cemetery of dwarves. One tomb contained a statue of a drawf, Per-Ny-Ankhu, which is considered to be one of the most unusual artifacts ever uncovered from the Old Kingdom period. Carved from basalt and measuring less than 2 feet in height, the statue is to be exhibited in the Cairo Antiquities Museum.

Another site of new discovery is about two miles southeast of the Sphinx, where a workmen's village and the tombs of their overseers have been found by a joint American-Egyptian team. The tombs, carved from limestone and colorfully decorated, contained hundreds of carved statues as well as pottery and other artifacts.

The Sphinx

Five hundred feet southeast of the Great Pyramid is the Sphinx, a recumbent lion with the head of a man. It was carved from natural rock, presumably in situ. Over the centuries as parts eroded or broke off, they were replaced, but the additions were fitted so well that they are hardly perceptible. (In early 1988, large chunks of rock fell off the body of the Sphinx, sending cries of consternation through the antiquities community and questions from many quarters as to the cause. The conclusions are not yet known, but you need not be a scientist to see the damage being done to all of Cairo's precious heritage by the pollution that has resulted from unbridled urban sprawl.)

The body of the lion—the symbol of kingship—represented might. The Sphinx's human head symbolized intelligence. Its headgear is called the Klaft, a striped hood with two flaps that are placed behind the ears and brought forward to rest on the shoulders. The Sphinx has a total length of 190 feet and is 66 feet tall at its highest point. The face alone measures 16.6 feet. Its paws seem out of proportion with the rest of the body, but the Sphinx was meant to be viewed from the front at the bottom of the valley. From there the paws are in proper perspective. The Sphinx faces east, from which it was meant to watch the rising sun—the return of life— each day.

The Greeks called the statue the Sphinx because it resembled a legendary hero of a similar name. It is probable that Abu-al-Hul, as he is known in Arabic, has the head of Cheophren, his builder. Successive pharaohs down to Roman times restored, venerated, and admired this remarkable statue. Some considered it the god of death.

Adjoining the Sphinx is the funerary temple of Cheops. At this temple the body of the dead pharaoh was mummified and sanctified by the priests. It is believed that this process could have taken as long as a year. From the temple, you may look up the causeway to the site of another temple at the base of the pyramid, where religious ceremonies took place before the body was entombed.

Son et Lumière (Sound and Light). The evening program for the Pyramids and Sphinx was one of the first in the *son-et-lumière* repertoire and is still one of the best. While floodlights play on the Pyramids, recorded voices apparently coming from the Sphinx tell their history. The lights display many unusual aspects of the Pyramids and vividly reveal their beautiful form and majesty. Shows are in English, French, German, and Arabic on different days of the week. Check locally to verify the time and language schedule. Admission: $10. You can hire a taxi to take you there, wait, and return you to town. Be sure to settle the price in advance. Local tour operators offer the excursion for U.S. $17 by motorcoach.

A word of warning—modernity has come to the Pyramids. Those who knew the area a decade or two ago will be startled to see it now. A four-lane highway runs from town to the Mena House and a two-lane asphalt road continues up the hill to the Great Pyramid. Progress—it is enough to make one weep. To alleviate the congestion created by dozens of tour buses disgorging groups at the base of the Pyramids, the government extended the roads another half mile to a plateau on the west side of the Pyramids and provided a parking area for tour buses. It has helped lessen the circus atmosphere—along with the camels and camel drivers—that had developed in the immediate vicinity of the Pyramids, but it has done nothing to enhance the beauty of the site.

There is great consternation locally and worldwide over the rapid deterioration of the Pyramids and the damage being done by continuing urban expansion and the urgent need to develop a rescue plan. There is no shortage of ideas, but, unfortunately, the experts themselves have continuously stymied efforts by their inability to agree on a plan. Their positions are aired often in the local press. It seems that unless the president of Egypt himself gets sufficiently aroused, demands action, and sets a deadline, the deliberations will be endless.

Memphis and Sakkara

The ancient city of Memphis lies 20 miles southwest of Cairo. Entrance: L.E. 15; Meit Rahini, L.E. 8. Hours—8 AM–5 PM.

Very little remains of the ancient city of Memphis, for centuries Egypt's capital. Near the little village of Meit Rahini, an ancient Egyptian name meaning "the ram-headed sphinx road," a small museum houses a magnificent recumbent figure of Ramses II carved in alabaster. On the grounds nearby are a large alabaster sphinx from the XVIII Dynasty, that stands on the site where it was excavated as well as several ancient statues.

Memphis was the city of the living; Sakkara, the city of the dead. The name Sakkara is derived from the word *sakr* (hawk), the god of necropolis in the netherworld. The necropolis contains over 14 pyramids, hundreds of mastabas and tombs, and art objects and engravings dating from the first to the XXX Dynasty. It was here that the oldest mummy and the oldest papyrus were found.

The Step Pyramid, thought by some to represent a staircase to heaven, was erected by Zoser, a pharaoh of the III Dynasty, and predates the Pyramids of Giza. Indeed, the Step Pyramid at Sakkara is considered the forerunner of the architectural style of the Giza Pyramids. It was the first major building in stone and was considered the greatest structure known to man at that time. Its architect, Imhotep (later known as the god of medicine), was the first to investigate the mystery of the Nile Flood in about 3000 BC.

A funeral chamber probably belonging to Sekhemkhet and an unfinished step pyramid (2750 BC) were discovered a few years ago near the Step Pyramid. The tomb is underground and composed of a main passage leading to a funeral chamber. Inside the chamber a large alabaster sarcophagus was found, but with no mummy.

Southeast of the Step Pyramid are the remains of an ancient colonnaded temple, probably the first of its kind in the world.

The largest and most beautiful mastaba in the necropolis is the Tomb of Teti, an important figure at the royal court in the late period of the VI Dynasty. The wall decorations have been extremely valuable to scholars in studying the life and customs of the ancient Egyptians in the early Dynastic period.

The Serapeum is the most curious tomb of the whole necropolis. It was dedicated to Apis, the ox, which was mummified in exactly the same ceremonial fashion as a human being.

Currently, five Egyptian and eight foreign teams are excavating at Sakkara and all have made extremely valuable discoveries, including a complete burial complex from the IV and V Dynasties. In 1985 an Anglo-Dutch team rediscovered the Tomb of Maya, Minister of Finance under King Tut. It was considered a major discovery. But there is much more to be done; scholars estimate that only a third of the area has been studied.

Among the latest discoveries, uncovered by a French team, are three Pyramids on the south side of the Pyramid of Pepi I. Ranging from 60 to 80 feet in height, the group belonged to queens of the Old Kingdom. One is the first Pyramid ever found that was dedicated to a specific queen; the hieroglyph was found in the chapel wall on the Pyramid's side.

Egyptian Antiquities Museum

Located on Tahrir Square (next to the Nile Hilton Hotel). Entrance: L.E. 15; entrance fee for Mummy Room, L.E. 40. Hours: 9 AM–4 PM daily, Friday 9 AM–11:15 AM and 1:30–4 PM.

This museum contains the world's most important collection of Egyptian antiquities, dating from earliest times to about the 6th century AD. The collection includes some of the artistic masterpieces of the world, including the famous mask of Tutankhamen.

The Department of Antiquities was created, and conservation and excavation services started, in the mid-19th century. The French savant August Mariette was appointed its first director, and the antiquities were housed and exhibited in a building in Bulaq. In 1891, the collection was transferred to Giza, and finally in 1902 they were placed in the present building. The collection has long since outgrown the space. A building 10 times larger would be only adequate—that's how much the collection has grown. What's more, the museum suffered for several decades from Egypt's hard times. In planning your sightseeing, you may find the museum less crowded with visitors early in the morning or late afternoon. The tour group crunch is mainly from 9:30 AM to 1 PM.

At the entrance of the museum a guidebook is available, and it is essential for viewing the exhibits on your own. Each exhibit in the museum is labeled with a number. The descriptions in the guidebook correspond to the numbers of the exhibit. More elaborate, expensive books and color slides and photographs are also on sale. Special permission is required to photograph in the museum. At least two hours are needed to see the main exhibits.

Guides can be hired for L.E. 20 for a tour that will take approximately two hours. Be sure to settle this price in advance.

The museum is in the shape of a rectangle. At the main entrance, turn left and follow its four sides. This will give you a chronological survey of ancient Egypt, beginning with the earliest period of recorded history, the Old Empire, about 3200 BC, followed by the Middle Empire and the New Empire comprising the XVIII, XIX, and XX Dynasties.

In the north gallery is the Akhenaten Room, and in the east gallery are numerous rooms containing monuments of the Ramasessid, Saite, Persian, Greco-Roman, and Nubian periods. On the second floor, the collection from the Tomb of Tutankhamen is displayed.

The museum is so full of marvels that you will want to return many times. From the paintings, statues, furniture, and models in the museum, visitors can draw a vivid impression of the ancient Egyptians. It would be impractical to describe all the exhibits in this museum, there are so many. We will point out only some of the most important.

The Rotunda at the entrance contains exhibits from recent excavations and those of the most colossal size. You may wish to save this section for the last stop, as you will have several opportunities to view it from the balconies of the second floor.

Turning left at the entrance, you'll come to the monuments of the first pharaonic period, the Old Kingdom (III to VI Dynasty, 2700–2200 BC), during which period Memphis was the capital. Its greatest surviving achievements are the Pyramids of Giza. In the galleries and corridors that make up the South and West Galleries on the ground floor there are dozens of statues and exhibits. In particular, note the group of statues in painted limestone representing workers at various tasks. The ancient Egyptians believed that the dead could still be served after death and that their eternal life depended in some measure upon their being properly supplied from earth.

In the first exhibit room on the right, Room 42 of the West Gallery, there is a diorite statue of Cheophren (No. 138), who built the second Pyramid. The statue was discovered in the temple of Cheophren by Mariette in 1858. It represents one of the finest pieces of sculpture ever found in the country. Two other excellently preserved painted limestone statues, discovered in 1871, are located in Room 32 on the right. These lifelike statues represent Ra-Hotpe (No. 223), high priest of Heliopolis (IV Dynasty), and his wife, Nofret. Different skin colors are used to denote man (dark or reddish brown) and woman (mustard yellow). This is one of the most photographed of all the exhibits. In the same room, you should note the larger-than-life statue No. 225, the priest Ra-hufer (V Dynasty). It is considered one of the best examples of Memphis art ever found.

The corridors have as many interesting and important exhibits as the rooms on each side. Note No. 286, Queen Nofret; Nos. 180, 158, and 149 of Mycerinus with Hathor. There are also statues in wood, as well as stone. Note especially the statue No. 116, with eyes of translucent stones.

After a period of internal discord in the Old Kingdom, during which time the country was divided into small kingdoms, there was a renaissance with the beginning of the first Theban or Middle Kingdom (2200 BC). It ended in about 1700 BC; when the Hyksos invaded Lower Egypt.

The character of the Middle Kingdom (Room 22) is quite different from that of the Old Kingdom and is reflected in the statues, such as those of Amenemhat III (XII Dynasty) and Senusret I (Sesostris). Notice No. 280, a wooden statue of King Hor (XIII Dynasty), which has the emblem of the *Ka* (two arms raised) placed on his head, signifying that the statue is a double of the king and is qualified to receive his soul if the need should arise.

Farther on in the hall is the small sphinx (No. 6152) in painted lime-stone portraying Queen Hatshepsut (XVIII Dynasty). The headdress is identical to those of the Hyksos sphinx.

Near the entrance of the hall (Room 12) of the XVIII Dynasty, which marked the beginning of the New Kingdom, is the white marble statue of Thutmose III (No. 428), the hero of the battle of Megiddo and the head of the Egyptian Empire at its zenith. During his reign and that of his predecessor, Queen Hatshepsut, architecture developed to a degree equaled only by Ramses II (XIX Dynasty), the greatest monument builder of all time.

In Room 12 are two of the most interesting of all the museum's exhibits: No. 445, a sandstone chapel with excellent reliefs depicting Thutmose III making offerings to Amen-Ra, and No. 446, a statue of a cow representing the goddess Hathor and Amenophis II drinking from the cow's udder, found in the chapel (XVIII Dynasty). Also note No. 6257, a fine ebony statue of Thy with intricate details. It was found at Sakkara, XVIII Dynasty.

In the Akhenaten exhibit, housed in Room 3 of the North Gallery, note exhibit Nos. 13247, 13248, and 3873. The jewelry in this room is exquisite. Also note the alabaster canopic vases (jars to hold the viscera of the deceased, embalmed separately from the body). There are also Nos. 6015 and 6016, statues of Akhenaten. A stele (No. 487) shows Akhenaten kneeling in adoration before the solar disc. It marks the founding of Tell al Amarna, his new capital. Another, No. 6056, is part of an altar with Akhenaten and his beautiful wife, Nefertiti. Among other important monuments is a sanctuary erected by Ramses II. It consists of two small obelisks that bear inscriptions glorifying the ruler.

Room 14 in the East Gallery is a continuation of the New Empire, XIX and XX Dynasties. You should note especially the statues of Ramses III, Horus and Set found at Medinet Hebu, dating from the XX Dynasty.

Also, No. 930, an alabaster statue standing in the hall at No. 30 position, is of Amenartais, XXV Dynasty.

Among the Greco-Roman antiquities, there is an extensive coin collection (Room 4, North Gallery).

There are fine mural paintings from Tuna El Gebel (ancient Hermopolis) near Minya, depicting the Oedipus legend, along with other art works belonging to the Greek and Roman periods (Room 34, East Gallery).

Also in the East Gallery (Room 44) is the Meroitic exhibit dating from about 300 BC, when the capital of Ethiopia was transferred to Meroe, an island between the White and the Blue Niles, well situated for control of the routes from Sudan into Egypt.

During the period of the Ethiopian Kings (XXV Dynasty, 750–656 BC) Piankhi and Taharqa, the latter was driven back to Sudan by the invading Assyrians. At Begerawien, there are 40 small Pyramids, which were the tombs of the kings of Meroe.

This hall also contains Nubian antiquities of the Byzantine period, which came from the royal tombs of Ballana and Qustul in Nubia. They have a strong resemblance to the objects found in the excavations near Wadi Halfa. The collection includes jewels, crowns, bracelets, and necklaces of semiprecious stones.

Leaving the Nubian Hall, you will once again find yourself in the South Gallery, and pass a number of sarcophagi from the Ptolemaic period.

The center hall contains a lovely painted wall from Tell al Amarna. There are also huge statues of Amenophis III. The stele of Ramses II, which some scholars say was the pharaoh of Moses' time, is the first mention of the Israelites found in Egypt.

The Tutankhamen Galleries. Located on the second floor. Visitors should note that these rooms are closed 30 minutes earlier than other parts of the museum.

The story of the discovery of the young pharaoh's tomb, whose marvelous treasure today fills a quarter of the museum, is well known. For years Howard Carter, a British archaeologist, searched for the tomb the length of the Valley of the Kings. Then, in 1922, just as he was about to abandon the search, he came upon the first steps leading to the hiding place.

When Amenhotep III (1402–1365 BC) died, his eldest son ascended to the throne as Amenhotep IV; but later he discarded that name, and history knows him best as Akhenaten. He has always been one of the most fascinating pharaohs of ancient Egypt. Although a great deal has been written about him, in fact very little is known about this unusual man. Only recently one of the temples he is known to have built was found near Luxor.

Akhenaten formulated a new faith that historians describe as the first monotheistic religion in the world. He conceived of Aton, the symbol of which is the sun's disc, as the one god, and he set about to destroy all the other gods, an act that directly threatened the powerful priests of Thebes. The conflict became so bitter that the revolutionary young pharaoh moved his capital from Thebes to Tell el Amarna, south of Minya, where he built a new capital, which he called Akhetaton (the Horizon of Aton).

Here he lived with his beautiful Queen Nefertiti, who gave birth to daughters only. The eldest married Semenkh-Ka-Re, for whom Akhenaten felt a deep affection and whom he named his successor. Semenkh-Ka-Re died, probably at about the same time as Akhenaten. He was replaced by Tutankhaton, who had spent his childhood at his brother's court and had married Akhenaten's second daughter. Egyptologists are not sure of the precise relationship between Tutankhaton and Akhenaten.

Tutankhaton was thought to be about nine years old when he acceded to the throne in 1334 BC. For the next three years, he remained at Akhetaton and continued the Aton cult. But the priests of Amon were too powerful for the young king, and he was forced to reestablish the court at Thebes.

This move was the first of a series of concessions that ultimately brought about a total rejection of the Aton faith and the reinstatement of Amon as the state-deity. The boy-king changed his name to Tut-Ankh-Amen and the name of his wife from Ankh-Es-Aton to Ankh-Es-Amon.

Because the ancient Egyptians believed that life on earth was transient and life after death eternal, the first thing a man did when he started to earn a living was to prepare his tomb and its funerary furniture, which included the objects he cherished and those he used in daily life. Tutankhamen is believed to have started work on his tomb when he came to the throne; but it was still rough when he died suddenly of an unknown cause in 1324 BC.

All the royal tombs in the Valley of the Kings were robbed except Tutankhamen's; this was spared unaccountably, and it is the only one to have been discovered almost intact. Because he died at an early age, about 19, his tomb might have been passed over as not containing enough treasures for the tomb robbers to bother with. At least this is one theory. Imagine—after you view the masterpieces in the collection—what the tombs of the great pharaohs must have contained!

After completing a tour of the ground floor, it is easiest to climb the east stairway from the South Gallery to the second floor. This will put you in the corridors numbered 49 and 50, where you can begin the tour of the Tutankhamen exhibit. Your walk will take you in descending order of the exhibit hall numbers, but by following the east corridor to the north side, you will have enjoyed the most dramatic way of viewing the collection and saved the best part for last.

At Station 50 at the entrance to the east corridor stand the lifesize statues of Tutankhamen (Nos. 96 and 181), which were found in the antechamber of the tomb. They were posted like sentries to the left and right of the entrance. They are wood painted with black and gold leaf. No. 447 is a carrying chest in the form of the god Anubis. You will notice that the Tutankhamen collection has a separate numbering system from those of the museum's other collections. It starts with No. 1 and runs consecutively in the order in which the pieces were received at the museum between the years 1922 and 1932.

Continuing along the hall, you will pass five cases containing about 30 small statues in gold that represent the pharaoh and various gods. Each is an exquisite piece of art and you will want to spend time examining them closely, but note especially No. 408—the King is carried on the head of Menkaret; No. 409—the King wears the White Crown of Upper Egypt; No. 425—the goddess Isis; and No. 427—the serpent Neter-Ankh.

Next is No. 1, the pharaoh's throne—one of the most photographed of all items. It is carved wood coated with gold and inlaid with faience glass, colored stones, and silver. The legs are in the shape of those of a lion, and the front ones are surmounted by lions' heads; the armrests are in the form of two serpents with wings outstretched for protection. On the back panel the king is portrayed sitting, while the queen, holding a perfume jar in her left hand, takes some with her right hand to anoint the king's shoulder. Above, the sun sheds its rays on the royal couple. The seat is covered with papyrus. Across from it is No. 3, a chair in dark wood that is in remarkable condition, and another chair, No. 983, which has exceptionally fine mosaic inlay. Be sure to examine these exhibits closely, as they are excellent examples of the master craftsmanship of the ancient Egyptians.

Nos. 6–9, 185, and 543 are lovely alabaster vases decorated with gold and ivory. They depict the symbolic plant of Upper Egypt, the lotus, and of Lower Egypt, the papyrus. No. 435 is the symbol of Anubis, two long stalks ending in a papyrus bud and fixed in an alabaster vase.

In the center of the north corridor at Station 10, there are several beds and couches, each supported by an animal representing a god or goddess, such as Hathor the cow. Note especially No. 521 and No. 221, No. 984, Nos. 437–440, and 455–458 where, in alabaster canopic boxes, there are a group of four vases that hold Tutankhamen's viscera.

Among the bowls found in the tomb was a translucent alabaster cup in the form of an open lotus flower. The handles also were shaped like lotus buds and flowers and surmounted by a figure symbolizing eternity.

Around the edge of the cup in hieroglyphics are phrases to wish the king long life and prosperity.

A number of toilet articles were found. One is an alabaster ointment jar in the shape of a lion standing on its hind legs, its right forepaw raised aloft, its left resting on the hieroglyphic sign for protection. The base of the jar is decorated with floral designs.

At the entrance to the coffin room is the collection of four funerary chambers made of wood, covered with gold leaf, and guarded by the four figures. One of the figures was part of the collection that toured the United States and Europe.

The Mask: In the center of Room 4 is the mask of Tutankhamen (No. 220), probably the most dramatic piece of ancient craftsmanship ever discovered. It is breathtakingly beautiful. The more often one sees it, the more beautiful it seems. Perfect in design and execution, it is in an equally perfect state of preservation. (The mask was the centerpiece of the Tutankhamen exhibit.)

The mask, which covered the face of the mummy, is made of solid gold and decorated with inlaid stripes of blue glass. On the forehead are the vulture and the uraeus (the scared asp) representing the gods of Upper and Lower Egypt; the eyebrows and eyelids are inlaid with lapis lazuli and the necklace with precious stones and glass.

In the case surrounding the mask is the collection of jewelry and other objects that were found on the body of the king. At the side of the mummy, a gold dagger with a richly decorated hilt was found; and the mummy itself was covered with jewels. One of these was a crown formed of a plain gold band in the shape of the vulture and the uraeus, inlaid with carnelian red, bright and dark blue glass; the feathers of the gods are outstretched in such a way as to form an almost complete circle.

A rectangular gold frame, filled with three large lapis lazuli scarabs and lotus flowers, made of polychrome glass and set in gold, hung down from one side. From the other, a chain of five rows of gold beads were attached to a plaque of gold that showed a seated man with the pharaoh's name in a cartouche over his head.

Tutankhamen's granite sarcophagus is in situ in his tomb in the Valley of the Kings at Luxor. It contained the three coffins: the outer coffin in wood, which in turn contained two more coffins, fitted one inside the other. On the left side of the room is the outer coffin (No. 222), and on the right side of the room is the third, or innermost, coffin (No. 219). Both are exquisite. The middle one is in situ and contains the mummy.

The innermost coffin is made of solid gold and weighs 495 pounds. It represents Tutankhamen as Osiris, god of the dead. His arms are crossed over his chest; one hand holds the scepter and the other the flail—the signs of royal power. On his forehead are the vulture and the uraeus, symbols of sovereignty; around his neck is a wide collar of two rows of multicolored stones; and on either side of the body are the deities of Upper and Lower Egypt represented in the form of a vulture and a bird with outstretched wings to protect the body.

Fifty-five out of the more than 3,000 pieces of the Tutankhamen collection were exhibited in the United States, Canada, and Europe from 1977 to 1981. It was the largest such collection ever to leave Egypt. Several of the pieces left the country for the first time. The entire exhibit is now back on display at the museum.

The Jewel Room. This houses collections from different excavations; jewels of the Greco-Roman period, silver vases, a boat with figures in gold and silver, a falcon head from Hieracopolis (near Abydos, the place where Egypt's first pharaohs originated). It was carved in wood and covered with copper plate. You will want to spend time examining the exhibits in this room, but note especially No. 4170—the links of gold. It would make a Cartier designer green with envy.

Room 2 holds the collection from Tanis in the Eastern Delta. The gold and silver vases and jewelry especially are to be noted.

In the Ostraca Room (from *ostracos,* a Greek word meaning oyster shell) are fragments of stone or pieces of pottery. The collection of figured ostraca is from Deir el Medina.

The Papyrus Room shows the methods used by the ancient Egyptians for writing, drawing, and painting on the materials of their day.

Another room shows the utensils of daily life: a collection of musical instruments, toilet articles, spoons for face cream or perfumes, equipment of the jeweler, weights and measures, working tools of the peasants, knife blades, razors, and other household objects.

Before leaving, be sure to see the model of the funerary temple and Pyramid of Sahu-Ra at Abusir, located on the second floor under the Rotunda dome. This exhibit will help you to better understand the Pyramids of Giza and Sakkara, since it shows how they were built. At the base, close to the Nile's bank, was the reception temple, containing the embalming and purification rooms and the funerary chamber, which contained the sarcophagus. The funerary temple was built outside the Pyramid, sometimes leaving room behind the Pyramid for storerooms, as in the case of Cheops's Pyramid. The small Pyramid of the queen in the funerary monument of Pepi II at Sakkara is also located outside.

The Mummy Room, on the second floor, is open once again, after a two-year closing for renovations. There is a separate admission fee of L.E. 40.

Restaurant and gift shop. On the east side of the museum's main entrance is a restaurant and *Onnig's,* a well known and long-established jewelry and gift shop. Prices here are fixed and reasonable, and the merchandise is reliable.

King Tut in America. A selection of 55 treasures from the vast Tutankhamen collection went on tour in the United States in 1976–77 to rave reviews and an unprecedented number of viewers. It touched off a wave of Tutomania, which resulted in the reproduction—good and bad—of ancient Egyptian designs on everything from towels and T-shirts to solid gold bracelets and pendants.

On the first stop on the tour at the National Museum in Washington, people stood in line for six to eight hours to see the exhibit. After that, museums in Chicago, New Orleans, Los Angeles, Seattle, New York, San Francisco, and Toronto tried to devise a system that would be fair and efficient without putting museum directors into their graves along with King Tut.

In the midst of the excitement, New York's Metropolitan Museum opened a new Egyptian wing, which enabled the museum to display its collection adequately. Soon after, the museum completed the installation of the Western Hemisphere's first complete Egyptian temple, the 1st century BC Temple of Dendur. It was one of the monuments that would have been flooded by the lake created by the Aswan High Dam had it not been moved. The temple is a gift from the Egyptian government to the United States in recognition of its contribution toward saving two dozen temples and monuments, including the most famous one, Abu Simbel.

The Temple of Dendur is small, measuring 41' × 21' × 21', with a gateway 11' × 12' × 26½', and is made of Aeolian sandstone. It has been reassembled as it appeared on the banks of the Nile and is located in the museum's new Sackler Wing.

Phase Two of the Metropolitan's permanent Egyptian collection was completed and went on view in late November 1978. Twenty galleries in all were opened, and they have had a steady stream of visitors ever since. They cover all the important periods of ancient Egypt and include study-storage areas housing material from the late XVIII (Amarna period) through the XXIX Dynasties: 1379–380 BC. The galleries contain exhibits from the time of Akhenaton and Tutankhamen, plus extensive material from the Museum's XXI Dynasty excavations.

COPTIC CAIRO

Summary of Coptic Cairo: There are churches of all denominations in the city, but the most interesting are the ancient Coptic churches in Old Cairo adjacent to Babylon Fort. Housed in the old buildings around the churches is the Coptic Museum, which has recently opened a new wing. It is the starting point of the tour. Coptic art is considered an evolution of pharaonic art—evidence of this as seen in the museum is surprising.

Egypt was one of the first countries to embrace Christianity, which it did with fervor; and it marked the beginning of another period in the country's history: the Coptic Age.

The word *Copt* (*Gibt,* in Arabic) comes from the Greek *Aegyptius,* meaning "Egyptian." The Greek word is said to be a corruption of Ha Ka Ptah (in the spirit of Ptah), the reigning deity and one of the names of Memphis, the ancient capital of Egypt.

The language of the Copts was ancient Egyptian as it was spoken in the early Christian era. After their conversion to Christianity, the Egyptians abandoned their ancient form of pictorial writing and adopted the Greek alphabet. They added seven demotic letters to represent sounds unknown in Greek.

Eventually Greek became the language of the government and scholars, but Coptic continued to be the common language. In education, it was restricted to religious instruction. At the time of the Arab conquest in the 7th century AD there was a brief revival of the ancient language, but by the 11th century Coptic literature had all but disappeared. Today Coptic is used only in the liturgy.

The history of Christian Egypt officially began with St. Mark, who founded the Church of Egypt about the middle of the 1st century. To this day, the Coptic patriarchs of Alexandria trace their succession directly from him. In 1968, St. Mark's relics were returned from Italy and reburied in a new Coptic cathedral, said to be the largest in Africa.

Traditionally, of course, Christianity goes back to the time when the Holy Family sought refuge from Herod in Egypt. The family is thought to have traveled along the route usually taken by merchants coming from the east. They arrived first at a place near Ismailia, from which they continued to the small town of Tal Basta, an ancient site near the present-day town of Zagazig. Here they met Aqloum, one of the townsfolk, who took pity on them and invited them to his home. Aqloum's wife, who was an invalid and had been bedridden for a long time, was healed by Jesus. Today the Church of the Virgin stands on the traditional site of the miracle.

When news of the miracle reached Jerusalem, Herod sent more soldiers to pursue the family and bring them back to Palestine. The family continued their flight until they reached the outskirts of Belbeis, where they saw a woman crying over her dying son. Jesus approached the crowd and, addressing the dying child, said "Rise, Jacob, for thou art well." Upon which, according to tradition, Jacob rose to his feet.

The family continued to Meniet Genah, near the present town of Samanoud, and then to Al-Sabbah. Finding no water to drink, Joseph asked Jesus to strike the earth with a piece of stone. He did, and water flowed immediately. Tradition has it that a church was built in the 4th century AD, where the stone was kept.

Near Senga, the family crossed the Rosetta branch of the Nile to the west bank and then traveled southward on the desert road (now the Cairo-Alexandria highway) till they reached the village of Hoaker (located near the Desert Road Rest House).

In Matarieh (Heliopolis), the Virgin's Tree is located where, according to tradition, Jesus made water spring from the ground. The well is still there, and the faithful drink from its waters or douse themselves for blessing.

Traveling southward, the refugees arrived at Babylon (Old Cairo), where they found shelter in a cave. The Church of Abu Sergah is built above the sacred crypt. The family resumed their journey until they arrived at Maadi (a suburb of Cairo), where they spent the night at one of the temples and in the morning continued to Upper Egypt by boat. Tradition says that on the site, Jesus told his mother a church would stand that would commemorate her name to the end of time. At present, the convent of the Sacred Virgin overlooks the Nile at the spot where the temple once stood. In the convent, a staircase leads to the water where the Holy Family took the boat. Patrons of the church celebrate the event annually, and the father of the church takes a boat on a short Nile cruise in commemoration.

According to tradition, the family arrived by boat at the small town of Al Fashn, 108 miles from Cairo, where they traveled by land to a village called Babar el Betouh (near present Bahnasa). Authorities claim that historical evidence in the region shows there were more than 360 churches here at the beginning of the 5th century.

From there the family journeyed southward to the village of Attsa, then to Hemopolites (now Ashmonin), Al-Qiussieh, and the nearby village of Qousqam, where they lived in a little room for six months. Word of the Child's miracles spread, and people rushed to him from all over the countryside to be cured. A church named after the Virgin has its altar in the room in which the family is said to have lived. The church has a slab of stone said to have been used by Jesus as a bed and a pillow.

Al Muharraq was the family's last stop. Here the angel appeared to Joseph to tell him about Herod's death. Before leaving Egypt, tradition says, they spent a night in a cave overlooking Assuit. Today it is known as the

Virgin's Cave. The family returned to Palestine by the same route they had come.

During the 4th century Deir Al Muharraq, once considered the greatest monastery in the East, was built. Near the monastery there is a church where, tradition holds, the Virgin appeared to Pope Theophilus, 22nd Patriarch of the Coptic Church (376 to 403). When he awoke he is said to have written the history of the Holy Family in Egypt as the Virgin told it to him in his dream. The church is said to date from the 1st century and is older than the monastery.

Coptic Churches

Babylon Fort in Old Cairo (about one mile south of the Meridien Hotel) is surrounded by many old and interesting Coptic churches. El Mouallaqa, Abou Serga, and St. Barbara are the ones most often visited by tourists, although there are six old churches in the area that may be seen. Between the churches is the Coptic Museum. *A Guide to the Ancient Coptic Churches of Cairo* by O.H.E. Khs-Burmester (Cairo, Societe d'Archeologie Copte, 1955) is one of the few books available that offer detailed information on these churches. The book has been reprinted and should be available in a Cairo bookstore. A booklet, published recently, is also available at the museum.

El Mouallaqa Church (The Church of the Holy Virgin). The name *Mouallaqa* (hanging) was given to this church because it is built over the Roman fortress as though suspended from it. The church, located next to the Coptic Museum, is the largest and loveliest in Old Cairo. It probably dates from the late 4th or early 5th century. Up to the 11th century it was the patriarchal seat of the bishop of Alexandria.

To visit the Hanging Church, a visitor must climb a flight of 24 stairs to the entrance. On the wall on the right after entering is a group of three icons. The large one in the center depicts St. George. On the south wall is a series of icons, beginning with a 10th-century one of the Virgin carrying Jesus on her lap, before whom St. John the Baptist kneels to kiss the Child's feet. The series ends with an ancient icon of St. Mark.

The door next to St. Mark's icon is made of carved wood inlaid with an intricate pattern of translucent ivory crosses. South of the sanctuary and in a direct line is the baptismal font.

In the main part of the church, and facing the altar at the eastern end, there is a wide iconostatis made of wood inlaid with ivory and ebony. Unlike their counterparts in other churches, the crosses in the design here do not consist simply of bands of ivory framed with ebony contours. Instead, they are elaborately carved and interwoven. From the ceiling and in line with the iconostasis hangs a row of ostrich eggs. An alabaster pulpit in the center of the church rests on 13 marble pillars, one of which is black marble, meant to symbolize Judas. The pulpit is used only once a year, on Palm Sunday.

Abou Serga Church. According to tradition, this church occupies the spot where the Holy Family stayed after their flight to Egypt. The church was founded during the late 4th or early 5th century and was dedicated to Sergius and Bacchus, martyred soldiers who died in Syria early in the 4th century. The most interesting features are the altars over the manger on the east side, the main nave separated from the two lateral naves by three rows of marble pillars, which bear the likenesses of saints, and a grotto, 30 feet below the surface of the ground, containing a tiny chapel. The Crypt, where tradition says the Holy Family stayed, is under the altar, but water from the Nile has seeped in and the chapel is not open to visitors at the present time.

St. Barbara Church. In the vicinity of Abou Serga Church and the Coptic Museum is a church originally built during the late 4th century and rebuilt during the 10th century with some of the materials being used at the time to restore Abou Serga. According to legend, when the caliph learned that a second church had been built, he ordered the builder, Yuhanna, to demolish one of the two. Unable to decide which to destroy, Yuhanna paced from one church to the other until he collapsed and died from exhaustion. Upon hearing the sad news, the caliph reversed his order and declared that both churches could remain.

The Saint George's Church (Greek Orthodox Church). Built on a bastion of Babylon Fort during the 6th century, the church was rebuilt several times and renovated again recently. It is approached by a great marble staircase from which there is a splendid view of Old Cairo. Inside is the Byzantine Icon Museum. It is one of the few examples of a circular church in the East.

The Coptic Museum

Coptic Museum, Old Cairo, adjoining the ancient wall of Babylon Fort. Admission: L.E. 8 and another L.E. 8 for a visit to the ancient churches. Hours: 9 AM–4 PM Friday 9–11 AM and 1–4 PM.

The museum was founded in 1908 to house the large collection of Coptic art and antiquities dating from 300–1000 and previously kept in the Antiquities Museum. Excavations at Baouit and Sakkara resulted in the discovery of two ancient monasteries, St. Appollon and St. Jeremia, from which many of the museum's objects were taken.

The exhibits are divided into seven groups: architectural fragments and funeral stelae; woodwork; glass and earthenware; textiles, considered the ancient Copts' greatest artistic achievement; metals; an interesting and valuable display of icons and frescoes; and manuscripts. A brief guide is available at the door.

The architecture of the museum building is in keeping with the collections it houses. The woodwork, taken from old houses belonging to the Coptic community, was adapted to the different rooms in the building. Particularly outstanding is the collection of *mushrabiya* windows.

The exhibits are well displayed on two floors of the museum. The ground floor is largely devoted to architectural fragments, while the second-floor rooms contain the famous textile fragments (the best, however, are in Paris), old manuscripts, and icons (none older than the 15th century).

Visitors are not allowed to take pictures inside the museum, and, unfortunately, the selection of photographs and slides on sale is of poor quality. You will need at least one hour for a hurried look at the museum, several churches, and the synagogue.

Within the compound of the Coptic Museum is Babylon Fort, the only Roman vestige in Cairo, dating from the 1st century AD. The Romans chose the site because of its strategic location. In those days, the area overlooked the edge of the desert on the east and was guarded by the Nile on the west, north, and south. According to historical records, Babylon Fort covered an area of one acre. During the 7th century the Arab armies battled for seven months to conquer it.

A stairway in the garden of the museum leads down to the south gate of the fortress. This gate, which is flanked by two great bastions, used to open onto the Nile. In addition to this gate, there are traces of other gates and towers.

Coptic Art

The evolution of Christian and Islamic art from pharaonic motifs is in evidence in many exhibits. For example, the Christian cross is said to have developed from the *ankh*, the pharaonic key of life, and the elevated pharaonic chair became a pulpit for the church and a minbar for the mosque.

Properly speaking, Coptic art flourished from the 5th to the 7th century and formed a transition between the Roman period and Byzantine art. It was influenced by the classical art of Alexandria as well as Persian and Syrian art.

Alexandrian art itself had been an evolution of the Hellenistic tradition, but with a difference—as a creation of the Ptolemaic court, it was half Greek, half Egyptian, and the Oriental element is pronounced.

The influence of Persian art resulted from a renaissance of ancient styles during the 3rd century AD under the Sassanid Dynasty in Persia. From it, Coptic art is said to have derived a number of characteristics: floral designs, animals, horsemen, hunting scenes, and the contrast of colors.

The influence of Syria on Coptic art might be called spiritual. In the beginning Christian art in Egypt was Alexandrian, but it was to Syria, geographically associated with the birth and life of Christ, that Egyptian monks looked for inspiration. Egypt, transformed by monasticism, which it had conceived, considered itself the spiritual heir of Christianity. In the monk's mind Alexandria was the refuge of Hellenism, and Hellenism was synonymous with paganism. From the 5th century, Egypt's affinity was with Syria and it was hostile toward all things Alexandrian.

By the 7th century, when it was beginning to develop in a new direction with an independent identity, Coptic art was redirected by the Arab conquest.

Monasteries

As many as 50,000 monks are said to have lived in approximately 500 monasteries in the Western Desert. The best known are located in Wadi el Natroun, where only four monasteries have survived. These are Deir Amba Bishoi, Deir es-Suryani, Deir el Baramus, and Deir Macarius.

There are also some in the vicinity of Aswan that are accessible.

St. Anthony and St. Paul monasteries are about 132 miles from Cairo near the Red Sea and can be reached by car.

Visitors to any of the places where there are monasteries or their ruins will be impressed by the devout and austere life the monks led in the solitude and serenity of the wilderness.

Tourists should request permission from the Coptic patriarchate in Cairo to visit the monasteries. His office is located at 222 Ramses Street; tel. 676–382.

ISLAMIC CAIRO

Summary of Islamic Cairo: The oldest and most interesting of Cairo's mosques and other Muslim monuments are covered here, butthis only scratches the surface. There are over 650 designated by the Islamic Monuments Preservation Society. Your visit to Islamic monuments and mosques should include a visit to the Islamic Museum. Restorations of all major Islamic mosques and monuments in Cairo are under way or planned, so some of the places you plan to visit may be closed.

From the time of the Arab conquest in 641 Cairo became a stronghold of Islam, but it was not until the decline of Damascus and later of Baghdad as Arab capitals that Cairo grew into one of the most important cities in the Muslim world. Ruler after ruler embellished it with mosques and monuments to the glory of Islam.

Islamic art is a tradition completely foreign to Western art after the Renaissance in Europe. No place is a better school for studying the development of this art than Cairo, whose ancient mosques are themselves an evolution of Islamic architecture and design and whose museums trace the history of this development.

Among the arts in which Islamic craftsmen excelled were calligraphy, textiles (a continuation of the Coptic tradition), carpets, lusterware, crystal, and ornamental decoration on metal and wood.

There are many excellent books on Islamic art and architecture that can be read in advance of your visit, but once you are in Cairo, the most useful book for sightseeing is *A Practical Guide to Islamic Monuments in Cairo,* by Richard B. Parker and Robin Sabin, American University in Cairo Press, Cairo, 1974. The book contains maps, which are essential for locating the monuments because many are located in old lands and alleyways that have no street signs and are known by their colloquial names. It is available in city bookshops.

No matter how fascinating you find the pharaonic antiquities, you will not have seen Cairo or known Egypt without a look at its Islamic heritage. Cairo's mosques are accessible to non-Muslims and the Islamic Museum is considered to have the most important collection of Islamic art and artifacts in the world.

Cairo Mosques

Cairo's mosques, said to number more than 500, represent some of the finest examples of Islamic architecture in the world. Each has a slight variation and point of interest, but only those of the most historic or architectural importance are described here. They are also those most likely to be visited by tourists. Even this number requires several days, but certainly no trip to Egypt is complete without seeing some of them.

Visits to mosques are not recommended at prayer time. Tickets to those mosques, which are designated as monuments, are sold by the caretaker and cost 50 piasters, unless indicated otherwise.

As a compromise with the Muslim tradition of removing one's shoes before entering the sanctuary, visitors are asked to cover their shoes with large cloth slippers provided by the mosque's caretaker. You are expected to tip 50 piasters for each pair. In mosques where slippers are not provided, as well as in mausoleums that are considered sacred to Muslims, you must remove your shoes before stepping over the threshold. Women must cover bare arms with a scarf.

Amr ibn el-As. Entrance: L.E. 3. In Old Cairo. Built by the Arabs during the 7th century following their conquest, this mosque was the first sacred place dedicated to Muslims in Egypt. It is situated in the heart of Old Cairo on the site of Fustat, the "first" Cairo. At that time the mosque overlooked the Nile. From the structure of this mosque came the model of an early style of minaret used in Egypt. Subsequently, it evolved into the final style of minaret now used throughout the Middle East. Reconstruction and expansion of the mosque were undertaken by later rulers. Today it is in a ruined state.

Ibn Toulun. Entrance: L.E. 3. In the area of the Citadel. Completed in 879, it is considered to be the oldest mosque in Cairo because it has not been altered from the original building (as has Amr's Mosque). The mosque was built of brick coated with stucco. The minarets are joined to the main structure by carved stones elaborately fitted to one another. The simplicity and perfect symmetry of the mosque make it one of the most beautiful buildings in the world. Its special features are the Kufic writing in bold, massive strips along the wall and the detailed stucco carving of its windows and arches, each in a different pattern from the other. Experts believe that the minaret was inspired by the minaret of the Samarra Mosque north of Baghdad and is therefore an evolution of the ziggurat. In 1296 the mosque underwent considerable restoration, and a school for teaching the Koran, medicine, and the four schools of Muslim law were added. Visitors whose time is limited might select this mosque to visit, as it is one of the best examples of pure Islamic architecture in the world.

Al-Azhar. Entrance: L.E. 6. In the district and street of the same name. Al-Azhar ("the splendid") celebrated its millennium in 1983. The structure was started in 969, soon after the Fatimids took control of Egypt, and was completed in 971. It is considered one of the best examples of Islamic architecture in the world and is intimately associated with the history of Cairo itself.

Throughout its long history, Al-Azhar has been a seat of learning, as well as a place of worship. Its university, considered the oldest in the world, has educated and trained the leading scholars of the Muslim world since the early days of Islam. The ulama (learned men) of Al-Azhar are considered Islam's most influential group of theologians. Today over 90,000 students from every Muslim country come here to study. The teaching staff numbers 3,600. Al-Azhar is also a place of shelter where the poor as well as Muslim pilgrims are given a free night's lodging.

Originally the mosque was intended simply as the main mosque of the capital, but in a short time judges began lecturing there on Shi'ite jurisprudence, the official sect of the Fatimids. In 988, under the second Fatimid caliph, Al-Aziz, the first professors were formally appointed and Al-Azhar became a seminary as well.

At first instruction was restricted to Shi'ite doctrine. Secular subjects such as philosophy, medicine, chemistry, and astronomy were taught at another university, Dar El Hekma, founded in 1005 by the caliph Al-Hakim. For a century the two vied for academic leadership.

At the end of the 12th century the Fatimids were succeeded by the Ayyubites, who were Sunni (orthodox) Muslims. They abolished all Shi'ite teachings and traditions. Salah ed-Din, known in the west as Saladin, even went so far as to cancel Friday prayers at Al-Azhar, thus divesting it of its status as the city's major mosque. Freed from sectarian restrictions, Al-Azhar was able to broaden its courses in medicine, astronomy, philosophy, and logic.

Then in the 13th century, with the fall of the Abbassid caliphate in Baghdad in the east, Cairo assumed unchallenged leadership in Islamic scholarship and Al-Azhar became the foremost university in the Muslim world.

For centuries under the Mamelukes, Al-Azhar continued to be a great center of Islamic and Arabic studies. Along with its academic prestige it enjoyed immense political and social influence until the Ottoman conquest in 1517. Its ulama occupied top legislative and juridical posts, and sometimes key political posts as well.

Even under the Turks, Al-Azhar was able to maintain its academic prestige and remain the stronghold of Muslim thought. This stability, as a focal point, is considered its greatest contribution to Islam and to the Arabic language.

The Turks, who feared its influence and regarded its professors and students with suspicion, could do no more than keep a vigilant eye on it. Al-Azhar became the refuge for the progressive and liberal students from Arab countries dominated by the Turks. It could even be said that the university nurtured the seeds of the Pan-Arab movement.

When the French invaded Egypt in 1798, they formed a council for governing Cairo made up of the ulama of Al-Azhar, regarding them as the political leaders of the people and hoping to gain popular approval through them. But the plan backfired. Al-Azhar sheikhs and students were responsible for many uprisings that provoked the French into retaliation. They bombarded the school, stormed the mosque with the cavalry and occupied it for three days. The Egyptians were outraged and finally got their revenge the following year when an Azhari assassinated Kleber, Napoleon's commander-in-chief in Egypt.

As the influence of European education and culture began to grow in Egypt and other Muslim countries, Al-Azhar's influence slipped. It needed reform.

The first move for reform started in 1872, and other steps to reorganize and revise its system followed. Finally, in 1936 Al-Azhar was transformed into a modern university made up of three faculties: theology, Islamic jurisprudence, and the Arabic language. Prior to admission to any one of these faculties, students have to complete general studies in such subjects as physics, chemistry, mathematics, and physiology, as well as foreign languages.

Al-Azhar stands on the same site on which it was founded a thousand years ago. Over the centuries, the mosque has been altered, expanded, and restored many times. The present entrance dates from the 14th and 15th centuries. On the left of the entrance is the library, which contains some of the oldest and most valuable manuscripts in the world. It contains more than 250,000 ancient and rare handwritten manuscripts, some penned in gold. The section behind the large courtyard is the oldest part of the building. The *mihrab* (prayer niche) dating from the Fatimids has been preserved. The old buildings underwent extensive renovation for the celebration of Al Azhar's millennium.

The cultural influence of Al-Azhar is still immense, and it remains the most prestigious center for the study of Muslim theology and jurisprudence and Arabic. There are students from other Arab and Muslim countries as far away as Mauritania and Indonesia. Scholars from abroad are lodged without charge, and many receive allowances in addition.

A detailed history is available in *Al-Azhar,* by Bayard Dodge, Middle East Institute Press, Washington, 1961.

El Hakim bi Amr Illah. Entrance: L.E.3. In the Bab Nasr area. Completed by the Fatimid ruler Al-Hakim in 1010, this mosque has many features in common with the Ibn Toulun Mosque. The most interesting architectural features of the mosque are the two minarets (no longer thought to be original) and the entrance. This was the first mosque in Egypt with a monumental entrance that jutted out from the facade. The mosque is located next to the old walls of Cairo between the two old gates Bab al-Futuh and Bab al-Nasr. The mosque was recently restored after six centuries of disrepair.

The Citadel and Muhammad Ali Mosque. Entrance: L.E. 14. Hours: 9 AM - 5 PM. The Citadel is situated on the slope of the Mukattam Hills and commands a complete view of Cairo, the Nile, and, in the far distance, the Pyramids of Giza. The Muhammad Ali Mosque (also called the Alabaster Mosque) within its compound is frequently used as an outstanding example of Islamic architecture. Its domed cupola and graceful minarets are second only to the Pyramids and the Sphinx as favored subjects for picture postcards of Egypt.

The Citadel was started by Salah ed-Din (Saladin) in the 12th century as a fortress and was constructed of stone taken from small pyramids at Giza. In later years, the Citadel was used as headquarters and official residence of the sultans until 1850, when Khedive Ismail transferred them to Abdin Palace.

The military career of Saladin conditioned his concept of city planning. In addition to the Citadel, he ordered all four of Egypt's earlier capitals— Cairo and its predecessors, Al-Fustat, Al-Askar, and Al-Qatae'e—to be enclosed within one fortified wall. Many sections of that wall still stand today, particularly the southeastern portions.

The Ayyubites, the family founded by Saladin, ruled Egypt for 80 years, during which time they embellished Cairo with new buildings of outstanding architecture that had a great impact on succeeding ages. Among the developments were the addition of halls and galleries in mosques, in place of the earlier cloisters, and a mastery of military construction.

During the early 19th century, Muhammad Ali rebuilt much of the inner part of the Citadel and doubled its area. He added the mosque bearing his name, the Jewel (Gawhara) Palace, the Law Court, the Mint and Archives situated opposite El Bab el Gadid, the New Gate.

The Muhammad Ali Mosque was designed by a Greek architect from Turkey and is a reproduction of the Nur-ed-Din Mosque in Istanbul. Its walls, both inside and out, are covered with alabaster. The facade is ornamented with quotations from the Koran and with the names of the caliphs of the Rashid Dynasty. The minarets measure over 255 feet in height. The chandeliers of the mosque consist of dozens of crystal balls hung from huge rings suspended from the ceiling (the caretaker never seems to tire of illuminating them for visitors).

The mausoleum at the southwest corner of the mosque contains the tomb of Muhammad Ali, who died in 1848. In the tower to the west is a clock presented to him by Louis Philippe of France.

Bir Youssef (Joseph's Well) was built by Saladin to ensure an adequate water supply in case of siege. The well is about 300 feet deep and is made of two superimposed sections, each fitted with a waterwheel driven by oxen. You may walk down the steps of the well to see the waterwheels with their fittings.

Part of the Gawhara Palace, within the compound of the Citadel, was destroyed by fire over a decade ago. Guides used to show visitors the room in which Muhammad Ali is said to have feted the Mameluk sultans before having them beheaded—all except one, who escaped by the daring feat of riding his horse over the wall of the Citadel. A more accurate account of the grim incident is related in *Cairo,* by James Aldridge. The only Mameluk who survived never got to the party. He was en route to the palace when news of the massacre reached him and he fled. The recently published book, *The Citadel of Cairo* by William Lyster (Cairo, Palm Press, 1990) is both a history and a guide with fascinating details that will greatly enhance your visit.

On the new drive to the Citadel from the south and east sides, the road passes the remains of a long aqueduct originally built by Saladin to supply the Citadel. It was rebuilt by Sultan el-Ghouri during the early 16th century.

Ibn Qalawun. Entrance: L.E. 3. In the Mouski area. This 13th-century mosque was formerly one of the leading places of worship in Cairo. It was begun in 1269 by Sultan el Mansur Qalawun and completed by his son, el-Nassir. Connected with it were a famous law school and a *maristan* (hospital). The mosque was once covered with beautiful marble and mosaic works. Except for the vestibule containing el-Nassir's tomb, the buildings are now in ruins. The vestibule has lovely stained glass windows and elaborately decorated walls and ceiling, parts of which have been restored. The interesting feature of this complex of buildings is its architectural appearance of being a Crusader church rather than a mosque. The archway entrance was taken from the Crusader Church of St. John in Akka.

El-Barquq. Entrance: L.E. 3. In the Mouski area. Adjacent to the Ibn Qalawun Mosque is a 14th-century mosque that recently underwent major renovations. The ceiling and decorative glass windows of the diwan and the vestibule containing the tomb of Barquq's daughter are worth viewing.

Mosque of El Zaher Baybars. El Zaher Square. One of the most outstanding monuments of the Mameluk age, this mosque was built in 1269. The wood and marble are said to have come from the Fortress of Jaffa, which Baybars captured from the Crusaders.

El Aqsunqur (also known as the Blue Mosque or Ibrahim Agha Mosque). Entrance: L.E. 3. In Bab Zuweila area. The mosque was built in the mid-14th century by Emir Aqsunqur but restored three centuries later by Ibrahim Agha. It takes its name, the Blue Mosque, from the panels of blue and green Persian tiles that decorate the east wall.

Sultan Hassan. Entrance: L.E. 3. In the Citadel area. This mosque, standing at the foot of the Citadel, is the most colossal one in Cairo and a masterpiece of Islamic architecture. It was built in 1356 in the form of a cross, each section representing one of the four schools of Muslim jurisprudence. The structure is massive. The gateway alone measured 85 feet in height, and the minarets are the tallest in Cairo. In the mosque the *kursi,* a stand on which the Koran is laid open for reading, is the oldest of its kind in Egypt. In the courtyard there is a lovely fountain surrounded by marble columns. The mosque is regarded by many as the masterpiece of the Mameluk Age and of Islamic architecture generally.

Al Hussein Mosque. Facing Al Azhar. The mosque is named for Sayyedna al Hussein, the son of Ali and the grandson of the Prophet, and is the principal congregational mosque of Cairo. Thousands of Muslims come to Cairo during the week of the Prophet's birthday to celebrate the occasion here. It houses some of Islam's most sacred relics, including articles that are said to have been used by Muhammad. It also houses a Koran that is said to have been written by Ali, the son-in-law of the Prophet.

El Muayyad. Entrance: L.E. 3. At Bab Zuweila. The mosque was built during the early 15th century and extensively restored during the late 19th century. The huge bronze gates were taken from the Sultan Hassan Mosque. The roof is supported by marble columns taken from nearby churches. One of the columns bears a cross in its capital. The restored walls, ceilings, and windows offer elaborate examples of Islamic art during the Mameluk period. The minarets rise high above the mosque on the two bastions of an 11th-century gate known as Bab Zuweila.

Imam el-Shafii. Imam el-Shafii, a descendant of the Prophet, was the founder of one of the four schools of Islamic law. In 1278 Saladin erected a mausoleum to the famous scholar. In the mid-18th century the mosque was built and was later reconstructed by Khedive Tewfiq. The canopy that surmounts el-Shafii's tomb is made of small geometric panels with carved Kufic inscriptions from the Koran and incidents from the Imam's life.

The Tombs of the Caliphs

In a huge burial ground known as the City of the Dead there are numerous mosques, mausoleums, and tombs, many of which are elaborately decorated. For those who have the time, this is one of the most interesting parts of Islamic Cairo. However, you will need a guide or someone with a knowledge of Arabic to help you find your way around. Richard B. Parker's book, *A Practical Guide to Islamic Monuments in Cairo,* will also be very useful. As a result of Egypt's population explosion and Cairo's inadequate housing, over a million poor people live in this burial ground, most having come to Cairo in the past decade.

Mausoleum of Qait Bey. Located in the northern cemetery behind the Citadel, this mausoleum is considered one of the most outstanding examples of Muslim architecture anywhere in the world and is especially famous for its minarets and elaborate dome. It was built by Sultan Qait Bey in 1474 and combines many features that are characteristic of Islamic architecture and art—marble, inlay, gilded ceilings, latticed wood, and colored glass. Entrance: L.E. 6.

The Gates of Cairo

The two most famous city gates are Bab al-Futuh (Gate of Conquest) and Bab al-Nasr (Gate of Victory), both of which were built by Gowhar, the Fatimid general who founded Cairo. Between the two gates run the old city walls (now restored), and adjacent to the walls is the mosque of Hakim bi Amr Illah. Entrance: L.E. 3.

All that remains of the southern wall of the medieval city is the Bab Zuweila, a most remarkable gate through which centuries of commerce have passed. You may climb to the top of the wall through the Muayyad Mosque, which adjoins the gate on the western side.

Museum of Islamic Art

This museum is located on Ahmad Maher Square and Port Said Street. Open 9 AM–4 PM daily except Friday, when it is open 9–11 AM and 1:30–4 PM in winter, 9–11:30 AM and 1:30–4 PM in summer. Entrance: L.E. 8. Tel. 903930.

During the late 19th century a museum was created by Khedive Ismail to house the valuable objects of Islamic art scattered in various Cairo mosques. The collection was kept in El-Hakim Mosque until 1902, when it was moved to its present location.

The museum's collection is said to be the most valuable and comprehensive display of Islamic art in the world. At the time of its opening, the museum had only 7,029 pieces, but over the years the collection has grown through donations and purchases and archaeological discoveries, especially the finds at Fustat. The museum now has over 78,000 pieces representing every type and school of Muslim art, although only about 8,000 pieces are on view. After years of neglect, the museum was recently cleaned and painted and some of its treasures restored. A new group of textiles and other discoveries from Fustat are now on display.

The museum is something of an institution for studying the history of Egypt in the Middle Ages. The names of the cities that played an important role in shaping events, the famous artisans and artists who formed schools of art, and the wide range of styles of Oriental art in different Muslim countries are available for those who want to learn about the development of Islamic art.

Exhibits from the 7th century, at the time of the Arab conquest, through the 19th century are displayed in 23 galleries and are grouped according to style and subject. Those grouped according to subject are arranged chronologically.

A careful study of these exhibits is useful for later visits to the mosques and other Islamic monuments throughout Cairo. The woodwork, rugs, and enameled glass are among the most interesting and extensive displays. A booklet describing the exhibits is available at the entrance to the museum.

Exhibits Representing Various Styles: Each of the Muslim ruling dynasties established in Egypt fostered its own artistic school, which developed a particular style and characteristics. The Umayyad style, Room 3, originated in its capital of Damascus. Nature is faithfully represented, and there are marked traits borrowed from other styles that prevailed in pre-Islamic Egypt, Syria, and Iran. One of the museum's oldest and most important pieces is a water jug of bronze dating from the 8th century at the time of Caliph Marwan II, the last of the Umayyad rulers.

The Abbasid and Tulunid styles are also represented in Room 3. Abstraction in art, as it is understood now, finds a forerunner in arabesque.

The decorative styles that evolved from writing were based on abstractions from nature. Among the most notable on display are the stucco decorations from Egypt and Iraq. About that time lusterware was first used for making vessels, instead of gold and silver, which were distasteful to strict Muslims. Ostentation was considered contrary to the true teaching of Islam.

Room 4 presents the Fatimid style, which was rich in decoration and detail. Most of the art works in this style are scenes of daily life, such as hunting, dancing, drinking, and singing. The Fatimid calligraphers excelled in the Kufic style of writing. There is also an impressive collection of ceramics.

Room 5 shows the Mameluk style of Egypt and Syria, especially copper and brass inlaid with silver and gold. This tradition continues to this day. One of the most extensive displays is that of mosque lamps (mishkat) enameled in a variety of colors and bearing minute decorations.

Colored mosaics in marble laid in geometric patterns and decorative forms are one of the best known of the Islamic arts. Among the most famous examples of this art is Al Hambra in Granada and the Cathedral of Cordova in Spain.

The Turkish style in Room 20 shows the European influence, especially in faithful representation of nature, and is thus a departure from the true Arab style. Also in this room is a collection of silver and glass pieces and a collection of prayer carpets.

The Iranian style, in Room 22, is characterized by an exactness in detail and a profusion of decoration and shows the influence of Chinese art on the Islamic art of Muslim Asia.

To view the ways in which Muslim artists have used materials over the ages, Rooms 6, 7, 8, 9, and 10 are devoted to displays of furniture from houses, palaces, and mosques. There is also a display of combs and jewelry boxes in different styles. Some are inlaid with ivory, mother-of-pearl, or woods of different colors; others are painted.

Rooms 9 and 11 contain metals that were used in making vessels and water jugs shaped like birds and animals. There are also statuettes, mosaics or tools for ornament, and candlesticks and censers with filigree decoration inlaid with silver and gold. A collection of weapons is displayed in Room 12.

The museum's porcelain collection is one of the most important and can be seen in Rooms 13, 14, 15, and 16.

The textiles in Room 17 were made in Yemen, Egypt, Iran, and Turkey. These include a wide variety of embroideries, some with Kufic inscriptions of prayers and the name of the city of origin. Tiraz, as the textile industry was then called, was of two types, one working for the caliph and his family and the other for the public. Both were directed by the government.

Room 17 also contains capitals with their bases and tombstones with Kufic and Naskhi inscriptions representing the development of Arabic writing in various stages.

Examples of marble mosaics that covered the floors in houses, palaces, and mosques are also on display.

Among the most outstanding artistic achievements of Islam were book illustration and calligraphy. Books penned in beautiful handwriting and abundantly illustrated are on display in Room 19. Some of the most elaborate are book covers and copies of the Koran.

Glassware, displayed in Room 21, includes vessels and fragments. It was an art in which Egypt and Syria excelled from ancient times. This hall has over 60 *mishkats* (lanterns) that belong to the Mameluk period and form the largest collection in any museum. Room 23 has a large collection of carpets belonging to different periods and places.

Woodworking: Historically, woodwork was one of the most important branches of Islamic art, and it flourished in Egypt. Even though Egypt has never been a producer of rich wood and has always had to import good qualities from neighboring countries—cedar from Lebanon, teak from India, and ebony from Sudan—Egyptian craftsmen have shown great skill in woodwork since ancient times.

The museum has a good collection of wood objects belonging to different Muslim periods. Many pieces were uncovered at Fustat and Ain es-Sira and had been used in buildings and as furniture.

Umayyad woodwork (661–750) continued to follow the Sassanid and Hellenistic traditions both in its deep cutting and its realistic style, such as the bunches of grapes, vine leaves, and scrolls with decorative motifs derived from Hellenistic art.

Those of the early Abbassid age (8th–9th centuries AD) can be distinguished by their decorations with concentric circles, interlacing arches, and small pierced oblongs with open work. But in 868, when Ibn Tulun became ruler of Egypt, an artistic evolution began and a new style was developed in both design and method. It was the slanting or beveled method, which used scrolls and lines that formed a stylized design of an animal or a bird. The technique was similar to the Abbassid stucco decoration found at Samarra.

The Fatimid woodwork (969–1171) is in good condition. It came from palaces, mosques, and Coptic churches, and the conditions under which it was produced make it obvious that it represents the highest artistic standards of Fatimid art.

During the reign of the caliphs Al-Zahir and Al-Mustansir (1020–1094), the art of wood carving reached its peak. Carving became more accurate and scrolls and leaves were more elaborately carved. Nature was honestly represented in rendering birds and animals.

The best examples of this style are the richly carved boards discovered in the Maristan of Qalaun. They are decorated with human figures, hunters, dancers and musicians, and other scenes that will give you insight into the life and customs of the Fatimid period.

The wood-carving style that begins with the reign of Al-Musta'li (1094) was a new method of decorating larger surfaces. The decoration did not form a continuous pattern but was split into small units such as hexagons and stars, each containing a separate design. An elaborate example is the beautifully carved mihrab of Sayyida Rukayaa. The *naskhi* style of calligraphy replaced Kufic script. Decorative animals and birds continued to be used, but the workmanship became less careful, and the figures were often treated as silhouettes with little surface detail.

During the Ayyubid period (1171), wood carving maintained the late Fatimid traditions, but the arabesque became more elaborate and some of the early Ayyubid wood carvings from Syria show Seljuk influence.

Under the Mameluks, carving became even more elaborate. Geometrical patterns of small panels became popular and usually consisted of hexagons arranged around central stars, all covered with intricate patterns of arabesque. The artists created outstanding works on pulpits, chests, doors, and chairs.

Another type of woodwork popular during this period was turned latticework, or *mushrabiya,* which has come to be known in the West as harem screens. The screens were used on the front of private houses and also to separate the sanctuary in mosques and churches. By varying the arrangement of the pieces, the artist was able to produce a great variety of designs.

With the weakened economic and political conditions of Egypt after the 15th century, the art of wood carving, along with the other Islamic arts, gradually declined.

MODERN CAIRO AND OTHER SITES OF INTEREST

Summary of Modern Cairo: Several old houses and former palaces have been made wholly or partly into museums and now serve as centers for art and handicrafts. They give a visitor the chance to meet Egyptians and to glimpse a side of the cultural activity. There are also innovations such as the Papyrus Institute and the Village of Harraniya, and such attractions as the zoo and the botanical gardens, Pharaonic Village, and excursions to Helwan and Fayoum.

Museums

Agricultural Museum. Ministry of Agriculture, Dokki. Hours: daily, summer 9 AM–2 PM; Fri. till 11:30 AM; winter 9 AM–4 PM; Fri. till 11 AM Tel. 702366.

Displays of village life, a collection of stuffed animals, and a variety of agricultural processes. The Cotton Museum (tel. 803802) is adjacent.

Egyptian Civilization and Gezira Museum. Gezira Exhibition Ground. Hours: Mon.–Thur. 9 AM–3 PM; Fri. to noon. Tel. 340–5198. Paintings and sculpture on the history of Egypt from prehistoric times to the present.

Khalil Museum. 1 Sharia el Sheikh el Marsafi, Zamalek. Hours: daily 10 AM–2 PM except Fri. Tel. 341–8672. A private collection of paintings and sculpture is open to the public. Exhibitions of contemporary artists are held regularly.

Modern Art Museum. Gezira Exhibition Grounds (near the new Cairo Opera House). Permanent exhibits of leading contemporary Egyptian artists. The new home for the collection was being readied and is expected to open in late 1991.

Mohammed Nagy Museum. 9 Mahmoud el Gendy St., Hadaak Alharam (off Cairo-Alexandria Road). Tel. 387-3484. Hours: winter, 10 AM–5 PM; summer, 10 AM–6 PM. Closed Monday. Admission free. Mohammed Nagy (1888–1956) was one of Egypt's leading contemporary artists who had a strong, definitive style that gave modern interpretation to traditional village life. The museum houses a vast collection of his works in what was once his studio.

Mukhtar Museum. Gezira, most easily reached by walking from Cairo Sheraton Hotel. Daily except Mon. Hours: 9 AM–1:30 PM. Tel. 340–2519.

In a building designed by the famous architect Ramses Wissa Wassef, it houses the works of Mahmoud Mukhtar, Egypt's best-known modern sculptor. The most famous piece is known as *The Winds of Khamsin,* often pictured in books on modern Egyptian art.

Papyrus Institute. Sharia el Nil, Giza (near Sheraton Hotel). Hours: daily 10 AM–7 PM. Tel. 348–8676.

At the research center, founded by Dr. Hassan Ragab, visitors learn how the ancient Egyptians made paper from the papyrus plant. Dr. Ragab spent seven years researching and perfecting the method. When he began in 1962, he had to bring the papyrus plant from Chad because the plant no longer grows naturally in Egypt, its importance having died in the 10th century with the introduction of rice paper.

The institute is situated in houseboats and adjoining buildings and includes an exhibition hall, museum library, and laboratory for research. Copies of drawings from tombs and temples painted on papyrus and other souvenirs are available for purchase at reasonable prices. Recently, a gallery for contemporary art and an art school were added, where the work of Egypt's leading contemporary artists and promising young ones are displayed. The school is directed by Liliane Karnouk, an artist and a designer and authority on modern Egyptian art. Due to visitor interest stimulated by Dr. Ragab's pioneering efforts, "Papyrus Institutes" have opened all over the city; despite their pretensions, they have no purpose other than commercial, several having been started by Dr. Ragab's apprentices. Dr. Ragab also has shops at the Cairo Marriott, Nile Hilton, and another on a houseboat in Luxor.

Pharaonic Village. On a small island in the Nile, 3 miles south of the city. Open daily 10 AM–4 PM. Entrance: L.E. 15. Tel. 729186. Dr. Ragab's last venture is something of an Egyptian version of Colonial Williamsburg and represents life during the New Kingdom, 1550 BC to 1070 BC. Visitors float on barges through canals to see scenes of ancient Egyptian life enacted by live actors while a guide provides running commentary explaining the action. The vignettes concern everyday agriculture, crafts, and industry. Visitors also tour a temple, complete with the mummification room and living quarters of a priest, and the houses of a nobleman and a peasant.

First-time visitors to Egypt find the village particularly interesting, for after viewing it, they are more able to relate the scenes drawn on ancient temple walls and tombs to present-day life in Nile Valley villages.

Old Houses

Anderson House. Near entrance of Ibn Toulun Mosque. Hours: 9 AM–3:30 PM; Fri. 9–11 AM and 1:30–3:30 PM. Tel. 847822. Entrance: L.E. 8.

Two houses built by Hajj Muhammad al-Jazzar in the 17th century are in excellent condition today because of the restoration by Major Gayer-Anderson, a British resident of Cairo during the 1920s. Anderson joined the two houses into one and lived here for many years. He furnished his home with interesting pieces of furniture and objets d'art he collected. After Anderson's death, the house was turned into a museum by the government. It gives a visitor a good idea of how a prosperous Cairo family in the 17th century lived. Attached to the house in the garden is a *sabil,* a public fountain from which members of the community could draw water, and a small tomb of a sheikh who was venerated as a holy and wise man by people of the neighborhood.

Beit el-Suheimi and Beit el-Tablawi. Adjoining houses from the 17th and 18th centuries located in the Mouski area on a street halfway between the mosques of Barquq and al Hakim. Entrance: L.E. 3.

Beit Sennari. Off Midan Sayyeda Zeinab on Haret Monge, south of Saneyya Girls' School, 9 AM–2 PM except Fri. Tel. 938565.

An old Islamic house is now used as a center for research in applied arts from the pharaonic period to the present. You may watch students at work and visit an exhibit of textiles, ceramics, batiks, kaftans, glass, silk-screen prints, and other handicrafts.

Musaferkhana. In a small lane several blocks from El Hussein Mosque. Hours: 9 AM–4 PM. Entrance fee: L.E. 3.

A grand old house built in 1779 was the birthplace of Khedive Ismail. It was restored by the Ministry of Culture a few years ago and now serves as an art center where several artists have studios. The building is difficult to find without a guide.

Wekalet el Ghouri. 3 Sharia el Sheikh Abdu, near El Ghouri Mosque, one block south of entrance to Khan el Khalil. Daily 8 AM–2 PM except Fri. Tel. 920–172. Entrance fee: L.E. 3.

A 16th-century caravanserai has been restored by the Ministry of Culture and is used to house a permanent exhibit of local crafts and folk arts from the different areas of Egypt. It also serves as a center where a number of artists display their works and as a workshop where pupils learn the traditional crafts of the country. The courtyard sometimes functions as the venue for open-air theater and concerts by foreign artists.

Former Royal Palaces and Rest Houses

Abdin Palace. Republic Square. Begun during the reign of Khedive Ismail and completed in 1874, Abdin Palace contained the living quarters of the former royal family as well as the reception rooms, the Belgium wing used for state receptions, the Byzantine hall, and the gardens. The building, used by the government, is not open to tourists.

Qubbah Palace. Attaba Square. Built in 1863 under Khedive Ismail, Qubbah Palace was used as the official residence of his successor, Tewfiq. The palace has some 400 rooms, including a museum, extensive gardens, swimming pool, and tennis courts. A railway station and engine shed accommodated the ex-king's train, in which he took trips incognito. The palace now houses apartments used for state occasions.

Manial Palace and Museum. Roda Island. Hours: daily 9 AM–2 PM. Entrance: L.E. 6. Tel. 987–495.

If your stay is too short to allow you to see many palaces and museums in Cairo you might opt for a visit to the Manial Palace. It will give you an idea of the grand style in which Egyptian royalty lived. The palace was built in 1901 by a prince of the royal family, Muhammad Ali. It is located on Roda Island and surrounded by lovely gardens. The palace is a mixture of Persian, Ottoman, Moorish, and Arab styles. It is divided into reception, residential, throne, and regency wings and the museum. Every inch of the palace is covered with mosaics, mushrabiya, or some intricate work of art—any one of which can be admired for its beauty. Taken together, it is overwhelming.

The reception quarters are located in a two-story building above the main gate. The west wing of its upper floor is in the Moorish style, the east wing in Syrian design. Its walls and ceiling are covered with wood taken from El Azm Palace in Syria and fitted by Syrian artisans brought to Egypt for the purpose.

The mosque is regarded as the loveliest of the palace's buildings. Its walls are plated with glazed tiles that frame panels inscribed with the attributes of Allah. Around the walls are hollowed marble casements and stained-glass windows; the floors are covered with Oriental carpets. The minaret, in Moorish style, has a clock that chimes.

In the residence the massive oak doors are framed in brass and inlaid with gold and silver. The ceiling designs, different in each room, are outstanding.

The Throne Room, 100 feet long and 21 feet wide, has white marble floors covered with red carpets. In the center of the ceiling an arabesque knob of hollowed wood inlaid with gold lets in the light in a symmetrical pattern. The decor is in the Ottoman tradition.

The palace museum consists of 14 galleries and contains masterpieces from the various periods of Islamic civilization: gold-decorated Korans, manuscripts penned by some of the most renowned calligraphers, Turkish carpets of the 17th and 18th centuries, ancient weapons, and candelabra. Also found here are costumes, a rare collection of nargilehs (pipes), furniture that once belonged to the Turkish sultan Abdel Hamid, and a 1,000-piece set of table silver engraved with the initials of Mohammad Ali, the caliph to whom it was presented as a gift from Louis Philippe of France.

The palace grounds now house a Club Med, which has an entrance on the west side.

Moses and Gardens

The Nilometer. This graduated column, said to date from 715, was used to measure the water level of the Nile and to anticipate the strength of the annual flood. Located at the southern tip of Roda Island, it is situated on the spot where, according to legend, the infant Moses was found in the bulrushes. Entrance: L.E. 3.

Zoological Gardens. Open daily 8:30 AM–4:30 PM. Cairo's 21-acre zoo is located on the Pyramid road and contains a rare collection of African and Sudanese animals and a museum of stuffed species. There is also a tea garden with restaurant.

Other Places of Interest

American University in Cairo. Founded in 1919 by a group of private citizens, the school has about 2,500 students, of which 80% are Egyptian. It offers bachelor of arts and science degrees as well as a master's degree in both disciplines. It has a large library and is especially proud of its Islamic Art and Architecture Library and the Debanne Collection on Egypt, which is available for use by scholars. The university's Division of Public Service offers an adult education program and sponsors cultural events throughout the year; it has 10,000 students.

The university is centrally located in the modern part of Cairo, only two blocks from the American Embassy and a short distance from the Nile Hilton and Shepheard's hotels.

Cairo University. With a student body numbering 125,000, Cairo University is the largest institute of higher learning in the Middle East and receives students from throughout the Arab world for study. Courses are primarily in Arabic. Among its leading faculties are medicine and engineering. The main gate to the campus is directly in front of the bridge leading from Roda to Giza.

Cairo Tower. Located on Gezira Island in the center of Cairo, the slim, modern structure dominates the skyline. The observation deck at the top offers a spectacular 360-degree view of the city. There's also a restaurant at the top. Entrance: L.E. 9.

Suburbs of Cairo

Cairo has now grown in every direction so that places that were once separate towns or villages are now part of the city. On the west side, Dokki and Giza, both of which are mainly middle-class residential areas, now stretch to the foot of the Pyramids, and the green fields that once surrounded them have given way to high-rise apartment buildings. Another rapidly growing district on the northwest is Mohandaseen.

South of the city is the elegant residential district of Maadi, connected by a superhighway. Farther on, the road leads to Helwan, which is both a spa and a developing industrial complex. The east side of the city is hemmed in by the Mukattam Hills, but the city is creeping in this direction, too. The greatest growth in the past decade has been in the area north of the city, especially with the addition of Nasr City, a low-cost housing project, and the expansion of Heliopolis, one of the oldest continuously inhabited sites and one of the main cities of Egypt throughout its ancient history.

Today Heliopolis—in Arabic, *Masr al Gadida* (New Cairo)—is 15 miles from downtown Cairo and is considered one of its suburbs. Its wide boulevards, spacious villas, and abundant gardens make it one of the loveliest sections in the city.

The old city of Heliopolis is referred to in the Bible as the city of On. Its only remnant is an obelisk. The section known as Matariya, once a village, stands on the original site of the ancient city. Located here is the Tree of the Virgin, which tradition holds was the resting place of the Holy Family on its flight to Egypt. Visitors are also shown an old well from which, tradition says, the Holy Family obtained water. The Church of the Nativity is within walking distance of the sacred well.

SUGGESTED ITINERARY FOR CAIRO

The hours suggested on these programs will vary according to season and city traffic. In summer, visitors should avoid sightseeing during the hottest part of the day—between noon and 4 PM—and should adjust the schedule appropriately.

First Day: Visit Egyptian Antiquities Museum—a brief survey of both floors will take two hours. (Prior to a visit you may want to read the exciting account of the discovery and opening of the tomb of Tutankhamen by Howard Carter, who discovered it.) Drive to Memphis and Sakkara to visit the Step Pyramid, the mastabas of the nobles, and other excavations in the area. Continue to the Pyramids and the Sphinx, stopping en route for lunch at a hotel or restaurant in the vicinity of the Pyramids. You may want to ride a camel or have tea at the café nearby and stop for a while to enjoy the view.

You can remain at the Pyramids for the son-et-lumière program. To pass the time before the show, enjoy drinks at the Mena House, where you have a spectacular view of the Pyramids.

Alternatively, you might stop at the artist village of Harraniya or Kerdassa, a short side trip off the Pyramids road before or after visiting the Pyramids. Depending upon the time and the location of your hotel, another alternative might be to return to the city for a visit to the top of Cairo Tower for the 360-degree view of Cairo and the Nile Valley.

In the evening, you might try the dinner cruise on the *Nile Pharaoh,* a large cruise boat in pharaonic decor offering dinner and dancing during cruises from Cairo to Maadi. *Le Scribe* (moored in front of the Semiramis Inter-Continental) is similar. *L'Egyptien*, the Nile cruise ship of Pullman Hotels, moored in front of its hotel in Maadi, also offers dinner cruises. Twice monthly on Thursday–Friday weekends, the ship sails to Beni Suef.

Second Day: Visit the Coptic antiquities in Old Cairo. Babylon Fort, old churches, and the Coptic Museum are located next to each other. Drive to the Citadel at the foot of the Mukattam Hills. View the Muhammad Ali Mosque and enjoy the view of the city. Afterward, visit the nearby mosques of Sultan Hassan and Ibn Toulun and the adajacent Anderson House. If time permits, Manial Palace on Roda Island can be included en route from the Citadel. Follow this with a felucca sail on the Nile at sunset.

Third Day: Visit the Islamic Museum and continue to the Mouski to visit the Khan Khalili bazaar, where you can wander through the labyrinth of lanes and alleyways watching craftsmen and chatting with shopkeepers. A visit to Al-Azhar can also be made if time permits. Those who have not yet been on a felucca might include a sail on the Nile and a visit to the Papyrus Institute or the new Pharaonic Island operated by the owner of the institute. After dinner, unwind by dancing at one of the nightclubs featuring an Oriental dancer.

If you are planning to spend five days to a week in Cairo, we would recommend the same itinerary, but at a slower pace, to allow you to spend more time at the museums and antiquity sites, shop, relax over meals, enjoy a sport, and to appreciate the serenity that is Egypt.

EXCURSIONS FROM CAIRO

HELWAN

Cairo has grown so much that Helwan, once a spa 15 miles south of the city, is now a suburb and the southern terminus of the new subway system, known in Cairo as the Metro. Helwan can also be reached by car on the Corniche. Despite the urban sprawl and industrialization of the area, Helwan still has sulphur springs, gushing water at 90° F., considered to have excellent curative powers. Visitors may swim for health or pleasure in open-air pools fed from the springs.

The quarries of Tura and Ma'sara near Helwan are today, as in pharaonic times, a source of supply for limestone. At the quarries you can see interesting old drawings depicting the ancient methods of stone working. Between Helwan and Ma'sara at Ezbet al Waldu, tombs of the first three dynasties contained exquisite vases and other artifacts that are now in the Egyptian Museum.

Wax Museum in Helwan. Established in 1934 and originally housed on Gumhuriya Street, the museum was moved to Helwan in 1955. It depicts the highlights of Egypt's history, especially under the pharaohs and Islam. The rooms include exhibits of Akhenaton in the company of his wife, Queen Nefertiti, their children, and a retinue on their way to Aton Temple at Tell al Amarna; Saladin's visit to his ailing enemy, Richard the Lion-Hearted; Caliph Umar Ibn el-Khattab making a charity call on a poor family; a wedding scene of the 19th century; Pharaoh's daughter sheltering the infant Moses rescued from the rushes.

The Japanese Garden. This is the only garden of its kind in the Middle East. There are statues of Buddha and Japanese-style arcades, as well as artificial pools. Unfortunately, it is in a rundown condition.

Helwan Rest House Museum. Situated on the Nile's banks about 4 miles from Helwan, it lies between the Pyramids of Dahshur on the west and the Helwan sulfur springs in the east. The Rest House belonged to ex-king Farouk and is open to visitors as a museum.

Helwan Observatory. The ancient Egyptians were the first to establish observatories, and records show that the scribes of the pharaonic university of Ain Shams, thought to be the first university of antiquity, were able to plot the stars. The present observatory in Helwan was built in 1903.

Fayoum

The largest oasis in Egypt, Fayoum lies 60 miles southwest of Cairo and can be reached by train or car. Fayoum is a popular hunting and fishing region. Its wooded countryside, flowering trees, old waterwheels, and cultivated fields offer a picturesque landscape in contrast to the barren desert surrounding it.

Fayoum was the center of one of Egypt's most ancient cultures and the earliest known site of pottery making and cultivation. Records of Fayoum's history indicate that the period of the XII Dynasty was the most prosperous. At that time Lake Qarun, known to ancient Egypt as Moeris Lake, occupied almost half of the Fayoum depression. Over the years the lake gradually shrank. The area is famous for migratory birds and ducks and has attracted hunters since antiquity. Now European, and more recently, American hunters are discovering it.

The Greek capital was called Crocodilopolis, after the local god Sobek, who was conceived as a crocodile. The province as a whole was called Arsinoite Nome, after the sister and wife of Ptolemy II. By the 1st century AD, the oasis had come to be known as Bion in Coptic, which later evolved into Fayoum, the present name of both the town and the province. *The Fayoum: A Practical Guide,* by R. N. Hewison, is a helpful book.

Kom Oshim Museum. Entrance: L.E. 3. There are also entrance fees of L.E. 3 to some Fayoum monuments. A few miles before the lake and the Auberge du Lac, a hotel near the turnoff south to Fayoum. Houses a small collection of antiquities. Immediately behind the museum is a huge site dating from Roman times, which was excavated by the University of Michigan.

Fayoum is noted for the famous wax-painted portraits, dating from the Roman period, found on mummies in place of the mask. The lifelike portraits, meant as pictures of the deceased, have astonishing force and character. Nothing similar has ever been found elsewhere. Some of the best are in the Cairo Antiquities Museum and the Greco-Roman Museum in Alexandria.

Among the monuments at Fayoum one of the most important is the Pyramid of Amenemhat III, XII Dynasty, 19th century BC, located nine miles southeast of Fayoum. It is made of dried bricks rather than stone. In 1956 the Tomb of Nefru-Ptah, daughter of Amenemhat III, was discovered a mile from her father's pyramid.

At Lahun, 30 miles southeast of Fayoum, are other pyramids and mastabas belonging to princesses and nobles. In the tomb of Princess Sat-Hathor were found exquisite pieces of jewelry, now in the Egyptian Museum.

Cairo travel agents can arrange a Fayoum tour, or one can negotiate a half- or full-day trip with a Cairo taxi. From the United States, information on duck-hunting tours is available from *Safari Caribe,* 800–9–SAFARI.

A new road continues south from Fayoum to the main highway along the Nile leading to Minya and Upper Egypt. For places to stay see the hotels under *Practical Information for Cairo,* above.

Towns and Antiquity Sites South of Cairo

Minya. Located on the main road west of the Nile, Minya is a four-hour drive from the capital. The road passes through Beni Suef, where a new paved road to the west leads to the Pyramid at Meidum. The Pyramid can be seen from the main road as well. Entrance: L.E. 8.

Minya, the capital of the governorate, has one of Egypt's 12 state-run universities. At the municipal building, which adjoins part of the University of Minya campus on the Corniche, the office of the inspector of the Antiquities Service is located on the first floor of the north wing. He is helpful and informed and, in lieu of any sophisticated tourist services, will be able to point you in the right direction to explore the antiquity sites on your own.

Hermopolis. On the west bank, 24 miles south of Minya and west of the village of Mallawi. This is the site of a fabulous temple whose ceiling was supported by statues of huge baboons. The patron of the city was the god Thoth, who was depicted as a baboon or an ibis. Hermopolis is also the site of a Greek agora, which has been restored by the Antiquities Service.

Tuna El-Gebel. The necropolis for Hermopolis west of the city. Entrance: L.E. 8. Here tombs of ibises and baboons, animals sacred to Thoth, were excavated in the rock foundation of the desert and extend in catacombs for many miles underground. Thousands of mummified ibises, baboons, ibis eggs, and the workshop of an embalmer have been found. A small museum in Mallawi displays many forms of the ibis. Entrance: 50 piasters.

The outstanding building at the necropolis is the Tomb of Petosiris, whose sarcophagus is now in the Egyptian Museum in Cairo. North of the tomb is one of the stelae of Tel al Amarna, which designated the city's boundaries.

Tell al Amarna. Entrance: L.E. 8. This was the city of Akhenaten and Nefertiti, who abandoned Thebes and the worship of Amon and embraced a new worship of one god, Aton.

To reach Tel al Amarna, drive eight miles south of Mallawi to the point where you cross the Nile. On the east side of the Nile the distance is less than a mile and can be covered on foot, donkey, or flatbed truck that has been converted into a wagon for tourists. Behind the present village, at the ancient site of Tel al Amarna, the ruins known as the Palace of Neferti-ti are among the very few remnants from the Akhenaten period. Tablets in cuneiform writing, which contained military correspondence between Egypt and Syria, were found here and are now in the Cairo Museum. It is a very long hike up the limestone hills behind the site to the tombs dating from the Akhenaten era. Only five of the 25 tombs that have been found are open to visitors. The drawings are badly damaged, but they do provide evidence of the profound changes in art and philosophy initiated by this unusual pharaoh.

To see any sights on the eastern bank of the river you must cross by ferry, which sometimes carries cars along with the usual donkey carts and local traffic. There are two docking stations. One is located at the southern end of town; the other is eight miles south across from Tel al Amarna. The ferries run throughout the day, but try to get on the first 6 AM crossing. The ferry does a brisk business, and you will need every available second for sightseeing.

Beni Hassan. On the east bank here, across from Minya, is one of the largest Christian and Muslim cemeteries in Egypt, used since the time of the Persian invasion. The cemetery with its beehive domes stretching far into the distance fills the land between the limestone cliffs and the water.

Just south of the cemetery in the limestone cliffs are several tombs of the Middle Kingdom—unusual because they are in the east rather than the west, as are all other pharaonic tombs. Some of these tombs are still unregistered. The Antiquities Service representative can arrange for you to visit them. They are particularly interesting because of the sporting scenes, which clearly show that the ancient Egyptians knew judo, karate, and wrestling, among other sports we practice today.

On the east bank, nine miles north of Minya, is the site of the Monastery of the Pulley. A new Coptic church stands on the foundation of the ancient monastery, where centuries ago the monks were lowered in baskets from the high rock by pulley to the banks of the river, to bless the journeys of the feluccas.

Note: One of the main problems of visiting the area of Upper Egypt from south of Cairo to Luxor is the lack of hotel facilities. See hotel listings under *Practical Information for Cairo* for details.

PRACTICAL INFORMATION FOR CAIRO

HOW TO GET AROUND. Rental car. You may rent a car with or without a driver, to be picked up at the airport on arrival. *Avis, Budget, Hertz,* and other international car-rental firms have offices at Cairo airport and major hotels. This is particularly useful in helping foreigners cope with taxi overcharge and language barriers.

On your first visit to Egypt, we do not recommend renting a car without a driver. Language becomes a problem when you strike out alone, and driving in Cairo is not easy. Besides, the cost of an English-speaking driver is so little (U.S. $7.50 per day from Hertz) that it is worth it. We strongly recommend it for those who are not on an organized tour and for business travelers who need to move around the city a great deal. In the latter case, it is smart to hire a car and driver by the week or longer, especially if you are likely to have several appointments each day. A car and driver can save you hours of frustration as well as time. It is important to hire a driver who knows at least a little English. You can ask your hotel doorman or travel agency to arrange for one, or if you find a taxi driver you like and with whom you can communicate, strike a deal with him on your own. But be sure to set the price in advance. On the other hand, you will probably do as well by going to a rental company, or at least checking their prices before putting your bargaining skills to the test.

In addition to car-rental firms, *Limo* (described earlier in "Facts at Your Fingertips") has cars for hire. Rates are higher than the usual tariff, but they are fixed prices.

Taxis. Taxis can be hired by the hour, half day or full day. By the hour the cost is L.E. 10–15; for a half day, L.E. 40–60, depending on your ability to bargain. For an eight-hour day, the cost will be about L.E. 100, including driver and gas, and more if the day stretches late into evening. Taxis engaged at deluxe hotels cost 30% to 50% more than those bargained for on the street—if you are good at bargaining. However, taxis such as those stationed at the *Semiramis Inter-Continental Hotel* in Cairo carry published tariffs of their fixed rates that you can ask to see anytime you think you are being overcharged.

River taxis. A novel way of beating traffic jams is to use the river taxis that ply the Nile from early morning until late afternoon. They are crowded and best avoided during rush hours, but they are a great way to go from city center to Coptic Cairo. Departure is from Maspiro Terminal between the Ramses Hilton and the Radio/Television Building. The cost is 10 piasters!

Metro. The first stage of Cairo's gleaming new subway was completed in 1989. Built by the French and called the Metro, it is a true copy of the Paris Metro in design, cars, color-coded direction signs, and pay and entrance/exit methods. The tracks run north–south along the city's most traveled routes and link two principal transportation hubs—Ramses Square, the main train station on the north side of town, and Tahrir Square, the major traffic circle of the city center where eight roads converge and the main city bus terminal is located. From Tahrir Square (also called Sadat Square on the Metro map) the line extends to its southern-most terminus at Helwan, a suburb. Several stops along the way provide access to major sections of the city. The entrances, exits, and station stops are well marked and directional information is clearly posted in Arabic and English. Tourists are most likely to use the sections between Ramses Station and Tahrir Square, and Tahrir Square and Maadi, a southern suburb. The maximum fare is 50 piasters.

City buses. City buses are simply too crowded to be recommended for tourist use. However, there are fleets of minibuses with guaranteed seats that leave from Tahrir Square to most parts of the city. Unfortunately, signs are in Arabic, and you will have to ask. Egyptians are very helpful and the first one who speaks even three words of English is likely to come rushing to your rescue. Deluxe and large first-class hotels in the suburbs have courtesy buses to Tahrir Square in the city center.

Walking. With a good map in hand, you can find your way around the major parts of downtown Cairo without difficulty. At major intersections, street names are posted in Arabic and English. Maps are available from the Tourist Office, travel agents, and bookshops. Egyptians are very willing, even eager, to help. You can stop in any shop and ask for directions. The shopkeeper will often leave his business to show you the way or send his helper along to guide you. People on the street who spot a foreigner looking lost will often offer to be of help.

HOTELS. Cairo is well equipped with hotels in the deluxe and first-class categories. Nine well-known American and European chains are represented. During the high season, it is wise for visitors to have confirmed reservations, especially between December and April, and to have their confirmation notice in hand upon arrival in Egypt. Regulations issued in 1990, required that the rates at deluxe, first-class, and some tourist-class hotels be quoted only in U.S. dollars. Pensions and two-star hotels may continue to quote rates in Egyptian pounds to foreigners. This reflects the introduction of a two-tier system—one for foreigners and one for Egyptian nationals—following the devaluation of the Egyptian pound in 1987. However, readers (or their travel agents) must check with hotels for precise rates. *Under no circumstances do we guarantee prices which do not include suites, listed here.* The following indicates the wide range in each category:

Deluxe: single with bath $72–$132; double $90–$169.
First Class (A): single with bath $35–$60; double $46–$105.
First Class (B): single with bath $33–$63; double $42–$79.
Tourist: single with breakfast $24–$37; double $35–$40.
Pension: single with bath and half board $5–$26; double $10–$36.

A 12% service charge is added throughout Egypt on the hotel and meal charge, plus a municipal tax of 2% to 5%, and a $15 per person, per night room tax, depending on the city.

English is widely spoken in hotels throughout Egypt.

The government designates hotels by stars, ranging from five (deluxe) to one (pension). In our experience all but a few hotels are overrated by at least one and sometimes two stars. Maintenance is a problem even in the hotels belonging to reputable international chains. The Ministry of Tourism has begun a review to reevaluate the rating of each hotel; however, it will be several years before the review is completed and new ratings assigned.

A current list of all hotels, their facilities, and official rates can be obtained from the Egyptian Government Tourist Office in New York. The hotels listed here are the best in each category.

Key to Abbreviations: swb—single with bath; dwb—double with bath; a/c—air-conditioned; TV—television; sw/ob—single without bath.

Note: All prices are approximate and subject to change.

Deluxe (five-star)

Cairo Marriott. Box 33, Sharia al Gezira, Zamalek, 1,250 rooms. Price: $110–$132 swb; $132–$170 dwb. Phone: 340–8888. Fax: 340–6617. Two high-rise towers were added around a famous old palace, originally built by Khedive Ismail as a guest house for Empress Eugenie at the time of the Suez Canal opening in 1869. It was later bought by a wealthy Egyptian pasha of Lebanese origin. The palace must have been considered grand at the time; it warranted a description in the 1895 edition of Baedeker's *Guide to Egypt.* The interior was elaborately decorated and gilded. The palace was converted into a hotel during the 1960s. It quickly became a favorite for wedding receptions—brides could make their grand entrance on the carved marble staircase of the main entrance hall, its most outstanding feature.

In the design of the new hotel, the palace has become the central pavilion. Marriott has gone to great effort to restore all the old furniture, wood, marble, rugs, tapestries, and objets d'art, most of which date from the late 19th century. These are used in the decor throughout the hotel wherever they are appropriate.

The facade with its original latticework portions is the most impressive. Inside, Damascene-painted high ceilings, elaborate arches, and mammoth old Oriental chandeliers help to retain the mansion's former grandeur.

The most beautiful restorations are on the north side, where the palace's original entrance hall has been made into a grand and elegant reception room with the famous marble staircase. It leads to the second level, with a grand foyer, magnificent ballroom, meeting rooms and terrace that have become the most popular in the city for special functions and wedding receptions. Other areas of the palace house the *Gezira Grill,* coffee shop, *Eugenie's Lounge,* nightclub and casino. The Zamalek tower houses a steakhouse and *The Library,* a lovely bar with a city view.

Situated on 12 acres, overlooking the Nile, the gardens include a swimming pool, fountains, and low-rise buildings housing health clubs for men and women as well as three lighted tennis courts. Most guest rooms have twin beds, but some have been fitted as businessmen's suites with desk and work area; and there are elaborate suites on every floor. The towers are connected to the palace by arcades of boutiques and services. The hotel also has apartments with kitchens for long-term stay.

Cairo Meridien. Corniche el Nil, Roda Island, 295 rooms. Price: $108 swb; $135 dwb. Phone: 362–1717. Fax: 362–1927. The hotel was taken over by Air France's Meridien Hotel chain in 1974. It has the most fabulous location of any hotel in the city, situated on a two-square-kilometer island in the Nile.

Rooms are spacious and comfortable; all are being refurbished and new bathrooms installed. The semicircular shape of the building gives each of the rooms a magnificent view of the Nile and Cairo. Rooms are equipped with air-conditioning, direct-dial phone and TV with two in-house video channels. Each room also has a nice-sized terrace on which guests may enjoy breakfast, sunbathe, watch the feluccas, the graceful sailboats of the Nile, or see the sun set over Cairo.

The hotel has several restaurants and a rooftop dining room featuring a nightly combo for dancing and a top-rated Egyptian belly dancer.

Facilities include photo, souvenir and book shops, florist, jeweler, several attractive dress and accessory shops, travel agent, car rental, bank, and airline office. There is a beauty salon, winter and summer swimming pool, sauna and massage. The hotel has a Business Service Center, with telex, copy machine, secretarial service, and private office space for rent. The hotel has a constantly changing exhibit of Egyptian art.

The hotel is near the British Embassy and within walking distance of the American Embassy. It is a short taxi ride from the Egyptian Antiquities Museum and the downtown shopping district.

Cairo Sheraton Hotel, Towers and Casino. 1 Galaa Square, Giza, 664 rooms, 112 suites. Price: $87–$115 swb; $127–$144 dwb. Phone: 348–8600. Fax: 348–9051. Located in one of the most attractive parts of the city, on the west bank of the Nile at Giza, within walking distance to the new Cairo Opera House and Cultural Complex. Rooms overlook the Nile or the public gardens and Gezira Island. They are equipped with air-conditioning, TV, and direct-dial phones. Rooms are large and nicely furnished. Facilities include bank, travel agency, two swimming pools. The hotel's nine restaurants are among the best in Cairo, and its casino the liveliest. The shopping arcade has a very good bookstore and camera shop among other boutiques, a patisserie and a quick-snack, stand-up bar. There is a Business Center and meeting facilities. The new tower is bridged to the old part, and between the two there is a swimming pool with Cairo's first swim-up bar. The new building also has a theater for 270 people and a large conference center. Rooms in the new tower are similar in size but more fashionably decorated; four floors have been designated as nonsmoking.

El Gezirah Sheraton. Gezirah Island, Box 34, Zamalek, Cairo, 520 rooms. Price: $99–$132 swb; $121–$154 dwb. Phone: 341–1333; Fax: 340–5056. Located at the southern tip of an island in the heart of the Nile and within walking distance of the Cairo Sheraton, its circular design of 27 floors enables all rooms to have a view of the river; those on the south side have a panorama that stretches from the Citadel on the east to the Pyramids on the west.

All rooms have air-conditioning, TV, and direct-dial phones; the top eight floors are devoted to deluxe rooms with Tower Service, including a private elevator and separate check-in. Facilities include bank, travel agency, swimming pool with sun deck and health club, and banquet and meeting rooms for up to 750 people. The 24-hour coffee shop, Oriental restaurant, and nightclub have lovely views directly overlooking the river.

Heliopolis Sheraton. Airport Road. In March 1990, this hotel, one of Cairo's most popular, was destroyed by fire. Gulf Hotels, the owning company, began rebuilding immediately and some restaurants and rooms are back in operation. However, completion of the 679-room hotel is not expected until 1992.

Mena House Oberoi. Sharia el Haram (Pyramid Road), Giza, 510 rooms. Price: garden, $78 swb; palace, $97 swb; garden, $98 dwb; palace, $122 dwb. Phone: 387–7444; Fax: 387–3424. Originally built as a royal hunting lodge for Khedive Ismail, Mena House is located at the base of the short, steep rise to the plateau on which the Pyramids and the Sphinx stand. The building was enlarged by the free-spending monarch and converted into a guest house in 1869 in preparation for the festivities marking the opening of the Suez Canal.

A decade later the property was converted into a hotel, expanded, and further embellished. The most outstanding feature of its arabesque decor was its windows of intricate woodwork, known as *mushrabiya* in Arabic and called harem screens by Westerners. These are said to date from the 14th century.

Mena House came to be one of the most popular places in Egypt, with a guest list that included kings, queens, statesmen, writers, actors, and other celebrities from around the world. Empress Eugenie of France, King Zog of Albania, King Gustav of Sweden, King Umberto of Italy, King Alphonso of Spain, Emperor Haile Selassie, and Mohamed V of Morocco all stayed here. Winston Churchill met President Roosevelt here.

From the hotel's front terrace, once the favorite place for British colonists and elite Cairenes to sip afternoon tea, visitors had a superb view of the Pyramids. In bygone days before the road to the Pyramids was paved, visitors would mount camels at stables in front of Mena House to carry them up the hill. It was a romantic scene, especially for the spectators who enjoyed their tea on the hotel's veranda while they watched the sun set behind the Pyramids. Today the terrace is the coffee shop, enclosed with large glass windows. The view is the same, but cars and motorcoaches breeze by and—no, it really is not quite the same.

The Oberoi Hotel chain of India took over the 44-acre property in 1972 and completely renovated the old hotel and the 200-room extension that had been added during the 1960s. Oberoi has upgraded all the hotel operations and added many new features and facilities. Another expansion has added a new lobby, a piano bar from which you get a view of the Pyramids, a new meeting complex for up to 1,000 people, and an Executive Business Center with five small conference rooms and a library. The latest addition is a casino.

The guest rooms in the original buildings are deluxe doubles with private bath, TV, and air-conditioning, and a group of them were redesigned into the most lavish, spectacular suites in Egypt, if not in the Middle East. They are furnished with authentic antiquities that were discovered in one of the hotel's storerooms, and completely restored to mint condition. The rooms on the front, or south, side of the main building have spectacular views of the Pyramids.

The main restaurant, bar, coffee shop, and halls have retained the original decor, although all the old wood had to be replaced and much of it has been painted gold. The walls of the public rooms, once painted white, have now been covered with white marble. The effect is more that of a maharajah's lavish palace than a small royal retreat.

Complete new kitchens with the latest American equipment were installed to supply *Al Rubaiyat,* the main dining room serving Continental food; the *Moghul Room,* offering Indian specialties; *Khan el Khalili,* the coffee shop open 24 hours daily; the *Saddle Room,* a stereo nightclub; *Abu*

Nawas, the inside winter nightclub; and the *Mameluk Bar,* the main bar of the old part.

Rooms in the garden buildings were refurbished and upgraded. These rooms face the Pyramids and overlook the swimming pool. Another 200 were added as an extension to the back side of the garden buildings. These rooms overlook the desert and the road to Alexandria. This part of the hotel is definitely not up to the standard of the renovated historic part, and this is reflected in the prices, which are about 25% lower. However, guests have full access to all the hotel's facilities, which are top-notch.

The hotel's facilities include four tennis courts, a nine-hole golf course, a health club, and a large swimming pool with a terrace restaurant that becomes the *Oasis,* an outdoor nightclub, in summer. There are several lovely meeting rooms, including the one in which presidents Carter and Sadat met to discuss peace.

While the location of the Mena House is fantastic, it could be a drawback for those who want to spend time in the city. The drive to Tahrir Square in the city center can take 30 to 45 minutes depending on traffic. The hotel offers shuttle-bus service for guests. It should also be noted that much of Cairo has grown in this direction. Because of the hotel's extensive grounds and facilities, Mena House should be thought of as a resort on the edge of town rather than as a downtown hotel.

Mövenpick Heliopolis. A half mile from Cairo International Airport Terminal; 412 rooms. Price: $105 swb; $130 dwb. Phone: 247–0077; Fax: 667–374. Operated by a Swiss company, Movenpick opened in 1983 in the rapidly expanding airport area. Attractively furnished, soundproofed rooms, all equipped with minibar, TV, direct-dial phone, and air-conditioning. Facilities include three restaurants, one of which is open 24 hours, executive business center, large swimming pool, two tennis courts, disco, casino, airline office, 24-hour room, and same-day laundry services, hair salon, boutiques, meeting rooms, and parking area. There is a free airport shuttle bus.

Mövenpick Hotel Jolie Ville Cairo-Pyramids. Alexandria Desert Rd., 252 rooms. Price: $85 swb; $105 dwb. Phone: 387–5612; Fax 855–006. This popular hotel, destroyed by a fire in 1987, has been rebuilt in the same bungalow-style set amid gardens and grouped around a large swimming pool—all with awesome views of the Pyramids of Giza. Reopened in early 1990, the hotel has been upgraded and now has air-conditioned rooms with bath, TV, minibar and direct-dial phone. Facilities include four tennis courts of which two are lighted, jogging track, heated pool, sauna, and gym. There is a 24-hour restaurant serving a mixed menu and one serving French cuisine, two bars, a take-out deli, shops, and a meeting center. A superior four-star hotel with five-star service, this is one of the most popular hotels in Egypt.

Nile Hilton. Corniche el Nil, 466 rooms. Price: $119 swb; $152 dwb. Phone: 765–666; Fax:760–874. The Hilton has become something of an institution in Cairo. Terrific location overlooking the Nile on one side and Tahrir Square on the other. The Egyptian Antiquities Museum is next door, and the hotel is within walking distance of the downtown shopping district and the American Embassy.

The Hilton has long been a favorite meeting place for foreigners, press and top-level government and business people, and its bars and poolside restaurant are usually crowded with Egyptians and visitors alike. Some people may find the constant crowds more irritating than interesting. The rooftop nightclub is tops. In summer it moves to an outside garden by the swimming pool. Its disco, *Jackie's,* is the leading one in the city. There is also a casino. Dining facilities include several restaurants, a coffee shop, pizzeria, and rotisserie.

The hotel uses a modern adaptation of ancient Egyptian motifs and colors throughout its decor. Most of the fabrics, furnishings, and objets d'art were made in Egypt. The hotel has many shops and services; prices tend to be higher than elsewhere, but the selections are good and the atmosphere pleasant. Several airlines and travel agents have offices in the hotel lobby. There is a beauty salon, barbershop, health club, sauna, swimming pool, and two tennis courts. Rooms are large and comfortable, with terraces that offer panoramic views of Cairo. For a view of the Nile, ask for a room on the west side. Rooms are equipped with air-conditioning, TV, in-house movies, minibars, and direct-dial telephones. On the city side there is a three-story extension, built around a lovely garden. The **Nile Hilton Centre** has 66 guest rooms and nine suites with kitchenette, and offices. The ground floor has a variety of boutiques, a bank, car rental, airline offices—including *Air Sinai*—and a parking garage.

Ramses Hilton. Corniche el Nil, 843 rooms. Price: $103 swb; $132 dwb. Phone: 777–444; Fax: 757–152. A completely separate hotel from the Nile Hilton, located on the Nile about three blocks from the latter and within walking distance of the Antiquities Museum, it is the tallest hotel and one of the tallest buildings in town. The rooftop lounge is a popular spot for cocktails and features a panoramic view from which, on a clear day, the Pyramids of Giza are visible on the western horizon, nine miles away.

Throughout the hotel touches of Egyptian motifs from all the important periods of its history are reflected in the decor. The walls of the lobby and main corridors are faced with a pharaoh's ransom of rose granite and Portoccino marble from Aswan. In the *Garden Court* of the central lobby, you can enjoy drinks under columns that soar to the second and third floors and resemble the great columns of Karnak Temple in Luxor.

A stairway curves up to the *Terrace Cafe,* a 24-hour coffee shop on the second level, which overlooks the Nile as well as the Garden Court. Nearby, the *Citadel Grill,* the main dining room, combines Egypt's Islamic heritage in design details taken from traditional tiles and in the use of mushrabiya latticework, with the village tradition of weaving, as seen in the beautiful tapestries from Harraniya. Enormous copper chimneys over the open grill are reproductions of bread ovens still in use in Upper Egypt. To the right of the grill is a cozy bar.

The lobby level and first floor have meeting rooms, a ballroom, and an Executive Business Service Center with full secretarial/translation services, open daily 9 AM–6 PM. A nightclub and the excellent *Falafel,* an Oriental restaurant/nightclub, are on the swimming-pool level, as are the hair salons. **Nile Beauty and Health Spa** for men and women is the most complete and sophisticated of its kind east of Rome. In 1989, a casino with very stylish art deco design was added.

Guests can also ride from the lobby to the first and second floors in what might be the world's plushest elevator. The two-ton glass and brass lift was made by the famous British manufacturer, Basingstoke. Its interior is finished in genuine suede leather and, according to one British newspaper report, so "lifted" the pride of the firm's employees that they invited their wives to see it.

Guest rooms are located on another 30 floors, and because of the building's unusual triangular shape, 80% of the rooms have views of the Nile. The rooms are beautifully decorated, even to the point of having original paintings by modern Egyptian artists and handmade ceramic wall plaques in pharaonic design in the bathrooms. Rooms have air conditioning, TV, in-house movies, direct-dial telephones, and refrigerators/bars. Two rooms are especially designed for the handicapped. A multistory car park, adjacent to the hotel, is the first of its kind in Egypt and has some very attractive shops.

Safir Cairo. 22 Rifaia St., Dokki, 280 rooms. Price: $74 swb; $92.50 dwb. Phone: 348–2424; Fax: 342–1202. Located in a residential area on the west bank of the Nile, this modern, elegant hotel has a lovely lobby and ground floor of marble and richly textured wood; shops and several restaurants have beautiful appointments. Guest rooms have TV, minibar, balcony, and 24-hour room service. Facilities include a heated, open-air swimming pool, health club, and meeting facilities.

The owning company also operates *Safir el Zamalek Apartment Hotel,* (Phone 414–865), a 30-story luxury building overlooking the Nile. It has 104 fully furnished, two- and three-bedroom apartments; two restaurants.

Semiramis Inter-Continental. Corniche el Nil, Box 60, Cairo; 840 rooms. Price: $100–$115 swb; $125–$144 dwb. Phone: 355–7171; Fax: 356–3020. Opened in 1987, this modern hotel is situated in a fabulous location overlooking the Nile on the site of the famous old hotel for which it is named. It is within walking distance of the American and British embassies, American University, Egyptian Antiquities Museum, and the major downtown shopping areas.

In the multitier high rise all rooms have balconies overlooking the Nile or Cairo and are equipped with air-conditioning; bedside-controlled TV with in-house movies and news service; minibars and direct-dial phones. The hotel has eight restaurants, including a tea garden and *The Grill,* an elegant dining room with a lovely view of the Nile. There are several bars, and the indoor/outdoor nightclub is on the third floor at the same level as the old Semiramis roof garden where generations of nobility, aristocrats, and other famous people danced under the stars. Throughout, the decor is elegant and stylish but understated.

Facilities include a full executive business center and private offices for daily rental; conference and meeting facilities with one of the largest ballrooms in the Middle East; a swimming pool plus a children's pool, an elaborate health club including a fully equipped gym, solarium, sauna and Turkish bath, and poolside snack bar. There is a two-floor shopping arcade, underground car park, concierge, 24-hour room service, and same-day laundry and valet service.

The Semiramis is Inter-Continental's first hotel in Egypt, but 13th in eight countries of the Middle East. Not surprisingly, a large percentage of their guests are business travelers from these countries, particularly the Gulf states.

Shepheard. Corniche el Nil, Sharia ala Hamy, 285 rooms. Price: $72 swb; $90 dwb. Phone: 355–3800; Fax: 355–7284. Under the direction of the Scandinavian Hotel Management Co., the hotel has been completely renovated and several new restaurants offering various cuisines—Indian,

Chinese, Italian, and Middle Eastern—and health club and meeting facilities have been added. The arabesque decor has been retained. The lobby and most rooms have views overlooking the Nile.

Samuel Shepheard, an Englishman who came to Cairo in 1841, opened the New British Hotel, later named Shepheard British Hotel. It catered to travelers en route to and from the Far East, and it thrived. Eventually the hotel was moved to the palace of Alfi Bey in Ezbekieh Gardens, which at one time had been used by Napoleon's commander-in-chief.

In 1861 ownership passed to a Dr. Zach, who restored and enlarged the building to accommodate the increasing number of tourists who came to Egypt following the opening of the Suez Canal. Its guest register began to read like an international *Who's Who,* and included Queen Mary of Rumania, King Leopold of Belgium, King Alphonso of Spain, and Winston Churchill. Its reputation was made.

Indeed, few hotels in the world have become so much a part of the history of their times that their destruction could symbolize the end of an era. When Shepheard's was burned to the ground during the riots of 1952, it signaled the beginning of the Egyptian revolution and the end of colonialism. The new Shepheard, built in 1956, tried to recapture some of the grandeur of the old one.

Sonesta. 4 El Tayaran St., Nasr City (en route airport/city), 209 rooms. Price: $80 swb; $98 dwb. Phone: 262–8111 or in United States, 800–343–7170. An attractive, small hotel on a quiet street, convenient to the airport. Rooms are nicely decorated, air-conditioned, and have minibars, TV/in-house movies, and 24-hour Reuters news. Facilities include several restaurants, coffee shop, tearoom, beauty salon, bar, disco, pool, sauna, tennis, business service center, and meeting rooms. The hotel offers business travelers a special airport "Meet and Assist" service, including free transfers by the hotel's air-conditioned limousine, and free sightseeing tours and daily transport to Cairo city center. Sonesta also operates a Nile cruise ship and is building a hotel at Hurghada on the Red Sea.

First Class Superior (four star)

Green Pyramids. Helmiat Alahram St., 78 rooms. Price: $55 swb; $68 dwb. Phone: 856–778. A hotel situated in the house and gardens of a former Egyptian actor, Yousif Wahbi, on a quiet street off the Pyramids Road in Giza. Several buildings housing guest rooms, restaurant/bar, and the pool have been added around the house. All rooms have minibars, TV, direct-dial phone and overlook the gardens. A fire in 1988 destroyed the restaurant and popular disco; these are being replaced by a new building which is intended to expand the hotel's capacity and facilities and upgrade its rating, and hence, its prices.

Manial Palace/Club Med. El Manial St., Roda Island, 183 rooms. Phone: 363–1710; Fax: 363–9364. Price and reservations on request from Club Mediterranee, U.S. 800–528–3100; London 01–409–06–44. The palace was the former residence of Muhammad Ali, an uncle of King Farouk and an enthusiastic collector of Oriental art. After the revolution of 1952 the palace was turned into a museum; later bungalows were added in the gardens to make it into a hotel. The palace is worth a visit even if you are not a hotel guest. It is set in beautiful gardens and has an outstanding collection of Oriental art.

Currently the hotel, which has a separate entrance, is being used exclusively by Club Mediterranee and must be booked through them. When the Club is not fully booked, it will accept individual guests upon request. Also, outside visitors are welcome to lunch, use the swimming facilities, or dine and see the show. Reservations a must. Phone: 846014.

Novotel Cairo Airport. Cairo Airport Rd., 215 rooms. Price: $55 swb; $69 dwb. Phone: 661–330; Fax: 291–4794. Located next to the airport; has a restaurant and coffee shop, pool, tennis, shops, 24-hour room service, and guest rooms with air-conditioning and video. Free shuttle bus to the airport.

President. 22 Taha Hussein St., Zemalek, 120 rooms. Price: $35–$41 swb; $46–$53 dwb, including breakfast, service, and taxes. Phone: 341–6751; Fax: 341–1752. Located on the first and top four floors of an apartment building in Zamalek, a fashionable Cairo residential district on the west bank of the Nile. Rooms are large and nicely appointed; most have an unusually large balcony overlooking the city. The hotel has a good rooftop restaurant with nice view, bar, and 24-hour room service. For newcomers the hotel might be hard to find, although large signs are posted along the way. It has become very popular with businessmen, as it is clean, well run and convenient, with telex and direct-dial for international calls. The hotel pub, *The Cairo Cellar*, serves food and drinks in a lively atmosphere.

Pullman Maadi Towers. Corniche El Nil, Maadi. 221 rooms. Price: $65 swb; $105 dwb. Phone: 350–6093. On the Nile just before Maadi, rooms have river views and look west toward the Pyramids of Giza and Sakkara. All rooms have a balcony, direct-dial phone, minibar, and TV. Facilities include pool, health club, business center, shopping arcade, bars, restaurants, disco, and 24-hour room service.

Medium (four-star)

Note: Many of the four- and three-star hotels in Cairo are really tourist-class hotels. The old ones are often very old, and have as their main asset convenient, in-town location and price. We have selected the best among them. Most of the new ones are in the new residential areas of Dokki and Mohandaseen, which makes them inconvenient without a car, but they are modern, and, hopefully, clean.

Atlas Zamalek. 20 Gameet el Dowal el Arabia, Mohandeseen, 74 rooms. Price: $49 swb; $61 dwb. Phone: 346–4175; Fax: 347–6958. Situated in a residential section, the hotel has two restaurants, swimming pool, roof garden, snack bar, coffee shop, disco, meeting rooms, sauna, and shops. Rooms are large and have air-conditioning, direct-dial phone, color TV; 24-hour room service. All rooms have minibars and small sitting area; some have terraces. Same owners as Osiris Travel, which has its own fleet of motorcoaches and minibuses.

Baron. Off Oruba St. (near Baron Empain Palace), Heliopolis. 126 rooms. Price: $63 swb; $79 dwb. Phone: 291–5757; Fax: 290–7077. Metropole hotel with 24-hour coffee shop, bar, disco, and business center. All rooms have air-conditioning, minibar, color TV, and direct-dial phone.

Cleopatra Palace. 2 Sharia Bustan, Tahrir Square, 84 rooms. Price: $36 swb; $45 dwb with breakfast. Phone: 759–900; Fax: 346–6785. A modern hotel with simply furnished, air-conditioned rooms. The hotel has a Korean restaurant and bar. The hotel is centrally located on a main square of the city, which makes it very convenient but noisy.

Nile Wena. 12 Sharia Ahmed Ragheb, Garden City, 232 rooms. Price: $43 swb; $55 dwb, including breakfast and service. Phone 354–2800; Fax: 354–2639. Conveniently located in Garden City on the Nile, near the Meridien and the British Embassy and within walking distance of the American Embassy; air-conditioned bar and restaurant; disco. The hotel was acquired in 1989 by the Shine group of hotels, an Egyptian company with Saudi investors, and has completed the first phase of a two-part renovation, installing totally new—and very nice—full bathrooms. Rooms on the Nile side have balconies with fabulous views, and at their current price they are about the best value in the city. The British hotel-management group, WENA, also has the newly renovated LUXOR WENA.

Flamenco. 21 El Gezira El Wasta St., Abu El Feda, Zamalek. Price: $44–$56 swb; $56–$70 dwb. Phone: 340–0815; Fax: 340–0819. Located in Zamalek, this new hotel near the Nile has a strong Spanish influence, including a Spanish specialty restaurant. There is a bar, video club, business center, and very friendly staff. Superior rooms have Nile views.

Maadi. At entrance to the suburb of Maadi. Price: $52 swb; $65 dwb. Phone: 350–5050. Popular with visitors whose business or friends take them to Maadi (it's the main residential area for Americans). Coffee shop, restaurant, small rooftop pool, video, and telex.

Salma. 12 Mohamed Kamel Morsi St., Mohandesseen, 54 rooms. Price: $33 swb; $42 dwb including breakfast, service, and taxes. Phone: 700901, Fax: 701–482. Very nice though small hotel. Located on a quiet street in pleasant neighborhood; rooms are small but nicely furnished and have air-conditioning, TV, phone, radio. Its bar has become a favorite neighborhood meeting spot.

Tourist Class (three-star)

Concorde. 146 Tahrir St., Dokki, 72 rooms. Price: $32 swb; $40 dwb with breakfast, service, and taxes. Phone: 717261; Fax: 717–033.. (This hotel is located within walking distance of Cairo Sheraton.) A small, modern and very attractive hotel that occupies the first and top six floors of a 12-story office/apartment building. It belongs to the same owners as the President Hotel and caters to business travelers and a European clientele. Rooms are nicely furnished and have air-conditioning, TV; there is a restaurant and bar.

Cosmopolitan. 1 Ibn Taalab St. (off Sharia Kasr el Nil), 90 rooms, all with bath. Price: $31 swb; $40 dwb including breakfast, service, and taxes; lower summer rates available. Phone: 393–3531. The hotel is located amid downtown office buildings, one block off the major shopping street. Rooms are modest. It has a bar and a restaurant. This is an old renovated hotel, but it's good value for the money.

Raja Hotel. 34 Mohi el Din Abul Ezz St., Dokki, 83 rooms. Price: $34 swb; $43 dwb w/breakfast. Phone: 360–4297; Fax: 349–3573. All rooms are double with two beds; air-conditioning, refrigerator, TV. Restaurant, bar, coffee shop, and nightclub; 24-hour room service.

Rehab. 4 Sharia Fawakeh, Mohandaseen/Dokki, 74 rooms. Price: $33 swb; $42 dwb, including breakfast, taxes, and service. Phone: 703112. Hotel has a 24-hour coffee shop, bar, 24-hour room service; air-conditioning, TV, and minibar are extras on room charge totaling L.E. 3.75. Hotel is located in residential district and is a little hard to find. Rooms have large bathrooms, clean linens; caters to European groups. *Marhaba Restaurant,* open for lunch and dinner, is part of the hotel.

Victoria Hotel. 66 Gomhouria St., 105 rooms. Price: $24 swb; $35 dwb with breakfast. Phone: 918038. An old colonial-style hotel, it was once the grand dame of Cairo and was patronized by the famous writers and aristocrats of its time. Room 418, a spacious, comfortable room with its original furnishings, was the favorite of Somerset Maugham and George Bernard Shaw. The hotel offers central Cairo location within walking distance of Ramses Station and the Metro. Rooms are large, comfortable, air-conditioned, and clean. All rooms have recently been renovated; phones, and modern private baths, most with bathtubs. It is all under the watchful eye of general manager Arthur Smith, a transplanted Australian who rattles off Arabic with the speed of a native. The hotel, patronized mainly by Europeans, belongs to the owner of Spring Tours, one of the country's largest tour companies that specializes in German and European groups and manages *Arabia* and *Giftun Tourist Villages* in Hurghada.

Economy and Pension (two-star)

Garden City House. 23 Kamel ed-Din Salah St., 38 rooms. Price: $14.70 swb and $23 dwb with half board. Room without private bath is slightly cheaper. Phone: 354–4126. An old but pleasant pension, centrally located only two blocks from the American and British embassies, it is a longtime favorite of professors, researchers, and students.

New Horus House. 21 Sharia Ismail Mohamed, Zamalek, 34 rooms. Price: $28 swb; $36 dwb with breakfast, and service. Phone: 340–3977; Fax: 340–3182. Small pension in the heart of Zamalek. Pleasant, friendly and comes highly recommended. (Not to be confused with a hotel in town named Horris.) Restaurant, bar, air-conditioning, phones, minibar, and TV in rooms; 24-hour room service. Same owners as President and Concorde hotels.

Pension Roma. 169 Mohamed Farid St., 34 rooms. Price: $5 single; $10 double; $13 double and $15.50 triple with shower, including breakfast, service, and taxes. Phone: 391–1088. Few private baths, but good value in downtown location for those who can settle for basics. Receives accolades from its young, budget-conscious guests.

Tulip. 3 Midan Talaat Harb, 20 rooms. Price: $8–$11.50 swb, $9–$14.50 dwb with breakfast. Phone: 392–2704. Good downtown location, recommended for the budget traveler. Some rooms with bath. All with telephone.

STUDENT FACILITIES

The *Youth Hostel Association,* 7 Sharia Doctor Abdel Hamid Said, Marrouf, Cairo, (tel: 758–099), can assist students in arranging accommodations in youth hostels and a program for visiting Egypt. The association's *Youth Travel Bureau* organizes excursions around Egypt to enable students to travel at low cost to most of the historic places and to modern projects as well. The bureau sometimes organizes excursions to remote places that would be difficult for individuals to visit on their own. The association has 15 hostels, open year-round, in historic and tourist towns. There is no age limit; men and women must sleep in separate dormitories. A booklet listing all the hostels, phone numbers, distance from Cairo, and other information is available from the association.

Hostels charge approximately $1 to $2, depending on location, per night per bed, second sheet, hot bath, and kitchen facilities. All bookings must be made directly with the hostels by letter stating name, address, and dates of arrival and departure. Or ask the association for assistance.

The *Cairo Youth Hostel*, Sharia Abdel Aziz al Saud, El Manial, is located at the foot of the Nile bridge leading to the University of Cairo.

OUTSIDE OF CAIRO

Fayoum. *Auberge du Lac,* on Lake Karoun in the Fayoum Oasis, 62 miles southwest of Cairo, 52 rooms. Price: $44 swb; $58 dwb. Phone: Cairo, 351–5717; Fayoum, 084–700–002. Initially built as a rest house and hunting lodge for the king, this establishment was turned into a hotel after the revolution but has been allowed to deteriorate. It has been completely renovated. The hotel, the first modern one in the Fayoum region, has a swimming pool and a restaurant. *Gabal Zeina,* a rustic restaurant overlooking Lake Qarun about one mile from the auberge, specializes in fresh fish from the lake—and it's delicious!

Pavilion de Chasse, 33 beds. Price: $17 swb; $20 dwb. The tourist-class hotel, located at the far end of Lake Karoun, specializes in handling hunters and has equipment and large lockers where birds are cleaned and stored.

Minya. *PLM Azur Hotel Etap Nefertiti.* On the west bank of the Nile. 96 air-conditioned rooms. Price: $60 swb; $75 dwb. Phone: 326–282. Fax: 002–086–326–769. The town's only first-class hotel has a convenient location for visiting Tel el-Amarna and Beni Hassan. The hotel has two restaurants, a coffee shop, shopping arcade, small swimming pool, and tennis court. The hotel, set in a garden, is on a hill overlooking the Nile.

For a less expensive hotel with only basic facilities, there is the *Ibn el Khassib,* 5 Ragheb St. Phone: 224–535. The hotel is adequate for a short stay. *Lotus,* 1 Port Said St. Phone: 324–576. This is a less desirable alternative, but it has a rooftop restaurant that gets good marks from recent visitors. Ask to see your room before booking, and look at several before you decide.

BUSINESS SERVICES. *American Chamber of Commerce in Egypt,* Cairo Marriott Hotel, Suite 1541. Phone: 340–8888. Established in 1982 to promote and facilitate business between American and Egyptian companies. The 400-member organization provides a wide variety of support and communications facilities, seminars, and networking. Monthly luncheon meetings at Cairo Marriott, are open to visitors. Its directory of members is a valuable reference book that can be purchased for L.E. 30.

International Business Associates. 1079 Corniche el Nil, Garden City. Tel. 350–1473; 355–0427. A comprehensive office service in Egypt ranging from instant, temporary office space with messenger, courier, telex, phone, and typing. Federal Express's managers and representatives also handle training and conferences for Egypt and have branches in *Heliopolis,* Maadi, and Mohandiseen. The company's American owner, William Harrison, is founder of *Cairo Today.*

Air Sinai, Nile Hilton Arcade. Tel. 760948. *Austrian Airlines,* Nile Hilton Hotel. Tel. 742–755.

British Airways, 1 Abdel Salam Aref St. Tel. 772–713 office.

P.B.S. (Professional Business Services) Osiris Building, Suite 32, Latin America Street (near Am. Embassy). Tel. 355–1913. Branch in Sonesta Hotel. Contact: Ann Wolfe. Full-service business support firm that rents office space with translation, telex, and international telephone facilities. Also in-house computer, messenger service, and conference management.

Ramses Hilton has a full-scale Business Service Center with telex, copy machine, and secretarial services— including IBM word processing, translation, courier, office rental, and desk space to use. It is conveniently located in the lobby corridor and accessible to outsiders as well as hotel guests. Similar business service centers are available at the *Nile Hilton, Cairo Marriott, Semiramis Inter-Continental, Baron, Sonesta,* and most other five-star hotels.

Apartment and Office Space. *American Egyptian Service Agency,* 8 Hassan Fahim St., Heliopolis. Tel. 291–8146. English-speaking owner has furnished houses, apartments, and commercial properties for rent. Wide experience with major U.S. corporations.

Arabian-American Real Estate Co., 19 Road 151 Maadi. Phone: 350–3488. Telex 20628 MAHUS UN. Full-service real estate company that can handle all negotiations with owners, write contracts, etc., for offices and apartments to accommodate individuals or an entire company in Cairo and Alexandria. Fees negotiated; references available; staff speaks six languages.

Conserv Co., 17A Mohamed Mazhar St., Zamalek. Phone: 340–1811. Wide listing of Cairo apartments and offices. Also handles refurbishing of property.

Arabic Language Courses. *Berlitz,* 165 Moh.Bey Farid St., phone: 915096; I.L.I. *(International Language Institute) Arabic Language Center,* Mahmoud Azmi St., Sahafeyeen, phone: 346–3087 and I.L.I., Mohamed Bayoumi St. (off Merghany), Heliopolis, phone: 666704. *Egyptian Center for International Cultural Cooperation,* 11 Shagaret El Dor, Zamalek, phone: 381–5419; and *American University in Cairo,* phone: 354–2969, main campus; and 346–7260, Mohandeseen Continuing Education Branch.

Photocopying. Several downtown photo and camera stores have photocopying service at 15–30 pts. per page.

USEFUL ADDRESSES. Emergency Numbers. *Ambulance:* Emergency calls 770123 or 123; Private service, Chabrawichi Hospital 701465. *Hospitals:* El Salaam, Corniche, Maadi. Phone: 363–8050. New, ultramodern, highly regarded. Misr el Dawli, Fini Square, Dokki. Phone: 716555; 713345. *Police:* Emergency, tel. 757–987; *Radio and International Calls:* tel. 777120.

Travel Agencies. *American Express,* 15 Kasr el Nil St.; *Thomas Cook & Son,* 17 Mahmoud Basyouni St. *Misr Travel,* 1 Talaat Harb, is the autonomous, government-owned agency and the largest one with offices throughout Cairo and the country.

Airlines. *Air Canada,* 26, Mohamed Bassoumi St. Tel. 758–939. *Air France,* 2 Talaat Harb Sq. Tel. 743300, 668903 office; 661028 airport. *Air India,* 1 Talaat Harb St. Tel. 742592 office; 966756 airport.

EgyptAir, 6 Adly St., 12 Kasr el Nil St.; 9 Talaat Harb St. Tel. 920999 office, 747–4444 reservations; 244–5982 airport. *El Al,* 5 Maqrezy St., Zamalek. Tel. 341–1620.

Japan Airways, Nile Hilton Hotel. Tel. 740809, office; 660843 airport. *KLM,* 11 Kasr El Nil St. Tel. 740999 office; 662226 airport. *Kuwait Airways,* 4 Talaat Harb St. Tel. 759874 office; 666500 airport. *Lufthansa,* 9 Talaat Harb St. Tel. 393–0343 office; 666975 airport.

Olympic Airways, 23 Kasr el Nil St. Tel. 751277 office; 664503 airport. *Pan American* (Emeco Travel), 2 Talaat Harb St. Tel. 747302 office. *Royal Air Maroc,* 9 Talaat Harb St. Tel. 740378 office. *Royal Jordanian,* 6 Kasr el Nil St. Tel. 750905 office; 671741 airport.

Sabena, 2 Mariette St., Tahrir Square. Tel. 777125 office; 669144 airport. *Singapore Airlines,* Nile Hilton Arcade. Tel. 762702 office; 291–5144 airport. *Swissair,* 22 Kasr el Nil St. Tel. 393–7955 office; 669537 airport.

Thai International (Bon Voyage Travel), 16 Adly St. Tel. 390–5090. *Transmed,* 2 Abdel Aziz Rashid St., Dokki; tel. 716–378 office; 291–32131 airport. *Trans World Airlines,* 1 Kasr el Nil St. Tel. 749900 office; 344–1050 airport.

United Airlines, (Bon Voyage Travel), 16 Adly St. Tel. 390–5090. *ZAS Airline of Egypt,* Novotel Hotel. Tel. 290–7836.

Shipping Agencies. *Adriatica* (De Castro), 12 Talaat Harb. Tel. 743144. *Cairo Shipping Agency,* 7 Abdel Khalek Sarwat. Tel. 745755. *Egyptian Navigation Co.,* 20 Talaat Harb. Tel: 759166; 26 Sherif, Immobila Bldg., Tel: 758278; 745598. *Misr Edco Shipping Co.* (Mena Tours) 14 Talaat Harb St. Tel: 776951. *North African Shipping Co.,* 171, Mohamed Farid Street. Tel. 391–4682.

Embassies. *Australian,* Cairo Plaza South, Corniche El Nil, Bulaq. Tel: 777900. *British,* Latin America St., Garden City. Tel. 354–0850. *Canadian,* 6 Mohamed Fahmy el Sayed St., Garden City, Tel. 354–3110. *United States,* 5 Latin America St., Garden City. Tel. 355–7371.

Banks. *American Express,* 15 Kasr el Nil; branches: airport, Cairo Sheraton, Marriott, Meridian, Nile Hilton, Ramses Hilton. *American Express Int'l Banking Corp.,* Mohandeseen. *Bank of America,* 106 Kasr el Aini, Garden City. *Bank Misr,* 45, Kasr el Nil. *Cairo Barclays Int'l Bank SAE,* 1 Latin America St., Garden City. *Central Bank of Egypt,* 31, Kasr el Nil. *Citibank,* 4, Ahmed Pasha St., Garden City. *Commercial International Bank,* 22/23 Giza St. (in front of zoo), Giza. *Lloyds Bank Int'l,* 48–50, Abdel Khalek Sarwat.

RADIO AND TELEVISION. Egyptian broadcasting is government controlled. Radio Cairo has regular programs of classical and popular Western music, in the morning and late evening, with news broadcasts daily in English. Voice of America and BBC are received in Cairo; reception is best in the early morning or late evening.

Cairo and Alexandria have three television channels. Most programs are in Arabic. They usually operate five hours a day and telecast in color. Some American serials are shown with Arabic subtitles. A new satellite ground station permits live local coverage of significant world events. There are newscasts daily in English and French.

NEWSPAPERS. Cairo has one English daily, *The Egyptian Gazette. The International Herald Tribune, USA Today,* and British papers as well as English-language publications from the Gulf States may be purchased at newsstands. A monthly magazine in English, *Cairo Today,* can be found at newsstands for L.E. 5.

BABY-SITTERS. The old English term "nanny" was imported to Egypt by the British and is still used. Inquire at your hotel—otherwise you will need to rely on friends to locate a nanny. There is no established baby-sitting service in Cairo, but the Maadi Women's Club telephone book lists names with phone numbers. Deluxe hotels can also provide this service.

The CSA (Community Services Association) in Maadi (350–5284) and the CLO (Community Liasion Office of the U.S. Embassy) can supply lists of students who baby-sit.

BARBERSHOPS AND BEAUTY SALONS. What was once the best bargain in Egypt has vanished with inflation, and in places that cater to tourists, such as deluxe hotels, prices are comparable to those in the United States An unfortunate practice that has developed at hotels during the past few years is that of charging foreigners double or more than Egyptians are charged.

A man's haircut is L.E. 15 but can be as little as L.E. 7 in neighborhood shops, plus tips to all who attend you. Most barbershops close on Mondays.

There are many good beauty shops. At salons in deluxe hotels, a wash and set is L.E. 35; cut, L.E. 25; manicure, L.E. 10; and pedicure, L.E. 15. But a wash and blow-dry is only L.E. 14 in neighborhood shops.

Most shops open from 9 AM to 7 PM and do not schedule appointments. Hairdressers close on Mondays, except those in hotels, but they are open on Fridays and Sundays.

You should tip the boy or girl who washes your hair and the one who helps the hairdresser (L.E. 1 is appropriate). A tip of a similar amount should be given to the manicurist and pedicurist.

Gharib, 15 Sharia Kasr el Nil, near American Express. Phone: 750950. Open daily including Sunday and Friday; closed Monday. Gharib, who has won the International Hairdressers' Competition in Paris several years in a row, gives the best haircut in town. Mrs. Sadat must think so, too, as he has been her hairdresser for more than 20 years. There's a new branch at Le Meridien Heliopolis Hotel. L.E. 35 wash and blow-dry; L.E. 60 with cut; L.E. 25 for cut only.

Sam and Hamdy, 158 St., off 105 St., Maadi. Tel. 350–4236. Great for color. L.E. 22 cut and blow-dry; L.E. 60 for coloring with cut and blow-dry; L.E. 75 for highlights.

Sayed Gouda, 9 Malek el-Afdal (near Villa Im Kalsum), Zamalek. Phone: 340–2104, 340–3878. One of the fastest hairdressers to be found anywhere. Gouda gives an excellent cut, but his apprentices do not.

Sheri Nile, Ramses Hilton and other locations around the city. Phone: 777–113. This is a full-fledged health-and-beauty spa for men and women. Offers a complete facial and body treatment from head to toe at very reasonable prices.

LAUNDRIES AND DRY CLEANERS. Cairo has many laundry and dry-cleaning plants that are adequate for normal needs, but few cope well with difficult fabrics. You are best off with 100% cotton clothes, which are handled beautifully and inexpensively. All hotels usually have speedy service at reasonable prices. Average rates: shirt, L.E. 6; suit washed and pressed, L.E. 9. Dry cleaning is more expensive: A suit cleaned and pressed is about L.E. 12.

Some residents hire a washerwoman and ironing man to come to their homes weekly; others make an agreement with a neighborhood shop to pay a flat rate per month. The price depends on the amount of work, but it is very little compared with prices for similar service in the States.

Egypt has much longer periods of hot weather than do most parts of the States or Europe. And that ever-present sand dust is hard on clothes. Summer clothing is used longer and washed more often. Good-quality, sturdy fabrics for clothing and linens are recommended. Bed and table linens of fine Egyptian cotton are readily available in Cairo at reasonable prices.

PHARMACIES. Many pharmacies are located in or near leading hotels and in neighborhood districts. Prices are set by the government. Many pharmaceuticals are medicines produced by leading American and European companies, bottled and packaged in Egypt. Most pharmaceuticals are available, but local packaging and labeling may make them difficult for a newcomer to recognize. If you have special health problems, bring your required medicines and prescriptions with you.

Pharmacies usually stay open until 10 PM. Among those centrally located with extensive stock are: *Dr. El Hakim,* across from American Embassy; *Zarif,* 1 Talaat Harb Sq.; *Kalisker Pharmacy,* 44 Talaat Harb St. Those open 24 hours include: *Isaaf,* 26th July St. and *Seif and El Ezaby,* Ahmed Tayseer St., Heliopolis.

REPAIRS. At many hotels, shoes left outside the hotel room at night will be shined by morning. For special repairs, consult your hall porter or the concierge.

Watch repair: Jewelers in leading hotels and downtown shopping areas as well as in the Mouski either have repair service or will know where to have such work done quickly and at reasonable prices.

THE NATIONAL CIRCUS. Initiated by the Egyptian Ministry of Culture in 1960 and trained by Soviet experts, the circus was inaugurated in 1966. Since then, the Big Top in Agouza, a Nile-side district of Cairo across the bridge from Zamalek, has been popular with old and young, residents and tourists. It has a seating capacity of 2,500, and its team of 200 performs nightly a classical repertoire of circus entertainment plus showstoppers by Arabian thoroughbred horses that prance and display their acrobatic skills to the beat of Arabic music.

On days of folkloric festivals or national holidays, the circus mounts shows in the different provinces of Egypt, and in July and August it takes up headquarters in Alexandria.

SPORTS. Egypt's climate is ideal for playing tennis, badminton, golf and squash, or for sailing, fishing, horseback riding, and waterskiing the year round. Most sports activities center at clubs in the city. Deluxe hotels have swimming pools, some have tennis courts, and often there is a club attached to the hotel that allows Cairo residents to use the hotel's facilities.

CAMPING. The Mediterranean coast offers camping on white-sand beaches near Alexandria, El Alamein, El Arish, and Mersa Matruh. Camping trips to the Red Sea are great fun if you have the necessary equipment and do not mind roughing it. Campers must take all provisions, including drinking water. The area is excellent for fishing and skin diving. The sea is crystal clear and the beaches are good.

The best camping in Eygpt is in the Sinai Peninsula. (See section *South Sinai* for details.)

FISHING. On the Mediterranean and the Red Sea. The Red Sea is one of the most famous bodies of water in the world for its variety of fish. The Sheraton Hotel at Hurghada has become the nucleus of the Red Sea area's development and a center for fishing, scuba diving, and snorkeling. It is also possible to rent a fishing boat in Suez.

FLYING AND GLIDING. Gliding facilities are available at the Embaba Airfield on Thursday and Friday. On other days private planes have the right of way, with flying lessons sometimes available. For information, call 805655.

GOLF. Two nine-hole golf courses—at the Gezira Sporting Club and at the Mena House Oberoi Hotel (with the Pyramids as a backdrop)—are open all year. The Mena House Oberoi's annual membership for golf, tennis, and pool is L.E. 1,100 per couple, plus an initial entrance fee of L.E. 800. The membership is L.E. 800 without golf plus L.E. 600 for entrance. Greens fees are L.E. 6 per person. Guests of members pay L.E. 45.

Equipment and instruction are available at both courses. Fees are part of the club's dues for membership and use of facilities, which are detailed below under *Sporting Clubs*.

In Alexandria, there is an 18-hole course at the Alexandria Sporting Club.

HORSEBACK RIDING. Good horses—with or without guides—can be hired from the stables near the Pyramids. Fee: approximately L.E. 5 per hour. A moonlit ride across the desert is great sport in Egypt, but it is not suggested for a novice. Desert riding is difficult and the terrain deceiving. Arabian horses are spirited, and in the desert nothing holds them back but the rider. The most comfortable gait for an Arabian horse is a canter or gallop. Only English saddles are used. Jodhpurs and English riding boots can be made locally at very reasonable prices.

Overnight or longer camping trips in the desert can be arranged through local stables. The cost depends upon the degree of luxury desired, but it is generally moderate. The best-known is *M.G. Stables,* located near the village at the foot of the Sphinx.

The five-hour ride from Giza across the desert to Sakkara and back is a popular excursion of Cairo residents and experienced riders. It would be very tiring for a beginner and is not recommended for an inexperienced rider. Reservations can be made directly with the stables.

The Ferrosia Riding Club is located at the south edge of the Gezira Sporting Club. Tel. 805690. The club boards private horses and horses for instruction. Visitors may obtain a three-month membership. There is another riding club in Heliopolis; stables are next to El Shams Club and the Hyatt El Salam Hotel.

HORSE RACING. Saturday and Sunday from mid-October to mid-May. Horse racing is available on alternating weekends at the tracks at the Gezira Sporting Club in Zamalek and the Heliopolis Horse-racing Course, near El Salam Hyatt. The racing form appears in the Saturday edition of the *Egyptian Mail* newspaper. Races begin at about 1:30 PM Pari-mutuel betting.

Many people enjoy going to the races for the pleasure of watching the beautiful Arabian horses. In Egypt, famous for its breeding of pure Arabian stock, racing is a sport. Purses are small.

The Egyptian Agricultural Society owns a famous stud, Al Zahraa, and breeds pure Arabian horses at Ein Shams. Visitors are welcome. For an appointment, contact Dr. Khalil Soliman or Ibrahim Zaghloul.

HUNTING AND SHOOTING. Hunting is excellent in Egypt, but there are few wild or nonprivate hunting areas. The Shooting Club at Dokki offers the best introduction, as it owns and maintains duck, snipe, and pigeon camps in Cairo and Delta areas; shooting ranges and a clubhouse. There are no set bag limits; licenses for guns and hunting are required. Most hunters use 12-gauge guns. Birds are plentiful. Fayoum is a popular hunting area where, in the past year, duck hunting has become more convenient due to the opening of the area's first deluxe hotel and the availability of hunting tours.

Duck season begins toward the end of November and lasts through January. It is supervised by the Shooting Club of Egypt. The quail and wild dove season comes twice a year: April and May in the Delta and Lower Egypt, late August and September along the Mediterranean coast.

Information is available from the Egyptian Shooting Federation, 37 Abdel Khalik Sarwat Street, Cairo; and from South Sinai Travel, Cairo.

BOATING. *Rowing:* The Egyptian Rowing Club is located on a boat moored near the Sheraton Hotel. Rowing is a popular sport in Egypt, and a visit by a U.S. team such as Harvard University is an annual event.

Sailing: You may enjoy sailing in Cairo, on the Nile the year round, and in Alexandria on the Mediterranean in all months except January and February, when the sea is rough. Alexandria, Cairo, and Maadi yacht clubs have their own boats. In Cairo, the 14-foot. Lightning class is excellent for Nile sailing.

In Alexandria, the favored classes are the Dinghy and the Fairey (an English class boat of approximately 25 feet with built-in center board). Club membership is open to foreign residents and visitors are welcome. Members and guests must pass a sailing test in order to man a boat.

Sailing on the Nile in a felucca is a delightful experience that no visitor should miss. These boats with crew may be rented at the dock near the Meridien and Shepheard hotels and in Maadi. Be sure to bargain for the price. The cost for a small boat should be about L.E. 15 per hour. The best time to go is about an hour before sunset. An evening cruise in summer is also fun.

For longer trips, the Cairo Sheraton has cabin cruisers. Boats hold up to 16 passengers and cost L.E. 60 per hour. You can either ask the hotel to supply food and beverages or bring your own. A favorite Nile destination is the Barrage, 14 miles north of Cairo.

WATER SPORTS. *Scuba, skin diving, and snorkeling:* The Red Sea is famous for the variety and colors of its fish. Underwater photography here is among the best in the world. (See *The Suez Canal and the Red Sea* for details.) *Cairo Divers,* Tel. 349–5638, a Cairo-based club, offers members diving lessons and weekend excursions. The group meets on the first Monday of each month at the Semiramis Inter-Continental Hotel.

Swimming: In Cairo from April to November you can swim in a pool at one of the sporting clubs or deluxe hotels. Hurghada on the Red Sea, Sharm el Sheikh, and the east coast of Sinai are now year-round resorts. In summer, the beaches along the Mediterranean at Alexandria or Mersa Matruh are popular resorts for Egyptians as well as visitors, and they are crowded.

The strong sun and highly chlorinated water in the pools are extremely wearing on bathing suits. Bring several changes if you plan an extended visit.

WARNING: *Do not* swim in the Nile. Its waters are heavily polluted.

Waterskiing: It is possible to water-ski in Cairo, but since the Nile isn't the cleanest body of water in the world, the sport is more popular in Alexandria and other seaside resorts.

TENNIS. Mostly clay courts are used in Egypt, and there are many in Cairo. The Gezira Sporting Club has 20 courts; instruction is available. Regulation white is generally required for men and women on most courts. The Nile Hilton and Marriott hotels courts are the most centrally located; clinics and private lessons are available.

Tennis is one of Egypt's most popular competitive sports. Tournaments by local participants, as well as visiting international groups, are held often. The Annual Tennis Open is held in late fall or early March.

SPORTING CLUBS. Cairo has excellent sporting clubs, similar to our country clubs, that offer facilities for outdoor and indoor sport, all within a few minutes' drive from the city center. At some clubs tourists and other transient visitors may obtain temporary membership. If you want to use the facilities of a particular club, ask your hotel to inquire. By law, sporting clubs cannot serve alcoholic beverages.

Cairo Yacht Club. 3 Sharia el Nil St., Giza. Tel. 348–9415. The club has facilities for sailing and waterskiing, and holds regattas in which guests who qualify are welcome to participate. The Club has no rental facilities, but members may moor their boats here. Initial membership, L.E. 3,000. The club has introduced 3-, 6-, and 12-month memberships at lower rates for foreigners living in Cairo.

Gezira Sporting Club. Zamalek. Tel. 340–6000 or 340–6006. Established in 1882 and covering 67 acres, this club derives its name from the island in the Nile on which it is situated. Once the epitome of British colonial snobbery when Egyptians were not even allowed to enter, the club is now open to all. It has two swimming pools, a nine-hole golf course, 20 tennis courts, croquet lawns, volleyball, basketball and polo grounds, squash courts, boxing and judo rings, a riding school and horse racing on weekends throughout the winter season. Indoors there are bridge, billiards, and table tennis rooms in addition to lounges, salons, restaurants, and a bar. There is a children's playground, a gymnasium, sauna, and barbershop. Annual membership fees are U.S. $400 per couple; U.S. $30 per child under 16; U.S. $60 ages 16–21; and U.S. $375 for singles. A one-month, nonrenewable membership is U.S. $90 for a couple. Day entrance fee, except Friday and Sunday, is L.E. 5 and does not include use of the club's sport facilities other than golf, for which there is a greens fee of L.E. 20. The business office is open daily 9:30 AM–2 PM except on Thursday.

Heliopolis Sporting Club. 17 El Merghany St., Heliopolis. Tel. 291–4800. Business office hours 10 AM–2 PM; closed Tuesday. One of the largest and oldest clubs, situated in the lovely suburb of Heliopolis, where there are facilities for 25 different sports. They include 10 tennis courts, seven squash courts, three swimming pools, billiards, and croquet, basketball and volleyball, judo, and gymnastics. Day use at nominal cost. Quarterly fees for members.

Maadi Sporting Club/Yacht Club. 8 Sharia Damashk, Midan El Nadi, Maadi. Tel. 350–5504. Located a few miles south of Cairo in the residential suburb of Maadi, the club has a wide range of facilities for indoor and outdoor sports, including its own sailboats moored on the Nile less than a mile away at the Maadi Yacht Club. Facilities include swimming pool, sauna, barbershop, beauty salon, and dining facilities. There are tennis and squash courts and horses for riding.

El Shams. Heliopolis (next to the Hyatt El Salam Hotel and available for use by hotel guests). Tel. 287–5920. Facilities for tennis, swimming, basketball, volleyball, handball, squash, and martial arts are available. There is a restaurant.

National Sporting Club. Gezira Island, adjacent to the Gezira Club and Botanical Gardens. Tel. 802112. The club includes tennis courts, swimming pool, gymnasium, and playing fields for other sports.

Sakkara Palm Club. Near Sakkara Pyramid ticket office. Tel. 018–200–791. New, private sporting club, with 60-room, four-star hotel under construction. Facilities include large pool with swim-up bar, horseback riding, tennis, squash, and health club. Annual membership U.S. $500 per person; day use of pool, L.E. 15. Good restaurant.

Shooting Club. Dokki. Specializes in trap shooting but has tennis courts, swimming pool, children's playground, and restaurant. Membership available. Business office in Dokki. Tel. 704353.

Tewfikia Tennis Club. Medinet El Awkaf, Agouza. Tel. 801930. The club has eight tennis courts, two swimming pools, squash and basketball courts, table tennis, children's playground, restaurant, and a summer open-air cinema. The annual open tennis championship of Cairo is held here in January.

SOCIAL CLUBS. In addition to sporting clubs, several social clubs might be of interest to visitors.

Automobile Club. 10 Sharia Kasr el Nil. The club has no sporting facilities in Cairo, but its dining room serves some of the best food in town.

Members of this club can use the Automobile Club in Alexandria, which has a seaside location in a convenient area of the city.

Egyptian Center for Cultural Cooperation. 11 Shagaret el Dor St., Zamalek. Tel. 341–5419. Offers interesting cultural trips and language courses.

Rotary International. 3 Ali Labib Gabr, (Kasr el Nil and Talaat Harb). Tel. 741737. Rotary has 20 chapters in Egypt—7 in Cairo and environs alone. Cairo Rotary meets for lunch at 2 PM on Tues. at the Nile Hilton Hotel; the Giza Club at 2:30 PM on Wed. at the Sheraton Hotel; Cairo South, 8 PM, Sun. Yacht Club Maadi; Cairo West, 2 PM, Mon., Meridien Hotel; Cairo North, 2 PM Wed., Nile Hilton; Alexandria West, 8 PM, Sun., Club of Alexandria; Alexandria East, 8 PM, Sheraton Hotel.

The Women's Association. 3 Salah el Din St., Mohandeseen. Tel. 346–3521. Meets monthly at Cairo Marriott Hotel; open to all English-speaking women. The group sponsors trips in Egypt and abroad. Also holds charity bazaars.

SPECIAL-INTEREST CLUBS. Archaeological Club of the American Research Center. Organization conducts lectures and tours to important sites, sometimes including those still in the research stage. Yearly membership is U.S. $75. Tel. 355–3052 or 354–8239.

MUSEUMS AND ART GALLERIES. Cairo offers a multitude of antiquity museums reflecting the magnificence of Egypt's ancient heritage. The *Coptic Museum,* the *Egyptian Museum,* and the *Islamic Museum* are just a few that are well worth visiting. For more information and a more complete listing, see the beginning of this chapter.

Modern Egyptian art is an interesting fusion of the country's art history—pharaonic, Coptic, and Islamic. Of all the country's modern cultural activities, art is the most outstanding in quality, quantity, and originality. Although many of the outstanding artists have trained or been trained by those who studied in Europe, the works of Egyptian artists reflect the influence, faith, and inspiration of their native land. In general, Egyptian artists have been influenced by their native art heritage more than those of other Middle Eastern countries—a characteristic that may be particularly Egyptian.

For those interested in more specific information, *Contemporary Art in Egypt,* Ministry of Culture, 1964, covers the history of the development of Egyptian art with details on outstanding painters and beautiful colored plates of the best art works. More recent books, all published by the American University in Cairo Press, are *Modern Egyptian Art: The Emergence of a National Style* by Liliane Karnouk (1988); *Crafts of Egypt* by Denise Ammoun (revised and translated from French; 1991); and *Egyptian Carpets: A Practical Guide,* by Luanne Brown and Sidna Rachid (1985), which describes Egypt's carpet industry and lists carpet stores.

The Museum of Contemporary Art, 18 Sharia Ismail Abdul Fetouh, Mohandaseen, maintains a permanent collection. The new cultural complex on Gezirah Island in Cairo includes an exhibition hall for contemporary Egyptian art.

Exhibits of local artists are held throughout the year under the sponsorship of the Ministry of Culture and various cultural centers, such as the *Egyptian Centre for International Cultural Cooperation,* 11 Shagaret el

Dorr St., Zamalek; the *Goethe Institute; French Cultural Center; Italian Culture Centre* and at leading hotels, particularly the Meridien. Check the newspapers and *Cairo Today,* a monthly magazine, for events during your visit.

Cairo has blossomed recently with art galleries that exhibit the works of Egyptian as well as foreign artists. Additionally, local artists welcome guests into their studios. Some of the leading centrally located galleries are:

Akhnaton Gallery. 1 Mahad el Swissry St., Zamalek. Open 10 AM–1:30 PM and 5–8:30 PM Saturday–Thursday; closed Friday. Frequently changing exhibits in an old Nile-side villa. Sculpture displays in the garden. The gallery, whose focus is modern art, recently opened its fifth exhibit hall.

Arabesque. 4 Kasr el Nil St. The long passageway of this stylish restaurant regularly presents exhibits of local artists.

Atelier du Caire. 2 Karim el Dawla St. (near Hannaux Department Store, off Talaat Harb Sq.). Often introduces relatively unknown talent.

Among others are *El Salam Mahmoud Khalil Gallery,* Gezira St. and *Karmah Gallery.* 27 Aboul Feda St. in Zamalek; *Mashrabeya,* 8 Champollion St.; and *Dr. Ragab Gallery for Modern Egyptian Art,* 3 El Nil Ave. (near Cairo Sheraton Hotel); and three at the Gezira Exhibition Grounds—*El Mustadira Gallery,* Syndicate of Plastic Art, Mahmoud Mokhtar St.; *El Nil Gallery;* and *Seray El Nasr.*

Teachers of art and others who want to have greater knowledge of art activity in Egypt might visit *Beit Sennari* and *Wekalet el Ghouri,* which have workshops attached to them. (See *Cairo Sightseeing* for addresses and description.)

Other places to visit are *Musaferkhana* (near El Hussein Mosque in the Al Azhar area) and *Harraniya* village on Sakkara Road. The former is a historic building where several artists have studios. The caretaker will show visitors each studio and you may purchase paintings from him. Or you can try to phone in advance for an appointment with an artist.

The village of Harraniya is quite a different story. Forty years ago an architect, Ramses Wissa Wassif, and his art teacher wife put a theory into practice that has turned out to be one of the country's best artistic expressions.

Wassif believed that children, especially Egyptian village children, when unencumbered by the restraints, restrictions, or inhibitions of adults, could find their own innate artistic ability if given the atmosphere, encouragement, and freedom for self-expression. He tried first with one orphan child and then another and another and, to his delight, found that the results exceeded his expectations. He and his wife taught the children to weave (a village craft from ancient times in Egypt) and put them to work on hand-driven looms, allowing their imaginations to run free and giving them only a minimum amount of direction and advice.

Over the years the tapestries they created found an audience and attracted the attention of collectors and critics. With the profits from their sales, which Wassif shared with the weavers, the group expanded from a handful of people to a small village, where today the families grow their own vegetables from which they make natural dyes. They live in a village Wassif designed, based on the old village architecture.

Today many of the artists are veteran weavers who have been with the settlement from the beginning, and a new generation of children are working at their side. To understand how the value of their work has grown, a tapestry a meter square that might have sold for $50 two decades ago is now $500. A small tapestry by a young student apprentice might be under $50, and the price climbs to $4,000 for large wall hangings of several meters, depending on the artist, intricacy of the design, and the dyes. For the most part, the motifs are taken from daily life and picture the birds, animals, plants, and trees of the Egyptian countryside in beautiful colors and shadings and often with great whimsy, something that is very much a part of the native Egyptian character. Ramses Wissa Wassif died in 1975, but the work of the village is being continued by his wife, who lives there.

We regret to report that fame seems to have distorted the perspective in this village somewhat. Mrs. Wassif has demanded that we remove our information regarding prices, claiming that it was misleading and made the endeavor appear "too commercial" for a school and that each piece is priced according to its artistic value and quality. However, since the tapestries are expensive and there are now so many tapestries being sold elsewhere for lower prices, we believe it is important for readers to know what to expect and to understand the differences. In our judgment, this knowledge in no way detracts from the beauty or quality of the Harraniya tapestries and, in fact, helps newcomers to better evaluate their worth. A recent innovation at the school is the making of batik with beautiful free-flow designs and colors. They are available in small squares for pillow covers or larger pieces for wall hangings and other uses, and range in price from $15 up.

Visitors should be aware that others claim to be selling the Harraniya tapestries to the extent that some have set up shop near the Wassif village and labeled their tapestries "Harraniya," but the only other place in town where the tapestries and batiks can be purchased is at *Senouhi,* 54 Abdul Khalek Sarwat Street.

There is no question that the tapestries made by Harraniya are the best from an artistic point of view. However, we do not want to give the impression that they are the only ones. Weaving is an art of many villages in Egypt and several have weavers whose skill and imagination are on par with the many of those at Harraniya. *Assiut* and *Beni Suef* are two of the best-known areas. Tapestries from Assiut are available from *Mousky Chic,* a shop in the Nile Hilton and Cairo Marriott arcades. Owner Louis Fanous does not have these on display but will bring them out of storage for serious buyers. Those we saw on our most recent visit were wonderful. In the Khan al Khalil, there is a shop that specializes in tapestries from Beni Suef. In both cases the prices are half those of Harraniya.

Another place that is very much frequented by tour groups is the village of *Kerdassa,* near the Pyramids, on a back road two miles beyond Andrea's restaurant. Most of what is made here is junk and covers the range from kaftans to camel saddles. Good traditional designs have been badly distorted and cheapened, but there are some good craftsmen, particularly among the weavers, if you are willing to persevere and are not after museum quality. Tapestries are good buys at L.E. 15–30 per square meter, provided you understand the nature of the works and do not take them to be great works of art. The best buy of all is handwoven stoles for only L.E. 5. They are wonderful gifts to take home.

At the shops of *Abdel Hamid el Issa* and *Golden Bazaar,* you can watch and photograph workers at their looms. Weaving has been a tradition for these families for generations.

The Sakkara/Harraniya road is becoming something of a center for Egyptian artists. Mohie el-Din Hussein, one of the country's leading ceramic artists, lives near Harraniya village in a house designed by Wissa. Here he creates modern pieces inspired by Egyptian designs from Islamic, Coptic, and pharaonic history, carrying forward one of the country's ancient traditions. The artist uses clay from Aswan and mixes his own glazes, which often results in a luminescent, metallic finish. Pieces are on display and are available for purchase at his home; prices are moderate.

Farther along the road there is a house on the west, marked by two large ceramic scarabs, that belongs to Zakaria el Konani and his wife, Aida Abd al-Kerim, artists who work in glass and ceramics. El Konani, a chemical engineer by training, has created a brilliantly toned turquoise paste, known as *faience,* which has a glazed finish when fired and therefore does not need glazing. At high temperatures it turns to glass. From these materials, his wife, a professor of art at Helwan University, makes wonderful pieces of jewelry and objets d'art. The couple receive visitors in their country house on Saturday and Sunday, from 11 AM to 5 PM, and their works are on display and for sale at moderate prices. Cairo address: 21 A Amin Elradie St., Dokki, Apt. 104. Tel. 348–6438.

Aida Gallery, Km. 6, Sakkara Road, is the latest addition. Open daily, except Friday, 10:30 AM–2 PM; 5–8 PM. Here, in a setting that is both modern and ancient, Egypt's major artists are represented.

MUSIC. During the winter season concerts and ballets by the Cairo Symphony Orchestra, the National Ballet, and visiting European and other artists are held at various cultural centers throughout the city. The United States Information Service sponsors American artists and performers from time to time, as do other foreign cultural missions. The new opera house, replacing the one that was destroyed by fire, is the centerpiece of the new culture complex built on Gezira Island.

The *Cairo Symphony Orchestra, National Conservatory of Music, National Ballet, Dramatic Arts Institute, Folk Art Institute, and the Cinegraphic Institute* are located in a complex of buildings just off the Pyramids Road, known as the *City of Arts,* where students can study for a B.A. and M.A. in a specialized field. It is operated by the Ministry of Culture.

The most famous singer of this century in the Arab world was an Egyptian woman by the name of *Um Kulthum.* Although she is no longer living, during the day or evening you might hear her voice on the radio in a shop, a local coffee house, or an apartment building. The Egyptians love her and become ecstatic while listening to her singing. When Um Kulthum gave public performances, she could draw crowds numbering in the tens of thousands. When she died, the entire nation went into mourning.

In recent years, the best-known classical musician in the Arab world has been *Muhammad Abd-al-Wahab,* also an Egyptian. In addition to his singing and composing of classical Arabic music, Abd-al-Wahab has written a number of interesting pieces adapting Western forms to the five-tone minor scale of Eastern music.

It is important for a newcomer to Egypt to understand that cultural activity of a Western nature extends as far as Western influence has penetrated Egyptian society. In other words, those attending and participating in such activities are mainly Western-educated Egyptians from the middle and upper classes—these being the strata of Egyptian society on which Western culture has had an impact. The bulk of Egyptians spend their leisure time enjoying the fruits of their own cultural heritage. Unfortunately for the visitor, these usually require a knowledge of Arabic for understanding and appreciation.

The *National Ballet* was created during the 1960s. It and several folklore and television dance groups give frequent performances. The best-known dance troupe, the Reda Group, is seen often on television and cinema and frequently performs at the Um Kulthum Theatre in Agouza.

Opera House. With a huge grant from the Japanese, Cairo now sports a magnificent *Education and Culture Center,* located at the southern tip of Gezirah Island overlooking the Nile in the heart of the city. The star of the complex is the Opera House, a modern interpretation of Islamic design, with lavish use of Italian marble and Scandinavian wood, producing a light, airy ambience. There are three theaters of different sizes and Egypt's first public facility equipped with features that facilitate the movement of the disabled. Here internationally known groups and personalities are featured. Other areas of the complex include theaters, classrooms, and a superb art gallery and museum along with a music library.

A serious problem for the Opera House is tickets. For major attractions, there are almost no tickets available. We were told that the Minister of Culture regularly takes half the allotment, not for distribution to students and other Egyptians who cannot afford to attend, but to give to friends, diplomats, etc.—the people most able to pay. Most of the remainder go to sponsors of the particular event for their friends, leaving only a small portion to be sold. The local press has been filled with criticism of the practice, but so far it has fallen on deaf ears. Readers should know this in the event they have trouble obtaining tickets.

LITERATURE. The greatest vehicle for artistic expression throughout the Arab world has been the Arabic language, which is richest and most highly developed in poetry. Even classical Arabic music is poetry set to music—the music being incidental to the verse.

Egypt has produced many of the leading philosophers and political and social thinkers of the Arab world in this century. The most famous is *Taha Hussein,* who, blind from the age of six, writes with a sensitivity and depth equal to the best in world literature. Several of his works have been translated into English. The best known are *From an Egyptian Childhood* and *Stream of Days.* English translations of these and other popular literature are available in Cairo bookstores. The Nobel Prize for Literature in 1988 was won by Naquib Mahfouz, an Egyptian whose books depict Egyptian culture. Many have been translated into English and are available in major bookstores.

THEATERS. Cairo has been the center of theater and film in the Arab world, staging high-quality productions regularly throughout the year. These productions have included original Arabic plays, as well as translations of American and European ones. Unfortunately, the past few years have seen an exodus of talent to higher-paying jobs in the Gulf and Tunisia, where much of the film industry has shifted. People in the industry cite bureaucracy, wages, and artistic freedom as points of concern. Another factor contributing to Cairo's decline as a leader in the arts was Egypt's isolation from the other Arab countries following the Camp David accords, but the country's preeminent position appears to be coming back now that it has made peace with its Arab neighbors.

The following is a list of leading Cairo theaters. Presentations are usually in Arabic. Performances are advertised in the local daily newspapers. Shows usually start at 9:30 PM unless otherwise indicated. The Nile Hilton Hotel also has a dinner theater.

American University at Cairo. Eward Hall, Sharia el Sheikh Rihan and New Theatre, Sharia Mohamed Mahmoud, New Campus. Occasional performances by local and visiting foreign artists.

Cairo Film Palace. 4 Salamlek St., Garden City. This new facility, established by the Ministry of Culture, has three minitheaters that show Egyptian feature films and documentaries. The Palace's goal is to document the history of Egyptian film and compile a computer catalogue of the 1,500 films made here during its 60-year history. A library and filmmaking seminars are also offered. Schedules change monthly.

Cairo Puppet Theater. Ezbekia Garden. Performances daily, except Tuesday, at 6:30 PM, plus Friday and Sunday at noon. Entrance: 50 pts. Performances are in Arabic but can be followed by non-Arabic-speaking audiences and enjoyed by adults as well as children. Occasionally visiting puppet troupes perform.

Cairo University Theater. Cairo University, Giza. Occasional performances by local and foreign artists.

Um Kulthum Theater (formerly Balloon Theater). Sharia el Nil, Agouza. Performances in Arabic by local folklore groups nightly from October to March.

Sayed Darwish Concert Hall. Sharia Gamal el Din el Afghany, off the Pyramids Road. Alternate weekly performances are given on Thursdays by the Arabic Music Troupe and on Saturdays by the Cairo Symphony Orchestra, with occasional performances by visiting foreign troupes, as well as local ballet, music, or dance troupes.

Sphinx Theater. At the foot of the Sphinx. On special occasions, plays, ballets, and musical concerts and shows are performed during summer in this open-air theater under the sponsorship of the Ministry of Culture.

Wekalet el Ghouri. 3 Sharia el Sheikh Mohamed Abdu (Al Azhar area). A restored caravanserai, which has been made into a handicrafts and folkloric arts center, is sometimes used for visiting foreign troupes. The courtyard serves as an arena or concert hall.

Zaki Tolaimat Theater (formerly known as Pocket Theater). Midan el Ataba and Sharia 26 July. Avant-garde productions in Arabic and translations of Western writers are performed during the season from October to May. The theater is named for a famous Egyptian actor who was also a director and producer.

CLOSING DAYS AND HOURS. *Modern Districts:* 9 or 10 AM–1 PM; 4 or 4:30 to 7:30 or 8 PM summer hours; 9 or 10 AM to 5 or 6 PM winter hours. Most shops close Saturday evening and Sunday, some close Thursday afternoon and Friday.

The Mouski (Khan el Khalil): 9 AM–1 PM; 3–8 PM. Some shops do not close for lunch, but the owner will probably not be around from 1–3, and his helper won't be much help. Some shops close on Friday, some Saturday, others Sunday. During Ramadan, stores often close all afternoon and do not reopen or reopen only after sundown.

SHOPPING. Cairo's modern shopping districts have a wide selection of clothing, shoes, accessories, and furniture made in Egypt, but for tourists the biggest attraction remains the old bazaar known as the Mouski—one of the best in the world. This is where you will want to spend your time leisurely—watching the craftsmen, sipping coffee with the shopkeepers, and examining the array of handicrafts that are so enticing it will be difficult to resist a wild buying spree.

Bargaining. Bargaining is an accepted pattern in Egypt. No one pays the original asking price—at least not in the bazaars. Your skill at the practice will determine the price. Egyptian merchants expect customers to bargain and enjoy it. If you end up at half the price originally asked, you deserve a blue ribbon. One-third off is the usual settlement. Remember, no one in Egypt is in a hurry—least of all the Mouski. If you browse in a shop for several hours, yet buy nothing, the shop owner will not object. In true Middle Eastern fashion, he will philosophize that if he does not sell it today, he will sell it tomorrow—if Allah is willing.

In Egypt, as in most countries of the world, guides are likely to take you to their favorite shops—those from which they get a commission. Look around first, and do not feel under any pressure to buy. Incidentally, one of the best ways to bring the price down in bargaining is to leave! Because most tourists neither enjoy bargaining nor have the time for it, more and more merchants are posting fixed prices. Even though they do not bargain, when you buy a lot from one shop, you can ask for a discount. It usually works.

Packing and shipping. Oriental stores in the Mouski and in hotels will ship goods to the States. They are reliable, but it can take six months or longer to receive parcels. Do not attempt to mail a parcel from Egypt on your own. An export license is necessary and the red tape is stupefying.

One of the most constant complaints of visitors is the long delays in receiving goods shipped from Egypt. There are two reasons for the problem: First, Egyptian bureaucracy is so layered that merchants can waste days and weeks getting the paperwork through; and second, there is no direct sea-freight service from Egypt to the United States, so this creates delay. Further, the backlog at the port of Alexandria is unbelievable. No matter what a merchant tells you, parcels shipped by sea will take six months or more; those sent by air can take up to three months.

Sending gifts to Egypt: Persons living in Egypt may receive gifts from outside, but to save them a great deal of trouble, give them your gift in person. Gifts are subject to customs duties and clearing a package through customs is a long, difficult, and exasperating process.

Shopping Districts

City Center. The main shopping streets are Kasr el Nil, 26 July, Talaat Harb, Sherif, Adly, Abdel Khalek Sarwat, Midan Mustapha Kamel, and the area encompassed by these streets. Cairo's modern district, unlike many Eastern cities, does not have well defined areas for specific goods. Rather, it is like a European city where several types of shop are found on any one street. Several leading hotels have new shopping centers. The largest are at the Nile Hilton, which has upscale shops, and the Ramses Hilton annex, where prices are moderate and often less expensive than those of the Mouski. Other shopping centers are found at the Cairo Marriott and Cairo Sheraton.

Residential districts. Garden City, Zamalek, Dokki, Giza, Maadi, Mohandiseen, and Heliopolis have neighborhood shopping areas. Those planning an extended stay or residence in Egypt should patronize neighborhood shops for everyday needs. Also, you might consult the *Practical Guide to Cairo,* American University in Cairo Press, which lists services and shops by commodities and is particularly useful for someone who is setting up housekeeping or opening an office.

Mouski. The old bazaars are situated in or near the street called the Mouski, the oldest commercial street in Cairo. Its narrow, picturesque lanes are lined with tiny shops sheltered from the sun by wooden awnings and teeming with milling crowds and mingled scents. You may watch a craftsman work in the same manner as his predecessors did five centuries earlier and wander through the bazaars full of copperware, ivory works, gold and silver jewelry, perfume, gems, spices, and silk. The owner of each tiny shop will invite you to enter and will offer you coffee or tea while you browse.

The Mouski is made up of several souks, or bazaars. About a half mile up Mouski Street is the *Souq al Nahassin,* where coppersmiths squatting on the ground hammer at pots, pans, vases, and trays. Nearby in the *Souq al Siyagh* are the booths of the goldsmiths.

On the street leading to Bab al Zuweileh are the perfume bazaars in *Souq al Attarin* and various shops selling native fabrics in *Souq Ghouriyeh.*

Walking southeast along Mouski Street you'll find *Souq Khayamia,* the tentmakers. You'll also find the tiny shops where the appliqué, often seen in tapestries of Egyptian motifs is made. *Bazaar Shop,* No. 18, has different types of the work, including calligraphy, and will make items to order. Another stall, *Hanafi Mohamed Ibrahim,* has tote bags of brightly colored canvas on which he does the appliqué. *Farahat Sosdy* has a catalogue of his designs. Farther along, another covered lane leads to *Souq Saramatiyeh,* where leather shops make camel saddles, ottomans, native sandals, and other leatherwork. Close by is *Souq Kariyeh,* where Turkish delight and other Oriental sweets are sold.

Farther along, in front of Al Azhar Mosque is the entrance to *Khan el Khalili*—the best of all the bazaars and the one in which you are likely to spend most of your time. Its narrow, devious paths lead past shops— jewelry, carpets, amber, brass, copper, antiquities, glass, leather, and silver, to name a few.

Some shops in the Mouski also have shops or displays in leading hotels, but to buy at hotels is to miss half the fun.

Because of the labyrinth of streets and alleyways, a newcomer can easily become confused. It is wise to go with a guide or friend who knows the way. On the other hand, if you decide to strike out on your own, you need not hesitate. Egyptians are enormously helpful to visitors. They will stop their work to help you, and it is not unusual to have someone walk several blocks out of his way to show you directions. If you are on your own, you might want to ask your taxi to wait for you, as it can be difficult to find a taxi when you want to return to your hotel.

Egyptian Crafts

The Mouski overflows with items made strictly for tourists. These do not need describing as they will be obvious immediately. The shopping guide here is intended to point out the more unusual items and the best buys in Cairo. Much, of course, will depend on individual taste.

Alabaster. Inexpensive vases, ashtrays, lamp bases, and figurines are available in Cairo at gift and souvenir shops, or you can buy them from factories in Luxor. Be sure to have your purchase packed carefully. It is more fragile than it looks.

Antiquities. Although several stores in the Mouski and in downtown Cairo are authorized to sell Egyptian antiquities, a new batch of regulations has made it virtually impossible for them to sell them and for you to buy them. Furthermore, customs authorities have become so difficult (they have even been known to search visitors on departure), that it apparently is not worth the risk. As a further warning, there are more fakes than real antiquities in the market—none but the trained eye can tell the difference—and even the experts sometimes get fooled. So, unless you are prepared to be taken for a ride and to run the risk of getting into big, big trouble with Egyptian authorities, do not buy antiquities.

As a matter of interest, small amulets are frequently used in designs for jewelry, or, as amulets, are sometimes encased or mounted in gold to be worn as charms. There are several types:

The *Ushabtiu* was the name given by the ancient Egyptians to representations in stone, alabaster, wood, clay, and glazed faience of the god Osiris made in the form of mummies. These were placed in wooden boxes or in the floor of the tombs. They were intended to do manual labor for the deceased.

Udjat or Uzait Horu, or the sacred eye of Horus, represents the human eye. This amulet was a divinity in itself and enjoyed independent existence. It was perhaps the most popular of all Egyptian amulets. It was meant to ward off the evil eye—a belief that pervades Africa and the Middle East to the present day. Those who wore it were supposed to be safe and happy under the protection of the eye of Re. The *udjat* was the principal design in the bracelet found on the right arm of the mummy of Tutankhamen. It is now seen frequently on the new jewelry and fabrics that have copied ancient Egyptian motifs.

The *scarab,* an Egyptian desert insect, was worshiped by the ancient Egyptians as being a living representative of a god. *Xepera,* father of the gods, was the hieroglyphic name given by the pharaohs to the scarab. He was creator of all things in heaven and on earth, and he made himself out of matter that he produced himself. In time, the scarab came into common use. People wore it as an act of homage to the creator of the world. Also, it served as a seal.

Nassar Brothers, Khan el Khalili, is one of the best and most reliable dealers. They have amulets made into charms, cuff links, or tiepins. Prices might be higher than in other places, but workmanship is outstanding. (See *Gold Jewelry*, below, for more information.)

Brass and copper. The Mouski is filled with tempting objects of brass, copper, and copper washed with tin. The new ones with pharaonic designs are popular, but the old ones with arabesque are more artistic. Copper plates encrusted with metal or silver (used for hanging or as trivets), tall pitchers and vases (excellent for making lamps), candlesticks, samovars, and braziers are among the best selections.

Although the products in most shops are similar, there is a great difference in the quality of the workmanship. You must shop around if you are looking for anything more valuable than trinkets and inexpensive souvenirs—and you must bargain. In Khan el Khalili, try *Embabi,* 2nd floor, and *Mohamed El Gamil.* One of the most attractive innovations is a handsome copper or bronze mug with your name in hieroglyphics or Arabic script, costing about L.E. 20, from *Essam,* 5 Rabeh el Salhidar, Khan el Khalili. Tel. 912–282. Allow five days for the order.

Carpets. The Egyptians make a plain beige carpet known as a western desert rug. It is sold by the square meter and the thickness of the pile determines the price. A good place to buy one is the village of Kerdassa.

Stores in the Mouski also have Oriental rugs from other Middle East countries for sale. *Ismail Ali, M. Fahmy al Kabany,* and *El Kahal* in Khan el Khalil have carpets and rugs. The latter dealer has a store at the Nile Hilton Hotel arcade, too.

Ceramics/glass. Charms, cuff links, brooches, and earrings are made from old pieces of mosaic glass. The lovely patterns run through the entire thickness of the piece and resemble the abstract designs of modern ceramics. Two types were made in ancient days: the mosaic bowls produced primarily at Alexandria and small, decorative plaques of high technical and artistic skill. The latter, mostly Ptolemaic, were used to inlay jewelry boxes and furniture or as ornaments to be admired at close range. This glass was one of the most amazing achievements in the history of glassmaking. Apparently experts are still not sure how the ancient Egyptians made it.

A new trend in jewelry using ancient motifs in modern ceramic designs is beginning to develop. All sorts of this inexpensive jewelry and gifts can be found at *Baracat,* 12 Brazil St., Zamalek (tel. 340–9651). *Al Fostat Gallery,* 21 El Mansur Mohamed St., Zamalek (tel. 341–3631), with some of the best designed pottery and ceramics in Egypt, is expensive but well worth visiting.

Egyptian accessories and objets d' art. Some of the most interesting jewelry in Cairo is found in the boutique of *Senouhi,* 54 Abdul Khalek Sarwat. Owners Leila and Omar Rachad have a great love for good Egyptian crafts and a good eye for bits and pieces that can be worked into contemporary coversation pieces. This unassuming atelier, where five people make a crowd, is located on the fifth floor; there is a name plaque at the building's entrance. The tiny elevator, to the left on entering, offers the ride up; customers, usually satisfied, walk down. Hours are 9 AM to 5 PM. Shop is closed on Sat. afternoon and Sun. and during September. Senouhi has the tapestries and batiks from Harraniya Village, and—on the high side. *Al Ain*

Gallery, 73 Houssein St., Mohandaseen, is a Cairo insider's favorite, but prices are on the high side and selections limited.

Two Zamalek shops are *Mamelouk,* 4 A Hassan Assem St., one of Cairo's outstanding gift shops for local crafts, with everything from pottery and hand-blown glass to old tapestries and mirrors; and *Nomad,* Marriott Hotel Arcade, petit shop with excellent selection of fine crafts at fair prices, which reflect the oases, villages of Upper Egypt, and towns of the Delta. *Om El Saad-Emeraude,* 58 Mosadeq St., Dokki and a branch in Heliopolis (54 Abou Bakr el Saddik St., Safir Square) also have local crafts, mostly ceramics.

Aida Gallery, Km. 6, Sakkara Rd., has crafts and objets d'art as well as works by Egypt's major artists. Open daily, except Fri., 10:30 AM–2 PM, 5–8 PM.

For more traditional selections, *Onnig's,* now retired, the gift shop at the Antiquities Museum, is reliable. Prices are reasonable and fixed. Onnig is a well-known jewelry designer and one of the leading gemologists in the Middle East. The popular and often copied wide gold band with multicolored stones, known as Cleopatra's bracelet, is his design.

Fabrics. Cotton is the best fabric to buy in Egypt. Material for skirts and ready-made shirts are inexpensive. Reliable stores are *Swelam,* Adly Street, and *George,* Talaat Harb Street. A man's tailor-made shirt costs about L.E. 30 or L.E. 60, including the cost of the fabric. Tailoring takes a week in Cairo but only three hours at the *Oriental Bazaar,* 15 Tourist Bazaar, in Luxor. Take a shirt to be copied for better results.

A variety of dress materials is available. The best selections are at *Salon Vert.* There are several smaller stores across the street, such as *Miss Paris* and *La Poupée,* which have a variety of fabrics. Good selections on all types of fabrics are available at *Hannaux* and *Cicurel.* On Kasr el Nil, Talaat Harb, and 26 July streets there are dozens of fabric stores where at least one clerk or the owner speaks enough English to be able to communicate.

One of the best of all buys in Egypt is *galabiyah* cloth. As the name implies, the fabric is used to make the galabiyah, the long outer robe worn by native-dressed Egyptian men. It is usually striped in soft colors, very sturdy, excellent for draperies and upholstering, and is inexpensive. You should buy it in the Mouski, where selections are unlimited. L.E. 5 per meter is the average price. *Abas Hegazi,* Khan Khalili, has a wide assortment of top-quality galabiyahs and will make them to order. Costs range from L.E. 35 to L.E. 75 depending upon the quality and amount of the fabric.

Among the most attractive caftans (which Egyptians call *galabiyah,* too) are those being made by local artists with block prints and other methods using pharaonic and Islamic designs. At the handicraft centers in *Beit Sennari* they cost L.E. 45 and up. One of the best collections is at *Mousky Chic,* in the Nile Hilton and Cairo Marriott. Prices are a little more expensive, ranging from L.E. 40, but the selection is good.

At *Elle,* a caftan of unpolished cotton is L.E. 25 and those of traditional polished cotton are L.E. 40, while the fancier acetate fabrics are L.E. 60. *Shahira Mehrez,* 12 Sharia Abi Emana, sixth floor, in Giza, within walking distance of the Cairo Sheraton, is a shop owned by seven Egyptian women from well-known families. Open 10 AM–1 PM; 4–7 PM. Tel. 348–7814. Several of the same women have another shop, *El Dokan,* in the annex of the Ramses Hilton. Here you will find modern and old dresses from different areas of Egypt. Most are reasonably priced but the unusual ones, such as those from Siwa, are very expensive.

Atlas, Khan el Khalili, and a branch in the Semiramis Inter-Continental Hotel, have stocks of caftans for women and men or will make them to order. Prices start at L.E. 40 and go up to L.E. 500 for the fancy ones made of wool with gold-thread embroidery. *Oriental Bazaar,* Khan el Khalili, also has a large selection for similar prices. They are available in hotel shops but are more expensive. The best selection and price for inexpensive cotton caftans are in Luxor. Prices range from L.E. 15 to 40, depending on the quality of the cotton and the extent of design or appliqué. Caftans can be made to order and completed in one day at no extra charge at many shops in Luxor and Aswan.

Gold jewelry. Gold is sold by weight and is one of the best buys in Egypt for its workmanship. Charms of the Pyramids and the Sphinx are available, but the most popular is a cartouche with your name in hieroglyphics. The price is determined by the weight, carat of gold, and the nature of the writing—engraved or applied. The cheap ones are very thin and have the hieroglyphics glued on. Those properly made are soldered and cost on average L.E. 130 and up. The characters can also be engraved on the cartouche—this is the most attractive. Deal only with reliable stores. *Onnig's* at the Antiquities Museum publishes a postcard that gives the heiroglyphic equivalent of the Latin alphabet and pictures various sizes of cartouches. In Khan el Khalili, *Gouzlan, Mihran & Garbis,* and *Sami Nassar* are jewelry stores which have them. At *Gouzlan's* in Maadi, you can have one made in 18-carat gold, worked in enamel, and set with diamonds for about U.S. $400 (L.E. 1,280).

A more unusual item is cuff links with your name inscribed in Arabic or hieroglyphics. Another popular product is the thin, plain, solid-gold bracelet used by native Egyptian women as their dowry. For an interesting experience, buy in the *Gold Souq;* for jewelry made to order, *Nassar Bros.,* Khan el Khalili, is excellent. The owners have their own workshop.

In a completely different vein, but no less outstanding is *Nakhla,* 10 El Nil St., Giza, a jewelry boutique owned by two designers who use masses of pearls, lapis, topaz, and other stones with gold to create fabulous necklaces and bracelets. The work is high style, original, handsome, and expensive—from L.E. 700 and up. No credit cards. Phone: 720938.

Inlaid wood. Trays, jewelry, and cigarette boxes inlaid with ivory and ebony are attractive. Also, mother-of-pearl mosaic inlay is available.

Mashrabiya and other woodwork: At the Mena House and on tours of old mosques, houses, churches, and palaces you will see examples of beautiful woodwork called *mashrabiya* (sometimes identified as harem screens). The woodwork from demolished old buildings is rare. The new, unfortunately, does not have the same grace and excellent workmanship as the old, but it is available. In the Mouski, you can watch the intricate pieces emerge from a raw stick of wood under the dexterous hands of a skilled Egyptian craftsman at any of the workshops specializing in wood.

Exquisitely carved wood to make tables and screens is also available. Copies of pharaonic furniture are interesting buys, especially the mahogany stool with a woven string seat. These are available from *Zaki & Boutros,* Khan el Khalili, or *Hatoun,* Mouski Street, both of whom will ship to the States. *Mashrabiya* is a new shop on a country lane near Felafel Restaurant in the Pyramids area, where latticework wood and carpets are sold.

NADIM, Dokki, south of the Coca-Cola Bottling Co. The firm, whose initials stand for the National Art Development Institute of Mashrabiya, manufactures quality furniture influenced by arabesque designs. Factory visits can be made daily 11 AM–1 PM except Sunday, or by appointment.

Leather work. Egypt is the place to buy the camel saddle you always wanted. Many decorative kinds are made for the tourist market, but the old type, free of brass design, is nicer. *Mustapha Soliman,* Khan el Khalil, is one of the few shops that sell the old type of camel saddles; the new models are available in any Oriental shop. Poufs or ottomans, sandals, and inexpensive leather suitcases can be found at shops in a small alleyway near the entrance to Khan el Khalili. Browse before buying.

Not to be overlooked in leather are sandals and shoes for about L.E. 19–30. Every other store on Kasr el Nil and Talaat Harb seems to be a handbag and shoe shop; *Bellina,* on Talaat Harb St. and *MM,* 26 July St., Zamalek (near Marriott Hotel) are good. Stores selling leather coats and jackets are not quite as numerous. *Lumbroso,* 19 Talaat Harb, has leather coats and jackets for L.E. 175 and up. *Mohamed Gadallah,* 5 Sayed el Bakry, Zamalek, carries high-fashion shoes. *K.M.,* 1103 Isis St., two blocks from Shepheard's Hotel, specializes in top-quality leather, snakeskin, lizard handbags, shoes, and belts. Handbags and shoes are often copies of European designer styles and may look good at a glance. But be sure to take a close look before buying. The copy in leather might be good, but the hardware is often of poor quality and shows signs of rust or other deterioration.

If you are planning to live in Egypt, bring the books in your library that need rebinding. Prices are low, and the workmanship is good.

Mouski glass. Inexpensive but fragile hand-blown glasses and dishes are made from melted-down glass of broken soda and beer bottles. A drinking glass costs 50 pts. The glass must be carefully packed for shipping, as it is very fragile. *Said Abdou Raouf,* Khan el Khalili, has a good selection. Hurricane lamps are especially attractive and inexpensive.

Perfumes. There are several perfume shops on Mouski Street. Scents are heavy and sweet, but their novelty is appealing, and they make inexpensive gifts to take home. Any of the perfume shops will give you an array of scents to sample, but the place that makes the biggest show of it is *Museum of Perfume,* Midan Tahrir (across from the Antiquities Museum). The owner claims to be one of the major suppliers of oils to many famous perfume houses in France.

Semiprecious stones. Alexandrites, aquamarines, topaz, and pearls are made into earrings, rings, pins, or bracelets at reasonable prices. Many jewelers offer designs inspired by pharaonic design. Workmanship is good. Amber, too, is a good buy. *Onnig's* has a good selection.

Silver. Egypt is a good place to buy silver, also sold by weight. Almost any type of dish, ashtray, tray, and candelabrum is available. A plain, sterling silver cigarette or jewelry box engraved with one's initials or name in Arabic (or English) is a lovely gift. *Saad* in Khan el Khalili (with a branch in Ramses Hilton) is Cairo's most famous silver artisan.

Stamps. Egypt has interesting stamps—old and new—and it is a good place for collectors to fill in Middle East issues that are missing from their collections. A hundred commemorative stamps of Egypt costing L.E. 10, and 50 stamps of pharaonic design, L.E. 5, are among those in the selection. A well-established shop is *Oriental Philatelic House,* Continental Arcade. It has a U.S. counterpart in New York, and you can deal with the Cairo store by mail. The shop also has slides and unusual postcards.

Modern Stores and Goods

Department stores. Even in the modern shopping districts, stores tend to specialize in one item—shoes, fabrics, sportswear, etc. There are a few department stores, but they are small in scale by comparison with those in the States.

Chemla, 11, 26th July Street. Cheap quality. *Cicurel,* 3, 26th July Street. Expensive. *Egyptian Products Sales Co.,* 2, 26th July Street. Household fabrics. *Hannaux,* Kasr el Nil Street. Good fabrics and linens. *Omar Effendi,* Moderately priced government-run chain. *Salon Vert,* Kasr el Nil Street. Largest selection of highest-quality Egyptian fabrics. Three of the most modern are *Sednaoui,* Talaat Harb Square, and *Gattegno,* Mohamed Farid Street, and *Galerie Hathout,* Mohamed Farid St.

Bookshops. Downtown Cairo and most residential areas have many bookshops. For books in English, our favorite is *Reader's Corner,* 33 Sharia Abdel Khalek Sarwat, which also has bookstores in the Nile Hilton, and Hilton cruise boats and an art shop at the Meridien. The store carries originals and copies of the famous Robert's prints as well. Also recommended are *American University in Cairo Bookstore,* 113 Kasr el Eini St. (Open to the public Sun.–Thur. 8:30 AM– PM and Sat. 10 AM– 3 PM ; tel. 357–5377) and *Anglo-Egyptian,* 165 Sharia Mohamed Farid, where you must be prepared to browse, as old and new books are stacked floor to extra-high ceiling. The shop's Middle East selection is one of the best in town. *Lehnert and Landrock,* 44 Sharif St., is probably the largest. *Les Livres de France,* Immobilia Building, Kasr el Nil St., has excellent French and some English selections. For old and rare editions, *Orientalist Print Shop,* 15 Kasr el Nil St. (next to American Express) is the best. This store also sells old maps and the famous Robert's prints of old Egyptian scenes. Once available for a few dollars each, they now sell for L.E. 1,000 per print! Magazines and newspapers are sold by vendors, but shops in major hotels have better selections.

Across the street from the Continental and around the fence of the Ezbekia Gardens there are outdoor stalls where, if you have the time and inclination, you can spend hours browsing through old books. Most are junk, but you never know when you might happen on a rare one.

Clothing. Many urban Egyptians and those of the younger generation dress in Western fashions. In the past few years Egypt has developed a ready-to-wear industry of chic fashions selling at a fraction of U.S. prices. Most women's boutiques are centered in Zamalek with one of the best being *Mix and Match,* 21 El Mahad El Swissry St., Zamalek. For pure woolen men's suits look for the Ismailia and Vestiaco labels in department stores; the former manufacturer has recently introduced a women's line. Prices are incredibly low. *Mobaco,* 19 Talaat Harb St., has good sportswear for all the family. The famous *Benetton* sportswear is made under local license in Egypt and is available at a fraction of the cost in the United States or Europe at shops throughout the city. *Octopus,* which has stylish sportswear for the whole family, and *Stefanel,* which carries Italian fashions for men and women, have stores in the main shopping areas in town and in the suburbs.

There are also a large number of shops on Kasr el Nil, Talaat Harb, and the side streets between the two, as well as many neighborhood boutiques in Zamalek and Heliopolis that have ready-to-wear items. Imported clothes and accessories are expensive; locally made ones are not.

The best buy of all is children's and baby's clothes. Dresses with pretty embroidery, playsuits, and other items are very inexpensive when compared with U.S. prices for similar products. *Bamco* and *Papillon,* Kasr el Nil, have clothing and toys, as do others along the same street.

Cosmetics and toiletries. If you have a favorite brand, bring supplies sufficient for your visit. Many American and European brands are packaged locally, but cost more than you would pay at home.

Egypt is the land of eye makeup (called *kohl* in Arabic), as is evident in the ancient tomb drawings and wall paintings. Some gift shops sell kohl, and the salesgirl will show you how to use it.

Florists. Cairo has a year-round profusion of flowers. They are inexpensive, especially when bought from vendors. Egyptians give and send flowers on the slightest occasion. If you have been entertained at dinner in an Egyptian home, sending flowers in advance or the following day is a popular way to say thank you. Bouquets average L.E. 10 to L.E. 15, depending upon the kind of flowers and time of year, and can be delivered. A box of candy is also an appropriate gift for a visit to someone's home or for a hospital visit.

Among the leading florists are *Fresh Flowers,* Garden City (across from the American Embassy); *May Flowers,* 116 Sharia 26 July, Zamalek; and *La Belle Jardiniere* 22, Kasr el Nil St. Florists in major hotels are also good but more expensive than others.

Food products. Few American and European food products can be purchased in Egypt. When they are available, they are expensive. Local fruits and vegetables are good, inexpensive but seasonal, although canning is one of Egypt's fastest growing industries. Refrigerated meats are limited. Meat is usually sold the day it is slaughtered and can be purchased fresh daily. Although Muslims do not eat pork, it can be bought in Cairo. Supermarkets in Zamalek, Maadi, and Heliopolis, where language is not a problem, have good selections. With only a few words of Arabic you can manage surprisingly well in food markets, and it is fun to try.

Linens. Bed and table linens of fine-quality Egyptian cotton with embroidery are reasonable in price. Try the department stores and specialty shops on Kasr el Nil, especially *Salon Vert,* and Talaat Harb streets. Fine cotton tablecloths and 10 napkins with lovely appliqué run about L.E. 20; bed sheets and pillowcases with embroidery and appliqué are also very reasonable in price. *Oeuf's* in Khan el Khalil, has very good value. *Farah,* in the Ramses Hilton shopping center, has exquisite hand-embroidered linens.

Tobacco and cigarettes. Popular American and English brands are now made locally and retail for about L.E. 3 per pack. Buy a carton on the plane before arriving and carry a lighter. Matches are not given away; they are bought, and smokers never have enough. The best Egyptian filters, *Cleopatra,* costs about L.E. 1.50. There are also nonfiltered cigarettes.

Toys and dolls. Locally made toys and dolls are available at department stores and specialty shops, especially in the shopping arcade between Sharia Adly and Sharia July 26.

DINING OUT. Some of the best restaurants are in hotels, although in recent years many new independent restaurants have opened that are especially popular with foreign residents, and more recently, the ubiquitous fast-food outlets, such as Pizza Hut, are beginning to appear. Those listed here are generally recognized as Cairo's best. With few exceptions, restaurants depend entirely upon local ingredients and offer whatever vegetables and fruits are in season.

In most good restaurants the maître d'hotel takes your order. He generally speaks French and English, often Italian, German, and Greek. Waiters usually speak only Arabic and a few words of English pertaining to food.

Breakfast can range from $3 to $5, lunch or dinner à la carte from $6 to $12; double this amount, or more, at luxury hotels and nightclubs. Twelve percent is added to the bill. There is almost no difference between lunch and dinner prices. Many hotel restaurants now impose an L.E. 10 or L.E. 12 charge or minimum to nonhotel guests to discourage the local habit of sitting for hours over one cup of coffee.

The price categories listed below are based on the approximate cost of an average meal, excluding drinks and service (tips) per person. The categories are: *Expensive,* L.E. 25 and up; *Moderately Expensive,* L.E. 15–L.E. 25; and *Moderate,* L.E. 15 and under.

Egyptian Cuisine

Egyptian cooking is a mixture of native tradition and Turkish, Lebanese and Syrian, Greek, Italian, and French cuisines. The choices offered in restaurants tend to be limited. You will get the wide range only in people's homes or at special banquets.

Do not judge an Egyptian-style restaurant by its exterior. Most are simple and specialize in the basic skewered meat and dishes made from *fool* (fava beans). They could be likened to a souvlaki place in Athens or New York. They are not for tourists who need to have special food or those who are not at all adventurous about trying new foods. Most are *Inexpensive* (under $6) to *Moderate* (under $10) in price. *Expensive* is over $10.

In recent years, several leading international hotels have added restaurants specializing in Egyptian and Middle Eastern cuisine. While they can be depended upon to be clean, their prices are often double or triple those in typical independent restaurants, but the food is not necessarily better.

Expensive

Arabesque. 6 Kasr el Nil St. Tel. 759896. Open 12:30–4 PM; 7:30 PM–midnight. Consistently good for food, decor, and service. The menu is Continental with a selection of Egyptian specialties. The decor, as the name implies, is Oriental and attractive.

Can Zamaan. Sakkara Rd., Km 6. Tel. 538–141. This cozy restaurant, attached to the respected Aida Art Gallery, whose name means "old times," presents a nightly musical show at 10 PM on Cairo in the 1920s. However, you may prefer to lunch in its outdoor garden where grilled food is the specialty. Open daily, noon to 1 AM.

Darna. Pullman Maadi Hotel, Corniche el Nil, near Maadi. Tel. 350–6092. The restaurant is modeled after a typical Egyptian farmhouse and serves Egyptian specialties for lunch and dinner.

Falafel. Ramses Hilton Hotel. Excellent restaurant featuring authentic Egyptian and Middle Eastern cuisine in clean and colorful setting. Fixed-price menu begins with a *mezzah* (Middle East hors d'oeurves) of a dozen different dishes and continues with four courses of meat, fool, vegetables, dessert, and coffee. A folkloric show performs twice nightly, at 8:30 and 10:30. Open 7:30 PM–12:30 AM.

Khan el Khalili. Heart of Khan el Khalili Bazaar. Tel. 903–788. This greatly welcomed addition, under the management of Mena House Oberoi, is a beautifully furnished restaurant. The facility also offers the Naguib Mafruz Coffeeshop, named for Egypt's Nobel prize winner who autographed a pillar in gold. Open 10–2 AM with menus featuring Oriental cuisine. Take-out service is available.

Moderate–Expensive

Abu Ali's Cafe. Outside terrace of Nile Hilton. Tel. 767–444. Favorite meeting spot; central location. Sandwiches and ice cream plus Egyptian specialties. Open 11 AM–11 PM.

El Bawadi Restaurant. 10 Hussein Wasef St., El Mesaha Sq., Dokki. Tel. 348–8173. Located one block from Safir Hotel, it is a find for those who like Middle Eastern cuisine. The Oriental decor is embellished with mashrabiya wood and arabesque designs; the menu has specialities from Saudi Arabia and the Gulf, which one is unlikely to find elsewhere in Cairo, as well as Egyptian dishes.

Kebabgy el Gezirah. El Gezirah Sheraton, Zamalek. Tel. 341–1336. Outdoor café on a terrace next to the swimming pool and overlooking the Nile; serves excellent Egyptian specialties made to order on open grill. You can also watch village women making bread—it's served to you directly from the oven.

Mashrabia. Ahmed Nessim St. (across the street from the Swiss Chalet). Phone: 725059. Very pleasant, clean restaurant serving good Egyptian and other Middle Eastern cuisine. No alcoholic beverages. An adjacent patisserie for Middle Eastern sweets.

Moderate

Abou Shakra. 69 Sharia Kasr el Aini. Tel. 848811. Specializing in *kofta* and *kebab;* refurbished every year during Ramadan. Home deliveries. A new, elegantly furnished branch opened recently in the Cairo suburb of Mohandesseen at 17 Gameat el Dowal el Arabeya. Phone: 344–2299.

Casino des Pigeons. On the Nile in Giza. Tel. 721–299. One of the oldest and best outdoor cafés on the riverbank. Specializes in roast pigeon, an Egyptian delicacy.

Felfela. 15 Sharia Hoda Shaarawy at Midan Talaat Harb. Tel. 740521. One of the best for fool, which is prepared in many ways; other local dishes. Pleasant garden in city center. Open 8 AM–12:30 AM.

Felfela has a country cousin located on Mariotia Canal St., a country road north of the Pyramids Road (opposite the road south to Sakkara). It is a garden restaurant with many features meant to bring traditional Egyptian life to city slickers—a donkey for the children to ride, a puppet show (one of the country's most popular forms of entertainment), dancing horses, and dance troupes performing traditional folk dancing of Upper Egypt. There is also the traditional coffee house, open-spit cooking, and a shop for Egyptian crafts. It's all by the same family that owns *Paprika.* (Incidentally, *felfela* means "pepper" in Arabic, as does paprika in several languages.) A third, equally popular *Felfela,* is located on the Alexandria Rd. near the Pyramids. It has take-out sandwiches, too. Open daily 9 AM–12:30 AM. And now there's a fourth *Felfela,* Ahmad Orabi St., Sahfeyeen.

European and Asian Cuisine

Although the following group of restaurants offer European, American or international cuisine, many also include Egyptian and other Middle Eastern dishes on their menu. Most are *Moderately Expensive* ($12–$15), or *Expensive* ($16–$25); some *Moderate* ($8–$12); and a few are *Very Expensive* ($26–$45). The coffee shops in international chain hotels—Hilton, Marriott, Meridien, Oberoi, Sheraton—offer American snacks, light meals, and sandwiches 24 hours a day.

Expensive

Aladin. Sheraton Hotel (second floor). Tel. 348–600. Lebanese menu, attractive decor. Considered one of the best in the city. Small piano bar adjoining dining room. Reservations recommended.

Al Rubayyat. Mena House Oberoi. Tel. 387–7444. The dining room generally gets good reviews from patrons. Continental cuisine and Indian specialties; open for lunch and dinner. Folklore show.

Angus. 34 B, Yehia Ibrahim St., Zamalek. Tel. 340–0928. Giant steaks, charcoal-grilled South American style, are the specialty of this attractively decorated restaurant. Open daily for lunch and dinner.

Le Champollion. Meridien Hotel. Tel. 362–1717. Fine French cuisine; open for lunch and dinner. Formal ambience; live classical music. Closed Fridays.

La Charmerie, 157, 26th July St. (on small side street), Zamalek. Tel. 340–9640. Elegant French Provincial setting for seafood, including nouvelle cuisine.

Le Chateau Swiss Air. El Nasr Bldg. Sharia el Nil, Giza. Tel. 348–5321. First floor of Cairo's most luxurious building, one block from former President Sadat's house and about two from the Sheraton Hotel. This is one of Cairo's smartest restaurants, with a wide range of European selections. Unfortunately, the service is indifferent to rude unless you are a regular. Lunch 1–3 PM; dinner 8 PM–midnight. Reservations recommended. *Le Chalet* its less expensive counterpart, is on the ground floor. Tel. 348–6270.

Citadel. Ramses Hilton. Tel. 777–444. The hotel's principal dining room overlooks the fabulous central, colonnaded lobby. Main room offers steaks and grilled specialties.

Don Quichotte, 9A, Ahmad Hismet St., Zamalek. Tel. 340–6415. French cuisine. Small, reservations required. It's considered Cairo's best by many European residents. Lunch 12:30–3:30 PM; dinner 7:30–11:30 PM.

Gezirat al Dahab. Safir Etap Hotel, El Mesaha Sq., Dokki. Tel. 348–2424. Probably the most elegantly designed restaurant in Egypt. Continental cuisine leaning to the nouvelle school; live music. Lunch and dinner daily.

Justine. 4 Hassan Sabry, Zamalek. Tel. 341–2961. Elegant restaurant is part of the Four Corners' gourmet quartet (along with coffee shop, disco, and bar) in the Egyptian American Bank Building. Specializes in classic and nouvelle French cuisine.

Kowloon. Cleopatra Palace Hotel. Tel. 759–831. Good Chinese and Korean cuisine.

Manial Palace. Club Med, Roda Island. Tel. 844–524. Buffet-style, good quality and quantity in the pleasant surroundings of the palace gardens. Lunch for L.E. 27, including wine. Nonresident guests may go for lunch from 1 to 2 PM and a swim, or dinner and a show from 8:30 PM; dinner L.E. 29; reservations required.

Moghul Room. Mena House Oberoi. Tel. 387–4999. Authentic Indian cuisine in beautiful surroundings and excellent service. Recommended ordering complete dinner. Lunch served noon–3 PM; dinner 7:30–midnight.

El Nile Rotisserie. Nile Hilton. Tel. 750666. Specializes in imported American meat; offers well-prepared European and oriental dishes in attractive surroundings. Reservations recommended.

Oasis. Mena House. Poolside restaurant with full view of Pyramids offers a very pleasant setting for lunch. It becomes the hotel's nightclub in summer. Indian specialties.

Omam Restaurants. 5 Riyadh Tower, Wissa Wassaf St., Giza. Tel. 737–592. Five stylish restaurants—**Sakura** (Japanese), **Il Camino** (Italian), **Al Fanous** (Moroccan), **Chandani** (Indian) plus a coffee shop—under one roof. Accolades go to the Japanese and Moroccan chefs. No alcohol.

The Pharaohs. Floating restaurants by Corniche Giza, near Cairo Sheraton. Tel. 726713; 738–957. The fanciful boats in the shape of a pharaoh's barge are operated by Mena House Oberoi. They serve Continental and Egyptian dishes in a buffet; no à la carte menu. Guests can enjoy a 2½-hour Nile cruise with lunch or dinner and entertainment; or a shorter sunset cruise. Check locally for departure times. Reservations required.

Semiramis Grill. Hotel Semiramis Inter-Continental. Tel. 355–7171. The elegant main dining room of the hotel is Cairo's best, truly gourmet restaurant with imaginative selections on par with leading New York and London restaurants. The Grill consistently receives rave reviews.

Moderate–Expensive

Andalus Coffee Shop. El Gezirah Sheraton Hotel, Zamalek. Tel. 341–1333. More than a coffee shop with large variety of American, European, and Egyptian selections; special daily buffet for lunch and dinner. Open 24 hours daily.

Caroll. 12 Sharia Kasr el Nil. Phone: 746434. One of the best in the downtown area; pleasant, mellow decor; good service and good food. Small, reservations recommended. Lunch 12:30–4 PM, dinner 7–11 PM.

Movenpick. Movenpick Hotel near Cairo International Airport. Tel. 664242. Attractive 24-hour coffee shop; wide variety of dishes, and excellent buffet.

Naniwa. Ramses Hilton annex. Tel. 346–5943. This Japanese restaurant, complete with tatami room, has a good sushi bar.

Nile Garden. Corniche el Maadi. Tel. 505121. Continental and Oriental selections. For lunch the restaurant has a very pleasant setting on the Nile with a superb view. The food and service are good. It becomes a nightclub in the evening.

Prestige. 43 Gezireth Arab St., Mohandeseen (near Wimpy). Tel. 347–0383. Specializing in European cuisine in elegant setting. Attached pizzeria with patio is very popular.

Scarabee. Floating restaurant located near Shepheard's Hotel. Tel. 355–4481. The bar is open from 11 AM to 2 AM; departs daily at 2:30 PM for lunch and 9:30 PM for dinner for two-hour Nile cruise.

Seahorse. By the Nile on the road to Maadi. Tel. 363–8830. Rustic thatched roof riverside restaurant under same management as Andrea's. Excellent grilled fish. Lunch with mezzah, grilled fish, and local beer will run about L.E. 30 per person. It's a wonderful spot to enjoy a relaxing afternoon watching feluccas sail by on the Nile against the outline of the Pyramids of Giza.

The Silver Fish. 39 Mohy el Din Abu el Ezz, Dokki. Tel. 349–2272. Wide, superb selection of fresh seafood; sleek, modern decor.

Taj Mahal. 15 Ibn Affan, Dokki. Tel. 348–4881. Attractive ethnic atmosphere for mughlai and tandoori cuisines. Very popular.

Taverne du Champ de Mars. Nile Hilton Hotel (ground floor). The restaurant's authentic Belle Epoque interior was brought piece by piece from Brussels and reassembled in Cairo. It is decorated with beautiful stained-glass windows and Tiffany lamps. The waitresses and waiters are also dressed in the style of the period. An interesting feature is a series of paintings done in Egypt during the last century. These apparently hung in the original Brussels tavern, although nothing is known about the artist. Drinks and snacks, noon to 2 AM.

Tokyo Okamoto. 7 Sharia Ahmed Orabi, Agouza. Tel. 349–5774. It was a sign of the times when Cairo got its first Japanese restaurant, which came on the heels of the Japanese businessmen invading the city. Open noon–3:30 PM; 6–10:30 PM. Closed Monday.

El Yotti. 44 Mohy el Din Aboul Ezz, Dokki. Tel. 349–4944. Ring the doorbell and gain entrance to Cairo's latest "in" place. The Lebanese chef turns out an incredible mezzah. Reservations necessary most nights. Lively bar, too.

Moderate

Andrea. About 1 mile north of the Pyramid Rd. at Tereit el Maryutia (opposite the road south leading to Sakkara). Tel. 851133. Specializes in barbecued chicken and mezzah. Rustic outdoor setting. Crowded on weekends.

Cairo Cellar Pub. 22 Sharia Taha Hussein, Zamalek. Tel. 340–0718. Open noon–2 AM. Located in the President Hotel, neighborhood sort of place. Popular meeting place for young executives.

Il Capo. 22 Taha Hussein St., Zamalek. Tel. 341–3870. Specializing in Italian and Continental food, this cozy and informal restaurant is managed by a personable Texan and an Egyptian from an old, well-known family.

Le Chantilly. 11 Baghdad St., Heliopolis. Tel. 669026. A sister of Cairo's Swiss Air restaurant featuring Continental entrées. Attractive decor, spacious garden dining and bar plus superb pastry.

La Chesa. 21 Adly St. Tel. 393–9360. Good Continental selections are served in this charming Swiss Air restaurant whose interior resembles an Alpine chalet. Located in the heart of the downtown business district, this is one of the few nonhotel restaurants that serves breakfast, daily 8 AM except Friday.

Estoril. 12 Sharia Talaat Harb (in passageway), near American Express on Kasr el Nil. Phone: 743102. Good European food; once was one of Cairo's best establishments, but not quite up to its old reputation. Lunch 12–3 PM; dinner 7:30–10 PM.

Hana Korea, 21, Mahad Swissry St., Zamalek. Tel. 711–098. Frequented by Korean businessmen and diplomats. Specializes in Oriental-style barbecue. It's really straight out of Seoul. Highly recommended.

El Patio. 5 El Sayed El Bakry St., Zamalek. Tel. 340–2645. Continental cuisine. Favorite with foreign residents.

Peace. Alexandria Desert Road (near Mena house). Tel. 738–263. Excellent fresh seafood is served here in a spacious setting.

Pub 28. 28 Sharia Shagaret el Dor, near Sharia 26 July, Zamalek. Small, intimate pub atmosphere. Lunch, noon to 3:30 PM; dinner 7 PM to midnight. Good meat dishes.

Tia Maria. 32 Jeddah St., Mohandeseen. Tel. 713273. Small, intimate restaurant with a wide variety of Italian food. Patronized by local residents.

Tokyo Japanese Restaurant. 4 Aziz Abaza St., Zamalek. Tel. 340–4229; open 5:30–11:30 PM Closed Sunday. Popular with Japanese residents of Cairo. Reservations recommended.

TEA HOUSES AND PASTRY SHOPS. Many hotels and sporting clubs have tearooms or outside gardens where you may enjoy afternoon tea or coffee. Some of the most pleasant are the Mena House, the rest house at the Pyramids, and the cafe at the foot of the Sphinx. Each of these has a view of the Pyramids and is particularly pleasant at sunset. Also, the Lido of the Gezira Sporting Club is usually lively at teatime.

Fishawi's. Perhaps the most famous tea and coffee house in Cairo, located in the Mouski. Its atmosphere will transport you centuries into the past. Fishawi's has had a tradition of being especially popular during the month of Ramadan, around midnight, when it is full and lively. There is now a new one, across from the old one, and both are located near the El Hussein Hotel within the shadow of the minaret of the El Hussein Mosque.

Groppi's. Kasr el Nil at Midan Talaat Harb. Tel. 743473. (Another with a garden at Sharia Abdel Khaled Sarwat and a third in Heliopolis.) Groppi's is a landmark in Cairo and its location and ambience made it a great rendezvous spot, but now more patronized for its candy shop.

Lappas. Kasr el Nil St. This long-established tea and snack bar, recently renovated, also serves ice cream and fresh fruit drinks. It has a small supermarket and an upstairs restaurant. *Moderate.*

Simonds. 112, 26th July St., Zamalek. Pleasant pastry shop that also serves fresh fruit juice and coffee.

Tower of Cairo. Gezira Island. Located on top of Cairo's modern version of the obelisk, the restaurant is meant to revolve slowly, enabling guests to view the fabulous panorama of the city while they eat. A full revolution takes half an hour (if it's working). A British paper once described its revolution as being like Nasser's: it turned once and stopped working. Not all Egyptians saw the humor. The restaurant revolves again! The elevator ride to the top of the tower costs L.E. 3. The best time to go is for afternoon tea.

ENTERTAINMENT. Cairo has a wide range of entertainment and cultural activities. It is one of the centers of the movie industry in the Arab world, and its air-conditioned cinemas show the best American and European films as well as Arabic ones. Nightclubs are numerous and the entertainment is varied. The highlight of the evening's performance is one of the famous belly dancers, of whom Egypt has the best. There are gambling casinos and horse racing in Zamalek and Heliopolis during the winter season.

Egyptians are fond of walking or lingering outdoors, which they do frequently in the many parks and public gardens throughout Cairo.

One of the most pleasant ways to pass an evening is a moonlit sail in a felucca on the Nile or at a desert party near the Pyramids. Either of these may be arranged through your hotel or travel agent.

Top priority during your visit should be the son-et-lumière show at the Pyramids. This sound-and-light show was one of the first ever created by the French firm that developed the concept, and it is still one of the best. The show is presented in English, Arabic, French, and German on different nights of the week. Check locally for schedule and prices.

Cairo Today, a monthly, magazine is the best source and is distributed through hotels and sold at bookstores for L.E. 5. *Places,* a magazine published six times annually and selling for L.E. 4.50, is also helpful.

GAMBLING. In Cairo there are casinos at the Cairo Marriott, Mena House Oberoi, Nile Hilton, Ramses Hilton, Movenpick Heliopolis, el Gezirah Sheraton, and Cairo Sheraton hotels. Egyptian citizens are not allowed in the gambling rooms and a foreign visitor must show a passport to enter. Roulette, 21, chemin de fer, and baccarat are played. Only foreign currency can be used.

BARS. There are dozens of bars around town, mainly in hotels. Cocktail time in Egypt is approximately from 7 to 9 PM. Among the nicest where women can go unescorted and feel comfortable are:

Al Gandool. Gezirah Sheraton Hotel. Low-key elegance and picture windows put you right on the Nile for great views.

Al Pasha. Baron Hotel, Heliopolis. Attractive, packed meeting place, especially popular with British visitors.

Eugenie's Lounge. Cairo Marriott Hotel. Lovely, elegant bar in former palace reception room furnished with antiques.

Felucca Bar. Semiramis Inter-Continental Hotel. Comfortable surroundings for people-watching.

Matchpoint. Four-corners complex, 4 Hassan Sabry, Zamalek. Sports and music videos as background.

Ramses Hilton. The lobby bar features towering columns resembling the Temple of Karnak, and the rooftop lounge has lovely panorama of Cairo but it has become very much a young romantic scene, especially after 9 PM. Ask the bartender, George, for a "Georgie"—it's a delicious cocktail.

Sultan's Bar. Mena House Hotel. Piano bar where you can enjoy full view of Pyramids and the sunset with your cocktails.

Tea Garden. Semiramis Inter-Continental Hotel lobby. Low-key elegance with wonderful Nile view. Classical quartet music in the evenings.

View Lounge. Cairo Marriott Hotel, top floor, Zamalek Tower. Nicest bar in the city if you want a lovely view in pleasant, quiet surroundings. It offers a New York deli-style buffet Saturday–Thursday from noon to 3 PM.

There are many other bars—often outdoors by a pool or on a terrace overlooking the Nile and Cairo.

NIGHTCLUBS AND DISCOTHEQUES. Cairo has a variety of nightclubs from which to choose. Many have romantic settings in outdoor gardens or terraces where you dance under swaying palms against a moonlit sky. Some of the best night spots are the nightclubs and discotheques of hotels. Large cabarets, mostly for men, are located on the road to the Pyramids.

Nightclub shows do not start before 11 PM. Some clubs have both local and European floor shows; others have none. Orchestras play all the latest international hits and Latin American or European music for dancing.

Cairo is the R and R center of the Middle East—especially for men working in the surrounding countries where the deserts are dry in more ways than climatically. As a result, Cairo has a large number of cabarets, and they are to be distinguished from the nightclubs and discotheques.

Also, in Cairo, the term discotheque has a slightly different meaning from that in most other countries. It is actually a small nightclub with stereo music, and sometimes a show, usually a performance by an oriental dancer, which will last 30 to 45 minutes. Prices are less than at nightclubs or cabarets. At some of the discos you can watch the show if you plan to stay at the bar only. At all the better nightclubs in the city you are required to reserve a table for dinner and dancing. Under social pressure in the current conservative atmosphere, some young Egyptian women do not go to discos as they did in the past. And, while many places advertise "for couples only," a quick check reveals a preponderance of men who seem to be there looking for Western women.

Contrary to what you might imagine, the age group at discotheques runs the gamut. It appears to be related directly to the decibel level of the music—the higher the count, the lower the age.

If you have the opportunity, be sure to see a performance by a leading Oriental dancer, or belly dancer, as they are known. When performed by a first-rate artist, the dance is one of tremendous beauty and artistic skill, and is not the bumps-and-grinds version too often passed off by third-rate dancers as the real thing.

Visitors might be interested to know that the standards for dancers are changing. During the past few years the impact of rock and other modern beats can be seen in the movements and heard in the music of the dancer, particularly in the tempo. The classic form is slower, with movements more elongated. There is an interplay and subtle flirtation between the dancer and the music. It is graceful and sophisticated. The form that is popular now is noisier and more detached. There is a frenzy to the movement that is not part of the old classical form.

The following are Cairo's major night spots. All are most crowded on Thursday and Saturday nights, therefore reservations are generally necessary—particularly at those night spots where dinner is required.

Abu Nawas. Mena House Hotel. The hotel's indoor winter nightclub.

Alaa el Din. Sheraton Hotel (second floor). Summer nightclub (next to swimming pool); oriental dancer, European chanteuse, good food, dancing; reservations essential.

Al Hambra. Sheraton Hotel (top floor). Panoramic view of Cairo; Western entertainers and a belly dancer. Reservations recommended.

Belvedere. Nile Hilton Hotel. Winter (October through May) supper club on the roof of the hotel; dancing; panoramic view; decor represents Egypt in the 19th century; Oriental dancer and show. French and oriental cuisine. You can sit at the bar to watch the show without having dinner. Nightclub moves outdoors near swimming pool in summer as the *Tropicana*.

Blow-Up. Vendome Hotel, Pyramids Rd. Phone: 850–977. Packed with young people.

Cave des Rois. 12 Sharia Mohamed Sakeb, Zamalek. A supper club with dance floor and band in the evening. Patronized by local residents.

The Churchill. Baron Hotel, Heliopolis. Recent European hits backed up by a large video screen.

Empress Night Club. Cairo Marriott Hotel, Zamalek. Two nightly shows, 7:30 and 10:30, highlighted by folkloric dances and one of Egypt's top belly dancers. Oriental and European cuisines. Nightly except Wednesday. Reservations recommended. Moderately expensive.

Good Shot. Corniche el Nil, next to Maadi Yacht Club. Restaurant on Nile with live music on summer weekends.

Jackie's. Nile Hilton. Continues to be the most popular spot of disco chic. It might be called Regine's-by-the-Nile as it's very reminiscent. Entrance is free for hotel guests and members. (Annual membership is L.E. 500, which allows members to bring two couples as guests.) With liquor prices having doubled, boozing here is not recommended for budget-conscious travelers, but the music and dancing are great, if you like discos.

It's a chance to see how Cairo's smart set swings. But because there are so many more men than women, some women guests may feel uncomfortable in this ambience.

Kasr el Rachid. Meridien Hotel. Housed in a large oriental tent by the dolphin pool, this club features Eastern food and a varied show, including a good belly dancer. Reasonably priced.

Merryland. Sharia el Lewa Ahmed Fouad Sadek, Roxy, Heliopolis. Spacious tea garden with restaurant and nightclub with show. Very popular with Heliopolis residents and worth the drive from downtown on Sunday evenings. Family-oriented. Men alone not allowed.

Nile Garden. Maadi Road by the Nile. Pleasant garden restaurant by the Nile; has live music and show in summer.

The Oasis. Mena House Oberoi Hotel. In warm weather you dine and dance at the poolside nightclub on an outdoor patio set in a garden of bougainvillea and geraniums under the moonlit silhouette of swaying palms and the Pyramids of Giza. Show has Western and oriental attractions; reservations recommended. Expensive by Cairo standards. Indoors in winter as *Abu Nawas*.

Regine's. Gezira Sheraton Hotel. One of the famous chain of discos, but hasn't quite made it here as the in place.

The Saddle. Mena House Oberoi Hotel. One of the most popular discotheques in town; music is by stereo but kept at a low enough volume for conversation. Western, ranch-style decor; so is the menu. Moderate.

Sahara City. Alexandria Desert Road. A nightclub in a fancy tent that boasts having the most belly dancers in town and no one disputes the claim. Show starts at 10 PM, and you are expected to have dinner, too. (It's included in the price.) Expensive.

Salt and Pepper. Sharia Abou el Fedda, at north tip of Zamalek. Has lost some of its earlier popularity. Hard rock and psychedelic lights, live and loud music; show has Oriental dancer.

Siag Pyramids Hotel. 59 Marioutia Rd., Giza. Large tent seating 600 people; dinner and nightly show with Oriental dancer.

Sinbad Disco. In Sonesta Hotel, Nasr City. Phone: 262–8111. A favorite of Cairo residents, who appreciate its down-to-earth prices and with-it music. Minimum charge is L.E. 10, Mon.–Wed.; L.E. 20, Thurs., L.E. 15, Fri.–Sat.

Tamango Disco. Atlas Zamalek Hotel, 20 Gameet el Dowal el Arabia St., Mohandiseen. Lively disco popular with both Egyptian and foreign residents. Spotlights latest recorded hits.

Tropicana. Nile Hilton Hotel. Poolside summer supper club. As the name suggests, decor is tropical with bamboo umbrellas, dancing under stars. Barbecue and Oriental cuisine, open hors d'oeuvres and dessert buffet; good dance orchestra, belly dancer; reservations recommended. Open from 9:30 PM but does not get rolling until 10:30.

Two Seasons Supper Club. Ramses Hilton. Phone: 744400. Floor show with top international talent. Nightly except Monday, 9:30 PM to 2:30 AM.

Vito's. El Salam Hotel, Heliopolis. Clubby atmosphere that is subdued early evening, lively with musicians 11 PM–3 AM. Minimum charge per person.

Amun, Patron God of Thebes

UPPER EGYPT

Luxor, Karnak, and the High Dam

A visit to the Egyptian Museum, or to Memphis and Sakkara, is only an introduction to the antiquities of Egypt. Not until you have made a trip to Luxor, Aswan, and the other sites of Upper Egypt does the magnitude of ancient Egypt's civilization become apparent. The 534 miles from Cairo to Aswan are dotted with ancient monuments and temples, with more being discovered all the time.

Strictly speaking, Upper Egypt is that narrow strip of green that stretches from the apex of the Delta 14 miles north of Cairo to the first Cataract at Shellal, about six miles south of Aswan. It resembles the long stem of the lotus of which the Delta, or Lower Egypt, is the flower.

Only the most important sites are described in this section, but those who have the time will find dozens of lesser known places with fabulous monuments and ruins to explore.

Over 700 tombs have been discovered on the west bank of the Nile at Luxor. If you were to visit only 15 of the best, you would be exhausted and probably saturated with Egyptian art for a long time to come. Do not overdo your sightseeing. If your time is limited, visit only a few tombs. You should not attempt to see all those listed below unless you are spending at least four days in Luxor.

If you rely only on a guide to explain the drawings, you will miss a great deal of their artistic value. For maximum benefit, familiarize yourself in advance with the names of the gods, the important pharaohs, and their representations in wall paintings. You should read, if you have not already

162

done so, or reread "The Egyptian Scene" chapter of this book prior to a visit to Upper Egypt. If you plan an extensive visit to the tombs, you will benefit immensely by carrying with you a book that details the drawings with pictures and explanations.

Other useful items for the trip to Upper Egypt are a flashlight, premoistened face cloths, and moisturizing cream. At sites of antiquity, on trains or in cars, dust from the sand will collect on your skin. Cleanse your face quickly with a moistened cloth, follow it with a moisturizer and you can feel refreshed quickly and easily. Also, bring fresh lemons, lemon drops or mints, a collapsible drinking cup, and a small thermos for water on sightseeing rounds in the open. Keep cameras, films, and lenses in plastic bags when not in use as protection against the sand and dust.

And last of all, you will need a strong pair of legs, comfortable shoes, and a zeal for tomb exploring—no matter what!

Photographing Antiquities

In summary, tourists who are taking pictures for personal use as souvenirs may photograph at all outside temples and monuments and inside museums, churches, etc., where it is allowed. However, in certain museums and tombs, tourists must buy a permit for L.E. 5 per tomb for still cameras. These permits must be purchased at the place where you buy your entrance ticket, as they are not available at the individual sites. Neither flash photograph nor video cameras are currently allowed inside tombs. Museum permits for still photography without flash cost L.E. 5. Only art specialists and professional photographers are given permission to photograph in the tomb of Tutankhamen, and permission must be obtained in advance from the Ministry of Antiquities in Cairo. (At press time Tutankhamen's tomb was closed for renovation. A reopening date had not been announced. Inquire locally.) Signs stating the fees are now posted at most museums and antiquity sites.

LUXOR

The present-day town of Luxor on the east bank of the Nile is situated 400 miles south of Cairo on the site of ancient Thebes, the capital of Egypt at its zenith during the Middle and New Kingdoms. The actual site of Thebes is said to have occupied all the area between Luxor and Karnak, a village a few miles north of Luxor. Today the area contains the ruins of the most gigantic monuments, statues, and temples in all Egypt. These represent the greatest artistic accomplishments of the ancient Egyptians from the XIII to the XXX Dynasty.

When viewing the monuments of Luxor and Karnak, you should remember that these marvels were once profusely decorated. The walls were overlaid with gold, silver, alabaster and marble, the gates plated with gold and the temples connected with each other by pillars, courtyards, and gardens.

On the west bank of the Nile is the world-famed Valley of the Kings, the burial grounds of the great pharaohs of the Empire. In the cliffs nearby

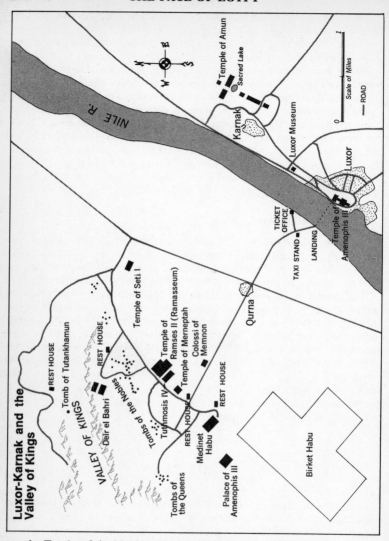

Luxor-Karnak and the Valley of Kings

are the Tombs of the Nobles. The inside walls and ceilings of these tombs are painted with beautifully detailed scenes and inscriptions in colors so vivid they could have been applied yesterday. On the plain at the foot of the monuments stand the mortuary temples of Deir al Bahri, the Ramesseum and Medinet Habu.

A guide for the day at Luxor should cost about L.E. 50–60. On your first visit a guide is necessary, especially for a visit to the west bank. In Luxor, horse-drawn carriages are a popular means of conveyance to antiquity sites. A ride costs L.E. 5–L.E. 10, depending upon distance and your ability to bargain.

East of Karnak Temple, an excavation by the University of Pennsylvania has revealed the outline of a temple built by Akhenaten. Scholars, using computers to piece together the stones that have been found in other parts of the Karnak Temple bearing the likeness of the pharaoh and his queen, Nefertiti, were able to locate the temple and to reconstruct the position of its walls. Akhenaten is said to have built eight temples in Thebes before he moved his capital to Tell al Amarna. The new discovery was the first of his temples ever found, although stones from them had been found as it was common throughout the history of Egypt for the builders to reuse the materials of an earlier period. In the case of Akhenaten, the priests of Amon had intentionally destroyed his temples to Aton. The discovery of any remains from this period are therefore remarkable.

Sites on the East Bank

Temple of Luxor. By the Nile, near Luxor Wena Hotel. Entrance: L.E. 11 daytime; L.E. 5 after 5 PM.

Less than a century ago, the Temple of Luxor was completely covered under a hill of rubble and hovels. It was discovered by accident, and it took two years to excavate the excellently preserved ruins that are now visible. The original temple was built during the reign of Amenhotep III and was dedicated to the trinity of the Theban gods: Amen-Re, his wife Mut and their son Khonsu. From the North Gate an impressive Avenue of the Sphinxes once connected Luxor Temple with the Temple of Karnak. Many have been uncovered and stand in situ. A walk or carriage ride along this road will help you understand the relationship between the two temples in ancient times.

Ramses II expanded the temple and added many statues of himself and two obelisks. One of the obelisks, given by Muhammad Ali to Louis Philippe in 1831, is now in the Place de la Concorde in Paris. The temple was also later altered by the Ptolemies.

Immediately inside the North Gate is the mosque of Sheikh Abu Haggag. The position of the mosque will help you to visualize the level of the debris that covered the temple at the time of its excavation. In February 1989, new statues from the 18th Dynasty (c. 1400–1300 BC) were uncovered by accident within Luxor Temple and are considered by scholars to be extremely valuable. The largest is an eight-foot high statue of Amenhotep III, surmounted by another statue, thought to be his wife or one of the gods. Unfortunately, the earth was cleared away and hastily put back without proper supervision and documentation, in order to have an "official" opening by Egyptian authorities. Egyptologists say valuable information was lost by the mishandling of these priceless treasures.

The best time to visit the temple is in the afternoon. The light of the afternoon sun softens the color of the temple's surface, and the reliefs are more easily distinguished. For photographers, too, the colors are deeper and richer. A visit to the colonnades at full moon is also recommended. A tour of the temple takes an hour. On the other hand, a detailed view of its many halls, columns, statues, and inscriptions could fill hours.

Temple of Karnak. About two miles north of Luxor. Entrance: L.E. 16; L.E. 5 open-air museum. Proceeding by the road through the village of Luxor, a few hundred yards before reaching the Temple of Karnak, the magnificent South Gate of the temple comes into view. The gate, which is in almost perfect condition, was built by Ptolemy III. It was the ceremonial gateway through which the festival processions passed from Karnak

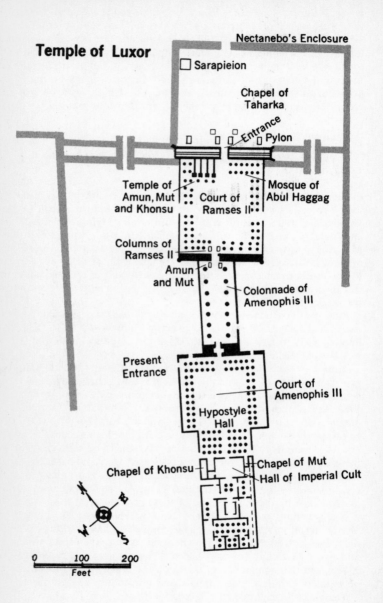

Temple of Luxor

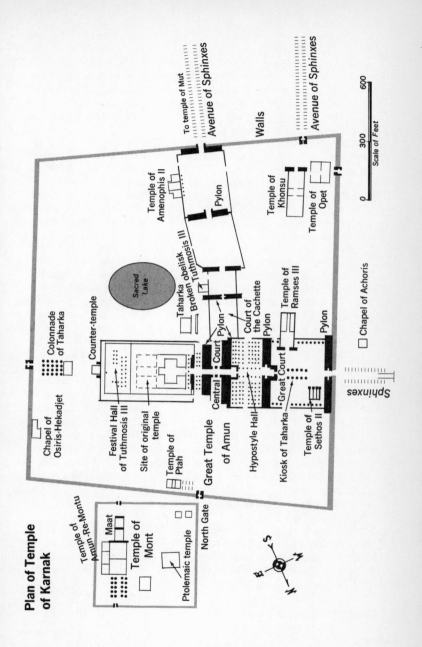

Plan of Temple of Karnak

to the Temple of Luxor. On both sides of the gate a wall originally enclosed a temple dedicated to Khonsu, god of the moon.

If you proceed from Luxor to Karnak by the road along the Nile, you will arrive at the North Gate of the Great Temple of Amen-Re. In front of it are the ruins of the Avenue of the Ram-headed Sphinx. The temple dedicated to Amen-Re, the patron god of Thebes, was the most important temple in the kingdom. Consequently, each pharaoh enlarged and embellished it as evidence of his faith. From the top of the temple entrance you get a full view of Karnak, Luxor, and the west bank of the Nile.

Inside the temple of Amen-Re is an earlier temple built by Ramses III. Its construction predates the forecourt of the Great Temple. From the forecourt you enter the Hypostyle Hall, reputedly the largest hall of any temple in the world. Its area covers 50,000 square feet. The roof of the hall (now fallen) was once supported by 134 immense columns.

From the Hypostyle Hall you will enter the original Temple of Amen-Re. Here stands the Obelisk of Queen Hatshepsut—97 feet tall, cut from one piece of pink Aswan granite. At the end of the temple is the Festival Hall of Thutmose III, used as a church by the early Christians.

Near the Amen-Re Temple are several smaller shrines. At the south end of the temple complex is the Sacred Lake, which the ancients used in connection with religious ceremonies. At Karnak, extensive restoration of the temple has been and continues to be made. The temple can be reached by carriage within 20 minutes from any Luxor hotel. The fee for the carriage and waiting time is L.E. 8–12. (Settle price in advance.) The best time to visit the site is in the morning. At least two hours are needed, but allow a full morning to view the temple in detail.

Son et Lumière. Karnak. Price: L.E. 10. Check locally for times and languages.

Every evening a son-et-lumière (sound-and-light) show is performed at Karnak Temple. The 1½-hour program brings to life the story of ancient Thebes. Starting at the entrance in front of the Avenue of the Ram-headed Sphinx, guests walk along the Great Hypostyle Hall to the Central Court, while voices and lights play on the great walls and drawings of the temple. Then at the Sacred Lake (where seats are available) the program continues with an impressive display of lights on the monuments, which reflect in the pool. Performances are given in English, French, German, and Arabic on alternating days.

Luxor Museum of Ancient Egyptian Art. Entrance: L.E. 8. Hours: 3–9 PM winter; 5–10 PM summer.

Between Luxor and Karnak temples, near the Etap Hotel, is the Luxor Museum of Ancient Egyptian Art, created with the assistance of the Brooklyn Museum for the municipality. It has only a small number of displays, but these are beautifully arranged and lighted and are definitely worth a visit.

Sites on the West Bank

For 25 pts. you may ride a local motor launch from the landing stage in front of the Luxor Temple to the west bank of the Nile. The tourist ferry costs L.E. 2 round-trip and leaves from in front of the Etap Hotel. At the landing stage and rest house on the west bank, cars with drivers may be hired to drive you to the sites. The cost is about L.E. 35 for half day; L.E. 70 for full day. Some of the large taxis hold up to 7 people and cost about L.E. 10 per person. There are donkeys, too, for about L.E. 2 per hour plus a tip for the donkey's owner. Hearty visitors can make the excursions on bicycles, but distances between the sites are too great to attempt the excursions on foot. Cars drive over a good asphalt road, well marked with direction signs. Visitors usually go first to the Valley of the Kings, where a rest house is located.

Our favorite driver is Gahlan Hassan Ahmed, taxi driver No. 94. You can contact him in advance by writing to him in Luxor, West Side, El Qorna. Give him the date of your arrival and the hotel where you will be staying.

In recent years, sightseeing on the west bank has been greatly facilitated. Nonetheless, it is very tiring. Be prepared to do a great deal of climbing, especially up and down stairs inside the tombs. Do not try to do it all in one day. There is too much to see. Furthermore, if you see too much at one time, everything will begin to blur and your enjoyment will be lessened considerably.

Tombs of the Kings. In the Valley of the Kings at the extreme west of the necropolis. Entrance: L.E. 19 for visiting any three tombs.

Sixty-four pharaohs' tombs have been found in the Valley of the Kings. The safest and most interesting are open to the public. Only the best preserved or those with the most interesting and elaborate wall paintings are described here, and they are listed in order of priority. Several tombs are being renovated and may be closed.

If you are not with a guide, you will need to tip the gatekeeper at each tomb 30–50 pts. Tombs in the Valley of the Kings are lit and a battery flashlight is no longer necessary.

Tomb 17: Seti I (XIX Dynasty, 13th century BC).

Many experts consider Seti's tomb to be the most interesting one in the necropolis. It is the largest and certainly the most impressive. The wall decorations begin at the entrance and continue all the way to the bottom of the tomb. The drawings and reliefs are exquisite and in excellent condition.

Tomb 623: Tutankhamen (XVIII Dynasty, 14th century BC). Separate entrance fee: L.E. 27. Closed at press time for renovation.

The golden mummy of King Tut lies in situ encased in the middle of the three coffins that originally held the mummy. You should take time to examine carefully the detail work on this world-famous masterpiece.

Tomb 35: Amenhotep (Amenophis II, XVIII Dynasty, 15th century BC).

The tomb is called the Tomb of Safety because several coffins, moved there by the high priests for safekeeping against tomb robbers, were found in it. The wall drawings are completely different from those in the tombs of Seti I and Tutankhamen. Note especially the painting of the goddess Isis kneeling on the emblem of gold, asking the god Gheb to protect the dead king.

Tomb 9: Ramses VI (XX Dynasty, 12th century BC).

The excellent wall drawings, especially on the ceiling and sidewalls of the last chamber, are an interesting variation from the other tombs.

Tomb 33: Haremheb (XIX Dynasty, 14th century BC).

In the small room of the inner chamber the colors of the drawings are excellent, but some are unfinished. Visit the tomb only if you have plenty of time.

Tomb 34: Thutmose III (XVIII Dynasty, 15th century BC).

The climb up to the tomb is very steep and the descent into it is long. Further, you need an explanation of the line drawings, or some knowledge of hieroglyphics, in order to appreciate them. There are no painted drawings like those in other tombs, and parts appear to be unfinished. The tomb is listed by many experts as one of the major ones in the necropolis, but for a novice it is hardly worth a visit.

Tomb 11: Ramses III (XX Dynasty, 13th century BC).

The drawings are badly damaged and smoked. Visit it if your time permits. Only about half of the tomb is lighted and accessible to visitors.

Tombs of the Queens and Princes. In the Valley of the Queens at the extreme south of the necropolis. Entrance: L.E. 6 for the three tombs open.

More than 57 tombs have been discovered in the Valley of the Queens, but very few are open.

Tomb No. 66, the tomb of Nefertari (wife of Ramses II), is the most outstanding tomb in all Egypt for its artwork. Entrance: L.E. 27.

Tomb 55: Prince Amenherkhepshef (son of Ramses III).

The wall paintings are quite different from those in other tombs, as pastel colors were used. The well-preserved decorations are definitely worth examining. Note the drawing of Ramses III leading the goddess Isis by the hand, and another of the king introducing his son to the god Ptah.

Tomb 52: Queen Thyti (Tyti, c. XX Dynasty).

Parts of the drawings in the tomb are in bad condition, but you should visit if you have time. Queen Thyti was the wife of one of the Ramseses.

Tombs of the Nobles. In various groups along the edge of the desert. Entrance: L.E. 6.for each two tombs in a group. Visitors are allowed to photograph; flash attachment required.

The private tombs of the priests and nobles in the courts of the pharaohs are famous for their fine wall decorations and drawings, which depict scenes from the daily life of the ancient Egyptians. The nobles' tombs are very small in comparison to those of the kings. After viewing the wall drawings in the Valley of Kings, those in the nobles' tombs appear as miniatures. The important tombs are located in the hills between the Ramesseum, Deir al Medinah and the Temple of Hatshepsut. The best belong to the dynasty between the 15th and 14th centuries BC.

It is from these drawings that Egyptologists and historians have been able to piece together much of the information found in popular writing on the daily life of the ancient Egyptians, their government, customs, and beliefs.

Tomb 52: Nakht, Scribe of the Granaries.

In this tomb is the famous drawing of the dancing girls (located on the left after entering). The banquet scenes are especially good. Note the detail in the drawing of the three seated women, one of whom is smelling a lotus blossom. The details of the hunting scene with Nakht are also lovely (located on the wall right of the entrance). The drawings in this tomb are among the most frequently reproduced in art books on ancient Egypt.

Tomb 55: Ramose, vizier or prime minister of Ikhnaton.

Although the tomb is damaged, it has some of the most beautiful drawings from antiquity and is definitely worth a visit. On the right and left walls immediately upon entering are the reliefs of Ramose and his wife. These are exquisite—be sure to study the detail. On the left wall, the upper panel is one of the most famous murals in ancient Egyptian art and the only painted one in this tomb. It shows the funeral procession and the wailing women, carrying the mummy of Ramose to the tomb. On the back wall on the right side are the badly damaged remains of the symbol of Aten, created during the time of Ikhnaton, which is the sun disc with rays that end in cupped hands.

Tomb 69: Menna, Chief of the King's Estate.

The details of the hunting scene, especially the beautiful birds, should be noted. The harvest scenes are interesting. In the first row, the land is being measured; in the second, the quantity of grain is being recorded; and in the third, grain is being harvested. On the back wall there is a well-preserved drawing of the scale of balance, weighing the heart against a feather, to judge the truth of the deceased's account of his life before Osiris.

Tomb 96: Sennefer, Prince of Thebes, Superintendent of the Granaries and Cattle of Amon (under Amenhotep II).

This is one of the best of the nobles' tombs. The ceiling decoration and formation are meant to represent grapevines. Be sure to visit this tomb, even though you will need to climb down many steep stairs. The tomb has two rooms and some of the best-preserved drawings in the necropolis, although the quality is inferior to others.

Tomb 100: Rekhmire, minister of Queen Hatshepsut.

The tomb has good drawings of daily life.

Other Tombs. *Tomb I* (also listed as No. 36 in some refences): Sennezen (Sennutem), minister to Tutankhamen.

Located near the French Archaeological Expedition. Guides will not take visitors here unless requested to do so. This tomb is small, but from my experience it has the best-preserved drawings in all the west bank. The tomb must have escaped the centuries of robbers, religious fanatics, and curiosity seekers because none of the drawings are damaged and the colors are so bright and fresh they could have been applied this morning. The walls are covered on all sides with drawings, as is the ceiling. Note especially the panel of Anubis, god of embalming, preparing the mummy; another complete panel at one end describes paradise. All the panels are wonderful, and photographers, particularly, will have a field day.

Tomb 359: Mennakhouey.

Located near the tomb of Sennezen. The tomb is small and so are the drawings, but they are very good and unusual, although parts are badly damaged.

The Temples. *Deir al-Bahri:* At the foot of the Theban Hills. Entrance: L.E. 8.

The mortuary temple built by Queen Hatshepsut (XVIII Dynasty, 15th century BC) is one of the most handsome monuments in Egypt. It is often pictured in books on Egyptian antiquities. Its plan—terraced and colonnaded—is unusual in ancient Egyptian architecture. Its location at the foot of towering cliffs enhances its majesty.

Upon the death of the powerful Queen Hatshepsut, her nephew and stepson, Thutmose III, attempted to obliterate all traces of her. As a consequence, many of the wall drawings at Deir al-Bahri were destroyed. The chapel dedicated to the goddess Hathor is the best-preserved section of the temple. You should allow yourself an hour to view it.

Ramesseum: South of the Valley of the Kings. Entrance: L.E. 6.

A mortuary temple built by Ramses II (XIX Dynasty, 13th century BC), this is one of the largest temples in Egypt. At the front on the east is the fallen head of Ramses' statue—the largest in Egypt, cut from a solid piece of stone. You should allow one or two hours to view the temple adequately. The colonnaded courts and wall drawings deserve close attention. The caretaker of the temple is very knowledgeable and can explain the drawings on the walls, the statues, etc. It is worth taking the time to study these carefully, as they will help you to understand similar carvings in other temples in Upper Egypt.

Medinet Habu: South of the Valley of the Kings. Entrance: L.E. 6.

A mortuary temple built by Ramses III (XX Dynasty, 12th century BC), this is one of the most colossal monuments in the world, considered second only to Karnak in architectural importance. The well-preserved temple is actually a complex of four temples—two built by Ramses III, one by Amenhotep I, and another by Queen Amenartas (700 BC).

From the top of the front pylon on the right, ascending by the original stairway, you get a magnificent view of Luxor and the Nile Valley. Throughout the temple the wall drawings are good and deserve careful attention. To view the temple complex thoroughly, you need half a day.

Deir el-Medineh: South of the Valley of the Kings. Entrance: L.E. 6.

A temple dedicated to the goddesses Hathor and Maat, built by Ptolemy IV in about 210 BC As it is similar but inferior to other Ptolemaic temples in Upper Egypt, you should plan to visit this only if you have ample time.

Colossi of Memnon: South of the Valley of the Kings.

Twin statues representing Amenhotep III in the classical sitting position are located on the edge of the desert, facing the Nile. Each statue is 64 feet in height. They apparently formed the entrance to a temple complex that no longer exists. In ancient times many legends were created about the statues because of a sound that was said to emanate from them each dawn.

Temple of Seti I: Located on the left of the road en route to the Valley of the Kings. Entrance: L.E. 6.

By comparison with other temples in the vicinity, the ruins and reliefs are in bad condition. Only if you are spending a week at Luxor would you find it worth a visit.

Sites Near Luxor

Nile steamers that cruise between Luxor and Aswan stop at sites mentioned below, enabling passengers to visit the monuments. Or you can travel by train from Luxor or Aswan to towns near the ancient sites. From the train station, you can either walk, ride a donkey or hire a carriage, car or boat to the site as the situation requires. Another way to go is to hire a car in Luxor or Aswan for the journey between the two points. This works very well for a party of two or more, but for only one person it can be expensive. If you decide to hire a car for a day's excursion, be sure to take along a box lunch.

An alternative is going by motorcoach from Cairo to Luxor, taken in two 200-mile sectors, or about 200 miles per day. This allows travelers to visit the site of Tell al Amarna near Minya, Assuit and Abydos, among the most interesting in Upper Egypt but less visited because of the difficulty of access. Fortunately, most of the longer (but more costly) tours now offered by U.S. operators include several of these sites, especially Denderah and Abydos.

Garagos, 15 miles north of Luxor, is a small village where potters make lovely, hand-painted pottery tableware—casserole dishes, cups and saucers, and other pieces. By taxi the trip should cost about L.E. 20 roundtrip.

North of Luxor

Denderah. 40 miles north of Luxor at Qena. Entrance: L.E. 8.

The train ride from Luxor to Qena (Keneh) takes about 1½ hours. A half-hour carriage ride from the station will take you to the river where you can cross the Nile by bridge to the west bank. From there you can either ride a donkey or walk to the site in a half hour. Nile steamers stop on the west bank near the site, and waiting buses take passengers to the temple in five minutes; or it is a pleasant 20-minute walk along a country road where you might get a close-up glimpse of rural life. Traveling by car or motorcoach from Luxor to Qena takes one hour. Here you'll cross a bridge for a short drive to the site.

Denderah was the capital of the sixth district of Upper Egypt under the Ptolemies. Here you may visit the *Temple of Hathor,* one of the best-preserved monuments in Egypt, built during the 1st century BC near the end of the Ptolemaic rule. The temple was dedicated to Hathor, goddess of heaven, joy and love, and patron deity of Denderah. It took about a 100 years to build, and some parts were never completed.

The temple is elaborately decorated, although the reliefs are not as fine as Egyptian art of earlier periods. Many of the drawings were defaced by early Christian and Muslim zealots.

On the roof of the temple are two chapels, one of which contains a reproduction of the zodiac (the original is in the Louvre). On the back wall are drawings of the last and most famous Queen Cleopatra (there were seven Cleopatras in ancient Egyptian history). From the side of the main chambers, steps lead to the crypts below. The drawings in the lower chambers are better preserved than those on the upper floors. The mud brick wall surrounding the temple also dates from the 1st century BC Be sure to climb the stairs to the roof to enjoy the view of the Nile Valley.

Abydos. 90 miles north of Luxor at Balianeh. Entrance: L.E. 8.

From Luxor, you can take a modern motorcoach or the early morning train. The latter arrives in Balianeh at about 11 AM. You can return by evening train, reaching Luxor by about 10:30 PM. The temple lies 7 miles west of the Nile. Donkeys, carriages, and early vintage autos are available to take you to the site. Another way is to hire a car for the day in Luxor and drive to Balianeh. It is a pleasant trip over a good road and takes three hours. The trip will cost L.E. 75 to L.E. 100. Nile steamers from Luxor on long itineraries stop on the second day at Nag Hamadi, 19 miles south of Balianeh, from which visitors proceed by bus to the site (an hour's drive). The road from Luxor along the west side of the Nile crosses by bridge at Nag Hamadi to the east side. This bridge has locks on the east side, that are opened twice daily—morning and afternoon—to allow the river traffic to pass through. From the bridge to the temples it is about a 40-minute drive. There is also a good road along the east bank, but it is desolate as it passes through the desert rather than the valley.

For centuries Abydos was a place of pilgrimage; the tomb of Osiris was supposedly located in the area. Abydos is situated on the site of the ancient city of This (Thinis), which was one of the earliest settlements of man in the Nile Valley. Tombs of the pharaohs from the First Dynasty have been discovered here.

The most important monument here is the *Temple of Seti I,* built on the site of an earlier temple. It was later enlarged and completed by Ramses II, son of Seti I. The Temple of Seti I, dedicated to Osiris, is considered one of the most important monuments in Egypt for its artwork. The art of Egypt during this period reached its peak and is unequaled for its beauty and delicacy. You should allow yourself enough time to carefully examine the wall drawings and reliefs; they are magnificent. The temple contains seven sanctuaries, each dedicated to a different god. Around the wall of the first hall a border of symbols represent the 42 provinces of ancient Egypt.

The most important feature in the temple is the group of some 70 cartouches of the pharaohs of Egypt arranged in chronological order. Upon discovery of these cartouches, Egyptologists, correlating them with information from other sources, established a definite timetable of the ancient dynasties for the first time.

Unfortunately, the location of Abydos is not convenient for the modern traveler. Nonetheless, a visit is very rewarding. Many experts consider the temple to be the most outstanding in all Egypt. A short distance from the ruins is the *Abydos Tourist Rest House,* which offers shish kebab and simple meals.

West of Luxor

The oases of the Western Desert, known as the New Valley, are located almost directly west of Luxor. Except for twice weekly air service from Cairo via Luxor, it's a bit of "you can't get there from here." The best road across the desert to the oases branches off from Assiut for a distance of about 135 miles.

Kharga. This is the administrative center of the New Valley, a new town built on the edge of one of the oldest settlements in Egypt. In ancient times the oasis of Kharga, Dakhla, Farafra, and Siwa served as links along the caravan highway that connected Europe and the Mediterranean with the Nile Valley and Africa, the Red Sea, and Asia.

With the passing of the caravans and the shift in trade to the New World these trails were all but forgotten except by pilgrims who crossed the desert en route to Mecca. During this century, even these travelers abandoned the old route in favor of the train, coastal motor routes, and the airplane.

During the 1960s under the Nasser government, interest was stirred anew in the Western Desert following the building of the High Dam at Aswan. The area has enormous development potential because of its mineral resources, particularly potash and petroleum, and its underground water supply is someday expected to sustain large numbers of Egypt's exploding population. Unfortunately, the initial campaign for development ran out of steam when Egypt's economy deteriorated after the 1967 war with Israel and the loss of the Suez Canal and had to wait for better times.

The area's potential for tourists has only recently been recognized and is very slowly beginning to be developed with the improvement of roads and bus service between the oases, and renovation of the Kharga Oasis Hotel in Kharga. The area is for adventure travelers who are prepared to accept minimal amenities for an unusual travel experience.

The most important antiquity site of the region is the *Temple of Hibis*, which was built during the XII Dynasty and rebuilt during the XXVI Dynasty by the Persians and again in the Roman era. It was built on the site of earlier structures since the town of Geeb was the first line of defense on the ancient road to Sudan known as the Road of the Forty. (It took 40 days to make the trip through the desert to Kharga.) The town was also known for its fruit, wine, and meat—as can be seen from ancient drawings. The people of Kharga come to the temple to spend the spring holiday of Shams el Nessim.

The large temple has three monumental gates. The first is Roman, the second Greek, and the third was built during the XII Dynasty but later embellished by the Persians. The temple bears many inscriptions of Darius and shows him wearing the crowns of Upper and Lower Egypt. One significant carving shows the goddess Mut feeding Darius (who was Persian) from her breast to give him the milk of Egypt; another shows the making of a new king.

One carving appears to contradict the Osiris legend and shows his brother Set slaying the dragon. The composition is so strikingly similar to the Christian story of St. George slaying the dragon that one cannot help speculating about the latter's origin.

In 1909 when the Metropolitan Museum in New York began excavations, the temple was filled almost to the top with sand. The temple was reconstructed in 1948 and now because of the danger of underground water weakening its foundation, it is being prepared for removal to a higher ground.

A visit should be made to the Christian cemetery, where crude drawings in Coptic burial chapels depict the stories of the Bible. Judging from the large number of tombs, the area must once have been thick with churches and monasteries.

Kharga is an important region for duck breeding, with farms that can be visited. It is also the center of carpet weaving. At the handicraft center you can watch and photograph village girls at work on looms, a potter molding vessels with hand-thrown clay, and blowers shaping glass—all using techniques little changed for centuries.

Dakhla. The drive from Kharga to Dakhla is one of the most interesting in Egypt and is dotted with unusual rock-and-sand formations. At Kilometer 20, the road passes through the "Great Sand Sea," which are endless miles of beautifully shaped, half-moon sand dunes that move about 5 miles in 10 years. Many historians theorize that Cambyses II, the son of Darius, and his legions were lost here. It would have been a more direct way to travel from Abydos to Kharga to Siwa, than the northern route from Memphis to Siwa.

Farther along, the road passes through a stretch of lunar landscape with giant rocks and natural pyramids reminiscent of Wadi Rum in Jordan. At several locations, there are petrogylphs on the rocks that have not been dated but are believed to have been made by prehistoric man in Egypt.

Several villages can be visited in the Dakhla Oasis. Some, such as *Bashandi,* have changed little in 20 centuries. The construction of the houses is surprisingly similar to the abodes of our Southwest. Each of the villages has remnants of temples and tombs from the pharaonic or early Christian periods. But the most interesting aspect of the villages are the people themselves, who are still unaccustomed to tourists. You will find the children very shy and likely to run away at your beckoning, or they might be so excited at seeing you that they will follow you around by the dozens just for a glimpse.

The road from Dakhla to Farafra is hard-topped, but onward to Siwa, it is not. When it is finished and additional accommodations have been built, this excursion could become one of the most fascinating for those eager to see the desert, oases, and view dimensions beyond the Nile.

Note: Unless you drive a car from Cairo or Assiut, travel around and between the oases is somewhat of a challenge. Transportation is limited and accommodations, except for the hotel in Kharga, extremely basic. The most convenient way to visit the area is to join a tour from Cairo. *Spring Tours* (3, Said el Bakri St., Zamalek; tel. 341–5972), which operates the Kharga Oasis Hotel as well as the Victoria and other hotels in Cairo, runs a fortnightly motorcoach tour to Kharga and Dakhla. It is sold mainly in Europe, but if you write or contact them in advance, you can probably be accommodated. For true adventurers, there is daily bus service from Kharga to Dakhla and Farafra. It can be booked in advance from Al Azhar Terminal near Attabaq Square in Cairo.

South of Luxor

All the Nile steamers for tourists that sail between Luxor and Aswan or vice versa stop at the locations described below. The journey takes three nights/four days and is sold as a four-night/five-day package. An alternate method, which is rapidly growing in popularity, is to travel by car or motorcoach the 250 miles between Luxor and Aswan. It is a long and tiring trip, but it will allow you to see more of the village life of Nubia and to take in other, lesser-known sites. The journey takes approximately four hours by car.

Esna. 30 miles south of Luxor. Entrance: L.E. 6.

By car from Luxor the drive takes less than an hour. By early morning train, you will arrive at Esna in about one hour. The temple is small and may be seen in 30 minutes, enabling you to return to Luxor by the morning train. By steamer, departure from Luxor will probably be late at night; you would arrive at Esna early the next morning.

The Temple of Khnum is Ptolemaic in origin. From other evidence, however, it appears that an earlier temple was constructed by Thutmose III (1500 BC) on the same site. Work on the Ptolemaic temple probably began in about 180 BC and ended in AD 250, as the emperor Decius is mentioned in a relief. The drawings in this temple were the latest representations of a pharaoh found in Egypt. The temple is well preserved and restored.

Edfu (Idfu). 70 miles south of Luxor, about halfway to Aswan on the west bank. Entrance: L.E. 11.

The morning train from Luxor arrives in Edfu at about 10 AM, and you may return on the afternoon train to Luxor. The steamers from Luxor stop here on the second day.

The ancient Greeks called the site Apollonopolis, after Apollo (or Horus), whose representation here is in the form of an eagle. The Temple of Horus is practically intact and is one of the finest examples of Ptolemaic art in Egypt. Its foundation was laid in 237 BC under the reign of Ptolemy III but was not completed until two centuries later.

On the side walls of the stairway to the roof are fine representations of the ceremonial procession of New Year's Day.

Kom Ombo. About 105 miles south of Luxor and 30 miles north of Aswan. Entrance: L.E. 6.

By train the one-hour trip is usually made from Aswan. From Luxor, the trip by road is long and duration will depend upon how much time is spent in Esna and Edfu.

Kom Ombo is situated on a hill overlooking the Nile at a point where the river makes a wide bend to the west. In ancient times it was a strategic location on the desert route to Nubia and Ethiopia.

The principal deities of the ancient town were Harwar, a hawk-headed god, and Sobek, represented in the form of a crocodile. The Temple of Kom Ombo is dedicated to the two deities and is unlike any other monument in Egypt. To avoid offending either god, a twin temple was constructed—the left half dedicated to Harwar, the right half to Sobek. Although only the bases of the columns and the back walls remain, the temple's majestic proportions and grace are impressive. The fine reliefs throughout the temple are worth your careful attention. At the side of the temple is a small sanctuary containing dozens of mummified crocodiles.

ASWAN

From its beginning, Aswan, located 534 miles south of Cairo, was the gateway to the south and the trade route from Egypt to Central Africa. Today, it combines the oriental and African influences of its history.

Before construction on the new Aswan Dam began, the population of Aswan was about 50,000. Today its numbers have swollen to 500,000. If you have time, stroll through the town. Along the way you may stop in a carpet-weaving shop to watch the owner and his small boys at work. This craft is similarly performed in hundreds of villages on the Nile in Upper Egypt. The market, too, is lively and especially good for spices and Nubian baskets. It is one street in from the main street along the Nile.

A folkloric group in Aswan has been widely acclaimed as being one of the best in the region. From Oct. to May, it gives nightly (except Fridays) performances of Nubian dances at the Aswan Palace of Culture located near the boat dock for the Oberoi Hotel ferry.

By train and steamer, you will arrive in Aswan on the east side of the Nile. By plane, you will land at the airport on the west side of the river and cross from east to west by a road over the Dam. The major hotels, travel offices, and shops are located on the east side.

If you are not careful, Aswan cab drivers will overcharge you. Settle the price before you start out. Quoted fares are for the taxi ride, whether there are one or five passengers.

If time allows, a sail in a felucca around the islands at Aswan is delightful. Boats can be hired at the landing dock by the Cataract Hotel or the docking stations of the Nile steamers in town and cost about L.E. 10 for a sail around the island. Some feluccas hold up to 20 people; the price has to be negotiated, depending upon the number. Stops can be made at Kitchener's Island to visit the Botanical Gardens and at the foot of the Aga Khan's Mausoleum, which is open to visitors. The walk up to the hilltop where the tomb is located takes about 10–15 minutes. There are donkeys and camels for those who prefer to ride. The trip around the islands takes about two hours—depending upon the wind, of course.

A felucca ride or cruise is often included in the sightseeing tour of Aswan on packaged tours. It should not be confused with the Nile cruise by steamer, which is an entirely different matter.

Sightseeing in Aswan

Aswan has long been a favorite winter resort because of its dry climate and beautiful location. The late Aga Khan maintained a villa in Aswan and asked to be buried there upon his death. His handsome mausoleum facing the Minarets of Bilal stands out on a hill behind his villa. His widow continues to winter at the villa.

In the desert behind the Aga Khan's mausoleum are the ruins of the Monastery of St. Simon, built by Coptic monks during the 6th century AD It is one of the largest and best-preserved Coptic buildings in existence.

From a hilltop on the west bank of the Nile, you get an excellent view of the old Aswan Dam, completed in 1902, the lovely landscape around Aswan, and the graceful white sails of feluccas on the Nile carrying visitors to Kitchener's Island and Elephantine Island, the ancient frontier fortress of Egypt. Elephantine Island also has an interesting museum and ancient tombs of the princesses of Aswan. Kitchener's Island, so named because it was presented to Lord Kitchener when he was consul general in Egypt, has botanical gardens created by him, with exotic plants from all over the Middle and Far East. (Another good view is from the top floor of the Oberoi Hotel.)

On the east bank of the Nile south of Aswan are the granite quarries where stones were cut for use in ancient monuments throughout Egypt. You should visit the quarries to see the partially completed giant obelisk. This will help you appreciate the colossal task that was involved in transporting the granite from Aswan to Luxor and even to Baalbek in Lebanon. There is an unfinished one, in situ, that measures 125 feet in length and is estimated to weigh 1,170 tons. Entrance: L.E. 6.

Temple of Kalabsha. On the west bank of the Nile overlooking the new High Dam. Entrance: L.E. 8. In 1962–63, a German group dismantled the structure at its original site and moved it to its present location to save the temple from future inundation. The work was done so well that only a trained eye can detect the reconstruction.

The temple, one of the best examples of Egyptian art from the Roman period, was devoted to the Nubian god Mandulis. It is the second-largest standing temple in Nubia after Philae. The temple is near the airport road about 11 miles from the Cataract Hotel.

The Kiosk of Qertassi. A small Roman temple with many Greek inscriptions. It resembles Trajan's Kiosk on the island of Philae.

The Tombs of the Nobles. Tombs carved in the cliff's face on the west bank of the Nile are opposite the northern tip of the island of Elephantine.

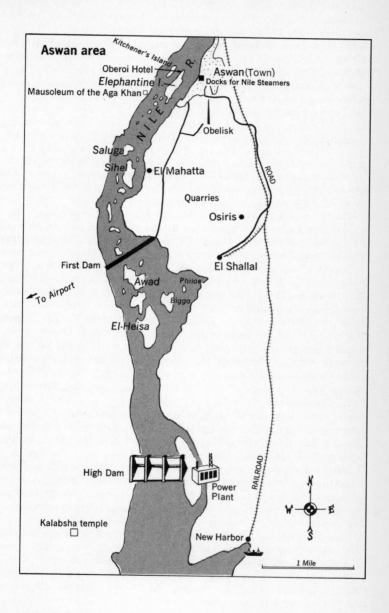

Aswan area

Kitchener's Island

Oberoi Hotel

Elephantine I.

Mausoleum of the Aga Khan

N I L E

Aswan (Town)
Docks for Nile Steamers

Obelisk

Saluga

Sihel

ROAD

• El Mahatta

Quarries

Osiris •

First Dam

• El Shallal

← To Airport

Awad

Philae

Bigga

El-Heisa

High Dam

Power
Plant

RAILROAD

Kalabsha temple

New Harbor

N
W   E
S

1 Mile

Entrance: L.E. 3. These tombs were constructed by nobles and princes of the region in about 2300 BC. Important among them are the tombs of Mekhu, Si-Renpowet, Pepi-Nakht, and Khuf Har.

Temple of Isis. South of town. This temple was the work of Ptolemy III and Ptolemy IV but was not completed. Entrance: L.E. 3.

The High Dam. Building projects of great magnitude—the Pyramids, the Suez Canal, and now the Aswan Dam—have been milestones in Egyptian history. All gained international attention, but to present-day Egyptians the new High Dam at Aswan represents the most important undertaking in their history.

Every year since ancient times, the flooding of the Nile has been the Egyptians' main concern. The necessity to cope with the inundation led the ancient Egyptians to acquire mathematical, astronomical, and engineering knowledge far in advance of other civilizations. Planning for the lean years during the years of plenty established law and order. This continuity of purpose for 6,000 years of Egypt's history is unique among nations. Now, with the building of the High Dam, the unpredictable behavior of the Nile has become a thing of the past.

The new dam is located four miles south of the old one at Aswan. During the first stage of construction, a diversion channel was cut through the east bank of the Nile. The rock removed in cutting the channel was dumped into the main riverbed to form a cofferdam and to create the foundation of the new dam. Upon completion of this cofferdam in May 1964, the course of the Nile River was altered by man for the first time in history. Now the river spills into the diversion channel and through tunnels where its water can be controlled.

The second stage of the project was the building of the High Dam itself to a height of 364 feet and a width of two miles across at the top. When it was completed, the billion-dollar dam created a lake 300 miles long to the border of Sudan. Its waters have allowed the cultivation of two million additional acres of land—one-third more than in 1965. The dam's hydroelectric plant, located halfway up the diversion channel, has tripled Egypt's power output.

The dam was built with Russian aid and technical assistance, but the construction and labor were Egyptian—about 35,000 in manpower. As one watched the orderly movement of thousands of workers, a similar scene at Giza 5,000 years ago sprang to mind.

On arrival at the dam site, you should go first to the dome-shaped exhibit building, where competent English-speaking guides will explain a model of the dam, maps, and pictures. Afterward, drive around the construction site. A hurried look will take an hour. Any Aswan taxi will drive you to the site. Set the fare beforehand.

The year 1990 marked the 30th anniversary of the initial construction of the High Dam. From the start it was controversial. Would the benefits outweigh the cost? What were the hidden problems?

Its supporters argued that the High Dam would expand Egypt's cultivated area, ensure water for irrigation even in the years when the river was low, increase productivity by converting 700,000 feddans from the basin irrigation system to perennial irrigation, improve productivity by improving drainage, protect the country against high floods, improve navigation conditions year-round, generate electric power for industrial and agricultural development, spawn a new tourist area and a fishing industry by the creation of Lake Nasser, and increase the annual gross national product by L.E. 234 million.

The jury is still out on the High Dam. There is no question that is has provided new productive land and new power. It has also brought a batch of new problems—many are technical and agricultural issues to which there are no immediate answers. Water seepage undermining buildings and foundations, salt residue in the soil, and erosion along the Nile banks, which had in the past received new layers of top soil annually from the mud carried by the river, are already creating problems at an alarming rate.

The Temple of Philae. Entrance: L.E. 11. On an island situated between the old and the new dams, this is the most interesting of Aswan's antiquities. Most of the temple was underwater except during the flood months from August to December when the old dam was open. When the dam was closed, only the cornices of the two pylons were visible.

With the building of the new dam, provision was made to save the temple by dismantling, crating, and moving it to another location where it has been reassembled. Here it is free from inundation and visible year-round. The rescue operation took three years.

The oldest part of the Philae Temple dates from the XXX Dynasty (4th century BC); the rest was completed during the Ptolemaic and Roman periods. The goddess Isis reigned here, and her cult continued to be followed even after Christianity had become the official religion of the Roman Empire.

Philae has several important temples. The largest was built by Nectanebo I, for the worship of Isis and her son Horus. This temple was renovated by Ptolemy II. The approach is made by an outer courtyard, flanked by western and eastern colonnades, each of whose 26 columns has a different design, topped with a distinctive capital. The columns combine pharaonic, Greek, and Roman motifs, revealing how much the cultures had, by this time, become mingled. Behind the eastern colonnade is the *Temple of Imhotep*.

The *Outer Court* leads up to steps flanked by two lions carved out of granite, and to the terrace of the First Pylon. On the walls, drawings show the ruler offering sacrifices to the gods Isis, Osiris, Khum, and others. In the temple's old location, when the waters were highest only the top portion of the pylon was visible. Water marks left by centuries of inundation are clearly distinguishable. An entranceway known as the *Portal of Nectanebos* leads to the forecourt of the temple and to the back pylon, which is the entrance to the *Temple of Isis*. At the back was the Holy of Holies, and a small chamber on the right, marked by a Greek cross, was at one time used as a church. There are other Christian drawings covering the ancient inscriptions.

West of the Isis Temple stands *Hadrian's Gate* and the *Temple of Harendotes,* and at the very north end of the complex, the *Temple of Augustus*. About 50 yards east of the large temple lies the *Temple of Hathor*. On one of the pillars there is a drawing of a flute player with Bes, the god of happiness, playing the lute and dancing. The building that has come to symbolize the island is Trajan's Kiosk of 14 pillars. It is among the most beautiful relics on the island.

There was considerable disagreement among scholars as to whether or not Philae should have been preserved, as it never ranked high on the list of artistic achievements of the ancient Egyptians. But there has always been a sentimentality attached to the temple.

A spectacular son-et-lumière is available at the temple in English, French, German, and Arabic on different nights of the week. Check locally for times and languages. Attending has been made easy with a package operated by Misr Travel. Buses pick up guests at their hotels and transport them to the dock on the east bank of the Nile, where boats then take them on the 10-minute ride to the Temple. The cost is L.E. 60 for one passenger; L.E. 50 each for two passengers.

A museum devoted to the antiquities of Nubia, designed by Mahmud el Hakim, who did the Luxor Museum, is under construction on the east bank and is scheduled to open in 1992. (Inquire locally.)

From Aswan, a brand-new road to Abu Simbel makes it possible for tourists to visit the great antiquity site by land for the first time. The distance is 180 miles and takes about 3.5 hours to drive. A daily bus departs from Aswan's central bus station in the morning; check locally for time. Also, Misr Travel offers a daily tour by air-conditioned bus, departing Aswan at 6 AM Cost: L.E. 172 round-trip including lunch, guide, and entrance fee.

ABU SIMBEL

On the edge of the Nile, 768 miles south of Cairo and 168 miles from Aswan, stands the *Temple of Abu Simbel,* the most colossal temple in all of Egypt and one of the best preserved. Situated on the western bank of the river, it was carved out of the side of a sandstone rock cliff and faces east to let the light of the rising sun penetrate the innermost sanctuary. Entrance: L.E. 27.

The huge complex was built between 1300–1233 BC by one of the greatest pharaohs, Ramses II, and dedicated to the three principal gods of ancient Egypt whose combined spheres of influence covered the entire land: Ptah, god of the underworld as he was worshiped in Memphis, the first capital of Egypt; Amen-Ra, patron god of Thebes; and Ra-Harakhte, a form of the sun-god Horus, worshiped at Heliopolis.

At the entrance to the Great Temple are four colossal statues of Ramses II in a seated position. Each is over 65 feet high. To the right and left of each statue are smaller statues of the royal family. On the left of the second colossus is Ramses' mother, Queen Ti, and on the right stands Queen Nefertiti, his favorite wife. On the facade of the temple are representations of Amen-Ra and Ra-Harakhte. On the south wall outside the temple is an inscription of a treaty of peace between the Egyptians and the Hittites. It is believed to be the first treaty of its kind in history.

From the facade to its innermost chamber, the temple measures 200 feet. The first room, the Great Hypostyle Hall, has a ceiling supported by eight columns faced with huge statues of Ramses II in the pose of the god Osiris. The ceiling and walls throughout the temple are beautifully decorated. The color in many places is in excellent condition. Note particularly the exquisite details of these wall carvings. To the side of Hypostyle Hall are several small storage rooms that also have wall decorations.

The second hall measures 36 by 25 feet and is supported by four pillars. The reliefs on the walls show Ramses II and Nefertari burning incense before the sacred ship of Amen-Ra. The reliefs of Ramses, his horses and chariots are exceptionally good.

The third hall is the innermost chamber and sanctuary. Four seated figures, Ramses II flanked by the gods to whom the temple was dedicated, keep watch in the Holy of Holies, which only the pharaoh and the high priests were allowed to enter. Twice a year at the equinox the sun rises directly in front of the temple, and its rays are meant to penetrate the innermost chamber, casting its light on the statues. This feature of the Abu Simbel Temple is considered to be one of the greatest engineering feats of all time.

Near the Great Temple stands the *Temple of Hathor,* also carved out of solid rock. This smaller temple was built by Ramses II for his wife Nefertiti and dedicated to the goddess Hathor. Outside the temple are six large statues, four of Ramses II and two of his wife, as well as smaller ones of their children. Inside, the Hypostyle Hall has a roof supported by six pillars topped with the head and face of the goddess Hathor, and reliefs similar to those in the Great Temple. The reliefs at the back of the temple that picture the queen and the goddess are particularly lovely.

Photographing Abu Simbel: The best time to take pictures of the temples is in the morning, soon after sunrise. You should be careful not to overexpose film, as the sun and its reflection on the temples are deceptively bright. You will need a flash for the temple interiors.

Note: The excursion to Abu Simbel is generally made as a one-day trip from either Cairo (via New Valley or Aswan) or Aswan. Be sure you have confirmed reservations and be at the airport early to claim your seat. Because of the limited number of flights, especially in high season, these flights have become notorious for overbooking and leaving passengers stranded en route.

Preserving the Antiquities of Upper Egypt

The temple of Abu Simbel was a place of worship as long as the ancient cults lasted—that is, well into the Christian era. In the centuries that followed, sands piled up around the temples until they were finally buried and forgotten. Then in 1813 the Swiss explorer Burckhardt discovered them. He was soon followed by other explorers and archaeologists who wrote about them excitedly, and by the turn of the century the great parade of Egyptologists had tourists at their heels. It was not, however, until the building of the Aswan Dam and the publicity to save the monuments of Nubia that an avalanche of visitors fell on this desolate spot. One of the best and most vivid descriptions of the trip to Abu Simbel, written before the salvage operation began, is given in Alan Moorehead's *The Blue Nile.*

Upon the completion of the new Aswan Dam, the area between Aswan and the Sudan border was inundated by the Nile waters. In anticipation, the Egyptian government, through UNESCO, sent a worldwide appeal to governments, schools, archaeological foundations, and cultural organizations for assistance in exploring the area and saving the most important ancient monuments, which would otherwise be lost forever. The response to this appeal was tremendous. About 20 groups worked in the area and made many important finds. In addition, some 30 monuments and temples were dismantled and transported to other areas.

The most difficult of all the projects was saving the temples at Abu Simbel. Hundreds of proposals were submitted, but the one, finally adopted seemed the most practical, certain and, perhaps, least costly.

The salvage project began in 1965, first by building a wall around the temple to protect it from the rising waters of the Nile. The temples were then dismantled (all 400,000 tons of them) by cutting them into parts that were crated and reassembled in the exact position as before at the top of the mountain cliff, 90 feet above the old site. The project was executed with such precision that only an inch-by-inch examination of the stones can detect the salvage work. It is truly a remarkable achievement and one in which the world can take pride. About 50 nations contributed to the rescue operations, and millions of people around the globe who have never been to Egypt, and may never have the chance to go, sent contributions to help defray the cost.

The project has been completed, and the water of the lake has risen almost to the same level it was at the old site in relationship to the temples.

After you have visited Egypt's monuments from Memphis to Abu Simbel, many of which were built by Ramses II and adorned with his colossal statues and wall paintings, you might have the impression—religious considerations aside—that Ramses II was the greatest egomaniac of all time! Yet, whether it was religious fervor or egomania, when you have seen Abu Simbel you will be grateful that time has preserved such a masterpiece, and that the efforts to preserve it for future generations were so successful. You may pass this way only once in a lifetime, but certainly, when you have seen Abu Simbel, you will know that you have seen one of the great wonders of the world.

SUGGESTED ITINERARY FOR UPPER EGYPT

The following itinerary covers the most important sites in the shortest possible time. It is not, however, the ideal way to see Upper Egypt and is suggested only for those who are pressed for time. By adding another day or two in Luxor, you may be able to see more and at a slower pace.

First Day. *Morning:* Depart Cairo by air for Luxor, arriving in time for lunch.

Afternoon: Visit Karnak and Luxor temples (start early). Depending upon time of arrival in Luxor, it might be possible to visit one of these temples in the morning. However, remember that the sun is very hot by midday and sightseeing should be avoided if possible at this time.

Evening: Enjoy the Sound and Light Show at Karnak temple.

Second Day. *Full-Day Tour:* Cross river and visit the Valley of the Kings. Ramesseum, Colossi of Memnon, Deir al Bahri (Queen Hatshepsut's temple) and, if time permits, visit at least one or two of the Tombs of the Nobles. In the late afternoon or evening, visit the Luxor Museum.

Third Day. *Full Day:* Depart by morning plane to Aswan. In Aswan, visit the new High Dam, the granite quarries, and the temples of Philae. Enjoy a felucca ride to Kitchener and Elephantine islands or visit the local market.

Fourth Day. *Full Day:* Fly to Abu Simbel by early morning plane. Two hours of sightseeing are provided at Abu Simbel before returning to Cairo.

As an alternative, you could eliminate Aswan altogether or fly directly from Cairo to Abu Simbel and pick up this itinerary in reverse order.

PRACTICAL INFORMATION FOR UPPER EGYPT

LUXOR

HOTELS. The following is a list of recommended hotels in the region. Prices quoted are approximate and are subject to change. Unless indicated otherwise, a 12% service charge and 9% tax must be added to the hotel prices.

Akhenaton Club Mediterranee. Khaled Ibn El Walid St. Phone: 777575. Price: $61 swb; $78 dwb. On the Nile south of town, 144 rooms. Booked as tour through Club Med. Accepts individual bookings when not fully booked by Club Med tours; request should be made through Cairo office. Non-guests may have lunch buffet and use swimming facilities, or dinner and show. Attractive four-star hotel in caravanserai-style with rooms on two floors grouped around swimming pool and central courtyard.

Egotel/PLM Azur. 10 Maabad St. Phone: 383–321; Fax: 383–316. 90 rooms. Price: $60 swb; $63 dwb, including 12% service and 9% taxes. One of Egypt's main hotel training schools came under the management of the French hotel chain, PLM Azur, to be operated as a full-fledged first-class hotel. Best value in town. Modern, attractive decor, air-conditioned rooms with twin beds, restaurant, bar, and shops. It is one block from Nile but rooms have views of Nile and Luxor Temple or gardens of the Winter Palace. Pool.

Emilio. Youssef Hassan St. Phone: 383–570; Fax: 384–884. 48 rooms. Price: $30 swb; $40 dwb with breakfast. New hotel for budget travelers. Basic rooms; air-conditioned; restaurant serves reasonably priced meals; bar. Roof garden with view of Nile and Luxor. Caters to European groups.

Etap Luxor PLM Azur. Corniche el Nil. Phone: 384–944; Fax 383–316. 306 rooms. Price: $69 swb; $91 dwb with service and taxes. The lovely, modern hotel is air-conditioned and has a swimming pool and garden, six restaurants, four bars, shops, bank, and telex facilities. The larger public rooms are richly decorated with marble and wood. Guest rooms are attractive and very comfortable. All have bath and a/c. The dining room has one seating with a fixed and an à la carte menu. There is a bar, disco, and shopping arcade.

Isis. Khaled Ibn el Walid St. (south side of Luxor). Phone: 383–356; Fax: 382–923. 530 rooms. On Nile south of town, Price: $89 swb; $116 dwb, including breakfast, service, and taxes. Reservations: Cairo 719591. A modern hotel; rooms simple, nicely furnished; air conditioning, phone, radio, balcony overlooking river. Two pools (heated in winter), tennis, bus service to town, hair salon, shop, exchange facilities. Seafood and Italian restaurants, poolside snacks; bars, nightclub; room service.

Luxor Wena. Opposite the Temple of Luxor, Phone: 580–620; Fax: 580–623. 80 rooms. Price: $73 swb; $90 dwb, including half-board, service, and taxes. Old-style hotel of Moorish architecture in garden setting, built at the turn of the century, it has been totally renovated and leased by WENA, a British hotel group. All rooms are air-conditioned and have balconies, direct dial, and TV. Facilities include a restaurant plus a Nubian Village for Egyptian cuisine, two bars, tea garden, large swimming pool, and snack bar.

Luxor Hilton International. New Karnak. Phone: 384–933; Fax: 384–657. 261 rooms. Price: $69 swb; $105 dwb. Located directly on east bank of Nile north of the Karnak Temple, Luxor's first truly luxury hotel was opened in 1988 and is a most welcome addition. Created as resort hotel, facilities include heated swimming pool, tennis courts, marina, several restaurants, bars, disco, shops. All rooms have balconies with Nile view; minibars; direct-dial phones. Meeting facilities. Horseback riding and rental of a felucca for a Nile sail are available. The Nile steamers operated by Hilton International embark from here for their Nile cruises.

Mina Palace. On Nile in town. Phone: 382–074. Price: $13 swb; $14 dwb, including breakfast, service, and taxes. Small, modest two-star hotel, appears to be well run; reports are good. Air-conditioning, restaurant, bar.

Mövenpick Hotel Jolie Ville Luxor. Crocodile Island, about 2.5 miles from Luxor. Phone: 384–855; Fax 384–936. 350 rooms. Price: $74–$104 swb; $105–$135 dwb with buffet breakfast, service and taxes. Laid out on 26 acres, it is a resort directly on the Nile with steps leading down to its own landing stage and a "sunset" theater where guests can watch Luxor's famous setting sun. Its location is a double blessing away from the honking and hawkers of town and adjacent to cultivated fields where you can enjoy the birds and nature of the river. Hotel operates continual bus service to town. Dinner buffet, an elaborate spread of Egyptian and European dishes, has received praise in the past. To avoid what appears to be indifference to diners who are not hotel guests, the management recommends non-guests to make reservations for dinner. Single-story bungalows in a garden setting. All rooms have air-conditioning, minibar, phone, bath/shower, and terrace. Two restaurants, bar and garden snack bar; tennis, pool, and jogging.

Savoy Hotel. El Nil Street. Phone: 580–522. 108 rooms. Price: $31 swb; $38 dwb, including breakfast, services, and taxes. Tourist-class. Set in nice garden. Rooms and furnishings adequate and have air-conditioning, pool, and a terrace overlooking the Nile that is a popular meeting place.

Sheraton Luxor. El Awameya Rd., Box 43. Phone: 384–544; Fax: 384–941; in U.S., 800–325–3535. 302 rooms in main building; 92 rooms in garden buildings. Price: $54 swb garden; $75 swb Nile view; $89 dwb garden; $93 dwb Nile view. Located on 14 acres in an area south of town that has grown in popularity as a hotel location, the hotel has a two restaurants, bar, two lighted tennis, croquet, and volleyball courts, swimming pool, marina for feluccas. Rooms are very small. Be sure to ask for a room facing the Nile; garden side is noisy and faces morning sun. Sunset concerts in setting overlooking Nile; all-day trips with lunch to Dendarah on hotel's own yacht.

Winter Palace. El Nil St., by the Nile, 268 rooms. Phone: 382–000; Fax: 384–087. Price: $80 swb; $101 dwb with breakfast. Finally, after years of promises and delays, the government turned over the management of this grand old dowager to Pullman Hotels. Renovations were under way at press time and its new look is eagerly awaited.

SHOPPING. Shops in and near hotels have the usual array of Egyptian crafts. Luxor is the best place to have inexpensive cotton kaftans made to order. *Oriental Bazaar,* 14 Tourist Bazaar, can make them in three hours starting at L.E. 25–40 and up. *A. A. Gaddis* in Winter Palace shopping arcade is a long-established store, but shop around before you buy—and bargain hard. Caftans cost L.E. 10–40 depending on quality of fabric and design. The street between the Tourist Bazaar and Luxor Temple is usually lined with vendors selling caftans and cotton shirts and dresses.

For workmanship and prices, a reader has recommended *Sami Abd-el-Malek,* a craftsman in the Tourist Bazaar who specializes in ivory and stocks superior-quality merchandise. What particularly impressed our reader was that the merchant was honest enough to say that real ivory hasn't been used in inlay mosaic in Egypt in 15 years. *Aboudi Bookshop,* next to New Winter Palace, has the best selection of books in Luxor. *Bazar Radwan,* a kiosk near the Luxor Wena Hotel, is recommended for high-quality caftans. For those who really want to try their skills at bargaining and get the real flavor of Luxor, Market Street is a must.

SIGHTSEEING. A spectacular hot-air balloon ride over the west bank and the Nile River is available. It is quite expensive—$250 for up to two hours—and due to wind and weather conditions, the balloon cannot always be inflated. Inquiries and reservations should be made at the office of *Balloons over Egypt* (tel. 386–515) at the Movenpick Hotel Jolie Ville-Luxor, or at Luxor Hilton.

ASWAN

Unless noted otherwise, hotel prices in Aswan have a 12% service charge and a 6% tax added to them.

Abu Simbel. Corniche St., 66 rooms. Phone: 322–453. Price: $8 swb; $12 dwb, including breakfast, service, and taxes. Tourist-class hotel with rooms facing river. All have bath, but most with shower only. Air-conditioning is extra. There is a restaurant, bar; elevator. The hotel is located next to the public swimming pool and in front of the docks for the Sheraton and Hilton Nile steamers.

Amoun. On Amoun Island. 56 rooms. Phone: 322–555. Price: $63 dwb with breakfast to $105 dwb with three meals. Housed in what was once a palace on an island in the Nile at the heart of town, Club Mediterranee's resort has a Beverly Hills–inspired pool overlooking the Nile. Guests reach it by the resort's private boat.

Aswan Oberoi. Elephantine Island, 244 rooms. Phone: 323–455; Fax: 323–485. Price: $87 swb; $98 dwb. Large deluxe hotel and one of the best in Egypt; wonderful location in the middle of Nile with view of Aswan and Nile Valley all around. Facilities include swimming pool, restaurant, gardens, bar, and nightclub, and fully equipped health spa with sauna, steam room, whirlpools, open-air sand baths, and other facilities. Aswan sand has long been known for its medicinal and healing properties.

Isis. Corniche el Nil St., 78 chalets. Phone: 324–905. Price: $63 swb; $88 dwb. Built directly along the bank of the Nile, this first-class hotel has a large pool, good Italian restaurant, bar. Affiliated with Isis Luxor.

PLM Azur New Cataract. Next to the hotel of the same name (below), 144 rooms, Phone: 323–434; Fax: 323–510. Price: $75 swb; $93 dwb. An exact duplicate of the New Winter Palace in Luxor. Air-conditioned and open all year. Facilities include 24-hour coffee shop, swimming pool, café, tennis, and nightclub.

PLM Azur Kalabasha. Located on the west bank of the Nile. Phone: 322–999. Price: $51 swb; $64 dwb. A hotel built about four decades ago catering mainly to European groups. It has been taken over by PLM and that is good news.

Pullman Cataract. Aqtal al Tahrir St., one mile south of Aswan on a hill overlooking the Nile, 129 rooms. Phone: 323–222; Fax: 323–510. Price: $90–$110 swb; $112–$130 dwb. For half a century this hotel was a famous wintering spot for European aristocrats. When President Mubarak visited Aswan in 1986, he was so appalled by the dilapidated condition of this once-grand lady that he ordered a total renovation. This has been completed and the building facade is back to its original ochre-and-white color; the original cutlery is back in use; and the famed terrace overlooking Elephantine Island is reserved for afternoon tea, served in the old tradition. The gardens were also renovated—one corner has a music nook for recorded concerts at sunset. A pub, disco, and lobby bar were added, and the Moorish-style dining room also serves as a supper club called Club 1902. There are plans to renovate the two royal and two presidential suites as they were when the czar of Russia and Edward, Prince of Wales, were guests.

Ramses. Abtal El Tahrir St., 129 rooms. Phone: 324–000. Price: $13 swb; $19 dwb, including breakfast and taxes. A two-star hotel, and some rooms are quite acceptable. Air-conditioned; restaurant, bar, and disco. Good value.

ABU SIMBEL

Nefertari. This hotel is about halfway between the airport and the antiquity site. Price: $61 swb; $77 dwb with half-board. After recent renovations and expansion to about 60 rooms, the hotel has become a three-star hotel with nicely furnished rooms, making an overnight stay at Abu Simbel a pleasant alternative to a hurried day trip. There is also a swimming pool. The hotel can arrange for a tour of antiquities and a visit to nearby Nubian village. At no time should you go to Abu Simbel with the idea of remaining overnight without first obtaining a confirmed reservation.

RESTAURANTS. In Luxor only hotel restaurants are recommended. In Aswan, the restaurants on the Corniche might be tried by adventurous travelers. Most specialize in simple fish dinners and they are cheap.

RECOMMENDED READING. *Luxor, A Guide to Ancient Thebes* and *Upper Egypt* by Jill Kamel are excellent paperbacks to have with you as guides during your visit in Luxor, Karnak, and on the west bank. They are available in local bookstores and contain good maps and descriptions without being academic.

Hathor, Goddess of Joy and Love

ALEXANDRIA

Ancient Queen of the Mediterranean

Egypt's second-largest city and chief port, Alexandria (in Arabic *Iskandariyah*), is 110 miles northwest of Cairo on the Mediterranean. Its excellent beaches, climate, and lively atmosphere have long made it the country's major summer resort.

When Alexander the Great conquered Egypt in 332 BC, he founded a city bearing his name on the site of the tiny fishing village of Rakotis, facing the rocky island of Pharos. Under the Ptolemies, the city grew rapidly and remained the capital of the empire throughout their reign.

The city also became a great cultural center and attracted the most famous scientists, scholars, philosophers, poets, and artists of the time. It had two celebrated royal libraries, said to contain 490,000 different scrolls. Around the museum housing one of the libraries rose what is considered one of the first universities in history. Under Ptolemy II, the great Tower of Pharos, one of the seven wonders of the ancient world, was built. The Tower, 220 feet high and lighted by night, is said to have been the world's first lighthouse.

During the time of Julius Caesar, Alexandria became the second-largest city of the Roman Empire. When Octavian entered the city in 30 BC, after the suicide of Anthony and Cleopatra, it became formally a part of the Roman domain. Under the Byzantine Empire, Alexandria was one of the great centers of Christendom and the see of a patriarchate.

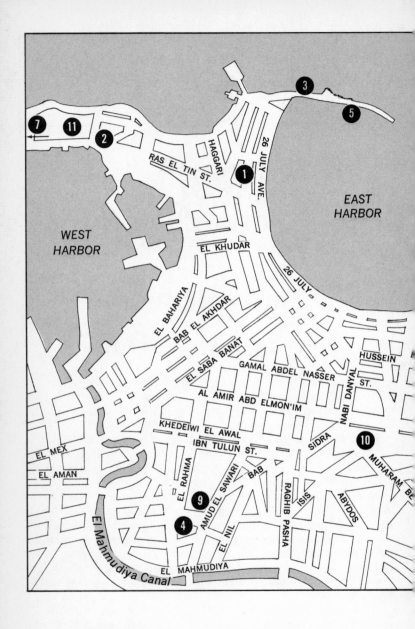

EAST
HARBOR

WEST
HARBOR

HAGGARI

RAS EL TIN ST.

26 JULY AVE.

EL KHUDAR

26 JULY

EL BAHARIYA

BAB EL AKHDAR

EL SABA BANAT

GAMAL ABDEL NASSER

HUSSEIN

AL AMIR ABD ELMON'IM

NABI DANYAL ST.

KHEDEIWI EL AWAL

IBN TULUN ST.

SIDRA

EL MEX

EL AMAN

EL RAHMA

AMUD EL SAWARI

BAB

RAGHIB PASHA

ISIS

ABYDOS

MUHARAM BE

EL NIL

El Mahmudiya Canal

EL MAHMUDIYA

Points of Interest

1) Abu el Abbas Mosque
2) Anfushy Necropolis

3) Aquarium
4) Catacombs of Kom-esh-Shuqafa
5) Fort Kait Bey
6) Greco-Roman Museum

7) Lighthouse
8) Nuzha and Antoniadis Gardens
9) Pompey's Pillar
10) Railway Station

11) Ras-el-Tin Palace
12) Sporting Club
13) Stadium
14) Zoo

By the time the city fell to the Arabs in 642, it had declined considerably. In 1798, when Napoleon's troops landed in Egypt, Alexandria was a mere village.

The city regained its importance once more under Muhammad Ali. In 1819 he ordered the construction of the Mahmudiya Canal to the Nile, thus bringing large areas in the city's vicinity under irrigation. Under Muhammad Ali's successors, Alexandria became the traditional summer capital of Egypt.

Today Alexandria has a population of about five million people and is one of the chief seaports on the Mediterranean Sea. Very little remains of the city's ancient past. Remnants of its onetime glory, especially the Greek and Roman periods, are housed in a museum in the center of the city, and excavations continue to turn up important finds, such as the almost perfect Roman amphitheater uncovered only a few years ago.

Alexandria is different from Cairo—its ambience is Mediterranean rather than Oriental. If you imagine it as the city described by Lawrence Durrell in his *Alexandria Quartet,* you may be disappointed to learn that it is no longer the same. But Alexandria has a charm and romance of its own, and no trip to Egypt is complete without a visit to this famous city.

Coastal Road and Beaches

The first and most remarkable look a visitor can have at Alexandria is the sweeping view of its crescent-shaped seafront, lined with stately palms and lovely old houses, hotels, and buildings.

A 15-mile east–west road, the Corniche, skirts the city along the Mediterranean from the port on the west to Montazah at its farthest limits on the east. From the western end at Ras el Tin, the peninsula that was once the Island of Pharos, the road passes the city's major hotels and cafés on the south to Midan al Tahrir (Liberation Square), the main square of the downtown area overlooking the eastern harbor, and Ramleh, the main tram station. On the far side of the harbor, the road continues along the Mediterranean to the city's most beautiful residential sections on the south and a series of beaches on the north. Many of the beaches have the same names as the city districts behind them: Chatby, Cleopatra, Sidi Gabr, Rushdi, Stanley, Glymenopoulo, San Stefano, Sidi Bishr, Mandara, and Montazeh.

Here cabins may be rented for the summer season. On both sides of the Corniche Drive, hotels, nightclubs, sidewalk cafés, and restaurants are the center of activity for the thousands of Egyptians who spend the summer here.

In bygone days the entire government moved from Cairo to Alexandria for the summer, and the diplomatic corps gladly moved with it. Now the country no longer indulges in this extravagance.

Sites of Antiquity

Opening hours for the antiquity sites: 9 AM–4 PM daily except Friday; 9–11:30 AM and 1:30–4 PM.

Pompey's Pillar. Entrance: L.E. 3. A column 84 feet high and about seven feet thick, made of polished Aswan rose granite, was erroneously called Pompey's Pillar by the Crusaders. In fact, it had nothing to do with

Pompey. It was erected by the Roman prefect Posthumus in honor of the emperor Diocletian and was part of the splendid Temple of Serapis. Some historians contend that it was originally within a portico surrounded by 400 columns, on the spot where tradition places the famous library of Alexandria. An entrance on the west of the pillar leads down a flight of stairs into long subterranean chambers that may have been part of the Temple of Serapis. Some claim the chambers were part of the famous library, but this is doubtful.

Roman Amphitheatre. Entrance: L.E. 3. Not far from the main railway station, an enormous area is now being excavated. To date the most important find has been an amphitheater in almost perfect condition. It is the first one of the Roman era to be found in Egypt. Carvings of the cross and other Christian symbols indicate that it was used long after the last Roman departed. The entire complex was discovered in the course of digging the foundation for a new building.

Catacombs of Kom el-Shuqafa *(Chofaga).* Entrance: L.E. 8. The funerary construction of the Kom el-Shuqafa dates from the 2nd century AD (Some authorities date it as early as the 2nd century BC) The dead were lowered through a shaft into the catacombs, which are three stories high. A winding staircase leads into the chambers of the first floor. The catacombs are unique both for their plan and decoration, which are a curious blend of Greco-Roman and Egyptian designs. They were discovered only in 1900. After you have visited the temples and tombs of Upper Egypt, it will be easy to see how the nation's art had sadly deteriorated by the late Ptolemaic period.

Anfushi Necropolis. Entrance: L.E. 6. In a park near the entrance to Ras-al-Tin Palace is a necropolis dating from the 2nd century BC Although it is older than the catacombs of Kom el-Shuqafa, it is less important because of its inferior decorations. All the tombs are carved out of rock and contain no other building material. A visit is recommended only if you have plenty of time.

Fort Kait Bey. Entrance: L.E. 6. On the spot where the Pharos Lighthouse once stood, a fortress and mosque were built by Sultan Kait Bey in the 15th century. These structures have recently been restored. The site is especially worth visiting for the view of Alexandria from the harbor. *Alexandria,* by E. M. Forster (*see* Suggested Reading List at the beginning of the book), has an interesting description of the history of the Pharos and the development of the island. The description of Pompey's Pillar, the catacombs, and the necropolis are useful for visits to these sites.

Museums and Royal Palaces

Greco-Roman Museum. Mataf Street at Gamal Abdel Nasser St., Hours: winter 9 AM to 4 PM Closed Friday from 11:30 AM to 1:30 PM. Entrance: L.E. 11.

The museum, founded in 1891, gives a visitor some idea of the grandeur of Alexandria under the Greeks and Romans. Further, it provides the link between the Egyptian Antiquities Museum and the Coptic Museum in Cairo. The museum recently had extensive renovations.

The collection includes statues, bas-reliefs, capitals, earthenware, jewelry, and amulets of mingled Egyptian, Greek, and Roman design. The museum has a large collection of coins minted in Alexandria during the

Greco-Roman period and an excellent display of Tanagra figurines. Note especially the exhibits of iridescent and fused glass and the fragments of Coptic fabrics.

Hydrobiological Museum. Hours: winter and summer 9 AM to 2 PM daily. Entrance: about 25.

Located on the south side of the street immediately before Fort Kait Bey, the museum houses a collection of fish from the Mediterranean, Red Sea, and the Nile River.

Ras el Tin Palace. Begun by Muhammad Ali in 1834 and completed in 1845, it was the official summer headquarters of the rulers of Egypt down through the mid-20th century. Its eastern gate is made up of six tall granite columns topped by the royal crown of Egypt and bearing inscriptions from the Koran. The room in which King Farouk signed his abdication is on the ground floor. After signing the document, Farouk descended the stairs leading to the wharf below, boarded his yacht, and sailed to Italy. The palace is not open to the public now but is being used as a guest house for official guests and visiting dignitaries.

Montazah Palace. Built by Khedive Abbas in 1892, the present palace dates from 1926 and is made up of several separate buildings. The estate is located east of Alexandria on the Mediterranean shore and is surrounded by 350 acres of beautiful parks and gardens. The main building is not open to the public at present. The Salamek (women's quarters) is a hotel. Visitors may swim at its beach or relax in the Palace gardens Entrance: L.E. 1.

Museum of Fine Arts. 18 Menasce St., Moharrem Bey. Hours: 8 AM to 2 PM daily except Friday. In addition to the art collection, the museum stages exhibits and has a year-round program of concerts.

Royal Jewelry Museum. 21 Ahmed Yehia Pasha St., Zizinia. Hours: Open daily 9 AM to 4 PM; closed Friday 11:15 AM to 1:30 PM. Entrance: L.E. 11. Housed in the former palace of the great-granddaughter of Muhammad Ali, it is as interesting for its architecture, art, and stained-glass windows as it is for the jewelry that once belonged to the elite of the old regime. The jewelry reflects the style in which Egypt's very rich once lived.

Library of Alexandria. An international committee sponsored by President François Mitterrand of France, Queen Sofia of Spain, Queen Noor of Jordan, and others and directed by UNESCO has launched a project to re-create the Library of Alexandria, once the seat of Greek scholars. Founded by Ptolemy II in the 3rd century BC, the library was located in the Brucheion district to the east of the main harbor. The area also contained the royal palace, museum, and tomb of Alexander the Great.

The new library, to be built near the original site and the present-day University of Alexandria, will have 200,000 volumes of books when it opens in 1995, but will be capable of housing four million. The focus will be on Alexandria, the Mediterranean region, and the Arab world. The collection starts with a donation of 76,000 rare documents in Arabic, Persian, and Turkish, preserved on microfilm, by the Egyptian Book Organization. In addition to special collections, it will be a general public library. It is also to be a center for the study of the ancient civilizations of the Mediterranean and will be connected to major world libraries by computer. It will also have a planetarium.

Sites East of Alexandria

Abukir. 18 miles: On the site of ancient Canopus, once a small fishing port, has now grown into an Alexandria suburb. It was here that Nelson's fleet defeated the French in 1798, thereby crushing France's attempt to gain a foothold in the eastern Mediterranean. The area contains the remains of ancient public baths, a temple dedicated to Serapis, and relics of Napoleon's expedition to Egypt. Four miles off the coast of Abukir divers have been excavating the wreck of an ancient ship that lies only 30 feet under the water.

Rosetta. 35 miles: The town, founded in the 9th century on the site of ancient Bolbitine, was once important as a center for commerce with the Orient. In 1799, near Rosetta at Fort St. Julien, one of Napoleon's soldiers found the now famous Rosetta Stone, a basalt tablet inscribed by the priests of Ptolemy V in hieroglyphics, demotic characters, and Greek. From this stone, Champollion found the key to deciphering Egyptian hieroglyphics. The town has many attractive Ottoman-style brick buildings.

Ras al Barr. The narrow extension of land between the Mediterranean Sea and the Damietta Branch of the Nile is a popular fishing area. Temporary bungalows of wood and dry reeds, put up each spring and removed in autumn, can be rented for the summer season. It is about a three-hour drive from Alexandria and is easier to reach from Port Said.

Sites West of Alexandria

The road west of Alexandria passes through Meks, the main industrial center of Alexandria, and skirts the sea. Another road slightly farther inland bypasses some of the town. The North Coast Highway is being widened to a four-lane carriageway from Alexandria to Mersa Matruh, and the first 30 miles along the coast are witnessing massive—and generally ugly—urban and tourist development.

Al Agami. 12 miles: The beach at Agami is one of the best in the vicinity of Alexandria and has become the most popular beach on the coast. Houses are available for rent during the summer season, and there are several hotels on the beach. Many Alexandrian and Cairo families own houses in the area and spend their summers here.

Burg al-Arab and Bahig. 27 miles: Near Abusir are the remains of a 3rd-century BC temple dedicated to Osiris, later turned into a fortress by the Arabs. Also in the area are the ruins of a Ptolemaic lighthouse believed to be one in a chain that stretched from the Pharos at Alexandria across the North African coast to Cyrene. Seven and a half miles south of Bahig, St. Menas is the site of a once great Christian city. Its ruins include several churches, monastery buildings, the sacred baths, and a cemetery.

Burg El Arab was formerly on a caravan route, and the village and the dress of its people are especially colorful, retaining a flavor of their Bedouin origins. From this village to El Alamein, the road once overlooked the white sand dunes bordering the Mediterranean's blue-green waters, but now the view is being rapidly obscured by tourist villages. What was once fig groves and scrub pastures for the Bedouins' goats and camel have been overtaken by a building boom completely devoid of architectural merit.

Wadi el Natrun. 63 miles southwest of Alexandria: Near the Natrun oasis is a complex of monasteries dating from the 2nd century AD. (Descriptions are available in Dorothea Russel's *Medieval Cairo and the Monasteries of Wadi Natrun.*) The monasteries can most easily be reached off the desert road halfway between Cairo and Alexandria. In the past, visitors needed advance permission from the patriarchate in Cairo (tel. 822256) to visit Wadi El Natrun, but now the monks are allowing tourists to visit more readily as a way of obtaining needed revenue to keep the monasteries alive.

A thousand years ago there were as many as 50 monasteries here, but now there are only four still occupied by monks. These can also be seen in the distance from the desert road just before the rest house situated at the halfway point between Cairo and Alexandria. A sign on the west side of the road designates the track to the monasteries.

Al Alamein. 64 miles on the Mediterranean: At this location one of the decisive battles of World War II was fought between the German Afrika Corps led by Rommel and the British 8th Army commanded by Montgomery. As you enter the village itself, the first monument on the south side of the road is the Greek monument, followed by the British Memorial, cemetery and garden. A pavilion at the cemetery bears this inscription:

> Within this cloister are inscribed the names of soldiers and airmen of the British Commonwealth and Empire who died fighting on land or in the air where two continents meet and to whom the fortune of war denied a known and honoured grave. With their fellows who rest in this cemetery, with their comrades in arms of the Royal Navy and with the seamen of the Merchant Marine, they preserved for the West the link with the East and turned the tide of war.

In the village of El Alamein is a military museum, directly on the north side of the coastal road. It contains material from the World War II battle as well as Egyptian military displays.

Nine miles beyond the village is the German monument, on a bluff overlooking the sea. After you leave the main road, at the fork in the sand track, bear to the right, and this will take you there. The caretaker, who speaks English, lives in the little house at the base of the memorial. Inside the enormous stone structure, in addition to the ashes of the known dead, is the grave of 31 unknown soldiers of undetermined nationality, bearing the inscription "Death knows no country."

Beyond the German cemetery (2.4 miles) is the Italian memorial, cemetery, and a small museum. The caretaker lives in the house to the east of the monument. Sound your car horn and he will appear with the key. Beyond this memorial, on the coastal road, are markers designating the Axis and British minefields.

Sidi Abdel Rahman. 92 miles west of Alexandria: The small village has a shrine mosque to Abdel Rahman, a venerated Muslim holy man, who was especially popular among the Bedouin.

Between El Alamein and Mersa Matruh there is only one gas station, located on the south side of the road about halfway into the village of El Dabah.

Mersa Matruh. 170 miles on the Mediterranean: The small port of Mersa Matruh is situated on a lagoon cut off from the sea by a chain of rocks. Its superb beach and crystal-clear waters have made it a favorite off-the-beaten-track vacation spot. It can be reached by car and train from Cairo and Alexandria. The train, however, is not recommended. There are no first-class coaches, and the journey from Alexandria could take six hours. Car travel from Alexandria is about three hours and from Cairo about seven hours. Express buses run from Cairo directly to Mersa Matruh, leaving from Tahrir Square. Buses also run directly from Alexandria, leaving from Saad Zaghlul Square.

Even before the Ptolemies, Mersa Matruh was a lively trading center. At the time of Alexander the Great the city was named Amonia, probably because it was the entrance to the desert route to the Siwa Oasis, where Amon was worshiped. Later, beautiful palaces were built at Matruh by Cleopatra, who chose to settle here with Caesar. In the hills north of the town is a church dating from the early Christian period.

West of town on the seaward side of a spit of land that forms another lagoon, is the beautiful Cleopatra's Beach. Here the coastline is a mass of rock columns and promontories gnarled and eroded by centuries of pounding seas. One of these outcroppings, known as Cleopatra's Baths, has been chiseled hollow and two carved tunnels—one the seaside and one the shoreside—allow seawater to flow in and out. Legend has it that Cleopatra bathed at this timeworn spot. The lee of this headland can be reached either by car or, during the summer season, by a sailboat ferry near the Beau Site Hotel.

Rommel's Cave is another favorite tourist spot in Mersa Matruh. It is located on the eastern edge of town and can be found by following the main east–west street, Sharia Galaah, through town to the east, where signs in English point the way. The cave where Rommel, in solitude, drew up his battle plans for Tobruk has been turned into a small museum. In 1978 Rommel's son donated several of his father's personal maps and clothing for display. Beyond Rommel's Cave and around the bend to the east is Rommel's Beach, noted for its excellent snorkeling. Leave your car parked at the little hotel called Marine Fuad and walk out to the beach; the sand is very soft.

Mersa Matruh is the capital of the Matruh governate, the largest in Egypt. It covers one-third of the nation's land area. There is a large government administration center, and the Ministry of Tourism maintains an office on the second floor of the municipal building located on the corner of the two main streets, Sharia Alexandria and the Corniche.

The town has a population of 60,000, and accommodates over 100,000 summer tourists, mostly Egyptians. Mersa Matruh has great tourist potential; its nearby beaches are considered among the most beautiful in the world.

The main road to the Libyan frontier at Sollum drops directly south after leaving Matruh and connects with the new road to the famous *Siwa Oasis*. Permission to visit Siwa must be obtained from the Office of Internal Security at the extreme eastern end end of Sharia Galaah in Mersa Matruh. Foreign visitors should carry passports, which must be shown at a checkpoint east of the city.

Some items from Siwa, such as handicrafts, dates and olive oil, may be purchased in a government-run shop on Sharia Galaah, next to the government dry-goods store called Benzione. The crafts store also sells items made by the Bedouins of the Western Desert. Prices are fixed.

West of the main mosque, whose minarets can be seen from any point in town, a secondary road leaves Mersa Matruh from the Corniche, the principal road along the harbor. This road, which is paved part of the way and is hard-surface gravel the rest, follows the coastline to the west and is one of the most picturesque and beautiful drives in all of Egypt. The road parallels the blue-green waters of the sea, framed with stark white sand dunes, and passes through olive and fig orchards.

The road first passes through a village called *Qasr,* which means "palace" in Arabic. It is believed that Anthony and Cleopatra built a magnificent palace here, from which Cleopatra sent out her armies to try to defeat Augustus. Qasr is five miles west of Matruh. Seven miles beyond Qasr is *Abyad,* a village renowned for its lovely beach. Signs in English on the main road indicate the way.

In the next village, *Om Rakham* (14 miles), at a small grocery store on the north side of the road, you may ask to be taken to the site of a Ramses II limestone temple, a few miles west of Om Rakham. It is situated only a few feet south of the road in an olive-fig grove, but is of marginal interest because the limestone has been severely pitted and eroded by water. Its foundation is now situated in a valley that floods during the winter rainy season. The desert between the temple and the road is overgrown with thistle. Should you undertake the short walk, be sure to wear closed shoes and cover your ankles.

Two miles farther west is *Ageeba Beach,* famous throughout Egypt and said to be one of the most beautiful beaches in the world. The road from Matruh winds up a hill and makes a horseshoe turn. At this point, you may leave your car and walk to the edge of the hill to see the sculptured cliffs plummeting to the water's edge. This location commands a breathtaking view of the Mediterranean, the beaches east and west, and the rock ledges meeting the blue sea below. A small but easily managed path leads down to the beach and caves. It is a good place for snorkeling; many varieties of fish can be seen. The drive from Ageeba back to Matruh takes a half hour.

PRACTICAL INFORMATION FOR ALEXANDRIA

HOW TO GET AROUND. Alex Limo. Phone: 482–5252 in Alexandria; 610–0470 in Cairo; has Mercedes cars driven by English-speaking drivers. Cost is L.E. 78 for half day within a 30-mile radius of city; L.E. 156 full day up to 10 hours, within 60 miles. For cars with air conditioning add 20%. If you are planning to stay at the Sheraton or at one of the other hotels at Montazeh and are arriving from Cairo by train, it would be closer to get off at Sidi Gaber Station rather than continuing on into Cairo Station in the center of Alexandria.

HOTELS. Agami Palace At Al-Algami Beach (west of Alexandria). Phone: 430–0386. $24 sw/shower; $27–$35 dw/shower, including breakfast, service, and taxes. It's not really a palace, but it is clean and services are adequate. Its advantage is proximity to the beach. Pool.
Hannoville Hotel, at Hannoville Beach west of Agami, 157 rooms. Phone: 430–3258. $23 swb; $30 dwb with shower and breakfast, services, and taxes.

Hotel Delta. 14 Champollion St., Mazarita. 54 rooms. Phone: 482–5542. $40 swb; $50 dwb with breakfast, taxes, and service. Modern hotel near the city center, one block of city seafront and convenient to Ramleh train station. Rooms are nicely furnished with twin beds; all have bath, air conditioning, TV, and phone. Good French restaurant, bar, telex, and photocopying service.

Metropole. 52 Saad Zaghloul St. Phone: 482–1467. $19 swb; $24 dwb including breakfast, services, and taxes. A recently renovated city-center hotel with Old World charm. Many rooms have balconies with sea views. Bar, restaurant, telex.

Montazeh Sheraton Hotel. Corniche el Nil, 307 rooms. Phone: 548–0550. Approximately $79 swb; $98 dwb. The 15-story hotel overlooks the gardens of Montazeh Palace and the Mediterranean Sea. The hotel has several restaurants and bars, pool, and conference center. The modern, air-conditioned, seafront hotel also has a nightclub, disco, tennis court, and can arrange water sports and fishing trips. All rooms have TV, direct-dial local calls, and offer free movies.

Palestine. Montazeh Palace. Phone: 547–3500; Fax: 547–3378. $78 swb; $97 dwb, service, and taxes. Directly on the beach of the palace grounds. Recently acquired by the same management group as Shepheard's in Cairo, the hotel has been renovated to return it to deluxe standards.

Pullman Cecil. 16 Saad Zaghul Sq. 87 rooms. Phone: 807–463. $44 swb; $54 dwb. Centrally located, overlooking the eastern harbor, the famous hotel, built in 1930, has been completely renovated and is now fully air-conditioned. All rooms have bath, minibar, and TV. Facilities include restaurant, bar, coffee shop, nightclub, disco, casino, shopping arcade, business center, and fitness club.

Ramada Renaissance. 544 Ave. El Geish, Sedi Bishr. 200 rooms. Phone: 549–0935; Fax: 431–1690. $75–$85 swb; $93–$105 dwb. Modern hotel in 12-story tower is part of an apartment/office complex. All rooms with TV, minibars, direct-dial phones, air conditioning; most have balcony and sea view. Several restaurants, bars, and shopping complex.

San Giovanni. 205 Al Geish Ave., Stanley Beach, 30 rooms. Phone: 852–258; Fax: 546–4408. $53 dwb; suites $95 with breakfast, service, and taxes. Simple, clean; good location, air-conditioning, TV, private bath, direct-dial phones, and in-house movies. 24-hour room service; bar, nightclub, and 24-hour coffee shop. Hotel has one of the best restaurants in town.

WEST OF ALEXANDRIA

Mersa Matruh: *Beau Site.* 43 rooms. Located on the beach, this is the best hotel and it is always heavily booked in summer. The owners, the Madpak family, take reservations at their home in Heliopolis. Phone: 259–9480; in Matruh, 03–943–319. The hotel is a collection of buildings along the beach, including the dining room. It has a pleasant and helpful staff, and the food is excellent. The hotel opens in May and closes in October. Rates are $25 swb; $33–$43 dwb; compulsory board, $21–$75 daily. Tents with two beds rent for $7 per night. A budget alternative is a Greek pension, *Hotel de Roses,* Sharia Galaah. Phone: 942755.

Sidi Abdel Rahman: *El Alamein.* On a beautiful white-sand beach a popular summer resort open year-round. Phone: (03) 492–1228; Fax: (03)

807–250. Hotel is located on the Mediterranean, 72 miles west of Alexandria. The PLM Azur-run hotel has a main building with 70 simply furnished guest rooms and 20 villas—all with private bath and terrace facing the sea. Prices: $50 swb; $60 dwb with breakfast. $185 per day for villa.

USEFUL ADDRESSES. *Airline Companies:* British Airways, 15 Saad Zaghloul Square; Sudan Airways, 6 Talaat Harb St.; TWA, 2 Gamal Abdel Nasser St.; Egyptair, 19 Saad Zaghloul Square. *Consulates:* United Kingdom, 3 Mina Street, Roushdy Pasha, tel. 546–7001; U.S.A., 110 Gamal Abdel Nasser St. (better known as Horreya St.), tel. 482–1911. *Club of Alexandria,* 32 S. Zaghloul St., tel. 483–4340, is a social, membership club of the city's movers and shakers. Annual membership for foreigners is U.S. $200 per couple. Dining room serves good food in old, elegant ambience.

SHOPPING. Although its bazaars do not compare with those of Cairo, Alexandria has a lively shopping district located in the area off Tahrir Square, known as Zankit el Sitat Square. Many of the well-known Cairo department stores, such as *Salon Vert* and *Omar Effendi,* have branches here.

Alexandria is the center of the leather and textile industries and prices might be lower here, especially for those who are good at bargaining.

RESTAURANTS. Alexandria is noted for its seafood, especially the large shrimp, which is excellent when grilled and served with lemon or butter. Try it at *San Giovanni* and you'll have the treat of your life.

Expensive

San Giovanni. 205 El Geish, Stanley Beach, tel. 852–258. Diners overlook Mediterranean in pleasant surroundings on city's best seafood; meat selections too. Adjacent nightclub starts after 10:30 PM

Moderate–Expensive

International Seafood. 800 El Geish Rd., Montazeh, tel. 873–951. Fresh Mediterranean seafood in elegant ambience.

Lord's Inn. 12 Moh. Ahmed el Afifi St., San Stefano, tel. 586–5664. Dinner only; disco after 11 PM. Sophisticated; excellent European cuisine.

Michael's. Agami/Bless section. Housed in villa; very trendy. Outstanding seafood.

Samakmak. 42 Ras el Tin Palace St. Popular, and deservedly so, seafood specialist. Try the crab *tajine.* Informal ambience.

Moderate

Kadoura. Beyram el Tonsi St. Inexpensive, very local café noted for seafood; owned by former fisherman.

New China. Hotel Corail, 802 El Geish Ave., Montazeh, tel. 548–0996. City's best for Far Eastern cuisine; sea view.

Pastroudis. 39 El Horreya St. Famous sidewalk café and pastry shop; good for snacks and people watching.

Saraya. Stanley Beach, tel. 850–885. Stylish restaurant with Middle Eastern food and sea views; daily show with good belly dancer.

Sea Gull. El Max, tel. 445–5575. Housed in old "castle" jammed with antiques, this popular spot specializes in fresh seafood.

Tikka Grill. Corniche, Eastern Harbor. Very pretty restaurant over-hangs sea with large outdoor terrace. Famous for grilled cuisine.

Xephyron. This seafood restaurant overlooking the Mediterranean in suburban Abu Kir is famous throughout Egypt for its excellent fish. You make your choice from the fresh fish and shrimp on display and have them cooked to order.

Inexpensive

Chez Gaby. 22 El Horreya St. Selections from pizza to Continental. Downtown location makes it a favorite.

Havana Bistro. Shurta Sherif, Horreya St. Bar atmosphere; excellent service; and best *calamari* in town.

Thoth, God of Science

THE SUEZ CANAL, THE RED SEA, AND SINAI

Passage to the Orient

The area of Suez, known as *Goshen* in the Bible, was strategically important in ancient times to the civilizations of the eastern Mediterranean because it formed a bridge of commerce and conquest between Asia and Africa. Many efforts were made to connect the two great bodies of water—the Mediterranean and the Red seas—which were separated by this narrow strip of land.

The first attempt to cut a channel was made about 2100 BC. It utilized an ancient branch of the Nile River. A second and different canal was cut in about 1900 BC., running from the Red Sea and Bitter Lakes to meet the Nile at a point north of Bubastis. It was called the Canal of the Pharaohs and was used for about a thousand years. This canal is pictured in a stele on the temple at Karnak and shows Seti I returning from victory in Asia by way of a canal at Suez. The same canal, after centuries of disuse, was redug in 606 BC but wasn't completed until 521 BC, during the time of Darius I.

A third canal was dug in about 286 BC during the reign of Ptolemy II and continued to be used as late as the Roman period. In AD 98 the Roman emperor Trajan had the canal changed so that it could meet the Nile near present-day Cairo. This canal came to be known as the River of Trajan.

202

The extent to which the canal was used during the following centuries is not clear, although references to it are found in historical records.

Apparently the last effort to use the canal was made at about the time of the Arab conquest. It was reopened and became known as the "Canal of the Prince of the Faithful." Historians agree that after the late 8th century the canal was no longer serviceable.

In modern times numerous schemes were suggested to revive the canal, but none were pursued seriously until the arrival of Napoleon's expedition in Egypt in 1798. Napoleon was particularly eager to rebuild the passage as an alternate sea route to India. Preliminary work was undertaken by the expedition but was unfortunately abandoned because Napoleon's chief engineer erroneously calculated the level of the Red Sea at 33 feet higher than the Mediterranean and declared that the project was not feasible.

Further efforts to cut a canal were not seriously considered again until several decades later when Ferdinand de Lesseps proved that the two waters were, in fact, at the same level.

In 1854 de Lesseps asked permission from the Egyptian ruler Said to begin work on the canal. Permission was granted two years later, but another two years were needed to raise the money for the project. Finally, construction of the canal was begun in April 1858. Eleven years later under Khedive Isma'il the canal was formally opened with magnificent ceremony. An opera house was built in Cairo to stage *Aida,* which Verdi had composed for the occasion, and royalty, including Empress Eugenie, and a host of dignitaries from Europe attended.

For the next century the Suez Canal was the lifeline of the British Empire and the pawn of imperial Europe. In one of the most blatant but brilliant manipulations in history, the British gained control of Egypt and the canal. The events culminated in an agreement in 1882, which gave the British control of the canal for 99 years.

Suez became the symbol of British imperialism to the Egyptians and the final bone of contention in the country's long struggle for independence. Little wonder that after the revolution of 1952 withdrawal of British troops from the canal zone became a cause célèbre. Finally, 100 years after the date of the concession to de Lesseps, the Suez Canal Company was nationalized by the Egyptian government. There followed quickly a series of events that ended in a joint attack on Egypt by the British, French, and Israelis in October 1956.

The canal became embroiled in international politics once again when it was closed for eight years as a result of the Six-Day War in June 1967. Fifteen ships were trapped in its waters, mines were laid, the Israelis dug in on the east bank, the people fled, and the towns on the canal became ghost towns. Then in October 1973 the Egyptians crossed the canal in a surprise attack, and the war that followed led ultimately to a negotiated settlement worked out by U.S. Secretary of State Henry Kissinger by which Egypt regained the canal.

Again, on June 5, 1975, the Egyptians celebrated the canal's opening. The occasion was marked by an impressive list of visitors, including the great-granddaughter of de Lesseps, some royalty, and press from around the world.

The Suez Canal from Port Said on the Mediterranean to Suez on the Red Sea is over 120 miles long. The breadth at water level is 200 meters. Ships drawing 53 feet can transit the canal. Transit time for a ship through the canal from Suez or Port Said is about 12 hours. The southern stretch from Suez to Ismailia, including the Bitter Lakes and Lake Timsah, is the most interesting part of the journey.

Port Said

Port Said is located 135 miles northeast of Cairo on the Mediterranean at the western tip of the canal. Passengers on ships transiting the canal may disembark here in order to take an excursion to Cairo and Luxor and to rejoin the ship at either Suez or Safaga farther down the Red Sea. Port Said was badly destroyed in the June war of 1967 and all but abandoned during the eight years the canal was closed. The town has been rebuilt, but it has lost its "old port" atmosphere except for a few buildings directly on the waterfront. There is a small military museum at the west end of town. A branch office of the Tourist Administration is located on the street along the waterfront a few blocks from the Canal Administration building.

Ismailia

The town skirting the desert and Lake Timsah, halfway between Port Said and Suez, was founded by de Lesseps to accommodate the staff of the Suez Canal Company. His home, still kept with his mementos, is used as a government guest house and can be visited through special permission of the public relations department of the Suez Canal Authority. The town's Antiquity Museum is nearby and is open daily, except Tuesday, from 9 AM to 4 PM. Closed Friday 11 AM–1:30 PM. Entrance: 50 pts.

The Suez Canal Company is now housed in a large, modern white building, and the town is built around spacious public gardens and wide tree-lined streets.

Ismailia has grown considerably during the past decade, but it's only the beginning. The first of several hotel projects overlooking the lake has been completed, launching the town as a new resort area near the capital. (See *Practical Information* section at the end of the chapter.)

Cross Canal Tunnel. A new tunnel *under* the Suez Canal, connecting the west and east banks for the first time, was a first step in the major developments planned for Sinai. The entry point is 27 kilometers (17 miles) north of Suez. The tunnel is open 24 hours daily.

Suez

Located 82 miles east of Cairo on the Red Sea at the southern entrance of the canal. Suez was the most heavily damaged town in the area during the Suez war and has been rebuilt but holds little interest to tourists except as an entrance to the canal. In front of the Suez Canal Authority offices there is a small promenade from which you can view the ships entering the canal at the port of Suez on their way to the Mediterranean Sea. Port Tewfiq is its counterpart town on the east side of the canal.

The coastline along the Red Sea south of Suez is backed by the barren cliffs of the Ataka Mountains, whose colors change from pink to purple at different hours of the day and provide some of the most beautiful scenery in Egypt.

South of the Suez on the Red Sea is an area that is rapidly becoming an important resort of vacation villages. *Ein Sukhna,* about an hour from

Suez, is noted for its beautiful beach. The town, which in Arabic means "Hot Springs," is known for its hot sulfur spring. There is a gasoline station here.

The next major intersection to the south is *Ras Zafarana,* 77 miles south of Suez. It has a lighthouse that can be seen for many miles north and south along the Red Sea coastal road. There is a gasoline station here, and a road on the west takes off into the desert and leads back to Cairo. Also in the area are the monasteries of St. Paul and St. Anthony.

Ras Ghareb, 146 miles from Suez, is a large community that is thriving because of the many oil discoveries in the area. Adequate tire repair facilities may be found here, as well as mechanics and a gas station. This is the last major stop before reaching Hurghada.

If you are traveling by car, make sure you are well supplied with drinking water, extra gas, water for the car radiator and battery, and a second spare tire.

While many of the deserted beaches along the way south may seem inviting, it is best to select a swimming area that is frequented by other travelers and local residents.

Hurghada

Located about 237 miles south of Suez, Hurghada, known locally as Ghardaga or Urgada, is one of the best places on the Red Sea for scuba diving and snorkeling. The capital of the huge Red Sea province, Hurghada is a small town tucked between the mountains, the desert, and the sea. It is made up of one-story houses and dusty streets crowded with children playing and goats and chickens scampering about. The Governor's Palace, as it is called, is far from being palatial; nevertheless, it dwarfs everything else in town except a pretty mosque with twin minarets.

At the water's edge, six miles north of Hurghada, a Marine Museum (soon to be renovated) and Aquarium contains small fish of unusual shapes and colors. The museum has displays of mounted fish covering the Red Sea's wide variety of marine life, as well as shells and coral from the area. There is also a small private aquarium near Shadwan, Golden Beach in the city center.

The resort area of Hurghada is about three miles south of town at *Abu Menka,* a U-shaped bay with its axis running east–west and sheltered at its southeastern end by several islands that offer some of the best scuba diving in the world. The waters around the islands are so clear that the bottom of the sea is visible at a depth of 60 feet, and they teem with a fantastic variety of shapes, sizes, and colors of fish and coral formations.

The area is being developed with resorts that have a broad appeal to a larger number of vacationers. The first resort, which was instrumental in opening the area over a decade ago, was the Sheraton, followed by Magawish Village, operated by Misr Travel. They were joined by Gifton Village and Jasmin Village, the first two of many all-inclusive villages and resorts that have opened or are under construction on the Red Sea mainland coast as part of an $1.5 billion investment by Arab and European interests. More than a dozen hotels are expected to open during the next year or so.

Above all, Hurghada's attraction is its underwater wonderland and the stark beauty of its scenery. Travelers who are accustomed to the lush palm-fringed beaches of the Caribbean or the South Pacific would be disappointed in Red Sea area's almost desolate landscape.

The bay is framed by a chain of rugged, barren mountains that protect the area from the desert's westerly winds. At the center of the bay there is an enormous coral formation so close to the surface of the water that from afar it looks like another island. The reef is only a few hundred yards from shore and within easy reach even for inexperienced swimmers. The sea bottom slopes gently from shore toward the center of the bay, and the absence of strong currents and undertows makes swimming here pleasant and safe. The entire area, undisturbed for so many years, is covered with shells of amazing shapes and colors.

With the area off limits since the 1967 war, Hurghada was left to itself—the inhabitants to their fishing and the fish to their coral. As the late Renzo Brilli of *Tours of Distinction,* New York, described it after his first visit: "There are no oil slicks, no floating cans, bottles, wrappings and the other signs of civilization, nor are there people spoiled by tourists. The blissful silence is broken only by the gentle splashing of the waves and, at times, the murmur of the wind blowing through the mountains in the distance. There is no commercialism, but honest and friendly, smiling people; no billboards or rows of hotels—only the pristine beauty of nature. The incredible colors of the waters contrast yet blend with the ocher of the bleak desert, and are framed by the stark and awesome mountains, beyond which, to the west, are all the wonders of the Nile and Ancient Egypt."

While this description still applies to parts of the Red Sea region, the recent mushrooming of holiday villages along the coast is beginning to bring about radical change. For Egypt, it means badly needed jobs; for naturalists, it means distress. There is bound to be an adverse impact on the environment here unless stringent regulations are made to safeguard it.

Red Sea Aquarium, 6 Corniche St. Hours: 9 AM–9 PM. Entrance: L.E. 4. This new privately owned aquarium, operated by a marine biologist, has a variety of Red Sea marine life, most with labels in English.

Safaga

Farther along on the coast, about 30 miles south of Hurghada and 132 miles east of Luxor, is the newest area of resort development where nine new resorts are being added in less than two years. Safaga, a town of about 35,000 people, faces some of the best reefs of the coast—with 18 dive sites in near proximity. Some of the town's prime resort and dive operators are organizing to avoid the mistakes that the sudden boom brought to the Hurghada area by better planning and building restrictions. Farther south, Quseir, which is directly east of Luxor, is also being developed.

SINAI, THE LAND OF TURQUOISE

Sinai is a peninsula east of the Suez Canal and the Red Sea. It was seized by Israel in the Six-Day War, and its return to Egypt was the major subject of negotiations between Egypt and Israel following President Sadat's historic visit to Jerusalem.

Sinai has been an important part of Egypt for as long as the country has existed, creating as it did a natural barrier between Egypt and her traditional Asian enemies. Many legends of the ancient Egyptians are set in Sinai. Isis went there to search for the body of her murdered husband, Osiris. The goddess Hathor, known to the pharaohs as "Our Lady of Sinai," sanctified the area.

The Bible mentions Sinai often—here Moses received the Ten Commandments, and it was by way of Sinai that the Holy Family fled into Egypt. Later the region became a place of refuge for Christians fleeing Roman persecution.

Today the Sinai is something of a refuge for adventure travelers and those who truly want an unusual travel experience. They can ski on mountains of sand, dive in the fantastic waters along the coast, trek across spectacular scenery of the interior, and camp under star-studded skies. With new hotels, resorts and sporting facilities, travelers who want greater comfort can now find it. At the same time, a network of excellent new roads and improved transportation services have brought once-remote regions of the Sinai within easy driving range of the coast or the interior.

On the east side of the canal a coastal highway runs south, skirting the Red Sea and bypassing new seaside towns and ancient settlements in the oasis at the foothills of the mountains that can be seen in the distance. At *Abu Rudeis,* the center of Egypt's oil industry, the road turns east into the mountains to *St. Catherine's.* (South of Abu Rudeis the road continues to Sharm el Sheikh.)

After turning east into the mountains, the road passes through the Firan Valley to the Oasis of Firan at the foot of Mount Serbal, which some authorities believe is the place where Moses received the Ten Commandments. Throughout the drive, the scenery is breathtaking.

Administration, not to mention roads, communication, and geography, divide the peninsula into two parts—North and South.

North Sinai

On the Mediterranean coast next to the Israeli border, *El Arish* is the main town and capital of the governorate of North Sinai. The town has a population of 80,000 and is noted for its beautiful white sand and palm-fringed beaches, which are crowded in summer. It got its biggest boost as a tourist resort in 1985 with the opening of the Oberoi Hotel, set on a lovely beach alongside a palm grove. (See *Practical Information.*)

El Arish is 168 miles from Cairo. Its newest addition is the *Sinai Museum,* located on the outskirts of town on the main road to Rafah, the crossing point for visitors to and from Israel. The regional museum is designed to portray the environment of the Sinai and the life of the bedouin of the region with displays of handicrafts, utensils, clothing, animal and bird life, and fishing activity. There is a large tent in a desert setting that is particularly popular with photographers.

South Sinai

Long before there were roads of any kind in Sinai, travelers were attracted to the region because of the *Monastery of St. Catherine,* situated deep in the mountain fastness of the Sinai Peninsula on the traditional site of the Burning Bush at the foot of Mount Horeb, known in Arabic as *Jebel Musa,* or Mount Moses.

Originally built in about AD 330 as a small chapel, the present Greek Orthodox monastery was constructed as a walled fortress by the emperor Justinian in the 6th century and dedicated to Catherine, an Alexandrian saint. The monastery consists of several buildings, each built or expanded at different times over the centuries. The most sanctified is the church with the chapel of the Burning Bush and its priceless icons and hanging lamps. In addition, the monastery has the world's most valuable collection of icons and many rare books. At present the library where the majority are stored is not open to the public. A new building designed for the collection is planned. Some are on display in the church.

Next to the church is a mosque, which tradition holds was built in the 10th century when the Fatimite caliph el-Hakim bi Amr Illah ordered the destruction of all Christian monasteries. The monks of St. Catherine's outwitted him by adding the mosque and, so the story goes, the slender minaret, which can be seen in the distance, was enough to deter the demolition of the other buildings. A wooden chair with Kufic inscriptions and a minibar in the mosque date from the 11th century.

Behind the monastery a footpath with 3,750 stone steps carved from the rock lead up Mount Moses, where, tradition holds, Moses received the Ten Commandments. Another less difficult path requires climbing 800 steps. There is a chapel at the summit at 7,500 ft.

Note: The monastery is open to visitors only from 9 AM to 1:30 PM, Mon. to Thurs., and Sat. Visitors must pay close attention to these times when planning an itinerary. It is not unusual to arrive after the monastery has closed and be turned away. It is, after all, a monastery.

St. Catherine's is located 273 miles from Cairo, and about 130 miles southeast of Suez. Less than a decade ago, this trip ranked as one of the most arduous a traveler could make anywhere in the world because it required driving through rock and boulder-strewn mountain valleys and trails for 12 hours or more. Now it is a comfortable three-hour drive from the coast or seven hours from the capital. The route from Cairo leads to Suez, where you will cross the Canal through a magnificent new tunnel north of the town.

The comfort of overnighting at St. Catherine's was also vastly improved with the addition of the *St. Catherine's Tourist Village,* located within view of the monastery.

Sharm el Sheikh

At the south tip of Sinai, 303 miles from Cairo is *Sharm el Sheikh,* which is both a town and a resort with lovely beaches and some of the best snorkeling and diving in the world. Less than a decade ago, the drive would not have been possible, and until 1986, it would have taken a full day. Now the drive from Cairo takes only five hours over excellent new highways all the way.

Sharm el Sheikh has several hotels and a youth hostel in town, but the best accommodations are on Naama Bay about three miles east of town. There are snorkeling and diving sites within walking distance of the hotels, but by far the most fabulous is *Ras Mohamed,* 32 miles from Sharm el Sheikh at the southernmost tip of Sinai.

Ras Mohamed is a nature reserve where snorkelers who are strong swimmers and experienced divers can enjoy the world's most spectacular underwater show. In the display, viewers can see acres of coral of every type and description and watch a dazzling variety of fish in schools numbering in the thousands pass near enough to touch. The site, named to the World Heritage List of UNESCO, was made into a national park in 1985, thanks to marine biologist Dr. Eugenia Clark of the University of Maryland, who almost single-handedly convinced the Egyptian government of the need to protect Ras Mohamed as an underwater park.

By car, the drive to Ras Mohamed takes 45 minutes; by boat, it takes two hours. Serious divers prefer the boat excursion because it enables them to explore more places around the rock-faced tip of Ras Muhammad than can be reached by swimmers from the beach. Quality diving centers in the Naama Bay area offer lessons, rental equipment, and daily excursions for snorkelers and divers to nearby places and to Ras Mohamed.

Sinai's East Coast

North of Sharm el Sheikh on Sinai's east coast fronting the Gulf of Aqaba are the resorts of *Dahab*, about 50 miles, and *Nuweibeh*, another 50 miles north, and *Taba*, 54 miles north on the Israeli boarder. The drive passes over excellent roads through magnificent mountain scenery. The two resorts have similar accommodations with lovely beaches and reefs accessible from the shore. Nuweibeh is also the port for a car and passenger ferry that runs daily between Sinai and Aqaba, Jordan.

From Nuweibeh and the coast another excellent road leads 66 miles through the mountains to St. Catherine's Monastery. The scenery all along this drive is spectacular.

North of Nuweibeh, the road leads 54 miles to Taba and the Israeli border. The exact location of the border had been in dispute since the peace treaty between Egypt and Israel was made. An agreement was finally reached in 1989. Less than a mile south of Taba and accessible by boat is Pharoah Island, a tiny historic island a few hundred feet offshore. It has a recently restored 12th-century fortress that offers views of Jordan, Saudi Arabia, and the Gulf of Aqaba. In February 1990, the Egyptian government began the first phase for the development of the area between Taba and Nuweibeh by signing a contract with the Taba Company for Tourist Development. Purchase of the Taba hotel and tourist village, now the Taba Hilton, was its first move.

PRACTICAL INFORMATION FOR
THE SUEZ CANAL AND SINAI AREAS

HOW TO GET THERE. Hurghada. *Egyptair* has daily morning flights from Cairo to Hurghada. Round trip is L.E. 458; flight time is one hour. *ZAS* also flies there daily from Cairo. Check schedules with the airline prior to travel as departure times vary according to the day of the week. Be sure to book early.

Arabia Village. located between Hurghada and the town's old port 440 rooms. Phone: 441–790. Reservations: *Spring Tours,* Cairo. Phone: 341–5972. This new hotel has air-conditioned rooms, all with sea views. Facilities include three restaurants, bars, disco, nightclub, health club with sauna, dive center, windsurfing, an Olympic-size pool, six tennis courts, four squash courts and billard room, plus 130 shops. Immediately in front of the hotel, there is a long coral reef for snorkeling and diving within swimming distance of the beach. The facility caters to packaged tours from Germany.

North Sinai. El Arish is connected with Cairo twice weekly by air service on *Air Sinai,* and daily bus service via *Qantara.*

South Sinai. *Air Sinai* flies from Cairo to St. Catherine and to Sharm el Sheikh, and between Sharm el Sheikh and Hurghada. *East Delta Lines* offers daily bus service from Cairo to South Sinai. Air-conditioned buses to Sharm el Sheikh depart at 7 AM, 10 AM, 1, 4, and 11:30 PM, and midnight. One-way fare is L.E. 17 for day buses; L.E. 22 for 11:30 PM and midnight service. Air-conditioned buses to St. Catherine leave Cairo at 7 and 10:30 AM Cost is L.E. 20 for early bus; L.E. 15 for others. Return is 6 AM and 1:30 PM each day. There is also a bus to St. Catherine's departing daily at 7 AM and 11 PM with onward connection to Nuweiba (L.E. 27) and Taba (L.E. 32).

There is also frequent bus service between Eliat, Israel, through the Taba border crossing to Nuweibah and Sharm el Sheikh. Air Sinai flies to Tel Aviv Wednesday, Friday, and Sunday at 7:30 AM. The fare is L.E. 396 one-way.

Daily ferry service between Hurghada and Sharm el Sheikh departs in the morning, with arrival six hours later. Cost is L.E. 80, including light refreshments. The sea between the two locations is often choppy and the trip rough, although new large ferries operated by *Spring Tours* make the crossing much smoother than it was in the past. Inquire locally for schedules.

TELEPHONES. Due to the rapid growth of resorts and holiday villages in the region, telephone area codes have been established for the various cities and areas: Hurghada, Suez, and South Sinai (including Dahab, Nuweibeh, Safaga, St. Catherine, and Sharm el Sheikh), 062; Ismailia, 064; Port Said, 066; North Sinai, 068.

HOTELS. The hotels are listed geographically beginning at the northern end of the Suez Canal and moving south along the Red Sea; and similarly from north to south in Sinai.

Port Said. Holiday Hotel. Gomhoria St. Phone: 220–771; Fax: 220–710. Price: $15 swb; $20 dwb, including breakfast, tax, and service. It is air-conditioned; rooms have refrigerator/bar, TV, phone.

Helnan Port Said. El Cornish Atef Sadat St., Box 1110; Phone: 220–893; Fax: 223–762. 58 rooms. Price: $34.40 swb; $43 dwb, air-conditioning, phone, TV, minibar. It has a restaurant, bar, and disco. Located north of town on the Mediterranean, the hotel overlooks the western entrance to the Suez Canal. There are also beach houses for rent.

Ismailia. PLM Azur Etap-Hotel Forsan. Box 77, Forsan Island. 152 rooms. Phone: 222–292. $50 swb; $61 dwb. The town's first hotel of international standard, fronts Lake Timseh (one of the Bitter Lakes and part of the Suez Canal waterway), and is designed to serve many purposes—a resort, business and meeting center as well as a traditional hotel. It is situated next door to the headquarters building of the Suez Canal Authority on a small island and is connected by a short bridge to the town.

Built around a swimming pool, the seven-story building takes full advantage of its location, with all public rooms and restaurants overlooking the pool, lake, and beach and an unobstructed view of the canal. There are tennis, sailing, windsurfing, and waterskiing facilities.

Suez. Visitors to the area may stay at the *Red Sea Hotel,* Port Tewfiq. Phone: 223334. 28 rooms. $32 swb; $42 dwb with breakfast. *Summer Palace Hotel,* on the sea at Port Tewfiq. Phone: 224475. 96 rooms. $22 dwb with breakfast, is even better. It was recently refurbished, and has a swimming pool and garden.

Hurghada. Gifton Village. On the bay south of the Sheraton. Phone: 440–779. 400 rooms. $52 swb; $71 dwb with half board. Phone: Cairo 918–038. Rooms are spacious, bungalow-style; facilities include large restaurant that serves buffets of international cuisine; three attractively furnished bars; tennis, squash, and full range of water sports, including windsurfing and four motorboats for snorkeling and scuba diving with professional instruction available. The resort also operates a fully equipped dive boat. The Village is operated by owners of Victoria Hotel in Cairo and *Spring Tours,* 3, El Sayyed el Bakri St., Zamalek, Cairo. Phone: 341–5972.

Hurghada Sheraton. At the northern end of the bay, six miles from Hurghada Airport. 85 rooms. Phone: 440–785; Fax: 348–8217. Price: $80 swb; $95 dwb including half board. Phone: 348–5571; 988–607. Rooms have private bath, air-conditioning, and terrace, charmingly decorated with Egyptian-made rattan furniture. The hotel is built in the round, with a central garden courtyard providing access to the restaurant, patio, and terrace bar and lobby areas. A huge swimming pool with barbecue facilities overlooks the sea and fishing, windsurfing, waterskiing, snorkeling, diving, and sailing services. Paddleboats and sailfish can also be rented, and there is tennis. Some accommodations are in cabanas around the pool; and there are 10 three-bedroom, beachfront villas with kitchenettes.

Fresh water for the area is piped in from Qena, across the desert on the Nile; thus the supply of fresh water (and, therefore, the functioning of the central air-conditioning) can be erratic.

Jasmine Village. On south end of bay, about four miles from airport. 450 units. (Reservation through Hamburg Hotel Bldg., 18 Borsa St., Cairo. Phone: 760–159 or 777–238.) Price: $44 swb; $68 dwb with half-board. Chalets of Mediterranean-style have air-conditioning, TV, and minibars. The all-inclusive resort offers fully equipped dive center, windsurfing, sailing, tennis, squash, two artificial lakes, large swimming pool, and gym. It faces a 600-foot-long coral reef. Three restaurants, several bars, and disco. Caters mainly to charter groups from Europe.

Magawish. At the southern end of the bay where the craggy mountains rise to their highest peaks. Price: $60 swb; $80 dwb, including meals. The resort village is owned by *Misr Travel* (630 Fifth Ave., New York, NY)

Each chalet has a small sitting room, bedroom with two single beds an a bath, and is air-conditioned. The emphasis is on scuba diving, snorkeling, and a wide variety of sports. The all-inclusive resort is spread along two miles of beach front, and includes a large reception-dining room building, a small theater, pool, and tennis courts. Misr Travel has air-conditioned motorcoaches stationed here for regular tours to Luxor. The water-sports center has windsurfing and sail boats, diving equipment, photo equipment, and lab. Facilities include a recompression unit. Dive boat goes daily for half-day excursions and twice weekly for full-day ones.

Al Mashrabiya. At south end of bay. 180 rooms. Phone 441–190; Fax: 348–5381. Price: $70 swb; $50 dwb; with half-board. The newest, four-star beach village has a large pool, restaurants, bars, and a disco on the sea with a glass floor for guests to view the marine life. It has a dive center, windsurfing school, glass-bottom boats, and full-service business center, which may account for the unusual guest mix of Arab sheikhs, foreign residents, and tour groups.

Sonesta Beach Resort Hurghada. On the beach; 73 hotel rooms and 30 villas with 120 one- and two- bedroom suites. Price: $105–$140. Phone in Cairo: 441–661; Fax: 619–980; U.S.: 800–343–7170. Opened in January 1991, this new five-star resort on 20 beachfront acres has two swimming pools, including one for children, indoor and outdoor restaurants, bars, shops, marina, meeting rooms, and boating and water-sports facilities. Future construction, scheduled to open in 1992, will include 205 more rooms and suites with added meeting, sports, and shopping facilities.

Safaga. **Movenpick Hotel Jolie Ville,** on the beach at Quseir, 307 rooms. This deluxe resort with three restaurants, lounge bar, disco, and conference facilities, is scheduled to open in spring 1992.

Safaga Paradise Village, Phone: 451–631; 244 rooms. $30 dwb plus $45 with meals. One of several new four-star tourist villages to have opened in the past year.

Serena Beach Hotel Jolie Ville, on the beach at Quseir, 120 rooms. Deluxe resort with restaurants, lounge, pool, bar, and diving facilities was slated to open in late 1991.

NORTH SINAI

El Arish. Oberoi El Arish. Overlooking Mediterranean Sea, 150 rooms. Phone: 778–033. $60 swb; $76 dwb, including breakfast, service, and taxes. Set on a beach alongside a palm grove. The hotel has a freshwater pool that is heated in winter, restaurant, bar, seawater pool, squash and tennis courts, jogging track, sauna, and water sports. Rooms have terraces overlooking the sea and are equipped with air-conditioning, TV, and direct-dial phone to Cairo.

SOUTH SINAI

Unless noted otherwise, the holiday villages in Sharm el Sheikh, Nuweiba, and Dahab are managed by Sinai Hotels and Diving Clubs, 32 Sabry Abu Alam St., Cairo. Phone: 393–0301; Fax: 392–2228. All have facilities for water sports; neither the lodgings nor the cuisine is brilliant, but the spectacular scenery of the Sinai and the underwater wonders more than compensate for the lack of luxury.

St. Catherine. St. Catherine's Tourist Village. Raha Valley, one mile from Monastery; 12 miles from airport. Phone: 770–221 or, in Cairo, 282–8112. 70 rooms. $45 swb, $70 dwb with half-board. Large, comfortable rooms in semidetached cottages built from natural stone in keeping with rustic and rugged nature of their surroundings. Each villa has bedroom with bath and sitting room with patio from which there are wonderful views of the monastery and the spectacular scenery of surrounding mountains. There is a restaurant. The hotel was built by Misr Sinai, a quasigovernmental organization that operates Air Sinai and motorcoach service from Sharm el Sheikh.

Other accommodations at St. Catherine's are strictly for trekkers and travelers accustomed to living with only basic necessities. A camping site with dormitory-style sleeping areas in permanent tented structures was constructed during the Israeli occupation. The facility is used by campers and trekkers or tours organized by travel agencies that arrange adventure-type excursions. While the camp is very short on comfort, the setting and its magnificent surroundings more than make up for its shortcomings. *El Salam* is a very simple hotel near the airport, to be used only as a last resort. Be warned! If you go to South Sinai during the winter months, it is very cold at night and warm clothing is a must. Even in summer, nighttime temperatures drop enough to require sweaters and warm socks for sleeping.

Taba. Taba Hilton. On the beach. 326 rooms. Phone: 747–616; Fax: 597–9660; Phone in Cairo: 777–444, ext. 3146. Price: $82–$102 swb: $90–$110 dwb. Located 250 miles from Cairo, on the Gulf of Aqaba, this hotel was on the disputed border between Egypt and Israel and was part of the peace settlement in 1989. Now operated by Hilton, it still has Israeli guests and offers attractive low-cost three- and four-night packages for Egyptians and foreign residents. The modern resort has a large pool and full restaurant, bar, and water-sports facilities with a fully equipped diving center. Featured is a special starlight dinner in the desert.

Salma Sinai. On the sea, halfway between Taba and Nuweibeh. Phone: 700–901; Fax: 701–482. 30 rooms. Price: $25 swb, $30 dwb, $33 triple, including breakfast, service, and taxes. This small, new hotel is located on miles of white-sand beach facing a long coral reef. It has bungalow-type accommodations, restaurant, bar, and a fully equipped dive center. Jeep and camel safaris into the Sinai are available.

Nuweibeh. El Sayadin. Overlooking Gulf of Aqaba, Phone: 757–398. 66 rooms. $33 swb; $54 dwb with full board. This resort has attractive and spacious accommodations in detached cottages along the beach; two restaurants. Contact *Sharm Tours,* 166 Hegaz St., Heliopolis, Cairo.

Nuweibeh Holiday Village. Overlooks Gulf of Aqaba, Phone: 770–393; Fax: 392–2228. 66 rooms. $48 swb; $60 dwb. An older resort, recently renovated, offers basic, clean accommodations in semidetached cottages. Restaurant, bar, extensive beach, reef directly off shore, windsurfing. Camping facilities are also available for $5.75 per person.

Dahab. Holiday Village PLM Azur. Phone: 062–770–788. 142 rooms. $77 swb; $90 dwb with breakfast. This is a small new resort and dive center on the east coast of Sinai overlooking the Gulf of Aqaba, an hour's drive north of Sharm el Sheikh. All rooms are air-conditioned with private bath and phone. Restaurant, snack bar, dive center, and water sports.

Dahab Movenpick Hotel Jolie Ville. 280 rooms. Similar to the new Movenpick in Sharm el Sheikh (below), this place was scheduled to open in winter 1992–93. Inquire at Movenpick.

Sharm el Sheikh. Fayrouz Village Sharm el Sheikh/Hilton International. 150 units. Price: $88 swb; $103 dwb. Phone 679–400 or 800–HILTONS or Ramses Hilton, Cairo, for reservations. Hilton's dive and beach village has air-conditioned bungalows with minibar, TV, hairdryers, and direct-dial phones. Facilities include three restaurants, snack bar, conference facilities, open-air theater, swimming pool, tennis, squash, health club and sauna, golf driving range, horseback riding, private beach, extensive water-sports facilities, and one of the best dive centers in the Red Sea area. The **Sharm el Sheikh Hilton Residence.** Phone: 2–062–70501; Telex: 66036 HISHK UN. Was scheduled to open in October 1991.

Ghazala Hotel. Naama Bay. 168 rooms. $60 swb; $75 dwb. Phone for reservations: (062) 770–217. This first-class resort catering to divers is the creation of South Sinai Travel, a pioneer in Sinai travel and diving. Rooms are in the main building and in bungalows and have phone, air-conditioning, and baths with shower. There is a restaurant, 24-hour coffee shop, bar, disco, pool, tennis, squash, private beach, and fully equipped dive center with recompression room.

Hotel Aquamarine PLM Azur. 30 bungalows and 86 rooms. $77 swb; $90 dwb with breakfast. Phone: 62–771–838. Situated on the Gulf of Aqaba, this diving center is air-conditioned and has restaurant, coffee shop, pool, and tennis.

Sharm el Sheikh Movenpick Hotel Jolie Ville. On Naama Beach. 280 rooms and suites in 42 bungalows. $95 swb; $115 dwb. Phone: 62–771–881; Fax: 62–771–533. This new hotel, scheduled to open in summer 1991 is the area's first deluxe resort. It has four restaurants, two bars, disco, two swimming pools, Turkish bath and sauna, tennis and squash, dive center and water sports, and shops. All rooms have extra-large beds, TV, direct-dial phone, minibar, and hair dryer in bathroom.

Helnan Marina Sharm. Naama Bay. Phone: 770–175; Fax: 768–385. 148 rooms. $48 swb, $60 dwb. Camping facilities are also available for $5 per person. Restaurant, bar; diving center. Walking distance to snorkeling/diving areas of Red Sea.

WATER SPORTS. As would be expected, you can find plenty of *swimming* along the beaches dotting the Red Sea and the Mediterranean. You might wish to choose one that isn't totally deserted. El Arish, on the Mediterranean, has beautiful palm-lined beaches. Bordering the Gulf of Aqaba are the seaside resorts of Sharm el Sheikh, Dahab, Nuweiba, and Taba, offering spectacular *scuba diving* and *snorkeling*. (Check the dive centers in Sharm el Sheikh for details.)

There are numerous dive centers in Hurghada and Sharm el-Sheikh that offer instruction, equipment, and dive packages, as well as assistance to those with their own equipment. For tourists not staying in luxury hotels with their own snorkeling facilities, day-long boat excursions to nearby coral reefs are available for about L.E. 25 or 30 in Hurghada through any small city-center hotel or pension. Snorkeling gear, except fins, is provided along with a simple fish lunch cooked aboard. One of the best operators is Emad Mohamed of Sunshine House, city center.

Fishing is also outstanding and you can charter a boat and captain directly from the new port or through the Hurghada Sheraton Hotel, which acts as the center for the town's annual fishing competition. Anglers must bring their own tackle.

South Sinai Travel, a private company for adventure travel, has a series of four- and six-day programs for trekking and camping in the interior and diving along the Red Sea coast beginning from Cairo. SST is located at 79 Merghany St., 10th floor, Heliopolis, Cairo. Phone: 664–013; 672–064.

DINING OUT. Port Said: *Maxim's,* on the Corniche, offers good fish and a wide selection of entrees, along with a view of the sea. *Reana House* is good for Far Eastern specialties.

Ismailia: *George's,* El Thawra St., is a well-established bistro-style restaurant for good seafood; bar. Moderate.

Hurghada: *Red Sea Restaurant,* rooftop dining on moderately priced seafood. *Three Corners,* located by the Shadwan Hotel on the beach near town, is a European-style sidewalk terrance where good pizza, croissants, ice cream, and lobster are available. Moderate.

Nivi, next to Shadwan Hotel, is an outdoor restaurant with great shish kebab, grilled chicken, seafood, and homemade ice cream. *Moderate.*

Chez Miky, near the old port in Hurghada, has excellent seafood, including lobster. *Moderate.*

ENGLISH–ARABIC
TOURIST VOCABULARY

There are many systems for the transliteration of Arabic words into English equivalents. In the following glossary the system has been made as simple as possible.

—All long vowels appear as double vowels except "a," which is written with a circumflex: â.

—The   (ain) in Arabic has no English equivalent. Its presence (when necessary to avoid confusion with other words) has been indicated by: '.

. . . The   (hamza), a glottal stop, is indicated by: '.

—H, h—the first is hard, the second is like the English "h" in *hat*.

—T, t—the first is hard, the second is like the English "t" in *tip*.

—D or th (like the "th" in *this*) are almost the same sound in Egyptian speech: hatha, ooDa.

—The   is indicated by "kh," pronounced gutturally as the German "ch" in *Bach*.

217

—The (jim) in Egypt is pronounced hard as the "g" in go.

Greetings

Good morning	*saida*
(reply)	*saida*
Good evening	*masa-l-khair*
Good day	*naharak sa'eed*
(reply)	*ahlan wa sahlan*
Hello	*zayak*
(reply)	*zayak inta*
Greetings (Peace be with you)	*as-salâm alaikoom*
(reply)	*alaikoom salâm*
Goodbye (the one departing)	*saida*
(the one remaining)	*ma'-salâma*
How are you?	*zayak innaharda*
Well, thank God	*kwayes elHamdu lillâh*
Welcome (host says)	*ahlan wa-sahlan*

Useful Phrases

Yes	*aywa*
No	*lâ*
Please	*min fadlak, min fadlik (f.)*
If you please	*tismah*
After you, I beg you to (enter, eat, take)	*tfaDDal, tfaDDali (f.)*
If God is willing	*inshallah*
Thank you	*mshakreen awwe, mutashakir geddan*
What is your name?	*ismak eh?*
My name is . . .	*ismi . . .*
Do you speak English?	*Bitkallam ingleezi?*
I do not speak Arabic	*ana ma bakallimsh 'arabi*
How? (In what way?)	*izzay?*
How much? (cost)	*aday?*
How many?	*kam?*
What?	*eh?*
What is that?	*eh da?*
What is it? What's the matter?	*fee eh?*
What do you want?	*awiz eh?*
Who?	*meen?*
Why?	*lai?*
For what purpose?	*min shân eh? alla shan eh?*
I do not want	*mish awiz*
I do not have	*ma 'indish*
I am hungry	*ana gu'an, ana gu'ana (f.)*
I want to eat	*awiz akul*
Give me	*iddeeni*
Bring me	*hatli*
Excuse me	*bil-izin*
Take care, watch out	*ou'ak*
Go away!	*imshi*
Hurry up	*yallah*
Get up	*oom*
Stop	*wa'if*
Stop, enough	*bass*

Slower please	*'ala mahlak minfadlak*
Slowly	*wish-waysh*
Take me to the hotel	*khudni 'al otel*
Wait here!	*istenna hena*
Open the door!	*iftaH el bâb*
Shut the door!	*ifil el bâb*
Let me see!	*wareeni*
Come here!	*ta'a la hena*
I do not know	*ma arafish*
See!	*shoof!* I saw *shuft*
Never mind	*malaish*
Again	*kaman, min gedeed*
Another time	*marra tânya*
Once	*marra*
Twice	*marratain*
Everything	*kulla haga*
All of us	*kullina*
Together	*ma'a ba'th*
Here	*hena*
There	*henak*
Yet	*lissa*
Not yet	*lissa bardu*
When	*emta*
After	*ba'd*
Later	*ba'dain*
Never	*abadan*
Always	*daiman*
Perhaps	*yimkin*
Is it possible?	*mumkin?*
Please wash these	*wahyatak, ighsili dol*
Please press these	*wahyatak, tikwili dol*

At the Airport

Airport	*maTâr*	Porter	*bawwab*
Car, taxi	*arabiyeh, taxi*	Office	*maktab*
Customs	*gumruk*	Suitcase	*shanta*
Handbag	*shanta*	Ticket	*tezkara*
Money	*fuloos*	Trunk	*sanduq kabeera*

In Town

Bridge	*kubri*	Place	*maHal*
Church	*kaneesa*	Hospital	*mustashfa*
District	*Hye*	House	*bait*
Harbour	*mena*	Shop	*dukkân*
Market	*souq*	Square	*midân*
Mosque	*gami'*	Street	*shârhi'*
Museum	*matHaf*	Town	*medineh, balad*

At the Hotel

Ashtray	*manfatha*	Doorman	*bawwab*
Bath	*hammam*	Floor (story)	*dor*
Bed, mattress	*sarrir*	Hotel	*otel, lukanda*
Blanket	*bataneya*	Hot water	*mayya sukhna*
Door	*bab*	Lamp	*nagafa*

Light	noor	Window	shubbâk
Lightbulb	lamba	Is there air-	fee tabreed?
Pillow	makhadda	conditioning?	
Room	ooDa	Is there heat?	al bait medafa?
Sheet	millaya	Show me a room	warreeni ooDa
Soap	saboona	Where is the	fain al-ham-
Towel	foota		

On the Road

Above, up	foq	Left	shemâl
Behind	wara	Near	'areeb
Under	taHt	North	shamal
East	sharq	Over	'ala
Far	ba'eed	Outside	barra
Gasoline	benzeen	Right	yameen
Go down	inzal taht	Road, highway	tareeq
Go out	iTla'barra	South	ganuub
In front	'uddam	Straight ahead	ala tool
Inside	gowwa	Village	qariya
Water	mayya	Is the road far	et-tareeq ba'eed
Where	fain	from here?	min hena?
Where is the	fain et-tareeq	How many kilo-	kam kilometer?
road to . . . ?	'al . . . ?	meters?	

In the Restaurant

Bill	fatoora, hisab	Lunch	ghada
Breakfast	fatoor	Matches	kibreet
Cigarette	segayar (pl.)	Plate	saHn
Dinner	'asha	Restaurant	mat'am
Fork	shawka	Spoon	mal'a'a
Glass	kubaiyeh	Table	tarabayza
Headwaiter	rais, garçon	Table napkins	foota
Knife	sikkina	Waiter	sufragi

Food

Apricot	mishmish	Lettuce	khass
Banana	mooz	Meat	laHma
Beef	laHm ba'ar	Roast	rosto
Beer	bira	Skewer	meshwi
Bread	aish	Melon (yellow)	shammâm
Butter	zebda	Milk	leban
Cabbage	karomb	Olives	zatoon
Cheese	gibna	Olive oil	zait zatoon
Chicken	farkha	Onions	basal
Coffee	'ahwa	Oranges	bortuân
Cucumber	khiyar	Peaches	khûkh
Cutlet	castaletta	Pepper, black	filfil
Eggs	baid	sweet	filfil hellu
hard boiled	baid maslooq	Preserves	murabba
soft boiled	baid brisht	Rice	ruzz
omelet	omelette	Salad	salata
Eggplant	batingan	Salt	milH
Figs	teen	Soup	shurba
Fish	samak	Squash	koosa

Fruit	*fak-ha*	Sugar	*sukkar*
Garlic	*toom*	Tea	*shy*
Grapes	*'enab*	Tomatoes	*tomatum*
Green beans	*fasulya*	Veal	*laHm 'ijl*
Honey	*'asal*	Vegetables	*khudra*
Ice	*talg*	Vinegar	*Khall*
Lamb	*kharoof*	Watermelon	*baTTeekh*
Lemon	*limoon*	Wine	*nbeet*
Lentils	*'atas*	Yogurt	*leban zabadi*

Weather

Cold	*bard*	Weather	*taqs, gaw*
Hot	*Harr*	Wind	*hawa*
Rain	*matar*		

Colors

Black	*sawda*	Grey	*rumadi*
Blue	*azraq*	Red	*aHmar*
Brown	*bunaya*	White	*abyaD*
Green	*akhDar*	Yellow	*asfar*

Personal Pronouns

I	*ana*	We	*iyHna*
You	*inta, inti (f.)*	You	*intu*
He	*huwa, heeya (f.)*	They	*huma*

Adjectives

Bad	*baTTâl, wehish*	High	*'ali*
not bad	*mesh baTTâl*	Hot (food)	*sukhn, harr*
Beautiful	*gameel*	Large, big	*kbeer*
Bitter	*murr*	Little (amount)	*shuwaiyeh*
Broad	*'areeD*	Long, tall	*Taweel*
Cheap	*rakhess*	Low	*wâti*
Clean	*naDeef*	Much	*kteer*
Dear, expensive	*ghâli*	Narrow, tight	*Dayyi*
Dirty	*wusikh*	New	*gadeed*
Empty	*fâDi*	Old, antique	*adeem*
Good	*kwayes*	Short, small	*zaghyar*
Not good	*mesh kwayes*	Sour	*had'a kida*
Very good	*kwayes awwe*	Sweet	*Helwa*
Great	*'azeem*	Tired	*ta'bân*

Parts of the Body

Arm	*Dra'*	Head	*râs*
Blood	*damm*	Heart	*alb*
Bone	*'athm*	Kidneys	*klâwi*
Chest	*sadr*	Leg	*rigl*
Ear	*wedan*	Liver	*kibd*
Eye	*'ain*	Mouth	*famm*
Foot	*rigl*	Stomach	*baTn*
Hair	*sha'r*	Tooth	*sinn, snan (pl.)*
Hand	*eed*		

Topographical Terms

Coast	shaTTi	River	nahr
Country	balad	Sand	raml
Desert	saHara	Sea	baHr
Earth, soil	arD	Spring	'ain
Fortress	al'a	Tower, fort	borg
Garden	genaina	Tree	shagara
Head, top	râs	Valley	wadi
Mountain	gebel	Well	beer, saqi
Plain	saHel		

Useful Words

Antiquities	asar	Iron (metal)	Hadid
Baker	farrân	(instrument)	makwa
Barber	Hallâk	Jar	olla
Bedroom	ooda-t noom	Judge	qâDi
Boat	safeena	King	malak
Book	kitâb	Kitchen	matbakh
Bookshop	maktabi	Letter	resâla
Camel	gamal	Lighthouse	fenar
Candle	sham'a	Living room	sâlon
Caravanserai	khân	Monastery	deir
Cards (playing)	kusheena	Moon	qamar
Carpet	siggâda	New Moon	hilâl
Castle	qasr	Pain	waga'
Chair	kursi	Pigeon	hamam
Coat	balto	Pilgrim	Hâjji
Column	âmood, awamid (pl.)	Pilgrimage	Hâjj
		Policeman	bolees
Consul	'unsul	Police station	karakoon,
Diarrhea	is-hâl		makfar
Dining room	ooda-t sufra	Prophet	nebi
Doctor	hakeem, doctor	Prayer-niche	miHrâb
Dog	kalb	Pulpit	minbar
Dome, cupola	goobah	Reception room	diwan, dar
Donkey	Hmâr	Religion	deen
Dress	fustân	Seamstress	khayyâta
Elder man	sheikh	Servant	sufragi
Eyeglasses	naddara	Shirt	amees
Fever	harâra	Shoes	gazamadi
Fire	nâr	Stone	Hajar
Girl	bint, benât (pl.)	Sun	shams
Headache	râsi bewugani	Tailor	tarzi
Heaven, sky	sama	Tomb	turab
Holiday	'eed	Toothpick	khel
Horse	hosân	Trousers	bantalon

PHARAONIC GODS AND SYMBOLS

Pharaonic gods were many, and often had the same or similar characteristics. In addition to possessing all human virtues, each god also possessed a particular attribute of an animal or bird. For example, Sekmet, the god of war, had the strength of the lion; Anubis, the swiftness of the jackal, and Horus, the keen sight of the hawk. During religious ceremonies the priests wore masks of the animals associated with the gods they represented, and the animals and birds associated with the gods were likewise considered sacred.

Supreme among the gods was Re (Ra), the god of the sun, also called Amen-Re. Osiris, his son, ruled on earth until he was murdered by Set, his brother, god of darkness. The mate of Osiris was Isis, goddess of heaven and earth. Their son, Horus, became lord of earth, and Osiris became god of the underworld and judge of the dead.

Some of the major deities and the animals with which they were associated were:

Amen-Re, the sun-god, patron deity of Thebes—the ram, also the hawk.

Anubis, god of the dead, patron deity in certain districts of Upper Egypt—the jackal.

Aton, god of the setting sun, local deity—the lion and the snake.

Hathor, goddess of heaven, joy and love, deity of Denderah and protector of the necropolis of Thebes—the cow.

Horus (and Ha-Rakhte, a form of Horus), usually represented by the winged sun disc—the falcon.

Isis, goddess of heaven and earth, patron goddess of Philae, wife of Osiris and mother of Horus—the vulture.

Khnum, patron god of Elephantine Island and the Cataracts—the ram.

Maat, goddess of justice—the ostrich feather.

Osiris, god of the dead—the "tet."

Ptah, patron god of Memphis and father of the gods—the bull.

Sobek, god of the waters, patron god of Fayoum—the crocodile.

Thoth, god of science and patron god of Hermopolis—the ibis.

With a little practice, you can often recognize the gods by their headdresses in wall paintings. Emblems of rule, sovereignty, and dominion were represented by the crook or sceptre and the flail.

The symbol of the key-of-life is known as the *ankh.*

The double crown indicated the union of Upper and Lower Egypt.

INDEX

(The letters H and R indicate hotel and restaurant listings.)

FACTS AT YOUR FINGERTIPS

(See also Practical Information sections for each region.)

Air travel
  in Egypt, 29–31
  to Egypt, 3–4
  airport transportation, 15–16
Arrival procedures, 14–20
Auto travel
  in Egypt, 35–38
  rentals, 27
  to Egypt, 5
Background information, 43–49
Bus travel, 5
  intra-city, 34–35
Climate, 1
Clothing, 11
Credit cards, 19
Currency & exchange, 17–19
Customs
  arrival, 16–17
  departure, 38–39
Distances from Cairo, 29
Egyptian calendar, 1
Egyptian literature, 141–142
Electric current, 21
Export regulations, 38–39
Food & drink, 68–71
Guides, 21
Health precautions, 25
Health regulations, 10
History, 50–67
Holidays, 1, 3
Horse carriages, 27
Hours of business, 22
Information sources, 12, 20–21
Language, 21
Mail, 22–23
Metric conversion chart, 22
Metro (Cairo), 27
Nile steamers, 31–34
Package tours, 5–9
  American, 5–8
  British, 9
  special interest, 8, 9
Packing, 11
Passports, 9–10
Personal checks, 19
Pharaonic gods & symbols, 223

Photography, 24–25
Public transportation, 25–27
Rail travel, 27–29
Recommended reading, 12–14
Registering on arrival, 17
Ship travel, 4
  Port procedures, 16
Subway. *See* Metro
Taxis, 5, 26
  intra-city, 35
Telegraph, 23
Telephones, 23
Temperature chart, 2
Telex, 23–24
Time, 21
Tipping, 19–20
Tourist police, 20
Tourist vocabulary, 217–222
Traveler's checks, 18–19
Vaccinations, 10
Visas, 9–10
Visiting Upper Egypt, 33–34
Weights & measures, 22
Women travelers, 20

ALEXANDRIA & VICINITY

Practical Information

Beaches, 189, 192, 195, 196–197, 198
Hotels, 198–200
Information sources, 200
Museums and Royal Palaces, 193–194
Restaurants, 200–201
Shopping, 200
Transportation, 198

Geographical

Abukir, 195
Abyad, 198
Ageeba Beach, 198
Al Agami, 195
Al Alamein, 196
Alexandria, 189–194, H198–199,
  R200–201
Anfushi Necropolis, 193

Bahig, 195
Burg al-Arab, 195
Catacombs of Kom el-Shuqafa, 193
Corniche, 192
Fort Kait Bey, 193
Greco-Roman Museum, 193–194
Hydrobiological Museum, 194
Library of Alexandria, 194
Mersa Matruh, 196–198, H199
Montazah Palace, 194
Museum of Fine Arts, 194
Om Rakham, 198
Pompey's Pillar, 192–193
Qasr, 198
Ras al Barr, 195
Ras el Tin Palace, 194
Roman Amphitheater, 193
Rosetta, 195
Royal Jewelry Museum, 194
Sidi Abdel Rahman, 196, H199–200
Siwa Oasis, 197
Wadi el Natrun, 195–196

CAIRO & VICINITY

Practical Information
Airlines, 129–130
Art galleries, 137–140
Babysitters, 131
Banks, 130
Barbershops & beauty parlors,
    131
Bars, 159
Boating, 134–135
Buses, 117
Business services, 128–129
Camping, 133
Car rentals, 116
Circus, 132
Dragoman. *See* Guides
Embassies, 130
Emergencies, 129
Entertainment, 158
Fishing, 133
Gambling, 158
Gliding, 133
Golf, 133
Guides, 77, 80–81
Horse racing, 134
Horseback riding, 133–134
Hotels, 117–128
Hours of business, 142–143
Hunting & shooting, 134
Information sources, 77, 80–81,
    129–130
Laundries & dry cleaners, 132
Literature, 141
Metro (subway), 116–117

Museums, 83–84, 85, 96–97,
    104–108, 114–115, 137–140
Music, 140–141
Newspapers, 131
Nightclubs & discotheques, 159–161
Pharmacies, 132
Radio & television, 130
Repairs, 132
Restaurants, 152–157
River taxis, 116
Shipping agencies, 130
Shopping, 143–152
    alabaster, 145
    antiquities, 145–146
    bargaining, 143
    bookshops, 150
    brass and copper, 146
    carpets, 146
    ceramics/glass, 146
    clothing, 147–148, 150–151
    cosmetics and toiletries, 151
    department stores, 150
    Egyptian accessories and objets d'art,
        146–147
    fabrics, 147–148
    florists, 151
    food products, 151
    gold jewelry, 148
    inlaid wood, 148–149
    leather work, 149
    linens, 152
    Mouski, 144–150
    Mouski glass, 149
    packing and shipping, 143
    perfumes, 149
    semiprecious stones, 149
    silver, 150
    shopping districts, 143–145
    stamps, 150
    tobacco and cigarettes, 152
    toys and dolls, 152
Sightseeing, 77, 80–81, 111–112
Social clubs, 136–137
Sound and Light program, 84–85
Special-interest clubs, 137
Sporting clubs, 135–136
Sports, 132–136
Studios & workshops, 138–140
Taxis, 116
Teahouses & pastry shops, 157–158
Tennis, 135
Theaters, 141–142
Tourist police, 80
Tours, 77, 80–81
Transportation, 116–117
Travel agents, 80–81, 129
Walking, 117
Water sports, 135

Youth hostels, 127–128

Geographical

Abdin Palace, 109
Abou Serga Church, 95–96
Agricultural Museum, 107
Al-Azhar Mosque & University, 99–101
Al Hussein Mosque, 103
American University in Cairo, 110
Amr ibn el-As Mosque, 99
Anderson House, 108–109
Bab el Luk, 77
Babylon Fort, 95, 96–97
Beit el-Suheimi, 109
Beit el-Tablawi, 109
Beit Sennair, 109
Beni Hassan, 115
Cairo, 75–161, H117–128, R152–158
Cairo Tower, 111
Cairo University, 111
Caravanseri, 108–109
Cheops Funerary Temple, 82–84
Citadel & Muhammad Ali Mosque, 101–102
City of the Dead, 103
Convent of the Sacred Virgin, 94
Coptic Cairo, 93–97
Coptic Museum, 96–97
Coptic Patriarchate, 97
Deir Al Muharraq, 95
Deir Amba Bishoi Monastery, 97
Deir el Baramus Monastery, 97
Deir es-Suryani Monastery, 97
Deir Macarius Monastery, 97
Dokki, 111
Egyptian Antiquities Museum, 86–93
Egyptian Civilization & Gezira Museum, 107
El Aqsunqur Mosque, 102
El-Barquq Mosque, 102
El Hakim bi Amr Illah Mosque, 101
El Mouallaqa Church, 95
El Muayyad Mosque, 103
El Zaher Baybars Mosque, 102
Ezbet al Waldu, 113
Fayoum, 113–114, HR128
Gates of Cairo, 103–104
Gezira Island, 77, 110
Giza, 82–84, 111
Great Pyramid, The, 82–83
Heliopolis, 94, 111
Helwan, 112–113
Helwan Observatory, 113
Helwan Rest House Museum, 113
Hermopolis, 114
History, 75–77

Ibn Qalawun Mosque, 102
Ibn Toulun Mosque, 99
Imam el-Shafii Mosque, 103
Islamic Cairo, 98–107
Japanese Garden (Helwan), 113
Khalil Museum, 107
Kom Oshim Museum, 113–114
Lahun, 114
Maadi, 111
Manial Palace & Museum, 109–110
Matarieh (Matariya), 94
Mausoleum of Qait Bey, 103
Memphis, 85–86
Midan al Tahrir (Liberation Square), 77
Minya, 114, HR128
Modern Art Museum, 107
Modern Cairo, 107–111
Mohammed Nagy Museum, 107
Monasteries, 97
Mouski (Khan el Khalil), 144–150
Muhammad Ali Mosque, 101–102
Mukattam Hills, 76–77, 111
Mukhtar Museum, 107–108
Musaferkhana, 109
Museum of Islamic Art, 104–107
New Cairo (Heliopolis), 94, 111
Nilometer, 110
Observatory (Helwan), 113
Old Cairo, 76, 93
On, 76
Papyrus Institute, 108
Pharaonic Cairo, 81–93
Pharaonic Village, 108
Pyramids, The, 81–84
Qubbah Palace, 109
Rest House Museum (Helwan), 113
St. Barbara Church, 96
St. Georges' Church, 96
Sakkara, 85–86
Sekhemkhet funeral chamber, 85
Serapeum, 86
Solar Boat Museum, 83–84
Sphinx, The, 84–85
Step Pyramid, The, 85
Sultan Hassan Mosque, 102–103
Tel al Amarna, 115
Tomb of Maya, 86
Tomb of Teti, 86
Tower of Cairo, 76–77
Tuna El-Gebel, 114–115
Tutankhamun Galleries, 89–91
Virgin's Cave, 94–95
Virgin's Tree, 94
Wadi el Natroun, 97
Wax Museum (Helwan), 113
Wekalet el Ghouri, 109
Zoological Gardens, 110

SUEZ CANAL, THE RED SEA, AND SINAI

Practical Information

Camping, 213
Hotels, 210–214
Museums, 205, 207
Restaurants, 215
Sports, 214–215
Telephones, 210
Transportation, 209–210

Geographical

Abu Menka, 205
Abu Rudeis, 207
Arabia Village, 210
Cross Canal Tunnel, 204
Dahab, 209, H214
Ein Sukhna, 204–205
El Arish, 207, H212
Hurghada, 205–206, H211–212, R215
Ismailia, 204, H211, R215
Monastery of St. Catherine, 207–208, H213
Mount Moses, 208
Nuweibeh, 209, H213
Port Said, 204, H210, R215
Ras Ghareb, 205
Ras Mohamed, 208–209
Ras Zafarana, 205
Red Sea, 204–206
Red Sea Aquarium, 206
Safaga, 206, H212
Sharm el Sheikh, 208, H214
Sinai, 206–209, H212–213
Sinai Museum, 207
Suez, 204–205, H211
Suez Canal, 202–204
Taba, 209, H213

UPPER EGYPT

Practical Information

Felucca (boat tours), 178
Hotels
    Abu Simbel, 188
    Aswan, 187–188
    Luxor, 185–187
Itineraries, 184–185
Nile steamers, 173, 176
Packing and accessories, 163
Photography, 163
Recommended reading, 188
Restaurants, 188
Shopping, 187
Transportation, 164, 169, 172–173, 174, 175–176, 177–178, 182

Geographical

Abu Simbel, 182–184, 185, H188
Abydos, 173–174
Aga Khan Mausoleum, 178
Aswan, 177–182, H187–188
Aswan Dam, 178, 180–181
Bashandi, 176
Colossi of Memnon, 172
Dakhla, 175–176
Deir al-Bahri Temple, 171
Deir el-Medineh, 172
Denderah, 173
Edfu, 176–177
Elephantine Island, 178
Esna, 176
High Dam, 180–181
Karnak, 165, 168, 168
Kharga, 174–175
Kiosk of Qertassi, 178
Kitchener's Island and Botanical Gardens, 178
Kom Ombo, 177
Luxor, 163–172, H185–187
Medinet Habu Temple, 172
Monastery of St. Simon, 178
Qena, 173
Quarries and obelisk, 178
Ramesseum Temple, 172
Temple of Hathor, 183
Temple of Hibis, 175
Temple of Isis, 180
Temple of Luxor, 165, 168
Temple of Kalabsha, 178
Temple of Karnak, 165, 168
Temple of Philae, 181–182
Temple of Seti I
    Abydos, 174
    Luxor, 172
Thebes, 163
Tombs of the Kings, 169–170
Tombs of the Nobels (Aswan), 178, 180
Tombs of the Nobels (Luxor), 170–171
Tombs of the Queen & Princes, 170
Valley of the Kings, 163–164, 169–170

Fodor's Travel Guides

U.S. Guides

Alaska
Arizona
Boston
California
Cape Cod, Martha's
  Vineyard, Nantucket
The Carolinas & the
  Georgia Coast
The Chesapeake
  Region
Chicago
Colorado
Disney World & the
  Orlando Area
Florida
Hawaii

Las Vegas, Reno,
  Tahoe
Los Angeles
Maine, Vermont,
  New Hampshire
Maui
Miami & the
  Keys
National Parks
  of the West
New England
New Mexico
New Orleans
New York City
New York City
  (Pocket Guide)

Pacific North Coast
Philadelphia & the
  Pennsylvania
  Dutch Country
Puerto Rico
  (Pocket Guide)
The Rockies
San Diego
San Francisco
San Francisco
  (Pocket Guide)
The South
Santa Fe, Taos,
  Albuquerque
Seattle &
  Vancouver

Texas
USA
The U. S. & British
  Virgin Islands
The Upper Great
  Lakes Region
Vacations in
  New York State
Vacations on the
  Jersey Shore
Virginia & Maryland
Waikiki
Washington, D.C.
Washington, D.C.
  (Pocket Guide)

Foreign Guides

Acapulco
Amsterdam
Australia
Austria
The Bahamas
The Bahamas
  (Pocket Guide)
Baja & Mexico's Pacific
  Coast Resorts
Barbados
Barcelona, Madrid,
  Seville
Belgium &
  Luxembourg
Berlin
Bermuda
Brazil
Budapest
Budget Europe
Canada
Canada's Atlantic
  Provinces

Cancun, Cozumel,
  Yucatan Peninsula
Caribbean
Central America
China
Czechoslovakia
Eastern Europe
Egypt
Europe
Europe's Great Cities
France
Germany
Great Britain
Greece
The Himalayan
  Countries
Holland
Hong Kong
India
Ireland
Israel
Italy

Italy 's Great Cities
Jamaica
Japan
Kenya, Tanzania,
  Seychelles
Korea
London
London
  (Pocket Guide)
London Companion
Mexico
Mexico City
Montreal &
  Quebec City
Morocco
New Zealand
Norway
Nova Scotia,
  New Brunswick,
  Prince Edward
  Island
Paris

Paris (Pocket Guide)
Portugal
Rome
Scandinavia
Scandinavian Cities
Scotland
Singapore
South America
South Pacific
Southeast Asia
Soviet Union
Spain
Sweden
Switzerland
Sydney
Thailand
Tokyo
Toronto
Turkey
Vienna & the Danube
  Valley
Yugoslavia

Wall Street Journal Guides to Business Travel

Europe
International Cities
Pacific Rim
USA & Canada

Special-Interest Guides

Bed & Breakfast and
  Country Inn Guides:
  Mid-Atlantic Region
  New England
  The South
  The West

Cruises and Ports
  of Call
Healthy Escapes
Fodor's Flashmaps
  New York

Fodor's Flashmaps
  Washington, D.C.
Shopping in Europe
Skiing in the USA &
  Canada

Smart Shopper's
  Guide to London
Sunday in New York
Touring Europe
Touring USA